*Photo by O. J. MacCord.*

Edith Wynne Matthison as Medea. Students of The Bennett School of Liberal and Applied Arts.

*Used by courtesy of Charles Rann Kennedy*

# A SHORT HISTORY
# OF THE DRAMA

By

MARTHA FLETCHER BELLINGER

NEW YORK
HENRY HOLT AND COMPANY

6831

*To*

JANIE

THE DEAREST OF COMPANIONS

AT THE PLAY

# PREFACE

The basis of this book is a series of lectures given before various classes and study groups, among others the Century Theater Club of New York and the Brooklyn Institute of Arts and Sciences. In conducting such courses I found that an outline survey of the drama of past centuries is a necessary preliminary to a just understanding of any play. Modern drama especially, to be rightly estimated, needs to be aligned beside the drama of other periods. The history of this art is continually presenting to the student the revival of old themes, the resurrection of stock characters, and the recurrence of stock situations; as a consequence what often seems strikingly original to the novice in the art is but the reincarnation of an ancient favorite of the boards.

I have had three main objects in the writing of the book:

1. to offer an easy narrative of the history of the art, giving occasional attention to forms of production and to theories of construction, but in the main trying to tell who the chief playwrights were and what they tried to do;
2. to supply a book which could handily be used as a reference work by critics, teachers, playwrights and students generally;
3. to indicate here and there the effective results gained by criticism, by conscious efforts on the part of reformers, or by the more or less organized revolt against established forms.

So far as has been possible I have read representative plays; and while sometimes bewildered by the difference of opinion among scholars of repute concerning certain plays and movements, I have generally come to the conclusion that my readers would enjoy best having the varied opinions set before them and being allowed to judge for themselves. In the Supplement I have supplied a short reading list of books about the drama;

also a chronological list of the chief playwrights of each period with dates and the titles of important plays.

I wish here to thank the many authors whose opinions I have consulted. I wish also to express my acknowledgments to several librarians and their assistants, especially to those of Columbia University, of the University of Chicago, and of the Public Library of New York City, for kindly help and the opportunity of seeing unusual books and pamphlets. My sincere thanks go to a friend and a classical scholar, Henrietta Josephine Meeteer, Ph.D., formerly head of the classical department at Swarthmore College; to Roy C. Flickinger, Ph.D., head of the classical department at Northwestern University, both of whom have made valuable suggestions and corrections; and to my husband, Franz Bellinger, Ph.D., for constant help in the preparation of the manuscript. It is unnecessary to add that no one of these helpers is responsible for whatever opinions or errors may appear.

In so brief a history many interesting playwrights must either be omitted or too sketchily considered; but I have tried to present the pageant of play-acting from its human and charming side. My sincere hope is that the story here set forth may enhance the pleasure of going to the play, and may perhaps arouse an appreciation of the rich background which lies behind even the most unpretentious theatrical entertainment.

M. F. B.

Wayne, Maine.
June, 1927.

# CONTENTS

### SECTION ONE: UNCONSCIOUS DRAMA AND PRIMITIVE LEGENDS

CHAPTER                PAGE

I. DANCING AND PLAY-ACTING . . . 3

II. HOW THE STORY-TELLERS SUPPLIED DRAMATIC THEMES . . . . . 9

III. HOW THE PLAY-ACTOR AND THE STORY-TELLER COMBINED TO MAKE DRAMA . 19

### SECTION TWO: CLASSIC DRAMA

IV. ÆSCHYLUS, THE FIRST GREAT PLAYWRIGHT 27

V. SOPHOCLES, THE MOST POLISHED OF THE TRAGIC POETS . . . . . 35

VI. "EURIPIDES, THE HUMAN" . . . . 45

VII. ARISTOPHANES AND THE GREEK COMEDY WRITERS . . . . . . 51

VIII. ARISTOTLE, CLASSIC TECHNIQUE, AND THE LATER GREEK DRAMA . . . 61

IX. GREEK PLOTS, THEATRES, COMPETITIONS, AND AUDIENCES . . . . . 68

X. HOW GREEK DRAMA INVADED ROME . . 78

XI. HORACE, ROMAN SPECTACLES, AND THE DECAY OF THE CLASSIC DRAMA . . . 89

### SECTION THREE: DRAMA OF THE ORIENT

XII. INDIA, CHINA, AND JAPAN . . . . 99

### SECTION FOUR: DRAMA OF THE MIDDLE AGES

XIII. A THOUSAND YEARS OF QUIESCENCE AND THE BEGINNINGS OF SACRED DRAMA . 115

CHAPTER                                                                 PAGE

XIV. MYSTERIES AND MIRACLES ON THE CONTINENT . . . . . . 122

XV. MYSTERIES AND PAGEANTS IN ENGLAND . 132

XVI. MORALITIES, INTERLUDES, AND FARCES OF THE MIDDLE AGES . . . . . 138

SECTION FIVE: THE GROWTH OF NATIONAL DRAMA

XVII. NATIONAL DRAMA: ITALY TO 1700 . . 147

XVIII. NATIONAL DRAMA: SPAIN TO 1700 . . 159

XIX. TRAGEDY IN FRANCE BEFORE 1700 . . 167

XX. COMEDY IN FRANCE BEFORE 1700 . . 177

XXI. THE KINDS OF ENGLISH DRAMA BEFORE 1700 . . . . . . . . 182

XXII. ELIZABETHAN PLAY-HOUSES, ACTORS, AND AUDIENCES . . . . . . . 207

XXIII. THE SCHOLAR POETS . . . . . 214

XXIV. SHAKESPEARE . . . . . . . 223

SECTION SIX: MODERN EUROPEAN AND AMERICAN DRAMA

XXV. THE FIRST HALF OF THE SEVENTEENTH CENTURY IN ENGLAND . . . . 235

XXVI. THE RESTORATION DRAMATISTS . . . 249

XXVII. THE EIGHTEENTH CENTURY IN ENGLAND . 260

XXVIII. THE EIGHTEENTH CENTURY IN FRANCE, ITALY, AND SPAIN . . . . . 268

XXIX. THE EIGHTEENTH CENTURY IN GERMANY AND SCANDINAVIA . . . . . 280

XXX. FRANCE: 1800-1875 . . . . . 292

XXXI. THE VICTORIANS AND THEIR PREDECESSORS . . . . . . . 302

# CONTENTS

CHAPTER     PAGE

XXXII. GERMANY, AUSTRIA, ITALY, AND SCANDINAVIA: 1800-1875 . . . . . 310

XXXIII. IBSEN, STRINDBERG, AND THE DRAMATIC AWAKENING . . . . . . 317

XXXIV. THE LAST FIFTY YEARS ON THE CONTINENT 326

XXXV. THE LAST FIFTY YEARS IN ENGLAND AND IRELAND . . . . . . . 338

XXXVI. DRAMA IN RUSSIA . . . . . . 347

XXXVII. DRAMA IN AMERICA . . . . . 352

XXXVIII. LATEST PHASES OF DRAMA . . . 365

A BRIEF READING LIST FOR STUDENTS OF THE DRAMA . . . . . . 373

A SUPPLEMENT CONTAINING A CHRONOLOGICAL LIST OF PLAYWRIGHTS, WITH DATES AND REPRESENTATIVE PLAYS . . . 381

INDEX . . . . . . . . 439

# LIST OF ILLUSTRATIONS

Edith Wynne Matthison as Medea . . . *Frontispiece*

FACING PAGE

Setting for the Garden Scene, *The Toy Cart* . . . 100

Mystery-stage in the 16th Century . . . . . 126

Jesus and the Apostles. From the Oberammergau Passion Play . . . . . . . . . . 136

*The Taming of the Shrew* . . . . . . . 232

Mrs. Fisk in Sheridan's *The Rivals* . . . . . 266

Firmin Gemier as Mephistopheles in *Faust* . . . 288

*Interior,* by Maurice Maeterlinck . . . . . 332

*The Dybbuk* as produced by the "Habima" Troupe . . 348

The Playmakers Theatre, Chapel Hill, North Carolina . 370

# SECTION ONE

## UNCONSCIOUS DRAMA AND PRIMITIVE LEGENDS

## CHAPTER I

# DANCING AND PLAY-ACTING

Religious Dances, it may be observed, are sometimes ecstatic, sometimes pantomimic. . . . Pantomimic dances, with their effort to heighten natural expression and to imitate natural process, bring the dancers into the divine sphere of creation and enable them to assist vicariously in the energy of the gods. The dance thus becomes the presentation of a divine drama.—HAVELOCK ELLIS, *The Dance of Life*.

Among certain peoples of the Malay Peninsula, there is sometimes enacted a play which has for its subject the punishment of coquetry. A young girl appears, wreathed with flowers and ready for the dance. She is looking for a husband. A youth approaches with gifts for her, and sings of birds, sunshine, and the joys of wedded love. She does not listen, but with a toss of her head she dances away. Still entreating her the youth follows; but she eludes him, and he retires in confusion and anger. A second admirer comes on, and a third; but each is rejected by the reckless maiden, who flouts their offerings and humiliates them. Presently the situation is changed by the appearance of three other young girls, who quickly capture the disappointed suitors and dance off with them. The girl then sees her mistake and begins to cry. At sight of her contrition the first man returns and renews his suit; but this time he proposes to make her his second wife only; and with this offer she has to be content.

*Drama defined.* It requires no great stretch of imagination to link this bit of primitive play-acting with the art of the drama as we know it today. The single "scene" described above may be given without any special setting or costumes, without music, footlights, prompter, or scenery. In its whole length no word need be spoken for its complete understanding.

It is a story told by imitation. Every play, from this little drama of slighted love to *Hamlet* or *The Emperor Jones,* is composed of the two elements: story or literary element, and imitation or play-acting. In pantomimes and farces the play-acting element is more important; but sometimes, especially in decadent eras, the literary element is given the greater prominence, and we have closet drama and problem plays. It is evident that in the ideal play the good story will be combined with the opportunity for good pantomime. When that end is achieved, we have, for example, an *Œdipus* or a *Cyrano de Bergerac.* In its essentials, therefore, the art of drama is simply telling a story by means of imitation.

Dancing, with mimicry, is one of the ancient accomplishments of man, inseparably connected with religion, warfare, the getting of wives and the getting of food. The movements of animals were imitated, costumes and masks were devised, the cries of the young were skilfully repeated. Since death was often associated with the idea of reincarnation in the form of some animal, it was but natural that many primitive rituals, intended to ensure protection for the living, should imitate the movements and cries of beasts.

A further incentive to imitation and play-acting was the wide-spread belief in sympathetic magic, which is based on the idea that the imitation of an event will bring that event to pass. When the savage wants rain, he climbs a tree and goes through the motions of pouring water from a bucket upon the ground. A second performer strikes two stones together to represent thunder, while a third waves a firebrand until the sparks fly in imitation of lightning. If a warrior wishes the death of an enemy, he makes a clay image and sticks it full of thorns and nails. If the hunter wishes to enlist the help of the gods he pretends to chase his prey, and when the victim is caught he goes through the motions of killing and skinning him. Thus the image of the deed is made, and the actuality will soon follow.[1]

A play called *The Battle of the Corn* is an Indian ritual de-

[1] Several of the illustrations used in this chapter have been taken from *The Drama of Savage Peoples,* by Loomis Havemeyer.

signed to win the favor of the gods in whose hands lies the prosperity of the crop. A slight setting is arranged, the front of which is made to represent roughly a field of maize. On the background are painted the symbols of the tribe. The performance begins by the appearance of angry demons representing Hail, Drought, Storm, and the like. These devils rush in, trampling down and destroying the grain. Presently come the owners of the field, hastening to the rescue of their crops. They attack the demons and wrestle with them, until at last the struggle becomes a pitched battle. A wounded demon falls, yelling in pain, and the defenders spring forward with renewed energy. A mortal falls, and the demons dance for joy. Just as the triumph of the devils seems assured, a new champion comes into the fight on the side of the rescuers, and the tide is turned. The weary men gather their strength for one more onslaught, the evil forces are put to rout and the crop is saved. This play, though more complex than many primitive scenes, can of course be performed entirely without words.

*War dances.* Rituals preceding wars often take the form of rather elaborate pantomimes, also based upon the idea of sympathetic magic. The dancers pretend to steal upon their foes, to discover and chase them, finally to slaughter them and join in the march of victory. These ceremonies are often like the pictures painted round a vase, merely a succession of incidents that might begin anywhere. Sometimes, however, a more subtle arrangement is contrived, with the outlines of a real plot. From one of the tribes of Sumatra comes a war play with a dramatic situation, though still no words are required. The scene is some distance from the place where a battle has been in progress. A weary warrior sits on the ground, plucking a thorn from his foot. His weapons are lying near, and he keeps a sharp lookout. In spite of his watchfulness, however, one of the enemy (supposedly) creeps up stealthily from behind and attacks him. He makes what defense he is able, but he is soon overcome, receiving the death wound and going through gruesome contortions. At last his head is cut off and the victor holds it up in triumph; but, as now for the first time the assailant has a clear view of the face, he discovers that he has killed not one of the enemy, but his own brother. There follows a lengthy portrayal of grief and remorse.

*Primitive plays a school for youth.* Play-acting and dancing occupy an important place in the social system of many tribes. There exist mystic societies, in possession of tribal secrets, initiation into which is a solemn ritual. The selected candidates, generally boys of suitable birth and skill, having arrived at the proper age, are cleansed by ceremonial and brought into the presence of the elders. With dancing, music, and pantomime, the instructors then enact the legends concerning their famous warriors and huntsmen. In some cases these exercises extend over a period of years and include a whole system of education for youth. In each dance or pantomime there is a sermon, or a lesson in geography, history, or craftsmanship.

One of the strange dramatic relics from the remote past is a "kind of nocturnal Egyptian Passion Play." [2] It is the portrayal of the struggle between Osiris, god of light, and Set, god of darkness, and was enacted at night on the shore of a lake near the great temple at Saïs. It was given with pomp and splendor, Osiris being robed in white, and the whole performance carried on to the accompaniment of music. Set, the enemy, hunts down the carrier of light and buries him beneath the waters of the lake; but Horus, son of Osiris, avenges the death of his father in a bloody battle. After the combat, Osiris again appears as the ruler of the shadow land of death. The symbolism of the conquest of Day by Night is obvious; and perhaps the still deeper symbolism of the conquest of Good by Evil, with the final rescue of the Good.

Certain ceremonies are of the nature of elaborate prayers for favorable weather and protection from disaster. One of the most noted of these ceremonies is the Rain Dance of the Hopi Indians. It is in reality a complex and highly symbolic play, lasting at least nine days and requiring for its performance some twenty warriors, all of whom must belong to certain tribes. There is the representation of a long series of events, the essential feature of which is the journey of a "stain-

[2] Edward A. MacDowell, *Critical and Historical Essays.*

less youth" to the underworld, in order to learn the secret of the rain.

One of the first adjuncts to the early dancing ceremonies was the drum, or some other simple percussion instrument, with which to mark the rhythm. Sometimes the audience sang or clapped, while the braves went through the movements of the dance. The next step was the use of chanting, the singing of appropriate songs, and the elaboration of the instrumental music.

*The Dionysiac procession.* To the historian of the drama the most important of all early rituals were the dithyrambic choruses and dances with which the festivals of Dionysus were celebrated by the Greeks. We know comparatively little about them. Looking back in the light of later developments, however, we can see that there were two groups of participants: those in the sacrificial processions through whom tragedy developed; and the bacchanalian revelers through whom, a little later, developed comedy. The former were dressed in goat skins and represented the companions of the god. Singing the dithyrambic hymn they marched to the altar and sacrificed a goat. It may have been true also that certain incidents in the life of Dionysus were enacted, and that one of the leaders of the procession himself impersonated the god. The second group of participants was called the *komos* (comus). The members of this group also paraded at the Dionysiac festivals, acted out crude farcical incidents, and imitated coarse episodes. Up to the middle of the seventh century before our era, these Greek ceremonies were probably in no way superior to many other examples of unconscious drama. In them, as in nearly all the early rituals, the three arts of singing, dancing and play-acting were combined.

*Significance of unconscious drama.* These few examples illustrate perhaps fully enough the extent and character of the great body of "unconscious drama," a large portion of which must have come into existence long before the art of writing was commonly known. The plays were often more or less improvised; though the tendency was, of course, for them to settle into form as they were handed down from one generation to the next. As they were witnessed in the beginning of history, so they may be seen today among Indians and other tribal peoples. Unlike most of the plays produced on what we call the civilized stages of the world, the unconscious dramas were always given for some purpose other than entertainment. Usually they were a part of a religious ritual in which the tribe more or less participated. There was little distinction between spectators and performers. Lessons in conduct were inculcated, the history of the tribe was taught, the principles of courage and honor were exemplified. Most of the religious ideas familiar today,—such as the belief in a Spirit, in the power of intercession, in immortality, and in the appearance of a Saviour for the tribe,—these were all portrayed. Furthermore, the subjects used were the same subjects which are in use today: the fight of man against fate or against great odds; the warfare of sex; the tragedy of mistaken vengeance; the symbolic presentation of the changes from night to day, or from winter to spring.

The art of the stage is rooted in these practices of primitive peoples, from whom the play-actor learned the making and use of disguises, the manner of painting the body or draping it with skins, the way to use animal faces and heads, the making of headdresses and masks, and the imitation of the sounds of animals and of nature. The early ceremonies were the school for historic drama, and the stories told by tribesmen are the very stories which have been told and retold on the stages of the world. Moreover, while civilized drama has had long periods of quiescence, seeming to have disappeared, unconscious drama has persisted.

## CHAPTER II

# HOW THE STORY-TELLERS SUPPLIED DRAMATIC THEMES

In books lies the soul of the whole past time: the articulate, audible voice of the past, when the body and material substance of it has altogether vanished like a dream.—THOMAS CARLYLE.

However interesting may be the unconscious drama of primitive peoples, there is nevertheless a wide gap between it and the conscious art of the historic stage. Unsophisticated play-acting needed the cross fertilization of a sister art—that of the story-teller—before the new art of the drama could be created. This new art was a fusion of play-acting and story-telling: masterpieces of epic poetry interpreted by masters of imitation. Long before the playwright appeared the pantomime and the epic had reached a high degree of perfection; and when the playwright at last came, he was little troubled about the invention of plots. He took what he thought good, from whatever source offered itself. He was in a sense a composite product of the play-actor and the story-teller, both of whom were most interested in portraying an exciting experience. Now a fight, a conflict, is the most exciting experience in the world; and primitive legends all have for their subject some sort of struggle,—men against gods or demons, heroes against the enemies of the tribe, rebels against tyrants, laws of god against the commands of men. Conflicts such as these became the prime material of the playwright.

*Chief sources of story material used in drama.* There are four principal sources from which the playwrights of various periods have drawn material for their plots or fables. They are (1) the ancient mythologies; (2) the Bible and other sacred books, together with the associated legends about saints and holy places; (3) tales of chivalry and knighthood, Italian

9

*novelle,* and the like, all generally grouped together under the name of medieval romances; (4) chronicles and other historical records. These four groups are not of course mutually exclusive. They overlap at many points; but as a working classification they will serve.

*Mythology.* In many nations there exist legends, half heroic and half religious, which appear to have preceded the beginnings of written literature. These legends were preserved, probably often much improved, and handed down to succeeding generations by professional story-tellers, whose business it was to entertain the court, the camp, or the marketplace. In Greece these story-tellers were called rhapsodes, in northern countries skalds, in Celtic countries bards, in medieval Europe minstrels or gleemen. Through these bards were disseminated legends going back to the dawn of history, exaggerated reports of commonplace events, or sometimes the composite record of several tribal heroes whose exploits came to be ascribed to a single popular figure. Patriotism, self-sacrifice, pride, and courage were favorite themes.

One of the earliest examples of this class is the story of Job.[1] Its text, as we have it in the Bible, is probably corrupted by numerous additions and deletions. As it stands, it appears to belong as much to drama as to pure literature; and it seems likely, as certain biblical scholars hold, that its author intended it to be enacted, but was opposed by the Jewish priesthood. It offers a good deal of spirited dialogue, thereby differing from most of the examples of unconscious drama described in the first chapter. Though *Job* is a work of religious speculation, yet the changes of situation, the suspense, the strokes of misfortune and the subsequent relief are of the nature of drama, and excellent drama at that. Beneath the outward struggle of the hero are speculations upon the nature of God, his relationship to man, and the purposes for which men live and die. In it are many eloquent passages upon the beauty and wonders of nature; there are pathos, irony, wit. The combination of play-acting quality, good story, and sombre strength make the same

[1] Produced in America about 1912 by Mr. Stuart Walker.

appeal on the stage today that they might have made some thirty centuries ago.

Of all the ancient mythologies, that of the Greeks has been most freely drawn upon by playwrights. During the time of Solon and the Pisistratidæ (sixth century, B.C.) the national legends and myths were collected into what was known as the *Epic Cycle,* considerable portions of which have now been lost. This *Cycle* included the history of the Trojan War, the legends of the House of Atreus (the Atridæ), of Laius and Œdipus (the Labdacidæ), of Hercules, Ajax, Philoctetes, Jason and the Golden Fleece, besides many other well known stories. By ancient writers this Epic Cycle was commonly attributed to Homer. At the period when the effort towards preserving the myths was being made, the Persians were threatening; and within a generation they had actually invaded Grecian territory. The dissemination of the legends undoubtedly had its effect in arousing the spirit of national pride, and in thus helping the Greeks to resist the invasions of what was then the dominant oriental power.

For the historian of drama, however, the important point is that all but one of the extant Greek tragedies are based upon incidents related in the *Epic Cycle*. Even concerning the lost plays, there is record of only two or three cases, in the entire history of Greek tragedy, when the Homeric poems were not used as a source book. Sometimes a slight episode, occupying but a few lines in the poem, was elaborated into a full length play; sometimes new characters were invented and associated with the well known hero; and sometimes the entire emphasis was changed, so that a minor character in the poem became the hero of the play.

Let us glance for a moment at some of the stories contained in the *Epic Cycle*. Probably the most used of all the stories of the world is that of the House of Atreus. It contains the great characters of Agamemnon, Clytemnestra, Electra, Orestes, Cassandra, and Iphigenia, as well as some of the most famous scenes of all literature. The *Oresteia* of Æschylus, the only complete trilogy extant, is built upon it. Sophocles, Euripides, Voltaire, Alfieri, and Dryden all wrote plays upon the single theme of the revenge of Orestes; and this list includes only the most distinguished names. The sacrifice of Iphigenia has tempted the giants of literature, being used at least once by Sophocles, twice by Euripides, and twice by Goethe. The Latin poets, Nævius and Ennius, composed tragedies on the subject. The play of Euripides called *Iphigenia in Aulis* was translated into Latin by Erasmus in 1524. An Italian version appeared in 1560. At least three French versions of the same play appeared during the seventeenth century before Racine wrote his *Iphigénie*. Gluck's opera, based on the play of Racine, was performed in 1674. The play of Euripides was translated into German by Schiller, and many English versions have been made. More than twenty operatic compositions, besides that of Gluck, have been made with the *Aulis* plays as a basis, while nearly a dozen composers have essayed to put the *Tauris* story into operatic form.

The myth of the Labdacidæ has proved almost equally fertile as a source of play material. It includes the Œdipus legend, and supplies us with the deathless character of Antigone. Three of the most admired of the extant plays of Sophocles were founded on it. Æschylus, Euripides, Voltaire, and many lesser poets have drawn upon it for dramatic themes. As in the myth of the Atridæ, the situations can be so transformed in their moral implications as to afford a variety of plots.

The story of Prometheus furnished Æschylus material for a trilogy, and gave Shelley one of his greatest subjects. The myths of Hercules and Hippolytus, each, formed the basis for plays by Sophocles, Euripides, Seneca, and Racine. The three greatest Greek playwrights used in turn each of the following stories: the return of the Trojan captives, the Argonautic Expedition with its story of Medea, the fate of Andromache, the legends of Ajax, Hecuba, and Helen. Nine other myths were used by both Æschylus and Sophocles. When national drama, in different countries, began to take shape after the Renaissance, these Greek plots were rewritten again and again by French and Italian writers of tragedy; and the poets of today are still using the same themes.

*Sacred books as sources of plots.* The famous myths and symbolical legends of the Orient, in many cases, are embedded in what are known as the sacred books. The Asiatic play best known to Europeans, *Sakuntala,* is founded upon events related in the sacred book of the Hindus, the *Mahabharata.* The *No* plays of Japan are uniformly founded upon legends connected with sacred shrines and holy people. Many of the characters in the long oriental plays have powers far exceeding those of mere mortals, and are looked upon, by the populace at least, as partaking more or less of the divine nature. The most striking illustration, however, of the use of sacred literature as a source for play material is in the drama of the Middle Ages, which was based on Bible stories and the traditions connected with the lives of saints. Professor Flickinger has pointed out that what the Homeric poems were to the Greek dramatists, the Bible and biblical legends were to the makers of pageants, miracles, and mysteries during the six centuries when these forms of entertainment flourished in England and Central Europe.

*Medieval romances.* The third great source of plot material consists of epics and legends collected in different countries during the Middle Ages. As the rhapsodes had traveled about Greece reciting the Homeric poems, so the skalds, gleemen, and minstrels of Europe went from court to court, or from baronial hall to feudal fortress, chanting their songs, and relating their tales of love, death, and glory on the field of battle. There is a known list of two hundred and thirty skalds who flourished between the eighth and thirteenth centuries. Their songs fill more than two hundred volumes. The two *Eddas*—the *Elder Edda* in unrhymed verse, and the *Younger Edda* in prose—recite the story of Sigurd, Brunhild, the Volsungs, and the Rhinegold. In Germany the Middle Ages produced the *Book of Heroes* (*Heldenbuch*) and the *Song of the Nibelungs,* with the stories of Attila, Theodoric the Great, Siegfried, called the Achilles of the North, Brunhild, Hagen and Gunther. Among the romances of chivalry are those relating to King Arthur and the Knights of the Round Table, those centering about Amadis of Gaul, and still a third relating to the court of Charlemagne and his Paladins.  Dramatic and full of beauty and symbolism as these tales are, they have so far been much less used than the myths of Greece.

In Spain, where the institution of chivalry took firmest root, the thrilling tales of Don Roderigo and other knights fill more than seventy volumes.  These old romances expressed, in a special way, religious and national characteristics, and furnished material not only for Spanish writers, but for dramatists of other countries.  Botta describes this wealth of literary material as "a mine which has unceasingly been wrought by the rest of Europe for similar purposes, and which still remains unexhausted."

In many countries, heroic tales crystallized into epic poems; but in Italy they, with romantic legends of all sorts, were gathered into *novelle,* or short prose novels.  Stories, already current for generations, were retold with witty and often ribald additions, and in time were turned into such collections as the *Decameron,* and so disseminated all over Europe.  The *Decameron,* consisting of one hundred lively tales, was published in Italy in 1353.  Not only Italian playwrights, but, in the course of time, the greatest writers of England, Denmark, and France borrowed from these stores of romance.  In 1566 William Paynter published sixty of the *Decameron* stories in English under the title *The Palace of Pleasure;* and in a few years thirty more of the novels were printed in England.  As is well known, the story of *Romeo and Juliet,* as well as several situations in other plays, were taken by Shakespeare from Italian sources; and the germ of many a character, now familiar to every reader of English drama, may be found either in Boccaccio, Cinthio, or some other Italian novelist.

The Arabs never developed a drama of their own, but from ancient times they were famous for their professional story-tellers.  Jinns, fairies, demons, and beautiful female spirits, called Peris, lived in these Arabian romances, together with the characters which inhabit the world of trade and barter.  This oriental background has had a perennial fascination for dramatists; but it has so far proved difficult to reproduce successfully on the stages of the western world.

*History as plot material.* The fourth and last great source of plot material lies in the historians and chroniclers, especially Plutarch, Geoffrey of Monmouth, Holinshed, and Stow. The first Italian tragedy of the Renaissance, *Sofonisba,* is based on a story found in Livy; but it was Plutarch who inspired the greater number of modern European playwrights. He was born in Chæronea, Greece, about 46 A.D., and wrote studies of forty-six *Lives* in which, in every case, a Roman was made to parallel a Greek. The *Lives,* familiar now to every school child, were first translated into English by Sir Thomas North and published in 1579. North made his translation from the French version of Amyot.

Geoffrey of Monmouth, who died about 1152, was possibly a Benedictine monk; he was certainly made Bishop of St. Asaph not long before his death. It appears that he was at Oxford in the year 1129, at which time he was probably already at work on his *Historia Regum Britanniæ,* or *History of the Kings of Britain.* Two editions, and two translations, of this work made their appearance during the twelfth century, and many later chroniclers seem to have regarded it as a veracious account of early British history. It was written in Latin, translated into Anglo-Norman, and back again into "semi-Saxon or transitional English." More than one Elizabethan writer drew upon Geoffrey of Monmouth's *Historia* before Shakespeare found therein the weird story of "King Leir."

Raphael Holinshed, the most important among the authors of *Chronicles of England, Scotland and Ireland,* died about 1580. The work was probably begun about 1548, and two editions were published during the sixteenth century, the first in 1578. Holinshed and the other contributors to the *Chronicles* drew upon Geoffrey of Monmouth to some extent. John Stow, 1525-1604, was the son of a tailor and an all-round, competent historian for his time. He produced *A Summary of English Chronicles* in 1561, translated and published the *Chronicle of Matthew Paris* in 1571, and the *Historia Brevis* of Thomas Walsingham a few years later. His *Survey of London* appeared only two years before the end of the century. The work which was of most interest to playwrights, however, was probably his *Annales, or a Generale Chronicle of England from Brute until the present yeare of Christ 1580.*

The facts in these and other chronicles were often mixed with invention and superstitious ideas; but they formed a goldmine for dramatists, especially for those of the time of Elizabeth. Out of them came *Lear, Macbeth, Hamlet, Tamburlaine, The Jew of Malta,* and a score of other plays. Shakespeare rarely ever used contemporaneous plot material, but he crept up rather close to his own time in *Henry VIII.* Other writers took curious events, such as would today make merely a newspaper headline, and transposed them into terms of drama. The stories of the Cid and of Faust, half legendary and half historical, traveled abroad, the one from Spain and the other from Germany, finding important dramatizers in foreign countries.

The four groups, thus briefly indicated, give an idea of the richness of the reservoir from which the playwrights of twenty centuries have drawn a large proportion of their plots, situations and characters. The classic poets ignored all sources but the first; the makers of the sacred drama of the Middle Ages ignored all but the second. Dramatists of the Renaissance, and especially the Elizabethans, widened and enlarged the field until at last the world of the stage, at its best, was all but as broad as the field of life itself. Modern plays are not better plays, in themselves, than the ancient masterpieces; but the modern stage, taken by and large, exhibits a greater variety of character, a wider range of problems, than the stage of any earlier time.

*Characteristic themes of the story-tellers.* The themes which occupied the play-actors of primitive peoples, we found, were those connected with war, hunting, the getting of food, and, to a slighter degree, the getting of wives. There were exhibitions of rebellion against authority, the salvation of the tribe by the suffering of innocence, and the exaltation of family or tribal traditions. These themes were also part of the stock in trade of the professional story-teller. In the course of our study we shall have to name and rename these world-themes:

taking vengeance for personal or family wrongs, every form
of chase and struggle, patriotism, family feuds, romantic love
(this especially in modern times), the adventures of national
and tribal heroes, and the fight against real or fancied tyranny.
The actors in these struggles, both in primitive plays and
in primitive legends, included supernatural beings, gods and
demons, wrestlers, warriors and champions, ambitious tyrants
and overconfident kings. Not until modern times was the
middle-class or low-born person introduced into the serious
drama of any nation. In comedy, however, slaves, traders,
parasites and the like have always found a place. The affairs
of women, and women characters, for many centuries were of
little interest to the playwrights. For one character such as
Antigone or Phædra, there were certainly a score of salient
male characters. In both unconscious drama and in legends
there has been perpetuated the memory of practices which, in
Europe at least, long ago disappeared: such, for example, as
the habit of infant exposure, or instances of the marriage of
brother and sister.

*Importance of national and historical themes.* History has
constantly been remade by the playwright; or, if not remade, at
least illuminated with a light more dazzling and alluring than
that of the historian. Who would know or care about Lear
or Tamburlaine, were it not for a few pages engrossed with
gorgeous poetry and burning with passion? Kings, warriors,
and local champions have acquired a universal quality, a halo
of symbolism, which they never had in life or in the pages of
the historian. As national monuments, these creations are of
importance. When national ideals were forming, they helped
to establish a heroic tradition. They supplied a kind of training school, a standard of thought and conduct. Schlegel says:
"A single monument, like that of the *Cid,* is more valuable to
the people than whole libraries of wit and genius without national associations."

*General progress of the art.* The growth of the dramatic
art has not been a continuous advance from rudimentary forms
towards an ever increasing standard of perfection; rather, its
progress has been through sudden spurts of achievement fol-

lowed by a return to almost primitive forms. The first period
produced plays perfect in their own way; the last period can
do no more. If the advance of the art were to be roughly
represented by a chart, it would show a gradually rising line,
with several breaks for mountain peaks.

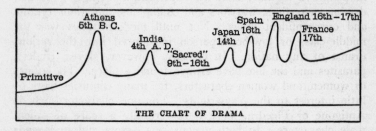

THE CHART OF DRAMA

The highest of these breaks, or mountain peaks, represent
the achievements of Greece, Spain, Elizabethan England, and
France. Smaller but still remarkable peaks stand for India in
the fourth century and Japan in the fourteenth. On the whole,
the trend of the art has been upward. Those periods are important in which new subjects, new ideas of national character,
more complex situations, and greater technical skill have appeared. If we find it interesting to ask: What sort of man
did the ancients admire? How will a man act when driven by
ambition or fear or selfishness or love? Is anything, in the
heart of man, stronger than self-interest? If we are desirous
of asking these and similar questions, it is in drama that we
shall find answers.

CHAPTER III

# HOW THE PLAY-ACTOR AND THE STORY-
# TELLER COMBINED TO MAKE DRAMA

Let us not deceive ourselves. Art is indissolubly bound up with men's spiritual forces. What we learn from . . . the Athens of Socrates is this: that art is able to assert man's moral nature at moments when it seems in other spheres to have been paralyzed or vitiated. —J. ADDINGTON SYMONDS, *The Renaissance in Italy*.

We have already spoken of the Greek Dionysiac festivals, and how, roughly speaking, there were two groups of cele-brants: the goat-singers (*tragodoi*) from whose hymns and ceremonies developed tragedy; and the group of revelers (*komos*) through whom, at a slightly later date, comedy devel-oped. The hymn sung by the goat chorus in the sacrificial procession was called the dithyramb, and at first it was prob-ably little more than a crude drinking song, often improvised. Arion, who flourished about 625 B.C., appears to have organ-ized it into a hymn with a prescribed form and meter. By tradition the dithyrambic chorus numbered fifty voices and was accompanied by the flute. The subjects of the verse were al-ways episodes from the life of Dionysus, the god of the vine, of music, and of poetry. It is supposed that the leader, with the singers, must often have indulged in pantomimic exercises suited to the story.

In the meantime, while the dithyrambic chorus was taking definite shape, the Homeric legends were becoming more and more familiar through the recitations of the rhapsodes, who were welcome guests at the courts of kings, at banquets, in the camps and at popular festivals. The tales which they sung or recited were of long-forgotten battles, of Olympian gods, and of superhuman heroes. Thus in Greece, during the sixth and fifth centuries before our era, the play-actors and the story-tellers encountered each other, with mutual profit. The bards furnished the plots, while the Dionysiac revelers or worshipers did the mumming; with the result that the unconscious drama of earlier days leaped suddenly into a more complex art. The sum of the two arts, however, unlike the sum in arithmetic, was more than the two put together,—it was a new creation.

One by one the Greek legends were refashioned. The struggle of the hero was made to stand out against a background of singing and dancing, "turning points" were emphasized, the climax was prepared for and rounded out. Nietzsche has pointed out, in *The Birth of Tragedy,* the combination of what he called the Dionysian and the Apollonian elements, that is, the choral and the epic. The singing of the chorus, with the dancing, became the framework within which the given story unfolded itself. Character took on a new importance, irrelevant or inartistic details of the original legend were slurred over or omitted, and each story was constructed with an eye to design, "with a beginning, a middle, and an end." The designer was the playwright. Furthermore, each detail of the story was contrived in such a way as to be interpreted by the play-actor, with the help of singers and dancers, and the whole performance was then shifted to a public dancing place near the shrine of Dionysus. The spectators no longer took part in the performance, which now became partly a religious ceremony, partly an entertainment given by playwright and actors, and exposed to the admiration, indifference, or censure of the crowd. The play, formerly improvised, was now carefully planned and written down. Dancers and actors were gradually differentiated; and through this differentiation evolved the professional actor. These changes, naturally, came about only by a series of steps, some of which can be traced.

*Thespis.* If tradition were to be taken literally, Thespis should be accounted as the Barnum of his age; for to him have been accredited striking innovations in the way of entertainment. His actual achievements, however, are sufficiently important. He belonged to the sixth century B.C., and came from Icaria, an important center of Dionysian worship. It is probable that he was a leader of one of the dithyrambic choruses; and his chief service to drama was the "invention" of the actor, or answerer (*hypocritos*), whose business it was to impersonate in turn each of the characters about whom the leader of the chorus was talking. Of course the play-actor had existed long before the time of Thespis; but with a difference. The primitive play-actor was one of a group, whose main business was the ritual prescribed. Skill was of secondary importance. The actor, as he now for the first time made his appearance, was a specialized performer, taking a part which lay far beyond the powers of the other participants. It was "invention" of the actor in the sense that a crude and haphazard custom was lifted out of the class of primitive activities and placed where it could develop into a fine art.

About the time of Thespis (but whether inaugurated by him we do not know) other important changes were made in the practice of Dionysian worship. Until then it is probable that events in the life of Dionysus always formed the subject of the dithyrambic hymn; now other themes, especially those embodied in the Homeric poems, were introduced. The performance was not improvised, as formerly, but planned out in advance; and the metrical form of the verse, which had been trochaic, was changed to iambic. The Thespian show also seems to have been the first to travel from place to place; though it is most likely that the performances were always given at the Dionysiac shrines and around an altar.

*The Thespian play.* Simple indeed was this first attempt at drama, and yet in principle quite different from the informal plays described in the first chapter. First appeared the actor, who delivered a short explanatory speech telling who the characters were in the coming play, where the action was supposed to take place, and, most likely also, what the point was. The chorus (which for some time after Thespis was to be the most important feature of the performance) then marched in; or perhaps it came with a solemn dance, singing the dithyramb. Meanwhile the actor had disappeared. At the end of the first hymn, or ode, he reappeared in costume and acted out, or narrated in a lively manner, the episode which was "on" at the moment. Sometimes he carried on a spicy dialogue with the leader of the chorus. When the first episode was finished, he again disappeared, and the chorus chanted another hymn. In the second pause he reappeared in different character, and so on until the end of the entertainment. The performance must have been something like an enlarged ballad, with alternating dialogue and refrain; or perhaps even more like the modern vaudeville, in which independent "turns" succeed each other.

It is obvious, in such an arrangement, that the actor must have some easily accessible place for making the changes in his masks and costume. For this purpose Thespis built a little hut, the Greek word for which is *skênê,* to which the actor could retire. This early *skênê,* which became of course our "scene," was purely a mechanical necessity, and not at all designed for decoration or identification of place.)

*The Thespian tradition.* In his time Thespis not only acted the chief parts himself—rôles of god, king, messenger, or victim—but he also wrote his own pieces, so far as they were written, trained his chorus, and was his own manager. It is thought that he not only used masks but also pigments to disguise the face of the actor. He appeared privately at Athens as early as 560 B.C., without the assistance of the state; but in 534 B.C., nine years before the birth of Æschylus, the old stroller took part in the first public competition in tragedy at the City Dionysia in Athens, and received the first prize. On one occasion Solon, archon of Athens and a contemporary of Thespis, condescended to witness a play. When the actor appeared before the wise man at the close of the performance, Solon rebuked him for "trying to deceive the people with his imitation gods and goddesses."

*Importance of Thespian changes.* The performance was not yet very dramatic, nevertheless it marks the difference between primitive, imitative dances and the drama of the schools. Unfortunately, no manuscripts are preserved illustrating this transition stage. In the thirty years between the last appearance of Thespis and the first play of Æschylus in 499 B.C., many writers must have experimented with the new form, but no complete work has survived. From the story-tellers there is a wealth of material; but from the Dionysiac plays there remain in all only a few fragments of the dithyrambic choruses:

twenty-eight lines from a fine work by Pindar, invoking the good will of the gods, and one or two other fragments.

*The forerunners.* The names of three playwrights are known: Pratinas, Chœrilus, and Phrynicus. In the contest in tragedy at the City Dionysia in 499 B.C., Chœrilus and Pratinas were successful, while among the defeated candidates was the youthful Æschylus. There are records to the effect that Chœrilus wrote one hundred and sixty plays, won the prize thirteen times, and lived for some years into the fifth century.

Pratinas contented himself with the well known Dionysiac incidents, gave them a humorous turn, treated them with considerable license and freedom, and so established the satyr play,—a form in which the goat-skin dress was retained for the chorus, though some of the newer features of tragedy were also employed. Chœrilus was also a writer of satyr plays.

Phrynicus was the most famous of the three forerunners, and in a literary sense the boldest. He struck out audaciously and used an event from recent Athenian history in a play called *The Capture of Miletus.* At the performance, people wept with emotion, so profound was the impression made; but in the end the state fined Phrynicus for portraying an event unflattering to the Athenians. Aristophanes called him a "writer of beautiful dramas." He had the reputation of being the first playwright among the Greeks to represent female characters on the stage—that is, to use masks representing women—and also of inventing many new and graceful movements for the dancers. Ancient critics, however, attribute to him as his chief merit the ability to lend more pathos, beauty, and dignity to his tragedies.

# SECTION TWO
# CLASSIC DRAMA

## CHAPTER IV

# ÆSCHYLUS, THE FIRST GREAT PLAYWRIGHT

. . . poetry has a universal and a moral function. . . . It is an art that has all time and all experience for its natural subject matter, and all the possibilities of being for its ultimate theme.— GEORGE SANTAYANA, *Poetry and Religion.*

Of all the miracles which dazzle mankind in the history of literary genius, none is more amazing than the advent of Æschylus. In his art he was bound by innumerable ties to Thespis and the forerunners, and to the half savage dancers round the drum; yet he reached far beyond them. Those primitive rituals and dances are alien to us, while Æschylus speaks as one of ourselves. With him appeared probably the first written play. He took the scattering, haphazard exercise of Thespis and made of it a coherent art form. He also began to think about the questions and problems with which we are still concerned, and tried to embody them in his work. He steps from the dim light of the primitive world into the relatively broad daylight of modern times; and he ushers in the great cycle of Greek drama which, in the space of a century, ran its course and decayed.

*Life of Æschylus.* 525-456 B.C. The last recorded public appearance of Thespis was in 534 B.C. Nine years after that, at Eleusis, not far from Athens, Æschylus was born, in a family belonging to the ancient Attic nobility. He and his brother Cynegeirus fought with distinction in various engagements against the invading Persians, and their portraits were included in the famous picture of the battle of Marathon on the Painted Porch at Athens. The first appearance of Æschylus in the competitions for tragedy was made, as has been noted, in 499 B.C., against Pratinas and Chœrilus, and was unsuccessful. The excitement of the contest brought such a great crowd of spectators to the theater that the wooden benches broke down. After this first appearance and defeat, Æschylus left Athens for Sicily; but in 490, the year of Marathon, he must have been back in Athens. Between the battles of Marathon and Salamis he achieved the first of his thirteen successes in the competitions. In 468 he was defeated by the young Sophocles.

Æschylus made many visits to Sicily, and seems finally to have adopted that island as his home, under the patronage of Prince Hieron. He must have returned frequently to Athens, however, in order to act in his plays and to superintend their production. Although greatly admired by the Athenians, yet he was almost mobbed on one occasion under suspicion of having revealed the Eleusinian mysteries. At his trial he was acquitted. He died at Gela, Sicily, in his seventieth year. The legend is that he was seated out of doors, writing, when an eagle, mistaking his bald head for a stone, dropped a tortoise on it and killed him. He was buried in the public tombs of Gela with great pomp and magnificence. Over his tomb was inscribed an epitaph which, it was said, was composed by himself, mentioning the fact that he had fought at Marathon, but saying nothing of his work as a poet.

*The seven extant plays.* Æschylus wrote about ninety plays, seven of which have been preserved. *The Suppliants* is probably the earliest of these. The story, taken from the *Epic Cycle,* tells how the fifty daughters of Danaus, sought in marriage by their cousins, the fifty sons of Ægyptus, fled for protection to a place near Argos. The fifty suitors overtook them and through a messenger commanded the maidens to give themselves up; but at this point the king of Argos interfered, sending the suitors off about their business. The play closes with a hymn of thanksgiving sung by the chorus.

*The Persians.* This play offers the only instance in the Æschylean tragedies of the use of a plot taken from other than Homeric sources. It was written to celebrate the final defeat of the armies of Xerxes, but was not exhibited until 472, seven years after the hostile army had departed, never to return. The scene is laid in Persia, among the very enemies against whom the Greeks had fought for more than eleven years. The successive scenes give the narrative of the defeat and ruin of the Persian forces. One sees the oriental setting, the fear of the down-trodden subjects in the presence of their despotic ruler, the votive offerings and libations of Queen Atossa, and finally the sorrow and wailing of Xerxes and his courtiers at the news of disaster. It is easy to imagine how such a play would feed the secret pride and exultation of a Greek audience. It is, however, far more than a boastful picture of Greek triumph and Persian defeat; rather is it a moral lesson on the subject of tyranny, designed to touch the heart and conscience of every oppressor, whether Greek or barbarian.

*The Seven Against Thebes.* A single incident connected with the Œdipus legend is made the basis of this play, whose underlying theme is the fulfilment of a curse. Of the two sons of Œdipus, Eteocles and Polynices, the prophecy had been made: "They shall divide their inheritance with the sword in such a manner as to obtain equal shares." When the play begins, Eteocles is in possession of the city, while Polynices with an army of Argive soldiers advances to attack it. In the battle which follows by the walls of Thebes, both brothers are killed. Their "equal share" is a grave. Antigone, the sister, here appears for a moment, announcing her determination to give her rebel brother the decent burial which had been denied him.

*Prometheus Bound.* This play shares with the *Agamemnon* the distinction of being the most admired of the Æschylean dramas. It has perhaps influenced more literary people than any other classic work. Like *The Suppliants* and *The Seven Against Thebes,* it was probably part of a trilogy. Prometheus is the friend and teacher of mankind. His services to men have brought upon him the enmity of Zeus who, through his messenger Hermes, demands that Prometheus shall consent to give up his practice of helping mortals and acknowledge him, Zeus, as the rightful ruler of Olympus. The Firebringer proudly and bitterly refuses, whereupon Zeus condemns him to long ages of punishment. He is chained to a rock by an abyss in the Caucasus. A vulture tortures him perpetually, and finally he is thrown into Tartarus. Before this catastrophe, however, there comes the promise of release and the justification of the hero.

Concerning this play Haigh, one of the ablest of modern critics, has said: "The central idea of the play—that of a god submitting of his own free will to ages of torment, in order to rescue mankind from their degradation—is a conception so sublime, and so alien to the usual spirit of Greek religion, that some of the early fathers perceived in it a dim presentiment of the Christian doctrine. But the drama may be regarded from many points of view. It may be looked upon, not only as a noble example of self-sacrifice, but also as a type of man's struggle against destiny, or of the conflict between liberty and oppression. . . . The great charm of the *Prometheus Bound* lies in its varied and perennial suggestiveness."

*The trilogy.* The regulations of the annual competitions were probably somewhat elastic, especially during the earlier part of the fifth century; but it is understood that in general each poet exhibited three tragedies and one satyr play, the four pieces being performed in succession in the course of a single day. Before Æschylus the poets had used for these plays, so far as we know, three different subjects; but Æschylus saw a way of deepening the impression by making the three tragedies all part of one story. Thus rose the trilogy. Each play is technically complete, yet gains in strength and meaning by being linked with the other two. The only extant example of this form is the celebrated *Oresteia,* which comprises the *Agamemnon, The Libation Pourers (Chœphori),* and *The Benign Ones (Eumenides).* The fourth play, a satyric drama called *Proteus,* is lost. In each play there is a distinct dramatic situation; but it is possible to regard the trilogy as a single three-act play, as it probably would have been written by a modern playwright.

*The story of the Oresteia.* The plot, taken of course from the Homeric poems, tells of the sorrow and successive disasters falling upon the House of Atreus. Its theme is the working out of hereditary guilt. The *Agamemnon* begins with the watchman's announcing the return of the warrior-king after his long absence at Troy. When he appears, bringing with him his captive maiden Cassandra, Clytemnestra greets her husband with scornful, haughty words which sound dutiful, but have a sting in their double meaning. Then with the help of her lover she murders him. The second play, *The Libation Pourers,* shows how Orestes, the son of Agamemnon and Clytemnestra, avenges the death of his father by murdering his mother and her companion Ægisthus. The third play, *The Benign Ones,* pictures Orestes pursued by the Furies, brought to trial at Athens, and at last obtaining pardon. With his purification, the Furies are transformed into protectors, and the long course of guilt and suffering is finished.

*Changes made by Æschylus.* Working conditions and materials, such as the outdoor setting, the use of masks, the presence of the chorus with its dancing and singing, were all inherited by Æschylus from the more primitive drama. The main characters and events of his plot were supplied by the legend. The single actor had already been "invented" by Thespis. One of the first things Æschylus did was to introduce a second actor. This innovation, made thirty years after Thespis had taken the first step, was a momentous event. Somewhat later Sophocles brought a third actor on the stage, and Æschylus quickly adopted the new style. Of course dummies were used, as in the scene where Prometheus was nailed to the rock; and in one or two later tragedies it seems as if a fourth actor would have been required. In general, however, after the early work of Sophocles Greek tragedy was limited to the three-actor play.

The physical setting of such a drama as *Prometheus* was probably somewhat more elaborate than that of any primitive play. Certain characters arrive on the stage in a wagon drawn by "a winged beast." Chariots had already become theatrical property, and other mechanical devices soon made their appearance. The custom rose for each entering personage by way of introduction to state distinctly his name, place of residence, and his office. Frequently also there was given, through the words of the prologue or one of the actors, a description of the scene of the play, with the landscape features. Such de-

scription, direct or indirect, is of course one of the stock theatrical devices. "How sweet the moonlight sleeps upon this
bank!" was only one of Shakespeare's ways of localizing his
scene.

The Æschylean chorus, composed originally of the singers
of the dithyramb, was continuously present. In the time of
Thespis and the early years of Æschylus it was by far the
most important portion of the play. The extant tragedies of
Æschylus, however, show a gradual but definite change. In
*The Suppliants,* an early work, more than half the lines are
given to the chorus, and the greater part of the dialogue is
between a single actor and the chorus, while the second actor
has but a slight part. In the succeeding plays, however, the
choral passages are much reduced in length, while the dialogue
is prolonged and made far more important. In *The Suppliants*
the fifty maidens form the chorus, but after a time Æschylus
reduced the number to twelve; and from then on the chorus
takes its place as a secondary though still necessary part of
tragedy, composed of appropriate characters, such as a council
of elders, courtiers in the palace of Xerxes, lawgivers, or
sympathetic expositors of the story. Occasionally they appear
as prophetic attendants to whom a happier future is visible.

Whatever changes he made, Æschylus always remained elemental and simple. He delighted in picturesque narrative and
phrases, such as "starry-kirtled night." He speaks of the
wrath of God as "trampling with heavy foot upon the nations
of Persia." He put more color and variety into the costumes
of the chorus and actors, and elaborated the dance movements.
For his time he was a specialist in novelties, such as torch-light
processions and choral effects of a striking character. He
used different rhythms in depicting varying moods, suddenly
transforming the expectations of the audience from delight
into anxiety and grief. Sometimes his characters indulge in
talk which at the moment seems trivial, but turns at a phrase
into tragic intensity, mystery, or dread. He was a master
of the dramatic situation and of climax, having an eye for
what was theatrical and spectacular in the best sense. "The
world," writes Haigh, "has seldom seen a more splendid com-

bination of the arts of poetry, music, dancing and stage management than was produced under the guidance of his genius."

*Patriotic and religious ideas.* Like most of the earlier
Athenian poets, Æschylus was intensely national. His plays
reveal a constant care and anxiety for Greece and the traditions
of greatness which she had inherited. *The Persians* is in a
sense the earliest specimen of Greek history in existence. It
was composed in the full flood of national pride, in the face of
the humiliation of the enemy. Æschylus sings,

> "Impregnable the walls of Athens stand,
> Her fearless children are her bulwarks sure."

Aristocratic in his principles, Æschylus believed that the government of the state should lie upon the shoulders of the
educated and the well-born. The rights of suppliant and guest
are sacred. Hospitality is one of the paramount duties. Liberty, reverence for the gods, generous suffering for the good
of others, and the ancient noble heritage of the Greeks,—
these are topics on which he loves to dwell. His moral earnestness is apparent in each one of his plays. To him Zeus was
the sublime and just ruler of the universe, punishing sin and
evil. There are laws of right and good in accordance with
which man must live; but patience in suffering disarms even
the wrath of the gods and brings rest at last.

Mixed with this deeply religious temperament were all sorts
of ancient superstitions, mingled with a tinge of wholesome
skepticism. In his plays, as in some of the examples of primitive drama, there are lessons in geography, in the history of
civilization, and in the origin of human customs. The very
core and kernel of one of his greatest plays, the *Prometheus,*
is the spectacle of an undefeated will struggling against an
enthroned power. Æschylus placed the wreath of immortality
upon him whose courage and determination held fast in the
face of threatened disaster.

*The eclipse of Æschylus.* Revered as Æschylus was in his
life and honored in his death, yet there rose a generation that
laughed at his archaic diction and ridiculed his plots. Even
within his own century, his simplicity was often scoffed at.

Aristotle, writing a century after his death, evidently regarded
him as one who had served well in his time, but was then out
of date. Beside Sophocles and Euripides he seemed antiquated.
To the modern reader or spectator his scenes sometimes seem
somewhat childish or improbable; and yet it is easy to accept
his fabulous, mysterious world of gods and heroes, which has
the same reality and truth that the ancient fables have, only
many times magnified and filled with poetic imagination. The
genius of Æschylus was flaming and volcanic, suggesting a
comparison with Marlowe, who, like Æschylus, ushered in a
brilliant period of dramatic creation.

With his remarkable gifts—his poetic power, his fertile
imagination, his flair for the thing that was theatrically effective, and his passionate earnestness for the right and good—
Æschylus was a worthy founder of one of the world's greatest
arts. For the Greeks he fixed and determined absolutely the
form of the tragic drama. It was left to later playwrights to
make plots more nearly perfect, and to achieve a more exquisite
finish; but in all essentials, classic tragedy was moulded by
Æschylus. It was as the great originating genius of drama
that he was honored at Athens. Although ordinarily a tragedy
was exhibited but once in the city, yet after the death of
Æschylus a special law was passed, authorizing the reproduc-
tion of his plays, annually, at the City Dionysia. A grant of
money from the public treasury was made to defray the cost.
This distinction was not conferred upon any other poet during
the fifth century.

## CHAPTER V

# SOPHOCLES, THE MOST POLISHED OF THE TRAGIC POETS

Creep gently, ivy, gently creep,
  Where Sophocles sleeps on in calm repose;
Thy pale green tresses o'er the marble sweep,
  While all around shall bloom the purpling rose.
There let the vine, with rich, full clusters hang,
  Its fair young tendrils fling around the stone;
Due meed for that sweet wisdom which he sang,
  By Muses and by Graces called their own.
    *Simmias of Thebes,* translation by Plumptre.

In Sophocles the supreme poetic gift was united with an almost unparalleled dramatic power, and with him the cycle of Greek tragedy came to its perfection. Technically he inherited practically everything. The setting of the stage and its appliances, the art of acting, the management of the chorus and the general structure of the play—all these matters had been worked out by Æschylus and his predecessors. Magnificent as the work of Æschylus had been, it was left to Sophocles to build up a more intricate yet symmetrical plot, to achieve a more polished verse, and to inculcate in his plays a more subtle and profound wisdom.

*Life of Sophocles.* 495-406 or 405 B.C. Colonos was the birthplace of Sophocles, who celebrated the beauties of his native town in one of the extant plays. As a lad of fifteen years he was probably sent away from home, with the women and children, to a place of safety when the Persians under Xerxes invaded Greece in 480 B.C. When, after their defeat, the day came for the celebration of the victory of the Greeks, the boy Sophocles was chosen to lead the triumphal procession.

During his youth the wooden theater which had broken down at the time of the competition of Æschylus against

Chœrilus and Pratinus was replaced, in part at least, by stone. During this period also Æschylus came to the height of his fame. The work of the elder poet must have had great influence upon the youth. In 468 he entered the competitions against Æschylus, when the two men were respectively twenty-seven and fifty-seven years of age. The legend is that the excitement over this contest was so great that the Archon Cimon resorted to the unusual method of taking with him to the play his ten generals representing the ten tribes of Attica, and known to be above any suspicion of unfairness. These generals he bound to act as judges. The play submitted by Sophocles was probably the *Triptolemos*, which received the prize. The text, except for a few fragments, is lost.

For twenty-nine years after his first success, Sophocles reigned supreme on the Athenian stage, though he did not always receive the first award. Of his hundred or more plays, seven are preserved. Like Æschylus and his forerunners, he acted both as director and stage manager; but, on account of his weak voice, early in life he withdrew as an actor. The *Antigone*, composed some time before 440 B.C., was greatly admired. A report, long current, had it that the *Antigone* brought to its author the odd reward of being appointed a general in the army of Pericles. He received flattering invitations from princes of neighboring states to make his home with them; but he seems never to have left Athens except in the course of official duty. In the year 440 he lost the prize for tragedy to Euripides, and in 431 lost it again to Euphorion, the son of Æschylus. When, towards the end of his life, news came of the death of his younger rival Euripides, Sophocles dressed himself in mourning and marched to the altar at the head of the funeral procession. He lived to a great age, loved, respected, and successful to the end. His life has been likened to that of Goethe, with its many years of fruitful activity, its comparative tranquillity, and its singleness of purpose. After his death, the Athenians remembered him by making a yearly sacrifice in his honor.

*The seven extant plays.* Probably the earliest of his surviving plays is the *Antigone*, always a favorite among classical

scholars. It is based upon incidents following the battle celebrated in *The Seven Against Thebes* by Æschylus. Upon the
death of the brothers Polynices and Eteocles, Creon has become
king. He issues a decree that the body of Eteocles, the defender of the city, should be buried with royal honors; but
that the body of Polynices, the so-called rebel, should remain
unburied without the city walls as a perpetual disgrace and
warning. Thereupon Antigone, sister of the two dead chieftains, declares her intention of performing the last burial
rites over the body of her dishonored brother. She goes outside the city wall, sprinkles the body with dust and pours
over it libations to ensure peace to the soul. Her disobedience
is reported to Creon, who sends for her and asks her how she
dared disobey his express commands. She answers that his
decrees are not strong enough to overpass

> "The unwritten laws of God that know no change.
> They are not of today, nor yesterday,
> But live forever."

Creon argues with her, pointing out that Polynices had dishonored himself by attacking his father's city. Antigone does
not repent. Her sister and her lover plead for mercy; but
Creon, feeling that lenience in this case would be but a poor
example of his rule, condemns Antigone to be buried alive in
a rock cave. To the Greek, it should be understood, proper
burial was not only an act of love and respect, but a service
demanded by the gods, a religious duty. Thus the play becomes a representation of the conflict between human and
divine law.

*Ajax.* The story of Ajax was related in one of the lost
epics of the Trojan Cycle, and is suggested also in the eleventh
book of the *Odyssey*. Upon the death of Achilles, the order
went forth that his armor should be given to the bravest and
best warrior in the Argive host. Ajax claimed it, since he
was a giant in stature, had many brave deeds to his credit,
and had rescued the body of Achilles from desecration. By
his arrogance, however, Ajax had incurred the ill-will of
Athena, who commanded that the armor should be given to

Odysseus. In his anger, Ajax would have murdered those about him had not Athena blinded him, so that he could not distinguish men from cattle. In the course of time he recovered, entered a contest and was defeated. Despair then drove him to self-destruction.

Temperance and moderation, even at the pinnacle of success—this is the lesson of the play, told in no uncertain terms. As a hero, Ajax had a peculiar interest for Athenians, for one of the Attic tribes bore his name, and from him certain distinguished families traced their origin. The dying warrior refers to the

> " . . . sacred land that was my home;
> O Salamis, where stands my father's hearth,
> Thou glorious Athens, with thy kindred race,
> Ye streams and rivers here, and Troia's plains,
> To you that fed my life, I bid farewell." [1]

Such an apostrophe, as Haigh reminds us, "would have a peculiarly touching effect when spoken in the open theater, from which the buildings of Athens and the sea-girt isle of Salamis were easily visible."

*The Maidens of Trachis.* (*Trachiniæ.*) This play has for its theme the tender faithfulness of a long-suffering wife, and her final revenge for great wrongs. When Hercules took Dejaneira as a bride to Tyrins, the pair had to cross a stream on the back of the Centaur Nessus. As he bore Dejaneira the Centaur laid rude hands upon her; and seeing this, Hercules shot him with a poisoned arrow. The dying Nessus, seeking to secure a future revenge upon his slayer, gave Dejaneira a rag which had been dipped in his blood, telling her that it was a love charm to win back her husband's heart, in case he should ever prove unfaithful.

For many years Dejaneira lived with Hercules, bore him many children, and forbore to use the supposed love charm in spite of many provocations. When he conquers Trachis, however, the crisis comes. For the sake of a beautiful girl, Iole, Hercules lays waste the city and takes all the women of

[1] Translation by Plumptre.

the city captive. Learning of this deed, in despair Dejaneira gives her husband the supposed charm. It is the "shirt of Nessus," which proves to be a poisoned garment, torturing its wearer to death. Thus an ancient prophecy was fulfilled, to the effect that Hercules should not die by the hand of a living person, but by "one who walked in the realm of Hades."

*Electra.* After Agamemnon had been slain, the city was ruled by his wife and her lover. Orestes, son of the murdered man and Clytemnestra, was obliged to leave the palace. Electra, his sister, secretly helped him and received messages from him through trusted servants. After eight years Orestes, having been commanded by Apollo to take vengeance upon his father's murderers, returns to the palace. With him is his friend Pylades. He contrives a secret interview with Electra, tells her of his purpose, and presently entraps Ægisthus and kills him. Wailing with grief, the mother now appears; and she too is led away to her death. The play closes with the opening of the palace doors showing the dead bodies of Clytemnestra and Ægisthus, with Orestes standing beside them. In theme and incident the *Electra* is, of course, a parallel to *The Libation Pourers* of Æschylus, and among the many plays based upon the legend of the House of Atreus.

*Œdipus the King.* Even to the Greeks of the fifth century, the myth of the House of Laius was a legend of great antiquity. It is touched upon in the *Iliad,* in the *Odyssey,* in Hesiod, and was probably the subject of the lost Theban Cycle of poems. Slight variations mark the different versions of the story. Like many of the Bible narratives, it must have sprung up during a period when infant exposure was a common practice, when the head of every petty tribe was a king, and when more enlightened teachers were endeavoring to abolish the practice of incest. The religion of this period was bound up with the methods of divination and belief in oracles.

The play begins at the point of the story when Œdipus sits proudly enthroned, honored by all. The Theban elders wait upon him, however, with a story of trouble. A plague is killing the crops and beasts, and an oracle has foretold that it will not abate until the murderer of Laius is found and punished. Œdipus, the great and powerful king, promises to rid the nation of its misfortunes and bring the guilty one to light. As the play advances, first one thread and then another is picked up, until in the end the evidence of guilt falls upon Œdipus himself. Jocasta his mother, whom in ignorance he has married, hangs herself; and Œdipus, but yesterday so triumphant, now sees the tragedy inevitably closing in upon him. In remorse he blinds himself; then, led forth by his daughter Antigone, he leaves Thebes and the court forever. In closing, the chorus utters the famous passage:

"Dwellers in our native Thebes, behold, this is Œdipus, who knew the famed riddle, and was a man most mighty; on whose fortunes what citizen did not gaze with envy? Behold, into what a stormy sea of dread trouble hath he come! Therefore, while our eyes wait to see the destined final day, we must call no one happy who is of mortal race, until he hath crossed life's border, free from pain."[2]

It is idle to dismiss such a piece of work as being merely the reincarnation of a ghastly story. It is more than that, for it reaches back into the history of the race. Two ideas are paramount: the futility and wickedness of disregarding the dictates of religion, and the sacredness of the natural family ties. Jocasta and Laius tried to outwit the gods; and Œdipus was in fact guilty of killing his father, although in ignorance of the relationship. Oriental stories abound in similar situations. This myth, like many of the stories of the Bible, relates through symbolism the history of man's efforts towards civilization, law, order, and purity. In addition to this, it portrays the downfall of one who, through prosperity, has become self-confident and arrogant. His trouble comes to him mainly, however, through error, for which atonement can be made. "Apollo is able to disclose and to punish impurity, but he will also give final rest to the wanderer, final absolution to the weary mourner for unconscious sin."

*Use of the Œdipus plot.* Comment has already been made

[2] Translation by Richard Jebb.

upon the wide-spread popularity of this legend. Æschylus used it in a trilogy, the three parts of which consisted of *Laius, Œdipus,* and *The Seven Against Thebes,* only the last of which has survived. A play by Euripides on the same subject is lost. There were at least eight Greek plays based upon this theme, and many parodies by comic writers. Suetonius reported that Julius Cæsar wrote a tragedy upon it, and tradition says that Nero particularly liked to play the rôle of Œdipus. No Greek version, except that of Sophocles, remains.

Among later writers, Seneca, Corneille, Voltaire, and Dryden used the plot. In Seneca, the ghost of Laius comes on the stage inciting his people to revenge, and Jocasta kills herself in sight of the audience. In the version by Corneille, a secondary or under-plot afforded the author a chance to develop an incidental love-story. Corneille followed Seneca rather than Sophocles in presenting scenes of violence on the open stage. Voltaire followed the Greek spirit somewhat more closely, in causing the suicides to take place behind the scenes; but he too used an under-plot, as he considered a love interest necessary to a good play. It was Dryden, however, who depicted the utmost horror. His final scene was too appalling in its butchery even for the strong taste of the times. Eurydice, Creon and Jocasta, Adrastus and the children are all killed on the open stage. Scott, writing in 1790, said that no audience could endure Dryden's *Œdipus.*

*Philoctetes.* The story of this play is found in the Trojan Cycle. Philoctetes was one of the Greek warriors who started out on the expedition against Troy. Being injured, he was left on the island of Lemnos, where he remained for nine years. Meantime the war had continued, and Hector, Ajax, and Achilles had been killed. Philoctetes is in possession of the bow of Hercules. The Greeks, almost in despair at the stubborn resistance of Troy, find that an oracle has foretold that Troy could never be taken except by a son of Achilles and with the bow of Hercules. The Greeks send to the island and try to get the bow away from Philoctetes by deception. During the quarrel that follows Hercules himself descends from heaven, commanding Philoctetes to acknowledge the will of the gods and go to the aid of his countrymen.

This story was used as the basis of a play by each of the three great tragic poets. One can read in it a plea for the burial of all private feuds at the call of country. Some classical students have seen in it a likeness to certain events in the career of Alcibiades, who was recalled to Athens at a time of political strife. Though there may be an analogy, yet the play is ideal in character, and should not be construed into a political tract. It was as near as Sophocles ever came to touching upon the events of his own time.

*Œdipus at Colonos.* The last of the surviving plays was written when the poet was nearing the age of ninety. It deals with still another fragment of the Labdacidæ legend. The blind Œdipus, expiating his guilt, has for many years wandered from land to land, finally coming to a lovely grove at Colonos. While he is resting there, a message is brought to him saying that the gods have now relented and will compensate him for his many sufferings; that in his death he will become a sacred figure, revered by Athenians and Thebans alike. At this point a messenger arrives asking him to come back to Thebes and settle a quarrel between rival claimants to the throne which he himself had once occupied. The old king, wiser now than in youth, refuses to have anything to do with worldly affairs. A clap of thunder and a stroke of lightning startle the company; and when again they look, the old man has been transformed into a strong youth. He feels renewed vigor, but he is not deceived. While his followers are rushing about in confusion and excitement, he calmly leads them to the place which, he knows, has been appointed for his grave.

The mere outline of these plays is sufficient to indicate the variety and richness brought by Sophocles into the drama. The mould so splendidly wrought by Æschylus was filled by him with even more precious metal. His varied characters, his brilliant scenes, his human understanding, his glowing and affecting poetry,—these elements were brought to a perfection which scholars still consider well-nigh matchless.

*The contribution of Sophocles.* Aside from the introduction of the third actor, Sophocles made no great technical innovations. He is supposed to have changed the number of the tragic chorus from twelve, the number fixed by Æschylus, to fifteen. He made sundry additions to stage equipment, caused scenery to be painted, and divided the single line of verse between two or sometimes three speakers. He returned to the earlier method of using three different subjects for the three plays submitted at a contest. While using the Homeric myths, he ignored the Dionysiac stories, and seldom presented the gods on the stage. Fifty-three of his plots were taken from the *Trojan Cycle*. His outstanding contribution lies in the elaboration of plot. Æschylus had never gone much beyond the dramatic situation or presentation of a single important episode. Sophocles took a whole series of episodes, and so arranged them that each one helped to develop the action and had its share in throwing light on the climax. He was able to keep the interest rising to the end. His work, when it left his hand, was as much a masterpiece as a cathedral, and as sound in construction.

*Position of Sophocles among the Ancients.* Much has been written concerning the brilliancy of the scenes, the beauty of language, and the subtle devices of characterization in the Sophoclean plays. Aristotle, the first to lay down principles of dramatic construction, turned to Sophocles, and especially to *Œdipus the King,* as the model of all that was just, beautiful, and illustrious in the art of tragic drama. Ancient writers quoted from Sophocles as moderns quote from Shakespeare. Many fragments remain, in which the reader can find a gentle, philosophic attitude toward life.

"Fortune ne'er helps the man whose courage fails,"

"None but the gods may live untouched by ill,"—

"The skilful gamester still should make the best
Of any throw, and not bemoan his luck."

"What may be taught, I learn; what may be found,
That I still seek for; what must come by prayer
For that I asked the gods."

The following extract, taken from *Philoctetes,* is the speech of the island recluse as he leaves his retreat:

> "Farewell, cave of my lonely watchings,
> Nymphs of the meadows and streams, a long good-by;
> Filling my cave with cries from the storm beaten cape,
> . . . Lemnos, adieu!
> Girt by thy waters! I leave thee at last and obey,
> Bowing my will to the gods' will, who finish all things,
> Bringing fulfilment out of men's obdurate pride."

In comparison with Æschylus, the younger man showed a broader humanity and a capacity for perfection, without the older man's austerity and ruggedness. Æschylus moulded the form, Sophocles harmonized and enriched it. He was not less religious than Æschylus; his whole life seemed to be a worship of the gods. He had, however, a more urbane style and a more human and sympathizing heart. His characters, like those of Æschylus, were to some extent personified passions; but they are pictured with greater compassion. He seems in a peculiar way to embody the spirit of Greece at its greatest and best.

## CHAPTER VI

## "EURIPIDES THE HUMAN"

If the Greek classics are to be read with any benefit by modern men, they must be read as the work of men like ourselves. Regard must be had to their traditions, their opportunities, and their limitations. . . . What we shall lose in reverence by this familiar treatment, we shall gain in sympathy for that group of troubled, uncertain, and very modern minds. The Athenian writers were, indeed, the first of modern men. They were discussing questions that we still discuss; they began to struggle with the great problems that confront us today. Their writings are our dawn.—H. G. WELLS, *Outline of History.*

Tradition has persistently claimed that Euripides was born in 480, on the very day of the naval battle of Salamis, fought between the Greeks and the Persians. If the tradition be true, then the three greatest of the Greek poets were linked together by an odd circumstance: the eldest helped to win the victory, the second was chosen to lead the triumphal procession, and the third was born on the day the fight occurred.

*Life of Euripides.* 485 or 480-406 B.C. In early youth Euripides was attracted to the study of philosophy and poetry. He began to write tragedies when he was eighteen, but did not win the first prize until he was about forty years old. He composed upwards of ninety plays, a few of which were satyric dramas, the others tragedies. Only five times in all—four times during his lifetime and once after his death—were his plays victorious. In 431, when he stood third among the competitors, his four offerings included the *Medea.* Like the *Œdipus* of Sophocles, this play, though accounted by later critics a masterpiece, failed to receive the first prize.

Euripides fell under the disfavor of his fellow citizens, probably on account of his alleged skepticism concerning the gods. He retired to the court of Archelaus, king of Macedon, by whom he was treated with consideration and affection. At his death he was mourned by the king, who, refusing the request of the Athenians that his remains be carried back to the Greek city, buried him with much splendor within his own dominions. His tomb was placed at the confluence of two streams, near Arethusa in Macedonia, and a cenotaph was built to his memory on the road from Athens towards the Piræus.

Euripides had a famous library—one of the first to be collected by a private individual. Although he lived most of his life in the midst of the cultured society of Athens, and was in some respects a leader in it, yet he grew bitter and despondent over the fierce rivalries and greedy ambitions which marked the life of the city. He loved the seclusion of his house at Salamis, where it was said that he composed his dramas in a cave.

*The plays.* Out of the ninety or more plays of Euripides, eighteen have been preserved. The *Rhesus,* for a long time attributed to him, is thought by most modern scholars to belong to some author of the fourth century. The success of several of the plays was owing, in part perhaps, to the fact that they flattered the pride of the Athenians. According to Plutarch, after the disaster of the Sicilian fleet many of the captured Greeks obtained their freedom, and others who had already escaped got food and shelter by repeating verses from Euripides, who was popular with the Sicilians. He was among the first, if not the very first, to use the theme of romantic love for a tragedy. This was done in the *Hippolytus,* one of the least bitter and most interesting of his works. The *Cyclops* is one of the two extant examples of the satyr play, a form which, at the City Dionysia, usually followed the tragedies. Of another work, the Euripidean *Helen,* Schlegel remarked that it was the merriest tragedy ever written.

*Hippolytus.* Phædra, the young wife of Theseus, is pining for the love of Hippolytus, her step-son, whose worship is given not to Venus, but to the chaste Diana. Through an officious nurse the plight of Phædra is revealed to the young man, whereupon tragedy ensues. Phædra, the lovable, is the ancestress of all the stage sirens of the world, down to Camille and

Roxane. The pride and purity of Hippolytus are those of a clean-minded youth not yet awakened from the innocence of adolescence. There are two choruses, one of Old Huntsmen, companions of Hippolytus; the other made up of country-women of Phædra's. In no other play does Euripides offer more buoyant or inspired poetry. Many scholars consider it his most characteristic tragedy. The subject had already been used by both Æschylus and Sophocles, and it has interested many playwrights of other countries.[1] It is the second version of Euripides' play which has come down to us, the first being lost.

*Innovations of Euripides.* Technically Euripides seems to have taken as many liberties as were possible at a time when the plays of Sophocles were set up as the inevitable model. There is no Euripidean play with the close and absolutely water-tight construction peculiar to the *Œdipus Rex.* Euripides was looser and more careless about form, while to the superficial glance he followed the classic model. He used the myths as subjects only because it was the custom, his real interest lying in the human situation and in the diversity of character. Instead of unfolding the details of his plot through the action, he often took the easy method of telling a good deal of it in the Prologue. Though he was contemptuous of the old-fashioned stage appliances, yet in nine of the eighteen extant plays he used the god-from-the-machine to extricate his characters from their troubles.

In comparison with his two predecessors, Euripides was somewhat of a radical. He tried many new themes, and invented many sensational episodes. He attacked political questions and suggested sex problems never before considered proper for the stage. He was a lover of epigrammatic sayings and of the long, set arguments characteristic of the oratorical contests. In all these ways Euripides showed himself resourceful, and proved himself a great poet. His career, however, was far from being the continuous triumph which had fallen to the lot of Sophocles. The Athenians liked novelty, as Saint Paul afterwards discovered; but it was necessary for the

[1] The most noted example in modern times is the *Phèdre* of Racine.

teacher of novelties to be wary. Only a few times was Euripides awarded the prize; and he was mercilessly scored by Aristophanes. His later plays are full of bitterness, with a tone which often tempts the reader to think that he is putting his own personal feelings into the mouth of his characters. Gilbert Murray, in his *Preface* to the *Hippolytus* and the *Bacchœ*, says:

"Amid all their power and beauty, there sounds from time to time a cry of nerves frayed to the snapping point, a jarring note of fury against something personal to the poet, and not always relevant to the play. . . . It is not really anything positive that chiefly illustrates the later tone of Euripides. It is not his denunciations of nearly all the institutions of human society—of the rich, the poor, men, women, slaves, above all of democracies and demagogues; it is not even the mass of sordid and unbalanced characters that he brings upon the scene—trembling slaves of ambition, like Agamemnon; unscrupulous and heartless schemers like Odysseus; unstable compounds of chivalry and vanity like Achilles in the second *Iphigenia;* shallow women like Helen and terrible women like Electra in the *Orestes;* . . . It is the gradual dying off of serenity and hope."

*Religion.* Besides criticism of men and political institutions, there was in Euripides evidence of independent ideas about religion. He despised necromancers and soothsayers, and had no belief in the "blind fate" which was seemingly such a reality to the earlier generation. He almost impeached the gods for making men their plaything. "Arrest the god, whose word we must obey. . . . His is the sin, not mine", one of his characters is made to say. Amphitryon rebukes Zeus himself, saying that justice and wisdom are not known to him. How different from the pious and devout words of Æschylus! Coleridge said, "Euripides . . . is never so happy as when giving a slap at all the gods together." Such a judgment, however, tells less than the whole story. At his best, Euripides filled the framework of the myths with the ideas of personal integrity and the reign of the universal law. Even to his keen skepticism there was the Great Mystery and the Great Obligation.

"And is thy faith so much to give?
Is it so hard a thing to see,
That the Spirit of God, whate'er it be,
The Law that abides and falters not, ages long,
The Eternal and Nature-born—these things be strong?"

In the *Hippolytus* the chorus of Old Huntsmen sing:

"Surely the thought of the gods hath balm in it alway, to win me
Far from my griefs; and a thought, deep in the dark of my mind,
Clings to a Great Understanding."

*"Euripides the Human."* It is evident that the three tragic poets of the fifth century wear their classic robes with a difference. While conforming superficially to the traditions of the Athenian stage, Euripides, for better or worse, was gradually transforming the type and destroying the classic mould. He was saying things which the older dramatists would have omitted, enlarging the range of subjects, and subtly changing the moral and intellectual tone of the stage. At heart a rebel against the classic mode, he injected into it a new spirit partly romantic, partly more "natural," bringing down those figures— Electra, Clytemnestra, Orestes and the others—from the idealized heights to which Æschylus and Sophocles had raised them, into a world at once more human and more teasing to the imagination. Human nature as it is seemed more interesting to him than ideal grandeur. That is what is meant by those who call Euripides more "human" or more "natural."

In him appeared also the romantic spirit. He united the telling fact, the crude details of real life with the romantic motive and atmosphere. Barbaric and picturesque settings, ghastly episodes, striking effects were for Euripides the materials out of which he was to weave a picture of sensuous interest. It was he, inevitably, whose temper permitted the conception of romantic love between the sexes to be used as a dramatic theme within the classic form.

The life of Euripides overlapped that of Æschylus by seventeen years, and was practically coterminous with that of Sophocles, yet he belonged in spirit to another generation. Like them he could sing of the glories of Athens with inspired breath;

and like them he used the Homeric myths. Like Sophocles, he sensed the irony of the mortal situation; but, unlike Sophocles, he was disillusioned with life and grew increasingly bitter as the years went on. He never pictured a saviour of mankind such as Prometheus; rather he set forth a strictly human code, within the reach of all men if they would only cease being greedy, vulgarly ambitious and ignorant.

Though perhaps not the greatest, yet Euripides must be considered the most important of the classical dramatists, because of his influence upon later poets. His ideas, subjects, and technique were transferred to the Roman stage through Seneca, and on through him to the stage of Europe after the Renaissance. His work tends towards the confusion of comedy and tragedy—a process which changed the nature of each. Of the three tragic poets, he is the most modern in tone and temper. Euripides gave the Athenians "plenty of politics, plenty of rhetoric, plenty of discussion political and moral, and now and then threw in a little skepticism." Such is the sketch made by Goldwin Smith. To this should be added the fact that he was a true poet, full of interest and charm.

CHAPTER VII

# ARISTOPHANES AND THE GREEK COMEDY WRITERS

The comedy of Aristophanes was a medley of boisterous comic-opera and of lofty lyric poetry, of vulgar ballet and patriotic oratory, of indecent farce and of pungent political satire, of acrobatic pantomime and of brilliant literary criticism, of cheap burlesque and of daringly imaginative fancy.—BRANDER MATTHEWS, *The Development of the Drama.*

With a burst of laughter, like the clown entering the circus ring, formal Greek comedy seems to spring instantaneously to life, only a little later than tragedy. We know nothing, except by inference, of any intermediate forms between the early pantomimic dance revels, and the finished, complex comedies of Aristophanes. There are only traditions of the *komos,* or revel-rout, which, long previous to the fifth century, must have been a veritable orgy of play-acting, topical songs, lampoons, and ridiculous antics.

The word *komos* (comus) originally indicated both the revel and the revelers—dancers, singers, and masqueraders taking part in the lighter ceremonies connected with the worship of Dionysus. These masqueraders impersonated birds, dolphins, ostriches, cocks, and other fantastic creatures. They rode upon the backs of their companions, carried aloft the phallic emblem, and padded themselves to look like deformed beings. A certain mask, worn with a tight, short jacket, indicated the clown. Other masks were accepted as stereotyped figures. The revelers marched in procession from house to house, pausing before each dwelling with a program of singing, flute-playing, and improvised topical songs. Personal abuse, comic lampoons, and sexual levity were always prominent features of these revels.

51

*Old Comedy.* As Arion brought order into the dithyramb, so Susarion, a fellow townsman of Thespis, brought some degree of order into the program of the comus, which was admitted into the yearly celebrations of Athens about 501 B.C. In 486 the archon granted a chorus for the performance of a comedy, which meant official recognition; and probably about 465 the comedy became a regular feature of the annual festivals. One of the earliest known comic poets was Cratinas, whose life was nearly coterminus with that of Sophocles. He exhibited twenty-one times and was victor nine times, triumphing once over Aristophanes. The titles and many fragments of his plays survive, but there is no complete play. As Æschylus is regarded as the creator of the tragic drama, so Cratinas is regarded as the creator of Old Comedy, giving it its political and personal turn.

*Aristophanes.* About 452 to about 380 B.C. The only peer, in comedy, of the three great writers of tragedy, was Aristophanes, the great representative of Old Comedy. He was a well-born and well-educated Greek. In his plays he carried on a vigorous war against the teachings of the Sophists, against the practices of the demagogue Cleon, against the jingo element of Athens which rendered impossible any long-standing peace with Sparta, and against the general fickleness, weakness, and credulity of the Athenian democracy. About 421 the Athenian legislators took measures to curb the writers of political satire, and for some years Aristophanes was silent. In 414 he appeared again with *The Birds,* in which is placed the famous Cloud-Cuckoo-Town, and with this play he won the second prize. From this time on, under one title or another he ridiculed, attacked, or maligned one institution after another. He embodied in his plays the idea of a communistic settlement and of a woman's conspiracy to bring about peace; he criticised the distribution of wealth and the manners of Greek youth, elaborated a new system of education, and noted the signs of decay in the Greek drama. In time of war he was an open advocate of pacifism, and talked of a Pan-Hellenic union when the rival governments of Sparta and Athens were at swords' points. With it all he contrived to keep the Athenian populace in a roar of laughter by means of his free-spoken and licentious wit.

Like most humorists, Aristophanes was a conservative, favoring the aristocrats against the foreign-born Athenians and political demagogues, having no sympathy with communistic ideas or freedom for women, and generally opposing all new things. He belittled and abused Sappho and the "foreign-born" Aspasia—the two ancient Greek women who, to the modern layman, seem the most gifted women Greece ever produced; yet he could imagine women intelligent enough to form a political party favoring peace, and did actually put such characters into a play. His patriotism took the familiar form of upholding the past. As tricky politicians more and more gained control of the one-time free Athens, bringing in contemptible and disastrous policies, Aristophanes grew more sarcastic and biting. So effective were his attacks on Cleon that at least on two occasions the demagogue attempted to bring an action at law against him. In later days he became the critic of social customs and conditions rather than of individuals.

Considerable pomp and dignity of style attended the Old Comedy. Farcical though it was at times, yet as a spectacle it was imposing, and as drama it was well composed, even formal. The chorus, numbering twenty-four, was gorgeously costumed. Masks were used for chorus and actors, and practically the same settings and machinery were employed as for tragedy. The verse was often marked by impassioned lyric beauty, elevation of diction, and vivid imagery.

The structure of a comedy was far more complicated than that of the tragedy of the same period. It consisted, first, of a set prologue; second, the entrance song of the chorus; then an argument or debating contest between two actors, each assisted by a half-chorus; next, the parabasis, which was an address to the audience, asking perhaps for lenience in judgment, or expressing the views of the author on some subject of current interest, or making witty or scurrilous remarks about people in the audience; then, a series of comic episodes separated from each other by choral odes; and lastly, the exodus, a companion piece to the entrance hymn of the chorus. The parabasis, it will be noted, had no structural connection with the plot, and was the first of the special comedy features to disappear. When the actors were offstage, the chorus united; but when the actors were present, the chorus was often divided, so that one part could answer the other in antiphonal fashion.

The Old Comedy kept the privileges of the early revel-rout in the way of slandering and persecuting prominent persons, and in making use of ribald subjects. Public characters were constantly attacked on the stage, frequently under their own names. Men like Socrates, Pericles, and Euripides were lampooned without mercy. While the prevailing tone of tragedy was religious, that of comedy was political. The plots were usually invented, or taken more or less from real life.

The fame and power of Aristophanes rested not so much upon any one given achievement, as upon the exuberance and abundance of his laughter-provoking spirit. It is almost an injustice to quote him; for while a single jest or even a page of fooling may seem childish, trivial, or unduly coarse, the sum of his work offers an almost inexhaustible volume of merriment. He was a Niagara of comic genius flowing over and about his age, drowning it in ridicule. He picks up jests, makes puns, indulges in personalities, cheap gags and wheezes, runs a joke to earth and then turns it into new laughter, makes topical songs, gives dialect scenes, parodies anybody and everybody. He makes Prometheus hide under an umbrella from the thunderbolts of Zeus, puts lines of poetry into the scales to see which are the heavier, uses slapstick methods with donkeys and slaves, invents queer oaths like "Gadzooks!" telescopes words as did Lewis Carroll, travesties the teachings of Socrates, and creates a topsy-turvy world.

*The Frogs.* This famous play was produced at the Lenæan festival at Athens in 405 B.C., when it won the first prize. It is concerned with the adventures of the god Dionysus and his servant Xanthias as they make their way to Hades. Dionysus is an absurd figure in lion-skin, mustard-colored silk tunic, and high-heeled shoes. He carries a club. Xanthias rides a donkey

and carries a huge bundle of luggage on his back. They
quarrel and bicker, get mixed up in adventures with Hercules,
with a corpse, with Charon, with a pretty girl. Master and
servant are mistaken one for the other, and only a beating can
determine which is which. They arrive in Hades, where there
is a trial by scales to determine which is the better poet,
Æschylus or Euripides. When they were starting on their
journey Hercules had said to them,

> "But aren't there other pretty fellows *here*
> All writing tragedies by tens of thousands,
> And miles verboser than Euripides?"

In Hades, however, nothing will do but a trial between the
two poets. They will weigh the poetry line by line,—but who
will be the judge? There are too many jail-birds in Athens,
and no critics, that is the trouble, says Xanthias. It is decided
at last that Dionysus himself shall be the judge. There follows
the most amazing trial of all literature. The chorus sings a
parody of the best known passages from each author. The
parody of Euripides runs:

> "Halcyons ye by the flowing sea,
> Waves that warble twitteringly,
> Circling over the tumbling blue,
> Dipping your down in its briny dew,
> Spi-i-iders in corners dim,
> Spi-spi-spinning your fairy film,
> Shuttles echoing round the room,
> Silver notes of the whistling loom,
> Where the light-footed dolphin skips
> Down the wake of the dark-prowed ships,
> Over the course of the racing steed,
> Where the clustering tendrils breed
> Grapes to drown dull care in delight!
> Oh, make me a child again just for tonight!
> I don't myself see how that last line is to scan,
> But that's a consideration I leave to our musical man." [1]

When Euripides sees Æschylus he cries, "I know him, I've
seen through him years ago, Bard of the 'noble savage',

[1] Translation by Frere.

wooden-mouthed, no door, no bolt, no bridle to his tongue, a torrent of bombast, tied in bundles!" It is some time before Æschylus gets a chance to speak, but when he does he retorts: "You phrase collector, blind beggar-bard and scum of rifled rag-bags! You and your dancing solos! You and the ugly amours that you set to verse!" Throughout the play there is a liberal criticism of plays, authors, and their methods. The lines are weighed. They argue over repetitions, over questions of truth, over figures of speech. In a word contest, Æschylus insultingly caps everything that Euripides tries to say with a tag—"lost your smelling salts!" In the end Æschylus is triumphant.

*Aristophanes as a critic of his times.* It cannot be claimed that Aristophanes always gave a fair judgment of men, or a true picture of affairs at Athens. He was a good hater, and could make the worse appear the better cause when he chose. He believed that Euripides was largely to blame for the decay of Greek tragedy; that Socrates, who to him represented the Sophists, was an absurd, farcical figure and a corrupter of youth; and that the political policy of Athens, as a "tyrant state", was suicidal and wrong. He loathed the vulgarity, and love of flattery, the greed, the passion for litigation and the low type of public men that had superseded the old Athenian aristocracy.

On the whole, Aristophanes must be recognized as one of the most vigorous and renovating forces in all drama. He claimed that he was always outspoken on the side of virtue against vice; and he made good his claim. He was extravagant, full of the motley spirit of carnival, turning the most solemn creatures of his world into comic pictures; but he was in dead earnest. The world to him was full of cowards, humbugs, liars and charlatans, and his business was to discredit them. Demagogues, philosophers, and rhetoricians were his especial abomination. His ideal was the plain, sturdy citizen of the old school which beat the Persians at Marathon. Two other characteristics, his modern tang of thought and his ability to write gorgeous poetry, should not be forgotten. With changed conditions, one could easily imagine him as a

political cartoonist of the present day, so striking is his gift
for epitomizing a bit of current history; and in his poetry he
could be as impassioned, as picturesque and as vivid as
Euripides himself.

*Middle Comedy.* The change from personal attacks to a
more general criticism of conditions marks the transition from
the Old Comedy to the Middle. Not only the themes, but also
the details of form were gradually altered. The parabasis
was abandoned, and later the chorus was given up for reasons
of economy. In the meantime a law had been passed prohibiting any mention of public characters by name. Aristophanes, with his genius, could to a certain extent elude these
legal restrictions; but in the nature of things the law did in
time effectively deprive the comic writers of the privilege of
personal attack.

Instead of criticism by direct attack, we find in Middle
Comedy insinuation, polished insolence, and the wit of innu-
endo. The gods of the old religion and old-fashioned religious
ideas, however, were still openly ridiculed. The Academy of
Plato, the newly revived sect of the Pythagoreans, and most
of the orators and poets of the day were slyly derided. The
Athenians were laughing over a satire on the myths in a play
called *Gigantomachia* (*The War of the Giants*) by Hegemon,
a Thasian, at the very moment when the news of the great
Sicilian disaster (413 B.C.) was brought to Athens.

The names of thirty-seven comic poets belonging to the
period of Middle Comedy are preserved,—many more than
are known to Old Comedy. The new mode leaned toward the
play of manners, with many interpolations of literary criticism, parodies, and burlesques of the myths. With Middle
Comedy began the creation of stock types—the fawning servant, the conceited cook, the stupid, sensual old man, the
bragging soldier. Under different names these characters, in
succeeding epochs, have appeared and reappeared on the stages
of the world with a kind of shameless immortality.

*New Comedy.* In its outward aspect the New Comedy can
scarcely be distinguished from the Middle. It is usually dated
from 338 B.C., the year of the conquest of the Macedonian

king. Slightly diversified stock types—the cunning slave, the roysterer, the gallant captain, the scolding wife—were added to the familiar stage figures, as these became more and more conventional. Before the middle of the fourth century the chorus had generally disappeared. Actors still wore masks. The love theme now became a common subject, but it was not the more delicate forms of romantic love which commended themselves to the writers of the New Comedy. The situations were almost invariably coarse, and the implications indecent. The work of "humanizing" the drama begun by Euripides a hundred years before, was now carried to its logical conclusion. Pictures of everyday life took the place of ideal conceptions. Human nature as it was replaced the portrayals of human nature as it should be.

*Menander.* 342-290 B.C. Sixty-four names survive from the New Comedy, the most famous of which are Philemon, Menander, and Diphilus. No single complete play of any one of these writers is in existence, but large fragments are known. Menander, the greatest of the three, was practically the last great original poet of Athens, as he was also the first writer of elegant social comedy. He wrote at least one hundred plays and gained the prize eight times. Fragments, discovered as late as 1905, give six hundred lines of a play called *The Guardians,* and four hundred and fifty from another called *The Shorn Lamb.* Menander was something of a popular idol during his lifetime, and became one of the prime favorites among the authors of antiquity. He was frequently imitated, and his plays were "adapted" for the Roman stage. Terence followed both the style and the plots of Menander. Saint Paul quoted him, and his epigrams and pithy sayings seem to have been on everybody's lips.

Menander's service to drama lies in the fact that he discovered a comedy formula for the play of contemporary manners—a formula with just the right mixture of ridicule, suavity, wit and flattery. He portrayed the fast life of Athens with quiet mastery. We can detect also, through the Terentian imitations, a more serious purpose, which is well described by Cruttwell in his *History of Roman Literature:*

"To base conduct upon reason rather than upon tradition, and paternal authority upon kindness rather than fear; to give up the vain attempt to coerce youth into the narrow path of age; to grapple with life as a whole by making the best of each difficulty when it arises; to live in comfort by means of mutual concession and not to plague ourselves with unnecessary troubles—such are some of the principles indicated in these plays of Menander which Terence so skilfully adapted, and whose lessons he set before a younger and more vigorous people."

*General nature of Greek comedy.* Sophisticated as Greek comedy was, yet it is interesting to note its reliance upon the same features which were used by the savage play-actors,—dancing and singing, song duels and debating contests, the use of grotesque masks, the impersonation and imitation of animals, and fighting an enemy by ridicule. The writers of comedy came much nearer to being a mirror of their own times than did the tragic poets, though great allowance must still be made for the exaggerations, the partisanship, and the lampooning privileges enjoyed by the former. The plays abound in local hits, references to events of the day and the slang of the moment. We see something of the real Athenian through the eyes of Aristophanes or Menander. We see their innate sociability, their democratic spirit, their literary tendencies, their love of novelty, frugality, and enjoyment in exposing the weaknesses of their fellow men. Sometimes they were cruel in their laughter; often their jokes seem amazingly modern. Was Aristophanes the first wag to accuse the sausage-makers of using dog and donkey meat? He makes fun of the high forehead of Pericles; makes Scythian policemen talk with a brogue, like the Irish stage policeman of our own day; jests about the married man, saying with mock pity that only the other day he saw the poor thing alive and walking about. He ridicules the Athenians for everlastingly bragging about their fine figs, their honey, their myrtle berries and their Propylæa. Menander, after losing the prize to a friend, asks him, "Don't you feel ashamed every time you take the prize away from me?"

Underneath the vivacity, the irreverence, and even the scurrility of Greek comedy can be detected two purposes: first to amuse a very shrewd and critical audience; and, secondly, to give vent to a running fire of criticism upon every phase of public and private life. Oddly enough, the judgments of these comic writers were often quite like the judgments of the moral reformers.

CHAPTER VIII

# ARISTOTLE, CLASSIC TECHNIQUE, AND THE LATER GREEK DRAMA

It is possible for a play to observe all the essential rules arising from the conditions of a performance in a theater, and before an audience, and yet be so lacking in poetry, in truth to life, in inherent worth, as to be undeserving the name of drama.—ROY FLICK-INGER, *The Greek Theater and Its Drama.*

The living center of Aristotle's criticism is a conception of art as a means to a good life.—J. MIDDLETON MURRY, *Aspects of Literature.*

It is to the Greeks that we owe not only the first great plays, but also the first principles of criticism and of dramatic construction. Not every Athenian was a good critic, as some would have us think; but we know that the comic poets took it upon themselves to deliver judgments, to compare one writer with another, and in some measure, to lay down the laws of drama. It fell, however, to Aristotle,[1] a philosopher and teacher born in the first quarter of the fourth century, to become not only the most important mouthpiece of Greek dramatic criticism, but also one of the most important influences in all the history of literature. He analyzed the plays of the fifth century as well as those of his own time, classified the kinds of drama, and laid down rules for the construction of tragedy.

Aristotle had the very human characteristic of harking back to the good old days, and thinking them much better than the days in which he lived. Taking scant account of Æschylus, he regarded Sophocles and Euripides as models in tragedy. His chief complaints were that the poets of his own time spoiled their work by rhetorical display; that the actor was

[1] Sometimes called the Stagyrite, from Stagyria, his birthplace.

often of more importance than the play; and that the poets tampered with the plot in order to give a favorite actor an opportunity of displaying his special talent. He said that the poets were deficient in the power of portraying character, and that it was not even fair to compare them with the giants of a former era; that the drama was greatly in need of fresh topics, new treatment, and original ideas; that it was polished in diction, but lacking in force and vitality. The playwrights too frequently made use of the god-from-the-machine for the purpose of extricating characters from their troubles. Such was the tenor of Aristotle's "reviews" and criticisms.

*The general principles of Aristotle.* The greatest tragedy, in the opinion of Aristotle, was *Œdipus the King* by Sophocles. The reasons for its supremacy lay in the excellent management of plot and chorus, in the beauty of language, in the irony of the situations, and in the general nobility of conception. Aristotle cited also the *Helena* of Euripides as a model of its kind, and lauded the author for the skill with which he had set forth the complicated plot. Euripides was to him the most tragic of the poets. At the same time, he found much in Euripides to censure. Only in Sophocles, the perfect writer, were united ideal beauty, clearness of construction and religious inspiration,—the three qualities which alone make tragedy great.

The subjects of tragic drama, Aristotle said, were rightly drawn from the ancient mythology, because coming from that source they must be true. If man had invented such strange incidents, they would have appeared impossible. The chief characters of a tragic action should be persons of consequence, of exalted station. The leading personage should not be a man characterized by great virtue or great vice, but of a mixed nature, partly good and partly bad. His errors and weaknesses lead him into misfortune. Such a mixture of good and evil makes him seem like ourselves, thus more quickly arousing our sympathy. The course of the tragic action should be such as to saturate the spectator with feelings of compassion, drive out his petty personal emotions, and so "purge" the soul through pity and terror *(Catharsis)*. The crimes suitable for tragic treatment may be committed either in ignorance, or intentionally, and are commonly against friends or relatives. Crimes committed intentionally are generally the more dramatic and impressive. (This in spite of the fact that the central crime in *Œdipus the King* was committed in ignorance.) As to style, a certain archaic quality of diction is needful to the dignity of tragedy.

*The three unities.* The most famous of the Aristotelian rules were those relating to the so-called unities—of time, place, and action. The unity of time limits the supposed action to the duration, roughly, of a single day; unity of place limits it to one general locality; and unity of action limits it to a single set of incidents which are related as cause and effect, "having a beginning, a middle, and an end." Concerning the unity of time, Aristotle noted that all the plays since Æschylus, except two, did illustrate such unity, but he did not lay down such a precept as obligatory. Perhaps tacitly he assumed that the observance of the unity of place would be the practice of good playwrights, since the chorus was present during the whole performance, and it would indeed be awkward always to devise an excuse for moving fifteen persons about from place to place. The third unity, that of action, is bound up with the nature not only of Greek but of all drama.

*Greek drama more concerned with plot than with character.* Aristotle conceived the action, or plot, of a play as of far greater importance than the characters. This conception he gained from the plays of the fifth century, which, in general, centered around a personified passion rather than around a character. The action was "the vital principle and very soul of drama." Again he says, "Tragedy is an imitation, not of men, but of actions." Second in importance was characterization; and third were the sentiments aroused by the action. He insisted very clearly that in tragedy the plot does not rise out of the characters, but on the contrary the plot tests the characters through the working-out of destiny—"blind fate." The main duty of the dramatist was to organize first the action, then display the moral character of his people under the blows of fate. "The incidents of the action, and the structural ordering of these incidents, constitute the end and purpose of tragedy." [2] Finally, and perhaps most important of all, was Aristotle's belief that although tragedy should purge the emotions through pity and terror, yet all drama was meant to entertain: tragedy through the sympathies, comedy through mirth.

*Perversion of Aristotle's principles.* In this manner was begun the formulated technique of the drama. The principles enunciated by Aristotle were deduced from a study of the plays which were effective in his time, and under the conditions of the Athenian stage; but as time went on, critics and playwrights often studied Aristotle instead of plays, and left out of consideration differing circumstances and conditions. In this way, rules, created for the open-air Athenian production, were applied indiscriminately to all sorts of stages, whether indoors or out. Many writers failed to recognize the new life in their own art, and missed seeing the truth that a first-hand observation of life is always of more value than rules of any sort. Therefore an immemorial war has been waged between the sticklers for old laws, on the one side, and, on the other, the genuinely creative writers. In no art has this war been more apparent than in the drama; and in no art have rigid rules been more oppressive. There have been long periods when the dominance of technical rules, wholly or partially outgrown, has sterilized and all but killed the theater.

*Records and preservation of the plays.* The archons of Athens kept records of the contests at both the city festivals, giving the names of the *choregoi* (citizens appointed to defray part of the expenses of the production), the poet-teachers (called *didascaloi*), the actors, plays, and victors in the contests. Aristotle published these records in the fourth century. In the meantime, special copies of the great tragedies of Æschylus, Sophocles, and Euripides had been preserved. The rapid growth of theaters all over the Hellenic world made the business of providing plays, both old and new, an important one. With the need of many new plays appeared the "adapters" and manipulators, who so corrupted the texts of the poets that

[2] From *Aristotle on "The Art of Poetry,"* by Lane Cooper.

the Athenians were forced to pass a law prohibiting the making of any change in the original version. When this law was passed, authorized copies of the plays were made; and whenever one of them was given, a public secretary was appointed to attend, with official copy in hand, to note any deviation from the genuine text. The producer who permitted such maltreatment of the lines was punished. Fragments of plays were often preserved, however, by the process of "contamination,"—a frequent practice of Latin producers,—which consisted of taking two Greek plays and combining them to make one Latin play.

In the third century before our era a collection of tragedies and satyr plays was made for the library at Alexandria. Scholars of that city also drew up a canon of famous writers, probably for educational purposes; and the works of the writers included in the canon were preserved in numerous copies. Many catalogues, chronological lists and yearly records must also have been published and placed in the libraries of the known world, together with authorized copies of the original works. But nearly all such copies, lists and catalogues have disappeared. The modern world owes the preservation of such plays as we have to the teachers and grammarians of the early Christian centuries, especially to those at Byzantium. Nearly a thousand years after the *Œdipus* was written, probably in the fifth century of our era, certain plays were selected for study in the schools. Seven were taken from Æschylus, seven from Sophocles, eight (or nine, if the *Rhesus* be included) from Euripides, and eleven from Aristophanes. Ten more from Euripides were preserved by other means. The dramas so selected were supplied with commentaries (*scholia*) and were given in the regular courses of study during the Middle Ages. Consequently these plays were reproduced in many copies.

*Followers of the great poets.* Even though we have no specimens of plays from the centuries immediately following the "golden" age, yet there was enormous dramatic activity. Theatrical entertainments were practically universal. The names of fourteen hundred playwrights are preserved, though their plays are lost. The theatrical tradition seemed to run in families. Phrynicus and Pratinas each had a son who became a playwright; and Euphorion, the son of Æschylus, took part in the contests, offering both his own and his father's plays. The two sons of Sophocles, Ariston and Iophon, were also known as tragic poets. Sometimes the gift descended to the grandson or grand-nephew, as in the case of Morsimus, son of Philocles, who was the nephew of Æschylus.

*The building of theaters.* From Sicily in the west to Phœnicia on the east—over the whole Hellenic world—appeared new theaters, many of which were built of stone. Dramatic contests were organized on the Athenian plan. For a time these contests were usually associated with the Dionysiac festivals; but in course of time they became a part of the program in ceremonies devoted to other gods. Later they were dissociated from religious festivals altogether, and used simply as secular entertainments, though never to such a degree in the ancient world as in the modern. Actors organized themselves into guilds. Kings and princes patronized the theater, often using it as the means of extravagant personal display. Haigh relates that Alexander the Great "was accustomed to celebrate the close of his campaigns with theatrical exhibitions on a scale of unapproachable splendor. Pavilions of silver and gold were erected, at such times, for the reception of the guests; the best actors were hired from every city of Greece; and subject kings were often compelled to fill the office of *choregoi.* On one occasion no less than three thousand performers were collected to take part in the various musical and dramatic competitions. From this time forward, gorgeous dramatic spectacles became the favorite amusement with the famous princes of the time. Antiochus the Great is said to have surpassed all previous monarchs in the splendor of his shows; and Antony and Cleopatra, in the winter before the final campaign against Augustus, wasted their time at Samos in a long series of similar entertainments."

*Weaknesses of later dramatists.* Such was the prestige that dramatic performances acquired in the course of a few centuries. The history of drama, however, is none the richer for these sumptuous imperial entertainments. If any masterpieces were written during those later days, they have been lost and all records of them forgotten. The names of some of the writers are known; also a few fragments, a few literary traditions, and the jokes of the comic writers—that is all. In Alexandria, in the days of its glory, there rose a set of brilliant poets, seven of whom became celebrated under the title of the Pleiad; and later still there appeared a group of "literary dramatists" who wrote not for the stage, but for public declamation or private reading. Such writers merely used the dramatic form, they did not produce drama. Many of them wrote in order to teach some political or philosophical doctrine. These were the signs of ebbing life; and as life went out, rules and dogmatic traditions were the more zealously followed.

*Meaning of "classic."* The word "classic" has at least two meanings in common use: first, as a designation of any work of art which has to a certain extent withstood the test of time; and secondly, as a designation of works of art which are modeled more or less after Greek or Latin examples. In this book the word is generally used in the second meaning. The representatives of the classic school are the Greek dramatists already considered, and the Latin writers who followed the models of the Greek. They established a certain kind of play, with heroic characters, and a remote and often majestic setting. Their style was usually marked by clearness, symmetry of form, restraint, and finish of detail. There were many lyric touches; but in general it was free from the extravagances, the surprises, the changes of mood and the individual emotion which belong to the romantic school.

Thus the great phenomenon of Greek drama germinated, came to its rich flowering, and fell into decay within a century. Its like has never reappeared. It was produced not in the midst of calm prosperity following the triumphs of war, as some writers have suggested, but in the very turmoil of political contentions in the state, and hostile attacks from without. It set up a standard of concentrated action, poetic imagery, and religious fervor towards which the playwrights of succeeding generations have struggled in vain.

## CHAPTER IX

# GREEK PLOTS, THEATERS, COMPETITIONS, AND AUDIENCES

The real standard of art is not comparative but qualitative. Art is not greater or less, it is good or bad, sincere or spurious. Not many intellectual workers are called to be Aristotles or Newtons or Pasteurs or Einsteins. But every honest piece of inquiry is distinctive, individualized; it has its own incommensurable quality, and performs its own unique service.—JOHN DEWEY.

With the Greeks, for the first time in history, we have drama that is also literature. With few exceptions, the plays were important contributions to religious ceremonials. In many cases they represent an age far more remote than that in which they were written. They present gods and the offspring of gods; and in tragedy they uniformly portray the vain struggle of man against fate. The form both of tragedy and comedy was determined by rather rigid rules. The *Œdipus* and *The Frogs* can be set forth, as to structure, like a geometrical design, symmetrical and complete in itself. All Greek plays were written in unrhymed verse, the lyrics of the chorus being susceptible of considerable variation in meter and length of line.

*The extent of the action.* The plot of a Greek tragedy did not cover the whole course of a story, such as is used, for example, in *King Lear*. As a rule it began at the culminating moment, when the long series of evil and mischance had come to a crisis. Thus it became necessary for the author to inform the audience of the preceding events. In the *Œdipus* this information is given naturally through the unfolding of the evidence, step by step. The dialogue discloses everything the spectator ought to know, just at the right time. Such a happy and natural disclosure, however, was a difficult thing to

68

achieve: hence the prologue, which in time became an integral part of every play. Since the action began, as it were, at the last chapter of the story, and the threads of the plot were already convergent, the chief purpose of the dramatist was to show the intensity of emotion, the despair, surprise, or horror attendant upon the catastrophe, which, as a matter of course, would be packed into a single scene, and limited in time to a few hours.

*Absence of death scenes.* The main outlines of the story would generally be known to the educated, and perhaps also to many of the uneducated members of the audience. The suspense lay in the variety of treatment, in the imaginative touches and in the poetic beauty of the situations. No portrayals of violence or death, as a general thing, were seen. Such events, as well as the news of distant battles and the like, were reported by the Messenger, whose speeches soon became an important feature. It is sometimes supposed that the Greeks were too refined to be able to witness scenes of bloodshed; but that explanation does not quite cover the case. The theater, during the Dionysiac festival, was the abode of the god: hence it was sacred. Temple traditions forbade any exposition of scenes of violence; therefore the actors, the chorus, and the playwright were protected and inviolable.

In many Greek plays there are excessively long speeches. Euripides and Aristophanes made popular concessions to the love of rhetorical contests by incorporating into their dramas set arguments or debates. The soliloquy and the aside, often called the deadly sins of the theater, were frequently used. The distinction between comedy and tragedy was always maintained; but the exact definition of each species was left then, as it has ever since remained, a doubtful thing. Not all Greek tragedies end unhappily. The *Eumenides* of Æschylus, the *Philoctetes* of Sophocles, the *Iphigenia* and *Electra* of Euripides,—all these plots end in some sort of happiness or success for the principal characters.

*Subjects and underplot.* A modern authority on Greek drama Professor Roy Flickinger, emphasizes the myth-element thus: "The subject matter of Greek plays is drawn from Greek mythology as inevitably as a sermon is founded on a biblical text." Of the extant tragedies, only one, *The Bacchanals* of Euripides, is founded upon the experiences of Dionysus; and only two plays, *The Persians* of Æschylus and *The Capture of Miletus* by Phrynicus, were founded upon historical incidents. In the brilliant period there was very little treatment of love between the sexes, either of the romance of youth or of married life. In the fourth century and later there was introduced a good deal of what has come to be known as comic relief; also there was often inserted another story about a subordinate set of characters, whose experiences ran parallel to the main story. This latter device was called the under-plot, or secondary plot. It was not used by either Æschylus or Sophocles, and was only hinted at in the work of Euripides.

One of the most striking discrepancies between actual contemporary life and life as represented by the dramatists lies in the portraiture of women. In reality, the Greek lady of the fifth century lived in almost oriental seclusion. She took no part in public affairs, and was seldom seen outside her home. The writers of comedy generally pictured respectable women in this light; but in tragedy the authors reverted to the period of Homer, when women were socially at least on an equal footing with men. In many other respects Greek drama fails as a mirror of the times. One would never suspect, from a reading of Greek tragedy, that the Athenian of the fifth century was one of the most political-minded of men. There are a few hints of political discussion in Euripides; but it is only in comedy that one can gain any adequate idea of the Greek's preoccupation with political questions.

*Greek irony.* The well-known classic irony showed itself mainly in two ways: a character uttered, unknowingly, the very curse which was destined to fall on his own head; or, knowingly, he spoke with veiled sarcasm in terms susceptible of two meanings. In the latter case, the person addressed naturally accepted the words in their obvious, innocent interpretation; but the audience, as well as the speaker, knew their sinister import. The entire plot in the *Œdipus* is based on irony. That a proud and deeply respected king should himself be the culprit whom he and his officers are seeking to bring to justice—that is the very essence of the ironical. The case is not subject to condemnation or tearful regret; the dramatist simply gives a stoical, sophisticated statement of the situation, which is complicated by the fact that often there is right on both sides, and that the contestants are blinded by fear or passion. Professor Flickinger reminds us that the drama frequently resembles a court-room trial, "when the irony arises from clashing intrigues, and the audience, admitted to the author's confidence, and sitting by his side, as it were, joins with him in awarding praise here and condemnation there."

*The Greek theater.* By the year 431 B.C.—the year in which the *Medea* of Euripides was exhibited—the drama had become firmly established at Athens and had also spread throughout Hellas. Many a man born during the lifetime of Thespis may have lived to see the rude vaudeville-like show transformed into an elaborate and beautiful spectacle. In the whole group of states there was scarcely a town so small or remote that it did not afford its theater and its yearly festival. Athens herself had been beautified beyond all precedent. Its Acropolis was resplendent with marble temples; and on the southern slope of this hill of beauty was situated the Theater of Dionysus Eleuthereus, in a natural open amphitheater. The old wooden benches had broken down in 499, when an immense crowd had come to witness the contest between Æschylus and Pratinas. Various replacements were made during the fifth century, until finally a stone structure was built, covering about three-quarters of a circle, and open to the sky. The seats accommodated perhaps as many as seventeen thousand people, and were set into the slope of the hill. The exact middle of the circle, which was of course the lowest spot in the theater, was marked by the altar (*thymele*) to Dionysus. Around this altar was the dancing place, called the orchestra. At the back was a permanent setting—the old skênê, or dressing hut enlarged with pillars and doors. This background represented a temple for tragedy, or a house for comedy. A part of it may sometimes have been painted to represent scenery; but there was no stage, in the modern sense, and no curtain.

In front of the altar, in the middle of the lowest tier, was a stone seat reserved for the priest of Dionysus. In the fourth century it was carved with an inscription indicating the office of its occupant. Examples of handsomely carved seats are still in existence. Other places in the front tier were for city officials, judges, and the archons. Three aisles radiated from the center, and a transverse aisle cut the three radii halfway up the slope. Far up, behind the topmost seats, perhaps there stood even in Sophocles' day poplar trees into whose branches truant boys sometimes climbed to steal a glimpse of the play. To the spectator facing the altar, the city market-place and the harbor of the Piræus with its ships would be on the right, and the open country on the left. The effect of this scene is thus described by Mr. Stark Young:

"In the theater of Dionysus the lighting was that of the sun; the scene was but slightly varied either through shifts or through light. The gestures were simple and restrained, as we may infer from the spirit and the style of the plays, and may be sure of from the difficulties that the costume, the onkos, the padding, and the high-soled cothurnus would have put in the way of animated motions . . . the larger part of the effect in the Greek theater was due to the voices, trained as we train for the opera, and exerted for a trained public taste. However beautiful the lines of those garments may have been, their grave and exquisite rhythm and their subtlety of color in the bright air, the blowing on them of the wind from the Bay of Salamis, it was the voices of the actors that achieved much of that effect of tragic beauty. . . . To all that antique world, the ear was the seat of memory."

*Stage appliances.* Nowhere in the world has there ever been used stranger or more artificial mechanism than on the Athenian stage. There were two ways by which an interior could be shown in the course of an outdoor scene. The general name for this device was *eccyclema*. One type was made with a revolving platform and an opening door; the other was a trundling platform, shoved out before the audience on tracks, carrying the set interior. The most famous of all the appliances was perhaps that which gave us the phrase "god-from-the-machine." This contrivance, sometimes called simply the "machine," was a crane-and-pulley arrangement by which the god could be lowered from heaven and caught up again. It may have been used for the first time at the performance in 431. The machine was often kept so busy that its use brought down ridicule from the comic poets. In earlier days the god stood on the roof of the dressing hut and spoke from there.

Besides the *eccyclema* and the machine, it was possible to represent falling or burning houses, to bring chariots, dragons, and winged beasts on the stage, to send spirits into the lower regions, and to produce thunder and lightning. Problems of stage lighting, however, did not exist; for ghosts walked by daylight, storms and night scenes were enacted under the same conditions. There were no playbills, no division into acts, therefore no intermission except between plays.

*The state as manager.* Neither the management of the festival nor the production of the plays was left wholly to private enterprise. The state owned the theater and determined what poets should be allowed to give their pieces. A committee first passed upon all the offerings, and granted a chorus to such as they deemed worthy of exhibition. The state paid the salary of the actors, supplied the prizes, and made the rules by which the competitions were governed. There still remained a heavy part for the private citizen to do. Each year it was decided by lot which of the wealthy Athenians should have the privilege of paying the salaries of the chorus, besides the cost of the trainer and the costumes. This citizen was called the *choregos*.

*The nature of the competitions.* About the time Thespis came to Athens, Pisistratus (called the Tyrant) organized competitions for the tragic poets, to be conducted at the annual festivals in honor of Dionysus. The most important of these celebrations, the City Dionysia, occurred probably toward the end of March and lasted at least for five or six days. Two lesser festivals, the Lenæa in January and the Anthesteria in February, were also in honor of the god of the vine. From a list of distinguished Athenians ten judges were chosen by lot. Prizes were awarded each contestant, first, second, or third, according to the rating. In the early days the prize for tragedy was a laurel wreath and a goat; later a tripod. For comedy the original prize was a jar of wine. By the year 431 a small sum of money was probably awarded, in addition to the wreath. Admission to the competitions was in itself a greatly coveted honor. Prizes were given not only for the best plays, but also for the best acting.

Women came to see the tragedies, but seldom remained for the comedies; if they did, the cloak of symbolism must have done duty in covering some very broad scenes. Men and women of all classes rubbed elbows, without much respect of persons. Slaves and children could come if their masters or parents would pay; and if a citizen were too poor to afford the two obols—about six cents—the state gave him the money for his admission. On certain occasions prisoners were released for the day. Schools were transferred bodily to the theater, and men of highest learning and position did not disdain to attend. Even Socrates, who did not ordinarily go to the play, might possibly have been seen at the festival in 431, since Euripides, his friend, was one of the competitors.

*Announcing and giving the play.* A few days before the City Dionysia began, a full announcement of the performances was given by means of a ceremony called the *proagon.* At a public meeting-place the poets, the actors without their masks, and the *choregoi* were presented by name to the public by a herald. It was made clear what pieces were to be presented, their subject, and what actors were to take part. With the arrival of the first day of the festival, all Athens would be alive very early in the morning to take part in the great procession which opened the event and was designed to escort the statue of Dionysus from the temple, his home, to the theater. The temple in Athens, however, was situated only a few yards from the stage; consequently the actual journey would have been short. But the Greeks did not always take the shortest cut. The statue was mounted on a wagon-ship and hauled by youths some distance out of the city towards Eleutheræ; from there it was hauled back to the theater and placed in a conspicuous position, where it remained as the silent witness of the festivities. On the journey to the edge of the city and back the entire free-born population of the city acted as escort.

The plays probably were given during the last three days of the festival, and were scheduled to begin at daybreak. Three tragedies and one satyr play from each competing poet made up the program. The first play opened by one of the actors coming forward and reciting the prologue, or by the advent of the chorus in a slow dance movement or march. The chorus, of course, was none other than the group of dithyrambic singers of the olden days; but the goat-skin costumes had been discarded, and never appeared except in the satyr plays. For tragedy, the chorus numbered fifteen; for comedy, twenty-four. Throughout the performance the chorus was present, sympathizing with the chief character, relating to the audience parts of the story which had taken place before the action began, or delivering a sermon on the moral lesson of the play. In the great days the chorus was an essential and important feature; but after the fifth century its connection with the plot became more and more relaxed, until it survived only as an ornamental addition.

*The actors.* In the early part of the fifth century the poet-dramatists were also the chief actors, and did most of the work of training the choruses. Æschylus and Sophocles had to invent and teach the art of acting, so far as it progressed beyond the primitive stage. The poetic character of the lines required great accuracy, and it is probable that all of the Greek actors of the great age were men of learning and breeding. Æschylus acted in all his own plays; but Sophocles early in life gave up speaking parts, on account of the weakness of his voice. The actors, three in number, were always men; supers and mutes were freely used. In the large amphitheater facial expression would naturally be lost; therefore the actors wore conventionalized masks, faces idealized for tragedy, caricatured for comedy. The stock figures—the garrulous old man, the god, the messenger, the slave—could at once be recognized by their masks. It is thought that the voice was magnified by a special mouthpiece, and that the height of the actor was increased by the use of the cothurnus, or thick-soled shoe. The actors stood on a level with the chorus in the space back of the altar; and with their long flowing hair, their graceful robes of gorgeous colors, and their stately movements they undoubtedly had the appearance of conventional beauty.

*The temper of the public.* If in imagination we could take our place among the throng present at the competitions of 431 B.C., we should feel a thrill at the beauty of the scene,—the sky brilliantly blue, the waters of the bay sparkling, the fields fresh with spring verdure. On the stage is a scene of stately magnificence. Poetry, music, and dancing are there, all supplementing and enriching the play. As the story unfolds, we too are swept away by the excitement of the crowd and the lure of the tragic story. As the day wears on, the place becomes the scene of many a noisy contention. The playwright has his own particular group of friends and partisans, and a well organized *claque*. When a daring speech is made the *claque* applauds, while another group hisses it down. Some of the audience whistle and boo, while others cheer and stamp their feet. Tragic as the story is, laughter and shouts break out if either actor or author should happen to offend some ruffian in the crowd. When the turn for comedy arrives, the audience becomes hilarious, undisciplined, full of dangerous whims. Figs, olives, and even stones are sometimes thrown at the comedians, who in turn make capital out of the occurrence by turning it into a joke. At the satyr play, the goat-chorus and Dionysus appear, full of ribaldry and merriment. At the end of the festival comes the decision of the judges, eagerly awaited. In those times, as in ours, "the decision of the umpire was often roundly cursed." The three tragic poets who were contending in 431 were Euphorion, son of Æschylus, Sophocles and Euripides. We do not know what plays were offered by the first two poets; but of the three tragedies offered by Euripides, one was the *Medea.* Euphorion won the first place, Sophocles the second, and Euripides the third.

Although many circumstances in the Greek play were not those of contemporary life, yet in certain ways Greek drama is a profound revelation of fifth-century Athens. In it was reflected the citizens' pride. All the poets brag about the splendor of their city, its reputation as a refuge, its hospitality, its impregnable strength. We see the native admiration for alertness, wit, and quick responsiveness. The Greek love of deciding questions by lot is reflected in the conduct of the competitions. The Greeks, like the modern French, were adept in making formal rules and in introducing order into their artistic enterprises,—and this trait is shown in their drama. Rhetorical contests and debates could always be counted upon to make a successful scene in a play.

"Crude in certain ways the Greek drama is, as we cannot help admitting; but still it is the most wonderful in all the long history of the theater, because it is the only great drama which has been wrought out by a single people, wholly without any aid from the outside, with absolutely no model to profit by. . . . This they did, and this no modern race has been able to do, because the dramatic literature of every modern language has come, at one time or another, directly or indirectly, under the influence of Greek tragedy." [1]

It is no exaggeration to say that the early masters of drama were teachers; this statement, however, does not mean that in Athens the playhouse was a school. In a sense it was both a school and a church; yet it was something more than that. The drama was a medium through which the playwrights could express their opinion, or their guess, about the riddle of human suffering, the relation of man to the gods, and the destiny of the human soul. Without the influence of these dramas, it is difficult to imagine what literary history would have been. The raw materials of the dramatic art were everywhere in the world; it was the Greeks who discovered it and moulded it into form. Almost instantly the new creation seemed to spring into life; and though it has lapsed and died, yet it has always sprung up again in new forms. With the possible exception of music, it is the most popular of the arts; and it is to the everlasting glory of the Greeks that they set a standard which has been a challenge to every succeeding generation of playwrights.

[1] Brander Matthews, *The Development of the Drama.*

## CHAPTER X

# HOW GREEK DRAMA INVADED ROME

For reasons to be sought in political and social history, the Latin drama never throve after its brilliant beginnings in the Middle Republic. . . . But the modern rediscovery of large portions of Menander has emphasized our appreciation of Plautus and Terence as dramatists of high genius, who fully deserve their traditional fame, and who may be not only studied, but read, with unabated interest.—J. W. MACKAIL.

Compared with the Greeks, the Romans showed little genius for the theater. In the nine centuries following the great period of the Athenian drama, they grew strong politically, conquered the larger part of the known world including Greece itself, established an empire, and contributed much to civilization; but in all that time almost nothing was added either to the technique of the theater or to the art of the dramatist. There was no Euripides, no Shakespeare, no Molière. In this art, as in others, they were conquered by the very people over whom they boasted conquest. They produced three great playwrights—Plautus, Terence, and Seneca; but the work of these men was based upon Greek models. Latin technique, plots, theaters and actors were all more or less copies of their Athenian predecessors.

*Traces of native drama.* The word *histrio,* meaning actor, from which our word *histrionic* is derived, came from the Etruscans—those mysterious people whose civilization preceded that of the Romans on the Italian peninsula. They had theatrical entertainments, but we know little about them. We do know something, however, about the early art of the Latins. Before they were overtaken by the passion for Greek art and literature, there were in existence several forms of mimetic art, mostly belonging to comedy and farce. The Fescennine songs, for example, seem to have been of the nature of lyrical dialogues accompanied by rude jokes and banter, and were frequently used at wedding celebrations. As a rule they were extemporaneous. The singers gave humorous representations of contemporary life, using current slang and often attacking respectable citizens with libellous insinuations. Like the Old Comedy of the Greeks, this entertainment gave too much opportunity for scamps to vilify their more decent neighbors, and its license was soon curtailed. The Fescennine singers wore masks which were sometimes made of bark.

The *Atellanæ*, another form of play-acting, consisted of comic episodes and pantomime, in which several actors took part. They were of the nature of rustic skits, much like a modern vaudeville piece, and became popular in Rome at an early date. The fun was generally restricted to the canons of good taste. Men of letters occupied their leisure time in composing these Atellan fables, while youths of fashion and of good family put on masks and acted in them. The *dramatis personæ* soon became stereotyped stock figures: Pappus, the old man; Bucco, the braggart; Maccus, the intriguing slave. In this conventionalized manner they continued for centuries, and survived in many out-of-the-way places during the changes from Republic to Empire, and so on into the Middle Ages.

There existed also in the early Roman days a sort of *potpourri* called the *satura,* consisting of flute playing, pantomimic dancing, songs and humorous dialogue. The *satura* was not extemporaneous, but regularly composed, with such subjects as the birth and adventures of Romulus and Remus, the rape of the Sabine women, and the wicked arrogance of Tarquin.

All these activities were indigenous. To an outsider, it would seem that the beginnings of drama in Italy were quite as promising as the Athenian comus dances and goat choruses. The promise of a national art, however, was not fulfilled. No poet rose to glorify the Roman legends on the stage. During the third and second centuries before our era the native entertainments, as well as the home-grown literature, were largely set aside in favor of importations. The group of Latin writers who followed the Punic wars (which formally ended in 241

B.C.) ignored the native traditions, translating or imitating the more highly developed literature of the conquered Greeks. Among these writers were five tragic poets, all of whom attained positions of considerable distinction.

*The early poets and the first formal play in Rome.* The earliest of the Latin tragic poets was Livius Andronicus, a Greek slave from Tarentum, who had the distinction of presenting the first formal play ever given at Rome. This première occurred in 240 B.C., and made a great impression upon the uncultured inhabitants of the city. The second poet was Nævius, an Italian though probably not a Roman citizen. He made translations from the Greek, both of tragedy and comedy. At least two of his plays, however, were built upon historical events connected with Rome. Plays of this sort, with the theme taken from Roman history but composed in Greek form, were called *prætextæ* or *togatæ*, in distinction to the *palliatæ*, which were Greek plots translated or freely adapted into Latin. Nævius considered himself, probably with some justice, a champion of the native modes of thought. His works continued to be popular for centuries after his death; but his voice was almost the only one lifted up in support of the native style and subjects. If, at that time, there had risen other poets bold enough to throw off the fast tightening bonds of Greek influence, perhaps Rome would have had a drama expressive of her own life. However, no such poet appeared.

Ennius (239-169 B.C.), called the "Father of Roman poetry," was only an additional power in behalf of the Greeks. In his youth he probably saw tragedies performed in Magna Græcia, and therefore was able to bring into Rome Athenian methods of production. He stands out as a manly, vigorous figure, an energetic and industrious scholar. At the same time it was surely he, more than any one else, who at the critical moment confirmed the taste of the Romans for their imported models. Largely through the work of Cicero, there are preserved a number of fragments and the titles of a score of tragedies from the hand of Ennius; and more than half of the plays are obviously based upon the Homeric fables. From his time, Latin drama wears the Greek dress without shame or apology.

Pacuvius (220-130 B.C.), a relative of Ennius, became celebrated as a tragic poet; but he did little more than to spread still further a knowledge of the Greek originals. Various ancient writers testify to his popularity, and Cicero relates how, at a certain performance, the audience rose spontaneously to applaud a passage in which Pylades and Orestes contend each for the privilege of dying for the other. The titles of one *prætexta* and twelve tragedies are known.

The last of the five early tragic poets is Attius (or Accius), who died in 94 B.C., and was celebrated for his learning as well as for his plays. He was both the friend and rival of Pacuvius. Attius introduced long set debates into his dramas, and carried on the habit of contamination (see definition, p. 65). After Accius, Latin tragic drama almost ceased to be written, although great actors like Æsopus kept the old plays alive to a certain extent. Whatever life the art had, was due to the patronage of the aristocracy. When wearied or disgusted with the sensational and brutal spectacles of the circus or the Coliseum, the patricians of Rome retired to their homes to listen to the reading of poems or plays from earlier times, or even to indulge in the writing of plays themselves. The art declined, however, growing more rhetorical and receding ever further from the stage. By the time of Seneca, tragic drama was no longer written to be played but to be read: the first of the closet dramas had arrived.

*Latin comedy.* The comic muse in Rome was in somewhat better state. The actor Roscius was almost as celebrated in comedy as was Æsopus in tragedy; and farcical or comic entertainments had more chance to live. Political conditions in Rome did not permit, for long, the Aristophanic type of play in which public men and national policies were held up to ridicule. Better suited to the Roman stage was the play of manners represented by Menander and the New Comedy, except that it was too refined and quiet. The average Roman spectator liked stronger and coarser stuff. The problem, therefore, of the Latin producer was to use the Greek dish, fill it with enough spice and ribaldry to make it acceptable to the Roman palate and at the same time escape the censor.

*Titus Maccius Plautus.* 254-184 B.C. The poet who succeeded best in concocting such a dish as that described above
was Plautus, a free-born Italian of humble origin, who is said
to have begun his career by working in a corn mill. In some
fashion he gained an education and became associated in a
practical way with a theater, for which he began writing plays.
There are in existence at least twenty authentic dramas, all
complete or nearly so. They were built for acting, as plays
should be; and in many cases it is the acting copy of the manuscript that has been preserved. In a large proportion of the
plays the author has used a Greek plot, kept the Greek names
of men and places, but portrayed the manners, weaknesses and
characteristics of the Romans of his own day. The work of
Plautus was a Greek crust with a Roman filling. This double
character gives rise to certain oddities in geography and settings. The spectators, as a rule, were familiar with the Greek
tongue but not with Greece itself; so that a slip in geography,
such as the familiar "sea-coast of Bohemia" in Shakespeare,
would scarcely be noticed.

None of the original plays from which Plautus took his plots
is in existence; but there is good reason to believe that he borrowed almost exclusively from the New Comedy, chiefly from
Menander. He did not translate, neither was he an imitator.
His method was that of a free-handed manipulator. In a prologue he said:

> "We lay the scene of all the play in Athens
> To make the dream seem more Greek to you."

Not only the scene, but costumes and many minor features were
Greek. Critics have remarked that in all the many references
to money in the Plautine plays, not a single Roman coin is
mentioned. At the same time, there is a tone of reality and
first-hand observation. Concerning one of his plays, he protests that he would never have dreamed of using a certain
situation, had he not seen just such a case for himself.

*Subjects of the Plautine plays.* Plautus did not touch the
private life of individuals, and makes comparatively few references to politics. His favorite subjects were love intrigues,

the ridiculous struggles of a character to carry out some ne-
farious plan, or the manner in which sly slaves and gay youths
outwit their masters and guardians. Frequently a play com-
bines all three themes. The original circumstances of his love-
intrigues are usually disgraceful; but when these are once accepted, the plays become quite moral in tone, enjoining all the
virtues of respectability. In the *Amphitryo* a risqué subject is
treated with far more delicacy than by either Molière or Dryden. Sometimes Plautus attacked the weaknesses and vices of
his time with the zeal of a real reformer. He ridiculed the
aged sensualist who often stands as the prominent and model
citizen, scoffed at the amours of the wealthy merchant, exposed
the evils which follow in the wake of slavery, and showed the
wretched end to which the life of the courtesan leads.

With Plautus the Roman lady of high station was always
virtuous, though often disagreeable; but he never tried to make
the life of a frail sister attractive. In *The Captives* there is a
fine picture of the devotion of two friends, and of the fidelity
of a slave to his master. Like the Greek playwrights, Plautus
emphasized the importance of giving asylum to fugitives and
travelers. He used both elegant and colloquial Latin with
ease and boldness, and had considerable skill in the use of
verse forms. As a specialist in the making of boisterous and
actable farces, with occasional passages of pure comedy, he
was particularly successful. His inventiveness, his knowledge
of stage-craft, his gift for theatrical effect, and his understanding of character gave him the title of "the greatest genius
of Rome."

Not a few of the themes of Plautus were used by later
poets. Molière and Dryden took the *Amphitryo* as the basis
for plays. *The Pot of Gold* was used by Molière in *The
Miser;* the *Haunted House* by Regnaud and Addison; the
*Threepenny Bit* by Lessing; and *The Twins* (*Menœchmi*) by
any number of later playwrights, including Shakespeare. It
was the opinion of Lessing that *The Captives* was the best
play ever put upon the stage. Plautus himself regretted he
could not find more plots like it, because (he said) the moral
lesson was so good. We can agree with him at least so far as

to admit that the details of the plot, unlike those of many early comedies, are mentionable in polite society. It is a mystery play, has no women characters, and does not hinge upon a love intrigue. It starts off with a punning joke about grace before meat, and depends for its liveliness somewhat upon the hungry parasite, who threatens every now and then to give up his job of sponging upon the rich, since it is such hard work. The style is racy, abounding in what must have been local allusions and current gags, and revealing an uncanny knowledge of those blasé, shrewd city-dwellers who made up the ordinary Roman audience. There are also occasional passages of genuine feeling.

Plautus said that in his prologues he always had three purposes: to tell the audience to keep quiet so they could hear the piece; to give very plainly the story of the play and an explanation of the stage setting; and lastly to banter everybody into a good humor. A list of the devices used in his plots reads like a catalogue of the ten-twenty-thirty thrillers of the last century: the abandonment of infants, kidnapping, piracy, shipwreck, tokens of recognition, change of identity, keyhole listenings, strange rescues. His world is peopled by scolding matrons, lying and thievish servants, money lenders, procurers and sycophants. In the end the knaves are generally punished, the stingy parent outwitted or won over, and the hero satisfied. The titles indicate somewhat the nature of his works: *The Play of the Hidden Pot of Gold, The Haunted House, How the Sham Steward Got Paid for His Asses,* and *The Play of the Caskets.*

*Publius Terentius Afer.* About 190-158 B.C. The second important writer of Latin comedies presents a remarkable contrast to the first. Terence, probably a native of Carthage, was a slave in the family of a Roman patrician. On account of his witty conversation and graceful manners, he became a favorite in the fashionable society of Rome and received his freedom. His work, so far as we know it, consists of two sorts: fairly close translations of Menander, and contaminations. There are six extant plays, three of which, *The Brothers, The Girl of*

*Andros,* and *The Eunuch,* are contaminations.  Each is made
from two Greek plays.  Of the remaining three, the *Phormio* is
based on a play by the Greek Apollodorus, and the others are
from Menander.  *The Brothers (Adelphi)* was first performed
in 160 B.C., at the funeral games of Æmilius Paulus.

The weakness of Terence lies in his lack of the bolder elements of action.  His characters are somewhat deficient in variety, and his situations are inferior to those of Plautus.  He is
superior to Plautus in refinement and taste, but never equal to
him in exuberance of spirits and in comic force.  Comparatively speaking, Plautus was the untutored genius, Terence the
conscious artist; Plautus the practical playwright, Terence the
elegant literary craftsman.  Plautus wrote for the crowd, Terence for the aristocracy.  Even with the equivocal subjects of
the new comedy, Terence did not make vice attractive.  As
with Plautus, when once the irregular situation is granted,
the plays are found to be full of moral sentiments and advice
of a prudent and wise nature.

*Stock figures.*  From the time of Plautus and Terence it is
possible to trace in European drama the same characters, the
same plots, the same old themes of a stupid husband outwitted
by a young wife, the stingy father fleeced by his rascally sons,
or the aged sensualist defrauded of the pleasures he has handsomely paid for.  In Terence, however, the young people are
somewhat superior to their prototypes in Plautus.  The courte-
sans are more refined in speech and manner.  The young men
are not wholly libertines, but approach more nearly to the type
of lover which the modern world enjoys in its fiction.  The
slaves are of a higher quality, and their masters more decent,
often treating them as trusted domestics.  The braggart soldiers are not quite such fools, but more like witty roysterers,
or half-philosophers.

*Position of Terence in the Middle Ages.*  Terence supplied
the standard of classical Latin for many centuries.  He was
studied and acted even during those dark periods when all sem-
blance of art seems to have died out in Europe.  In the tenth
century the learned Roswitha, a nun of Gandersheim, Germany,

wrote, in imitation of Terence, several plays which are still in existence.[1] The prologues of the Terentian plays contain valuable criticism and statements of dramatic principles. His sententious sayings have become the general property of mankind: "Many men, many minds!" "I consider nothing human alien to me," and "While there's life there's hope." It is through Terence, more than any one else, that the traditions of comedy can be traced back to the New Comedy of the Greeks.

*Lucius Annæus Seneca.* 3 B.C.-65 A.D. The eight tragedies and one *prætexta* attributed to Seneca are the only surviving specimens of Latin tragic drama. They were probably written by the philosopher of that name, who was born in Cordova, Spain, in the third year of our era. He was a brilliant youth, studying law and the Greek poets. Early in life he attached himself to the Stoics, later to the Pythagoreans. His remarkable oratory in the Roman courts of law awakened the jealousy of the Emperor Caligula, who hinted that the philosopher-orator would be in better health away from Rome. Consequently Seneca went into exile from which he was recalled, after the death of Caligula, by Agrippina, who placed him as tutor to her son Nero, the heir apparent. In this post of advantage Seneca gained fame and wealth. For five years or so during the early days of Nero's reign, the power of Seneca, and his colleague Burrus, was second only to that of Nero himself.

Seneca was learned and able, and his writings have the excellent quality of being conversational in tone, even when touching the most profound topics. His tragedies were written while he was in exile, and we do not know that they were ever enacted on any stage. He chose the dialogue form, but was more interested in his theories than in drama, and he knew more about the lawyer's platform than the stage. Moreover the ordinary popular play of his day, indescribably indecent and coarse, was highly distasteful to him. There was no public stage open to a writer of tragedy. Such works as Seneca's probably had little chance of performance, still less of popularity. They are more like dialogue-poems meant to be re-

[1] Three or four of the plays of Roswitha have been presented in the experimental theaters of New York in recent seasons.

cited at banquets or read in the library. They follow the classic form, and are based on classic themes; but the flair for the theater is lacking. The tone is too rhetorical, too artificial, and often insincere. The antithesis, the epigram, and the quotable saying were more important to their author than the sincere unfolding of the human situation.

Among Greek writers, Euripides attracted Seneca most. His *Agamemnon* is in imitation of Æschylus, his *Œdipus* after Sophocles; all his other plays are after Euripides. In most cases he retained the Greek names and plot, making slight changes in the arrangement of scenes, or shifting the action in order to bring a different character into prominence. Here and there a new personage is introduced; yet the Latin plays are generally shorter than the Greek originals. The chorus was retained, though there was no dancing place in a Roman theater. The lyrics given to the chorus by Seneca do not advance the plot or intensify the action; they merely serve for rhetorical display and seem therefore doubly redundant and artificial.

The *Medea*, the *Mad Hercules*, and *The Trojan Women* are among the best of his plays. In the first two, the action is practically identical with the Greek prototypes. *The Trojan Women* is a contamination of the *Hecuba* and *The Trojan Women* of Euripides. There are many differences in detail, and changes of scene not customary in a Greek play. Only three speaking actors are required to be on the stage at one time, but the taboo is lifted from portraying scenes of violence. The plays are far inferior to the corresponding Greek dramas. Seneca's artificiality and lack of sincerity proved fatal when it came to the delineation of passion. The Phædra of Euripides struggles against her unlawful love, but is overcome by Aphrodite; while the Phædra of Seneca is sensual and shameless, deceiving her nurse in order to gain her as an accomplice. Similar parallels can be found in other plays, proving Seneca the weaker and smaller genius, if genius at all.

*Seneca's importance in dramatic history.* It is obvious that Seneca's importance in drama does not lie primarily in the intrinsic value of his plays. Like Plautus and Terence, he was a link between the ancient and the modern stage. Through him the European world first became acquainted with classic tragedy. A translation of his plays, made by different writers, was published in London in 1581, just at the time when the Elizabethan poets were most strongly attracted to the theater. They were looking for a form more concise than the sprawling chronicles and miracles; and in comparison with medieval compositions the Senecan model was indeed neat, tight-bound, and effective.

In France the influence of Seneca was even greater than in England. There sprang up a neo-classic school which dominated the stage for many decades. To the modern student, it seems as if all that was least admirable and least characteristic of the classic writers at their best had somehow been salvaged by Seneca and handed down to the European stage. We miss the wisdom and the sincerity, the tender beauty and nobility of the Greeks; while we find ever with us the long, undramatic speeches, the soliloquies, the off-stage action reported by the messenger, as well as cumbersome rhetoric and artificial mannerisms. Nevertheless for better or worse, it was the fertilization of the Renaissance mind by the classic spirit, through Seneca in tragedy and through Plautus and Terence in comedy, which produced the remarkable European drama of the fifteenth, sixteenth, and seventeenth centuries.

## CHAPTER XI

# HORACE, ROMAN SPECTACLES, AND THE DECAY OF THE CLASSIC DRAMA

After the great period of tragedy, those men whose names make up the rôle of Alexandrian literature had personalities too petty for broad feeling, though some of them could express personal passion. The dominance of the intellect is no longer impressive, as with Æschylus and Sophocles, yet no dominance of great emotion succeeds it.—HENRY OSBORN TAYLOR, *The Classical Inheritance of the Middle Ages.*

A troupe of players immediately came in, clattering their shields and spears. Trimalchio sat up on his couch, and while the Homeric actors in a pompous fashion began a dialogue in Greek verse, he read a book aloud in Latin with a singsong tone of voice. . . . The Homeric actors set up a shout, and while the slaves bustled about, a boiled calf was brought in on an enormous dish with a helmet placed upon it. The actor who took the part of Ajax followed with a drawn sword, fell upon it as though he were mad, and hacking this way and that he cut up the calf and offered the bits to us on the point of his sword, to our great surprise. . . . —PETRONIUS, *Trimalchio's Dinner.*

The names of Plautus, Terence and Seneca, with Ennius and Nævius glimmering in the background, are all that redeem Latin dramatic literature during the course of nearly eight centuries. Rome did, however, make a contribution to dramatic criticism in the work of Horace, who lived from 65 to 8 B.C. In the famous *Letters to Piso,* later known as the *Ars Poetica,* he set forth in an interesting but disconnected manner canons of criticism and composition which were handed down from one group of scholars to another throughout the Middle Ages. Many of his principles apply to literary matters in general; but he devotes a portion of his work to the drama, and in a measure reaffirms the judgments of Aristotle. Horace, however, is far more superficial than the Greek; though in justice it should be said that his observations were not intended as a formal treatise, being rather the somewhat casual comment which one man of letters might naturally have written to another.

*Maxims of Horace.* Certain verse forms and meters, said Horace, have been established as appropriate to comedy, others to tragedy, and these recognized styles should be followed. A tragic hero should not speak in the same rhythm as a comic one. Characters should be consistent with themselves, and should conform to the general expectation: boys should be childish, youth fond of sport, reckless and fickle, mature men should be businesslike and prudent, while old men should remain praisers of the past, sluggish and grudging. The poet should not try to change the character of well-known figures of the stage, such as Agamemnon, Medea, Hercules; at the same time, he should not stick too closely to the stock subjects. When beginning a play, avoid pomposity and grandiloquence; but when once the play is launched, rush the spectator on through the action, leaving out the ungrateful parts of the story. Do not present ugly things on the stage. The traditional structure of plots should be used, but such contrivances as the god-from-the-machine should not be worked to death. Keep to the three-actor play, and remember to use the chorus for the expression of moral sentiments and religious tone. Above all things, stick to the Greek models. Some people may have been fools enough to admire Plautus, but that is no reason why every one should do so. Plautus is rude and barbarous, not worthy of study beside the Greeks. Every play should either instruct or delight,—better if it does both. "Mix pleasure and profit, and you are safe."

Such were the rather humdrum instructions of Horace, who indeed followed Aristotle, but a long way behind. It was the influence of Horace, however, which was largely responsible for the perpetuation of the so-called "rules of Aristotle" through the Renaissance to modern times. Some of the medieval and Renaissance writers, however, had a positive genius for misinterpreting and misreading both Aristotle and Horace; so neither one should be held to blame for all the crimes committed in the name of classicism.

*Latin writers after Seneca.* The names of thirty-six tragic poets appear after Seneca, with about one hundred and fifty plays. Among those who dabbled in tragedy were Quintus Cicero, brother of the orator, Varro, Varius, Pollio, and Ovid. Lucian, who died in 200 A.D., asserts that in his time original dramas were no longer written. The old Greek plays were occasionally given, however, for a chronicler belonging to the third century of our era reported that a play of Euripides was sometimes to be seen on the Roman stage. This would of course mean that there were capable professional actors.

*Ignoble position of actors.* In Greece actors had enjoyed a position of eminence and respect; but in Rome their condition was mean and contemptible. Like many other professions in the empire, that of play-acting was hereditary. Actors were foreigners, captives, or more frequently slaves who through skill had been able to purchase their freedom. During the republic and the early days of the empire, women actors never appeared; but in later years women acted both in the mimes and pantomimes. In either case the position was an infamous one. Julian, called the Apostate, made it a rule that the priests of his pagan religion should never be seen within the walls of a theater. Even the far-from-Puritanical Tiberius forbade people of the stage to hold any intercourse with the Roman knights and senators. The famous Acte, at one time a favorite concubine of the Emperor Nero, was an actress in the mimes. Tradition has it that she was converted through the teachings of Saint Paul; that she was banished by the Emperor; and that, after his death, she was the only person found willing to prepare him for decent burial. The Church, while condemning the obscenities perpetrated in the name of art, often fought for the enactment of laws which should release "these unhappy slaves of a cruel voluptuousness." [1] There were rules designed to regulate the movements of supposedly converted actresses; and these were characterized, even by indifferent writers of the time, as cold, cruel, and unjust. Dill describes them as showing "an inhuman contempt for a class whom humanity doomed to vice, and then punished for being

[1] Dill, *Roman Society.*

vicious." Legally the position of the acting class was never essentially changed; but in time the social standing was somewhat improved, and gifted artists, such as Roscius in comedy and Æsopus in tragedy, occasionally rose above their station and enjoyed the friendship of men of high standing.

*What the Roman play was like.* Latin plays were presented in the daytime, sometimes before, sometimes after, the noon meal. The average comedy was about two hours long. The characters wore the Greek dress, with or without masks. Paint and wigs were employed, a gray wig for an old man, black for a young man, and red for a slave. For the greater part of Roman history the profession of acting was confined to men, the women's parts being taken by youths. The ordinary setting was a stage with a street and three or four houses in the background. Two doors led from the wings on to the stage, the one at the left of the spectators for the entrance of persons from foreign parts, that to the right for ordinary citizens. The doors between led into the various residences of the characters in the play. There was no limit to the number of actors. The chorus was never as important as in Greek drama, and in time it was abandoned altogether. Division into acts or scenes was made only when the actor left the stage to prepare for the next appearance. During such intermission a flute player entertained the audience. In both comedies and tragedies probably some of the dialogue was sung, as in modern opera. Thus there rose curious artificialities. Livy relates that Livius Andronicus (who first replaced the Fescennine songs with a regular plot) was so frequently encored as actor and singer that he lost his voice; in consequence he obtained permission from the city officials to introduce a boy to sing by his side, while he himself interpreted the action by appropriate gestures.

*Theaters and spectacles.* Although the best Latin plays belong to the second century before our era, yet at that time Roman theaters were of the crudest description. They were built of wood at the foot of a grass-covered slope, with almost nothing in the way of accommodation for either actors or audience. The stage was a narrow platform, elevated, and backed by a simple architectural design. There was no curtain, no scenery that could be changed, no sounding board to carry the voice. An altar was placed on the stage, in front of the "set" described above. The audience, out on the sloping amphitheater, either reclined, stood, or sat on stools brought from home. In Rome the theater was never a place for worship, as in Greece; it was always a scene of noisy confusion, pushing, and crowding. The aristocracy would not mingle with the more or less disgusting crowd, which was, for the most part, deaf to the elegances of such a writer as Terence. Even Plautus, with his boisterous humor, his bustle and high spirits, was obliged to explain the subject and story of a play in a manner that almost seems suited to an audience of half-wits. In his prologue he tells the whole plot, then he points and re-points the facts during the performance. Terence, in one of his prologues, asked the spectators not to hiss his play off the stage until they had heard it out.

During the republic various attempts were made to improve the theater structures, and at least one temporary wooden auditorium was built after the Greek model. In the year 55 B.C., Pompey the Great erected the first permanent theater in Rome. It was of stone, seated perhaps seventeen thousand people— Pliny said forty thousand—was situated on the Campus Martius on level ground, and had separate sections for knights and senators. About the time of Horace roofed-in play-houses also began to be built, though even then the greater number of such structures were after the Greek style. Thirteen years before the beginning of the Christian era two new, roofed-in auditoriums were constructed for the purpose of staging huge and costly spectacles consisting of games, military exercises, combats between slaves, captives, condemned criminals, and not infrequently contests between beasts and men. Sometimes panthers or foxes, infuriated by burning firebrands tied to their tails, fought among themselves. Pompey is said to have furnished troops of cavalry and bodies of infantry for some of these performances, with real booty for the successful combatants. These spectacles naturally had little or nothing to do with drama, but their significance should be understood, for they explain its lethargy and final death. The money and enthusiasm which might have promoted the art of the stage was diverted to these noisy and brutalizing shows. Slaves who drove the chariots in the races won fabulous sums, and often became the petted favorites of nobles. Huge structures were required, and builders contrived curious plans to meet the need. In one case, two whole theaters constructed of wood, each in the form of a half-circle, were so placed that they could be united to form one immense amphitheater.

*How Roman plays were financed.* All games, sports, plays and spectacles were under the general supervision of an official called *ædile,* but the production itself was a private affair. In some cases it was purely a business enterprise; at other times it was of the nature of a festival given by a prominent person in order to gain favor with the popular political party. In the latter case, the giver, after gaining permission from the ædile, placed the management of his entertainment in the hands of an agent who got as much money as he was able, both from his client and the public. The permission from the city did not mean either official or monetary support from the state.

*Roman mimes.* The most popular of the stage entertainments which survived were the mimes,—short scenes given by two or three actors, with spoken dialogue. In these skits the actor took off rustics, sight-seeing provincials, pompous officials, and other decent but dull types, often with obscene and indecorous accompaniments. A contemporary writer has recorded how Horace and his friends laughed over the representation of a bombastic rural priest who wore a loud purple robe with broad stripes and carried a pan of coals, according to the requirements of his office. Of course such a figure, once connected with the ancient dignity of the patricians, could easily be converted into burlesque. The dialogue of the mimes was in verse, and Roman knights sometimes employed themselves in their composition. The prosperous, as well as the lower classes delighted in them.

*Pantomimes.* Pantomimic shows, usually given by a single dancer, were of three kinds: simple mimicry without music or words, but with dancing; secondly, mimicry with instrumental music; and thirdly, mimicry with music and words,—the latter frequently given to a chorus. Some of the pantomimes were modifications of the Atellan fables and *saturæ*. Often they reproduced to the life tales of abnormal depravity, and always they were salted with coarse buffoonery and indecent humor, exhibiting, fully and unmistakably, by exaggerated gestures, the various passions and emotions of mankind. Cymbals, gongs, castanets, rattles and drums were used. In time these entertainments became so gross that even easy-going citizens were forced to discountenance them. Dill, the historian of Roman society, writes: "The theater and the circus were for five centuries the great corrupters of the Roman world."

*Reasons for the decline of the classic drama.* It goes without saying that such associations did not improve the drama. The Roman world, or such part of it as frequented the spectacles, was not of the sort to find delight in the more subtle revelations of character. Thrilling scenes were for them almost daily enacted in real life: their malefactors were stretched on the cross, or tossed to the beasts of the arena; their generals, returning from war, led their captives in chains through the streets. Such plays as were given had to compete, very unequally, with the spectacles and circuses, as well as with the turbulent and sensational life of the city; and they were further degraded by being placed, on occasion, on the circus programs between the gladiatorial shows and the wild beast combats. Moreover, the political and social condition of the city was averse to the cultivation of the arts. As the empire expanded it was the custom for sons of patricians to serve in the wars and to administer the government in distant provinces. In consequence whole families became extinct and the aristocracy dwindled, while the prestige of the city drew into its confines a strange crowd of outlanders, barbarians, prisoners of war, tradesmen from foreign countries, hangers-on and scamps of all sorts. The result was that many of the people in a theater audience knew but little Latin—only sufficient to enable them to trade—and their taste was inevitably low. They honestly preferred rope dancing and the bloody sights of the arena. It followed naturally that playwrights found scant market for their wares; and even the lowest actors despised the verdict of the masses.

It is not wholly fair to say that Roman drama was smothered by the Greek; it is quite as true to say that it was starved out by the Romans themselves. Oratory and law interested them more than poetry. They were perhaps too impatient to sit quietly through a representation of an experience of the heart, to reflect on its meaning, and to appreciate its wisdom and beauty. It had been the aim of Ennius and other early teachers not only to familiarize the Romans with Greek literature, but also "to enlighten their minds and banish error." Gradually this purpose was forgotten. Seneca and such writers as he only arrested for a moment the national decay; they could not stop it. Although the mimes were popular, yet they reflected the worst traits of a debauched and crumbling civilization, and in time they were condemned by all decent Romans. It was not Christian bigotry but its own depravity which destroyed the Roman theater. As it then existed, Christian and pagan alike knew it to be simply a school of vice.

Moreover, the classic cycle had run its course, and had more than outlived the civilization which gave it birth. A new religion and a new view of life were painfully seeking to express themselves. The ideals portrayed in the most notable examples of classic drama were self-control, moderation, a manly submission to the blows of fate, and an ever increasing sense of the dark enigma of life. The Greek theater was mature, thoughtful, rational. When, however, an original drama next appeared in Europe—the biblical drama of the Middle Ages— it was childish, full of superstitions, extravagant; and it began with a new set of fables and legends. The very meaning of the words *comedy* and *tragedy* was lost. The playwrights of the new day were to work their way along, learning nearly everything anew for themselves.

SECTION THREE

DRAMA OF THE ORIENT

## CHAPTER XII

# INDIA, CHINA, AND JAPAN

What qualities are required in a drama? The qualities required in a drama are a profound exposition of the human passions; a pleasing interchange of mutual affection; loftiness of character; delicate expression of desire; a surprising story; and elegant language.—Opening passage of a Hindu play.

Pleasures of peace and prosperity.
> Chinese phrase for dramatic entertainment.

> . . . and when I am no more,
> I pray thee deign to offer prayers for me,
> That in the dark place there shall be a light
> For this blind man, and over evil roads
> A bridge. . . .
>> Closing lines of a fourteenth century
>> *No* play, translated by M. C. Stopes.

## I. India

India is one of the few countries which can boast of an indigenous drama, unaffected by any foreign influence. When Hindu plays first became known to the European world through Sir William Jones's translation of *Sakuntala* in 1789, it was then generally thought that Greek literature had penetrated into India, influencing their playwrights; but that opinion does not prevail today. Most critics agree that Hindu drama was neither a borrowing nor an imitation, but the product of native genius.

The dramatist Bhasa, or Bhrata, thirteen of whose works have recently been recovered and published, is traditionally considered to have been the founder and "Father" of Indian drama. There is considerable confusion concerning the authorship of many plays, owing to the fact that it was the custom to attribute a literary work to the ruler at whose court, or

99

under whose favor, the real author chanced to live. Thus the
earliest extant stage piece, *The Little Clay Cart*,[1] is ascribed
to a sovereign named Sudraka. It should probably be dated
sometime before 400 A.D. This is one of the few oriental
dramas treating, in part at least, of middle-class life.

*Language and conventions.* The long play opens with a
prayer, followed by a dialogue between the manager and one
of the actors, in which the audience is complimented and the
chief circumstances of the coming presentation described; then
by skilful management the dialogue merges into the play.
There is division into acts and scenes, the intermissions being
filled by musicians. The greater part of the piece is in prose,
while the more impassioned passages are in verse, the four-
line stanza being much in use. (Nearly half of *Sakuntala* is
in this form.) There are many lyrical scenes in which lovely
things in nature are described, also many moral reflections and
precepts of wisdom. Such lines are always put into the mouth
of an important character and are given in Sanskrit, which has
not been the common language of India since about 300 B.C.,
though it is still spoken in the courts of rulers and by the
Brahmin priests. While the gods, heroes and the few important personages speak in this aristocratic tongue, the women,
slaves, and all minor characters use the dialect of the lower
class. The play closes, as it opens, with a prayer.

The exhibition of undue ardor of love is not regarded as
decorous or æsthetically permissible; nor extravagant expressions of jealousy, hate, or anger—in fact, nothing sensational
or violent. Sorrow is toned down to a gentle melancholy.
Kissing, sleeping, eating, scratching, or yawning are considered
indelicate; and there is never any reference to such topics as
banishment, plague, or national calamity of any sort. There
are stock figures, such as the accomplished courtesan, the jester,
the humble confidant and friend of the hero. There are also
stock comic situations, like the complaining of the stubborn
servant, and mock grief over the death of a wealthy relative.
Other devices of the stage, such as the play within the play,

[1] Produced at the Neighborhood Playhouse in New York during the
season 1924-25.

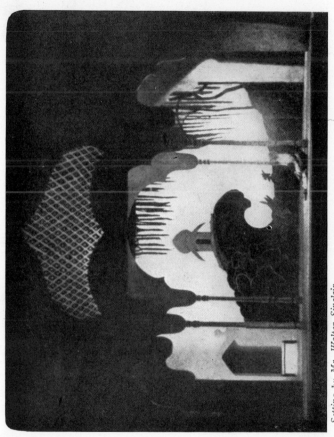

*Setting by Mr. Walter Sinclair*

Setting for the Garden Scene, *The Toy Cart*, as produced at the
Hart House Theatre, Toronto

the finding of hidden letters, and the antics of drunken men, are as well known and as popular in India as elsewhere. Magic and supernatural events have a large part in the action of many pieces: characters are put under a curse, bewitched, or caused to assume the form of an animal or a tree. In many of these cases, as in Greek tragedy, the intervention of a god is required to release the victim from his difficulties.

Unity of action in the Hindu play was rigidly insisted upon. Unity of time was interpreted as allowing, roughly, one act to represent the passage of one day, though this general rule was often disregarded. There was no attempt at observing unity of place; whenever it was necessary, the actor announced his whereabouts. The theater was usually a concert hall or the outer court of a palace. Scenery did not exist; and the curtain, instead of falling before the actor, formed the background and concealed the dressing room behind the stage. The stage properties were extremely simple, with perhaps seats, thrones, and occasionally chariots drawn by actors disguised as animals. Masks were not commonly used, and the costumes were usually those worn in everyday life. There was no chorus, and no official distinction between comedy and tragedy. In fact, pure tragedy was unknown, since every play was required to end happily. As in the Greek plays, there was frequent intercourse between earth and heaven.

The production of plays was almost exclusively an affair of the aristocracy, who gave them in honor of a coronation, a lunar holiday, a royal marriage, or the birth of a royal heir. The actor's profession was regarded with respect, and there was no objection to women being employed on the stage. In many ways, however, the drama reveals the social philosophy upon which the caste system is based, as well as a profound religious feeling. Great importance is attached to the idea of self-sacrifice as the highest form of self-realization.

*The brilliant period.* We know of about a dozen plays, written in India probably between 400 and 900, which have excited the interest and admiration of modern students. Sometime during those five hundred years lived the two greatest playwrights, Kalidasa and Bhavabuti, whose works were attributed to the emperors Sudraka and Criharsha respectively. Wide differences of opinion exist concerning the dates of these two authors, especially of Kalidasa, the difference ranging from half a century before the birth of Christ to the sixth century after. Professor Kunow, in *Das Indische Drama* (1920), places him at about 400; and with this opinion Professor Jackson (Columbia University) agrees. Bhavabuti was a Brahmin of southern India and probably belonged to the early eighth century. He must have been much admired, for the people called him Crikantha, "he in whose throat is fortune." Three dramas survive from each of these authors.

*Famous plays.* The drama best known to Europeans is the *Sakuntala* of Kalidasa, which was translated into English by Sir William Jones in 1789. It made a profound impression upon such scholars as Goethe, and created something like a literary sensation. It is in seven acts, and the story is taken from the first book of the *Mahabharata.* Its hero, Dushyanta, was a celebrated king of ancient times. The action moves in part within the realm of fancy and the supernatural; and the dialogue is always poetic and elevated. On account of its imaginative insight, lofty poetry, and emotional appeal, it has been regarded by people of every nation as one of the masterpieces of dramatic literature. Mr. Arthur Symons has called it the most beautiful play in the world.

*The Rise of the Moon of Knowledge* is an allegorical and theological piece in six acts, in which abstract qualities such as Will, Reason, and the follies and vices of man are personified and made to struggle with one another. The obvious parallelism between this play and the European moralities of the late Middle Ages is of considerable interest. A political work called *The Signet of the Minister,* written about 800, and another named *The Binding of a Braid of Hair,* are among the well known productions. Besides these, the titles of more than five hundred Sanskrit dramas are known; and more than a dozen have already been translated into various modern European languages. From them and from other sources, much has been learned concerning the technique and ideals of the ancient Indian stage.

## II. China

It is the opinion of modern scholars that drama was not native to China, but was introduced, probably in rather an advanced state, by the Mongols in the thirteenth century. During the one hundred and sixty-eight years of the Kin and Yuen dynasties the most celebrated plays were written. A famous collection known as the *Hundred Plays of the Yuen Dynasty* is preserved, and the titles of about six hundred others are known, as well as the names of eighty-five playwrights. Three of these authors were women belonging to a class similar to the Greek *heteræ*. During this period (1200-1368) the style of acting, the subjects to be treated, and the general conduct of the theater were determined. The Chinese stage at the beginning of the twentieth century was practically the same as that of seven hundred years ago.

*Theory of Chinese drama.* The ideal of the Chinese stage was that every play should have a moral. An article in the penal code of the Empire requires every dramatist to have "a virtuous aim." Both prose and verse are often used in the same play. The best plots satisfy the rule regarding unity of action, and many of them also observe the unities of time and place.[2] Many of the plays are short, a half-hour or so in length; and the longer ones are divided into acts and scenes. It is the custom in many places to give a series of short plays without any intermission, so that a performance sometimes lasts for several hours. In such a case of course there is no attempt at maintaining a single unified action. The second play may take up the career of a new hero after the first one has been killed or defeated, thus carrying the spectator over long distances and through many years. In order to keep the thread of the action clear, each important character pauses occasionally to announce his name and lineage, and perhaps to rehearse the course of the plot. A singular feature of the Chinese play is the singing actor, to whom are given the most poetic and beautiful passages. Like the Greek chorus, he sometimes repeats

[2] Neither the Chinese nor the Hindus knew anything of Aristotle's theories concerning the elements of structure.

the chief events of the play, and moralizes upon the conduct of the characters.

*Subjects of Chinese drama.* The field of the Chinese playwright is broad, as he has a choice of historical or contemporary affairs from which to draw his plots. He may portray parental or filial goodness, national vices and weaknesses, official corruption, difficulties and delays connected with the law courts, and the absurdities into which religious fanatics are drawn. Love stories are comparatively rare. National customs, such as arranging marriage through an agent and determining official rank by means of examination, are inexhaustible sources of comic action. Avarice is often ridiculed. There are burlesques on Buddhism, a religion to which nearly four-fifths of the nation subscribe. No class or section is exempt from the laughter of the stage. As the gods often intervene in Greek plays, so in a Chinese play the Emperor often saves the heroine from an unfortunate marriage, or an innocent victim from death. It is technically illegal, however, to represent the person of the Emperor on the stage.

One of the most revolting features of Chinese drama is the frequent representation of scenes of violence. Suffering and death by starvation, drowning, poison, flogging, hanging, and torture have been exhibited for centuries, and it is the distinction of many a famous actor that he can most vividly depict the intense sufferings incident to these punishments. Suicide is a custom honored in China, and therefore often seen on the stage. When an actor is about to kill himself, he sings a long chant before committing the deed; but whatever disasters occur, the end must be happy.

In general, Chinese drama is comparatively weak in the logical development of plot and in the delineation of character. Great stress, however, is laid upon verbal decoration and poetical ornament. There are pleasing contrasts between parallel scenes, and parallelism of language, as in the Psalms. In many passages a single word is played with, compounds being made upon the root, so that a speech in praise of a flower or of a royal person becomes an intricate linguistic labyrinth, like an English acrostic or anagram.

The Chinese stage usually has little scenery, no curtain, flies, or wings. The costumes of the actors are gorgeous and costly, of brocade or heavy silk, often embroidered and set with semi-precious stones. If, in the course of a performance, an actor has to travel to another country, he goes through the motions of cantering for a few paces, cracks his whip, dismounts, and announces: "I have now reached the country of So-and-So." A property man in ordinary dress, regarded as "honorably invisible" by everybody, remains on the stage all the time, providing articles needed by the actors. The latter have their tea on the stage; and dead men rise and walk away when their scene is ended.

The player does not stand high in the social scale in China. Neither he nor his descendants for three generations may compete in the public examinations for civil office. Since the eighteenth century women have been forbidden to appear on the stage, and women's parts are taken by young men. Those who would enter the profession of acting must undergo severe discipline from an early age, and must submit to the strictest physical training in respect to diet, acrobatic feats, contortions, and walking with bound feet in imitation of high-born women. There are five classes of actors, each being trained for certain stage types; and each actor is assigned to his own type. The regular companies consist of fifty-six actors, and every member must know from one hundred to two hundred plays. There is no prompter at the performance.

*Famous Chinese plays.* Not until the eighteenth century did any knowledge of Chinese drama come to Europe; and even now the greater part of the vast storehouse of oriental plays remains closed to the occidental world. In 1735 a Jesuit priest named Joseph Prémaire brought to France the translation of an old work called *The Little Orphan of the House of Tchao.* The play from which he had made his translation was of the fourteenth century; and it had been taken, he said, from a still earlier piece. Voltaire, who was writing plays about the time Prémaire brought his translation to Paris, declared *The Little Orphan* to be a masterpiece, far superior to anything that had been produced in Europe as early as the fourteenth century.

Voltaire appropriated the plot for himself, calling his play *L'Orphelin de Chine*. The action of the piece hinges upon the sacrifice of a mandarin and his wife, who yield their own son to the enemy in order to save the heir to the throne. At the final moment, when the child is about to be beheaded, the mother in her agony of grief rushes upon the scene and tells the conquering invader the truth. He is impressed by her beauty and spirit; tries by immoral means to cajole her; but at last is conquered by her youth and virtue.[3]

A celebrated play, reprinted in countless versions, called *The Story of the Magic Lute,* is also from the fourteenth century. *The Sorrows of Han,* whose plot resembles the story of Esther of biblical fame, is said to date from before the Christian era.[4] The Emperor in this play was a historical character, living about 42 B.C. The story is plainly designed to expose the evil consequences of luxury and self-indulgence, and the worthlessness of monarchs who neglect the welfare of their people. It is in five acts, contains many beautiful songs, and is a great national favorite.

## III. JAPAN

Many important elements of the dramatic art in Japan are similar to those developed by the Chinese. In many cases the story material is obviously the same, and there is great similarity in the methods of producing and acting. There were two periods of brilliance in Japan (the fourteenth and eighteenth centuries), and two distinct types of theater: the aristocratic and the popular. The former is associated with the famous *No* plays, which reached their period of perfection during the fourteenth century.

*The staging of a No play.* A square platform supported on

[3] This situation was taken over into Japanese literature, but the outcome was changed. With some modifications it was produced in New York by the Washington Square Players about 1912 under the title *Bushido*.

[4] This play is more or less familiar to Europeans and Americans. It was given in New York about 1910, the chief part being taken by Miss Edith Wynne Matthison.

pillars, open to the audience on three sides, and covered with a temple-like roof, forms the stage for a *No* play. It is connected with a green room by a corridor, or gallery, which leads back from the stage at the left, as the audience sees it. Here part of the action takes place. Upon the back scene is painted a pine tree, and three small pines are placed along the corridor. The orchestra, consisting of a flute, drum, and two instruments resembling the tambourine, is seated in a narrow space back of the stage; while the chorus, whose number is not fixed, is seated on the floor at the right. The actors are highly trained, and their speech is accompanied by soft music. There are rigid rules for acting, each accent and gesture being governed by an unchanging tradition. The actors are always men, wearing masks when impersonating females or supernatural beings. The costumes are exquisite and of medieval fashion. The performance is day-long; but as the *No* play is always short, occupying about an hour, several pieces are rendered during the day. Alternating with them are farces called *kiogen,* which are short, full of delicate humor, and given in the language of the time without the chorus.

*The No play.* The construction of the *No* play is always the same. It begins with the appearance of a traveler, perhaps a priest, who announces his name and purpose of journeying to such-and-such a battle-ground, temple, or other time-honored place. While he is crossing the stage, the chorus recites the beauties of the scenery or describes the emotions of the traveler. At the appointed spot a ghost appears, eagerly seeking an opportunity to tell of the sufferings to which it is condemned. This ghost is the Spirit of the Place. The second part consists of the unfolding of the ancient legend which has sanctified the ground. The story is revealed partly by dialogue, partly by the chorus. At its close the priest prays for the repose of the Spirit whose mysterious history has just been disclosed, and the play ends with a song in praise of the ruling sovereign.

The content of the *No* play, which is nearly always tragic, is treated with simple dignity. There is frequent reference to learned matters, and to the teachings of Buddha. The text is partly archaic prose and partly verse. Within this slight conventional form are themes relating to filial duty, endurance under trial, uncomplaining loyalty in the face of hardship and neglect, and tender sacrifice. The plays are uniformly austere and poetic, remote from the everyday scene, and full of imagination and beauty. Kwanami Kiotsugu, who belongs to the second half of the fourteenth century, was called the greatest poet of his time, and the founder of the *No* play. His son, Seami Motokiyo, was almost equally distinguished. He left instructions as to production and acting, stressing the necessity of avoiding realism on the stage. Other relatives and successors of Kiotsugu improved the music, and the Shoguns honored the authors. This type of play may well be considered unique in the history of the stage, and an important link between the classic plays of Greece and the poetic drama of modern Europe.

*The popular theater.* Tradition assigns the beginning of the popular theater in Japan to the early part of the seventeenth century, when the priestess Okuni ran away from her Shinto temple and built a theater in Kioto. This theater developed in two ways: a "legitimate" playhouse with living actors, and a marionette or puppet show. Both these forms of entertainment became popular in the seventeenth century, when the art of the actor and the dramatist improved. We may infer that it was then fashionable for members of the aristocracy to attend these plays, also that quarrels in the playhouse were not unknown; for about 1683 an ordinance was passed prohibiting the wearing of swords in the theater.[5] The *Samurai* (knights), being unwilling to lay aside their swords even for a short time, stayed away from the performances; and in consequence the shows promptly deteriorated.

As among the Chinese, the governing group in Japan looked upon the drama as a means of instructing the lower classes in loyalty and self-sacrifice. A very strict set of regulations crystallized about the stage. Every play was produced with elaborate exactness and precision. Much of the beauty of the pieces depended upon the skilful use of parallelism in language,

[5] A similar ordinance was passed in France in the days of Molière.

and in the employment of pivot or root words around which the author could display his verbal dexterity. The "invisible" property man was always on the stage, and realistic details abounded. Grief and passion were expressed by violent contortions. The hero would grimace, roll his eyeballs, bare his teeth, and go through every possible variation of distress, while the property man held a lighted candle near his face in order that nothing should be lost to the audience. When a man was killed, he turned a somersault before depicting the final agony. For many decades the most brutal crimes were performed before the eyes of the spectators,—scenes of torture and crucifixion, hara-kiri, and bloody scenes of every description.

After its period of brilliance in the seventeenth century, the popular stage became overloaded with conventions and began to decline. Doubtless the absence of the nobility from the theaters contributed greatly to this result. Genshiro, a native dramatist and critic of the nineteenth century, wrote that "the theater in Japan had reached the lowest depth of vulgarity, and so continued until the last year of the Tokugawa Shogunate in 1867."

*The Marionette Theater.* In the meantime another specialization of the art appeared in the development of the marionette stage.[6] The original basis of the marionette or puppet show was the history of the heroine Joruri, whose love stories were related by a chorus while the puppets walked the stage. Gradually dialogue was added; and soon the puppets became so popular that managers brought into their service extraordinary mechanical devices by which eyeballs and eyebrows could be moved, lips would seem to whisper or talk, fingers would grasp a fan, and tiny figures kneel, dance, or swoon with emotion. The stage was furnished with scenery, trap doors, turntables, trapeze appliances, and the like.

Along with this mechanical development there appeared, also in the seventeenth century, Chikamatsu Monzayamon (born about 1653), one of the most important figures in the whole

[6] This species is found also in Italy and Spain; and in recent years has been successfully produced in the United States by Mr. Tony Sarg and Mr. Jean Gros.

history of the Japanese drama, and completely identified with the marionette theater. His most famous play is said to be *The Battles of Kokusenya,* the hero of which was a celebrated pirate. The scenes are laid in Nanking and Japan at the time of the last Ming emperor. It contains one of the characteristic situations in oriental drama: namely, the conqueror asking the defeated enemy for the gift of his favorite wife as a tribute of war.[7] In this play are also the treacherous general, the substitution of another child in order to save the heir to the throne, much bloodshed, suicide, and fighting. Spectators have testified to the vividness and force of these representations, to the tenseness of the dramatic situations, and to the impressiveness of the dialogue. Chikamatsu had the gift of diverting the attention from improbabilities and of making his characters bear themselves like tragic heroes. Moreover, he had the great virtue of never being dull.

*The Forty-seven Ronins.* With the exception of the *No* plays and the works of Chikamatsu, nearly everything of note in dramatic literature belongs to the eighteenth century. Many pieces from that time had three or four collaborating authors. One of the best known of these collaborators was Idzumo, who had a share in making a play called *The Magazine of Faithful Retainers,*—one of the forty or fifty extant versions of the story of The Loyal Legion, or the Forty-seven Ronins, based upon a historical incident which occurred in 1703. A member of the *samurai* (knightly class) was unjustly degraded by his feudal lord for some trifling accident. His companions, all members of his own order, assembled in protest and drew lots for the privilege of killing the unjust master. The lot was drawn and the work done; but the code of their order required that the rebels, one and all, should commit hara-kiri. So the Forty-seven Ronins perished; and every year thousands of admirers make their way to the scene of their burial. In the many versions of the story, various additions have been made, such as a love affair, a tea-house scene, bloody and thrilling incidents, and many touches which reveal contemporary manners. As a play it is certain to draw a crowded house.

[7] A variation of this theme is found in *Monna Vanna* by Maeterlinck.

About the beginning of the eighteenth century the marionette theater began to decline, and writers ceased to produce
plays suited for puppets.  In the late nineteenth century vigorous attempts were made by both noblemen and scholars to improve the stage.  One of the first features to be condemned
was the presentation of scenes of violence and cruelty.  Many
of the restrictions as to attendance have been removed; women
are allowed to appear as actors; and the tendency towards excessive realism has been offset by the practical application of
æsthetic principles.

# SECTION FOUR
# DRAMA OF THE MIDDLE AGES

## CHAPTER XIII

# A THOUSAND YEARS OF QUIESCENCE AND THE BEGINNINGS OF SACRED DRAMA

"Quem quaeritis in sepulchro, Christicolæ?"
"Jesum Nazarenum crucifixum, O Cœlicolæ."
"Non est hic, surrexit sicut prædixerat,
Ite, nuntiate quia surrexit de sepulchro."
Dialogue upon which was based one
of the earliest of the sacred plays.

For nearly a thousand years after the death of Seneca in 62 A.D., the flame of dramatic genius was smouldering. The drama of the Orient was unknown to the western world, and that of Greece was all but forgotten. Of course play-acting did not altogether cease. Gorgeous spectacles were occasionally given by the Roman emperors, though with less and less frequency, until with the general decay of the empire they disappeared. The mimes and pantomimes remained alive, though their display, being already on the lowest rung of the ladder of art, could not descend much lower. Although Rome fell, yet merchants and porters and slaves required the Tired Business Man's entertainment. Small wandering companies, similar perhaps to the modern Punch-and-Judy show, lived from hand to mouth, preserving after a fashion the seeds of the most ancient Roman art. These low-caste companies seem to disappear, only to show up again wherever and whenever public opinion sanctioned them. Like the gipsies, they never entirely died out. During these centuries of quiescence they lived in the alleys and on the edges of civilization, but still they lived.

*Reappearance of play-acting in Christian ritual.* While the mimes belonged to the gutters, another class of play-actors emerged from the cloisters. From the very early days of the Church occasional attempts were made by monks and priests to utilize the beauties of the classic drama in the interest of religion. As early as the fifth century living pictures were introduced into sacred services, especially on festival days; and short Latin dialogues from the Bible were chanted by the clergy to illustrate the teachings of the Mass. There developed strange exercises, such as the *Feast of Fools* and the *Feast of the Ass* which, in the beginning, were doubtless religious in intention, but soon became boisterous and licentious travesties of sacred rites. These and similar exercises seem to indicate attempts on the part of the leaders of the Church to substitute for the pagan spectacles some sort of theatrical entertainment which would be in accord with the Christian spirit.

Another group, doubtless small enough, consisted of learned priests and nuns somewhat familiar with the classic plays, who endeavored to imitate them and to preserve the knowledge of the classic tongues and literatures. Here and there, in convents and monasteries, the plays of Plautus and Terence were read and sometimes acted. Imitations of them were written in medieval Latin. The most notable of these attempts was that of Roswitha, the learned nun of Gandersheim, Germany, who, in the tenth century, wrote so-called Christian plays modeled on those of Terence. Roswitha's plays portray the miracles of saints, and are especially concerned with the teaching of chastity. According to the usage of today Roswitha is not always decorous, and lacks the gift of individualizing her characters; but her plots are good and her dialogue is often brisk and pointed. For a woman to have achieved any excellence at all in the art of the drama in that long period of darkness and silence, seems remarkable enough.[1] Saint Hilary (a pupil of the celebrated Abélard), who is supposed to have been an Englishman, wrote three plays in Latin with refrains in old French. The subjects are Daniel, the raising of Lazarus, and the miracle of Saint Nicholas.

*Sources of European drama.* In the slow rediscovery of the pleasures of the theater, there were, generally speaking, three main sources from which the art renewed itself: first, whatever was left from Greece and Rome, including not only the great

[1] Three of Roswitha's plays were produced at the Studio Theater of Joseph Lauren, New York, in April, 1926.

plays (most of which were practically lost for centuries), but the stock characters of comedy and farce, with the lively methods of the mimes and pantomimes; second, a new source of plot material—the Bible, together with the Apocrypha, the lives of the saints, and events connected with holy people and places; and third, the romances of the medieval poets and story-tellers. From these three main elements were built up the medieval sacred drama and later the various national dramas in the European countries.

*How political unity fostered the growth of drama.* When the first signs of a revival of interest in drama began to appear, France, Germany, Italy and other European countries did not exist as nations. The general fashion of government, which reached its culmination in the latter part of the Middle Ages, was founded upon the feudal system, its chief and his body of retainers, and was practically alike throughout the different sections of middle and northern Europe. The unit of the social structure was the baron or feudal chief; and over all the units in a given section reigned a sovereign power, at least nominally supreme. This political situation created a certain similarity of thought and opinion. Ideas of conduct, pleasure, and the requirements of aristocratic life were very much the same from one feudal domain to another. There were visitations from castle to castle, and a popular song or story spread with surprising quickness. Merchants, scholars, musicians, priests, and troubadours traveled from country to country, carrying with them news, fashions, and polite learning. What more natural than that the mystery and miracle play should be carried from one end of Europe to the other?

*The religious unity of medieval Europe.* Even more important than the similarity of political ideas was the domination of the Roman Church. During the first thousand years of our era the religion of Rome extended over practically the whole of Europe; and it was the universal acceptance of the Church which made the sacred plays possible. The service of the Mass was the same everywhere, although the language used for it was equally unintelligible to both knight and serf: for, broadly speaking, neither could read nor write, much less understand

Latin. For the most part, only the priests understood what they were saying. Association with the Church had an importance in the medieval world that does not wholly obtain in the world of today. Every man was inside the Church. Then, too, nearly all intellectual and artistic activities, music, painting, and architecture, were closely associated with it. There spread over Europe a mania for cathedral building, so that many cities were supplied with beautiful houses of worship for the use of rich and poor alike. The officers of the Church stood with kings and emperors, sovereigns of the world. It was this powerful, unified, paternal body under whose protection European drama was born.

*Primitive nature of medieval drama.* The revived drama, born in the Church, is termed religious, sacred, liturgical, or ecclesiastical, and flourished from about the ninth century to the sixteenth. Mystery, miracle, and the Latin word *ludus* were names frequently used.[2] Some writers distinguish the terms *mystery* and *miracle* as meaning, respectively, a play based upon a biblical episode and one based upon the history of a saint or Church father. The nomenclature, however, has never been exact. Comparatively few of the plays were ever written down; and of the surviving manuscripts only a small number have been published.

Medieval playwrights began at the bottom of the ladder. In considering their first attempts, one would gain the impression that the art had never been tried before. All that had been learned by the ancients about constructing a play, about machinery for the stage, about acting, the use of masks, the rules of the unities, the proper subjects for tragedy—all these things were temporarily lost. Those who made the new plays neither knew nor cared about them. They began just where the Dionysiac revelers and the Hopi Indians began: with the attempt to represent an event in the life of the god whom they worshiped. This beginning of sacred drama is all the more interesting because it is the first and last time we are enabled to watch the process of development. We can trace it almost

[2] Many other names are met with, according to the region and century. See Chapter XIV.

step by step from the first simple scene before the altar to the latest spectacle of our own day. For three or four centuries this "new" art was left to flourish undisturbed by any influence from outside sources.

*The Easter plays.* The first scene suggesting itself to the priests for representation in dramatic form was the *Quem quæritis* episode, which takes place at the tomb the third day after the burial of Jesus. In its earliest form it was probably something like living pictures or dumb show. The dialogue, part of which is quoted at the head of this chapter, was recited in Latin by the priests. The next step was doubtless the presentation of the scene which immediately precedes the Resurrection—the laying of Jesus in the tomb. There are churches still in existence which have the sepulcher of wood or stone in the floor of the chancel. In this the crucifix was laid, to be taken forth again on Easter morning amid the joyous hallelujahs of the choir. In the course of time other scenes were chosen. It would be natural to precede the *Burial and Resurrection* with the *Entry into Jerusalem* and the *Trial before Pilate;* until finally a great part of the life of Jesus was represented.

*The Christmas plays.* Another event which became the nucleus of a series of plays was the *Birth at Bethlehem.* The picturesque scene at the manger, the visit of the Wise Men, the movement of the Star—all these things could be presented with ease. The Star could be moved forward on a wire until it paused in the right place, and the whole story could be made appealing and interesting, aside from its religious meaning. The stories embodied the central truths of the Christian doctrine, so that their representation, or attendance upon representations, was counted to the credit of the believer. Tradition says that there was a promise from one of the popes of release from purgatory for a thousand days to all who should attend the miracles performed at Chester. The Christmas play became even more popular than the Easter mystery. Saint Francis of Assisi in the twelfth century presented the Bethlehem scene at an altar which he had built for himself in the forest. There was a manger with a real child, and near by stood a real ox and a real ass.

Immediately after *Bethlehem* came the *Slaughter of the Innocents,* which was enacted on the twenty-eighth of December. It was strikingly presented by a procession of choir boys dressed in white, with the figure of the Lamb preceding them. From his throne Herod ordered the children to be murdered; and when the deed was accomplished the children were called to heaven. They made this journey by ascending to the choir-loft, where they sang the *Te Deum.*

A third center around which sacred plays were built was the story of the Old Testament Prophets, together with incidents in the lives of the early Church fathers. Saint Augustine is represented as preaching to the Jews, endeavoring to convince them of the divinity of Christ. He invokes Isaiah, Nehemiah and other biblical characters, adding to the group Virgil, Nebuchadnezzar and the mythological Sybil. At the close of the scene the whole company, being convinced of their error, fall in adoration of the Christ child.

Here then are the three most important nuclei around which the new drama arranged itself. It is not known just when or where these dumb shows and simple dialogues were first added to the service of the Church. The custom was pretty well established by the end of the ninth century, though it was not until three or four hundred years later that the plays were committed to writing. They became immensely popular and spread over all Europe. The Christian Church possessed many of the same external elements of worship as were employed in the rituals of primitive peoples: the procession, the bearing of the sacred emblems by the priest, the singing and chanting before the altar, and the use of special costumes and a distinctive speech. When these elements were combined with the story of the life of Jesus, the result was a dramatic spectacle full of human interest, and susceptible of harmless elaboration.

The writers and managers of the earliest plays, most of whom were probably monks, are not known by name. The dialogue parts were generally improvised or transmitted orally from one set of actors to another. There was no division into acts or scenes, and stage appliances were of the simplest description, since, up to the twelfth century, the chancel of the church was itself the stage. The actors were priests, and the occasion of the performances was some festal day of the Church. There were no professional actors, and if there had been the performance would not have been entrusted to them. In the chancel, or just without, on the floor of the church, would be placed the designated localities, or stations: the manger, Herod's throne, the House of Pilate, or whatever else was required by the play. At an early period lyrical passages were added to the prose of the dialogue; and though the original speech was Latin, the language of the common people quickly crept in. Hymns and chants from the service of the day provided music.

Until about the middle of the thirteenth century the story of the rise and development of the liturgical play is practically the same for all countries of continental Europe. It was not a French, German, or Italian product, but a popular European movement. From the thirteenth century on, however, characteristic differences began to show themselves in the various countries.

1. Sacred Drama

## CHAPTER XIV

# MYSTERIES AND MIRACLES ON THE CONTINENT

*All the sweetness of religion is conveyed to the world by the hands of its story-tellers and image-makers.*—BERNARD SHAW.

France seems to have taken the lead in the making of sacred plays, both as to time and quality. Manuscripts belonging to the twelfth and thirteenth centuries have been found and edited. There is also in manuscript an enormous number of plays still unedited—fifteen volumes, each containing from four thousand to thirty-seven thousand lines. The sacred play was called *jeu, histoire, représentation,* or *mystère;* and the stories were often grouped in cycles, according to the source, as the *Cycle of the Old Testament,* or the *Cycle of the Saints.*

*The Miracles of Our Lady.* As the taste for religious plays spread, the need for fresh material became insistent. One of the earliest subjects, outside the biblical narrative, was the miraculous power of the Virgin Mary. Hundreds of *Mary* plays were written and performed, especially in France, and the subject retained its popularity throughout the thirteenth and fourteenth centuries. Forty-one examples are preserved in one collection. The plot varies little from one play to another. Some one in distress calls upon the Virgin for help, and is delivered from his troubles. If the suppliant is a great sinner, so much the better. The playwrights were generous in their ideas of forgiveness. For example, one miracle portrays a hermit whose evil desires got the better of him. He seduced the daughter of a king and threw her into a well. Immediately repenting of his carelessness, he called upon the Virgin for help and imposed upon himself severe penance. Thereupon, after sundry minor episodes, the girl was restored to life and the hermit was promoted to a bishopric.

*The Miracle of Theophilus* by Rotebœuf consists of six hundred and sixty-six verses in dialogue. Theophilus is the Faust of the earlier Middle Ages. He sells his soul to the devil in order to regain a certain position he had lost. The bargain is made, Theophilus succeeds in his ambitions, and in due time the devil comes to claim his soul; but the man is too great a coward to stand by his bargain. He prays for help and is saved through the intervention of the Virgin. The famous legend of the Juggler of Notre Dame tells of a poor monk who knew no way in which to serve the Virgin but with his tricks and dances; so he performed them before her shrine at night. He was discovered and denounced by his brethren; whereupon the Virgin herself approached, blessed the Juggler, and wiped the perspiration from his forehead. The miracle of Sister Beatrice is equally famous, telling how the Virgin took the place of an erring Sister and pardoned her guilt. These two legends have been used by celebrated writers and composers as subjects for drama and opera, among them Maeterlinck and Massenet.

*Great length of French miracles.* The next step in the extension of subjects was taken by including events connected with the lives of the apostles and saints. The miracles of Saint Nicholas were especially popular. The story of the twelve apostles afforded material for endless elaboration, and tempted authors to write at astonishing length. One of the apostolic *histoires* contains more than 40,000 lines, and is probably the longest play ever written.[1] The plays are nearly all in rhymed verse, eight or ten feet to the line.

*Structure of the miracles.* The great majority of the sacred plays were rambling in form, with single scenes strung together without much thought of coherence, unity, or climax. Occasionally, however, a play is found which exhibits considerable skill. *The Wise and Foolish Virgins,* originating in France, belongs to the period when Latin was gradually being superseded by the common tongue. In this piece the chorus sings in Latin, but the dialogue is a mixture of French and Latin. The action is straightforward and lively, consisting of

[1] The length of a Greek tragedy is about 2,000 lines, while that of a Shakespearean play is about five times as much.

a request for oil from the Foolish Virgins, the reply of the
Wise Ones counselling them to go to the Merchant, his re-
fusal, and the final appeal to the Bridegroom. This happy man
is as relentless as the Merchant. He denounces them in Latin
and then curses them in French; and presently the devils come
and carry off the poor Foolish Ones. The plot has all the elements of dramatic wholeness: a motive, a theme, a coherent
action, and a climax.

In the course of time stock figures began to emerge from the
plays. The spirit of wickedness was impersonated in Vice,
who from the earliest days seemed determined to become a
comic figure, cutting up antics with the devil, and interpolat-
ing amusing scenes and farcical business into the most serious
play. Nameless people such as the wife of Noah, the servant
of Cain, the soldier at the tomb, were added to the conventional
stage *personæ*. God and the devil, both of whom had been
important from the first, now had well known features which
every one knew and expected.

When the plays came to be written down, toward the end
of the thirteenth century, there was still no division into acts
or scenes; indeed no such division was ever made. The use of
music often made natural halting places; otherwise the players
stopped whenever they chose. The scholar-priest Abélard,
whose works belong to the twelfth century, wrote three plays.
One of these, the *Miracles of Saint Nicholas,* has refrains in
old French, while the body of the play is in Latin.

Whether in prose or in verse, in Latin or in the vernacular,
the plays were above all things popular, written and acted by
amateurs for the amusement or edification of the common
people. They had all the crudities, the lapses in taste, and
lack of artistic judgment which popular movements are apt to
possess. There was no historical sense, no attempt to give the
play the setting or costumes appropriate to the period in which
the action took place. Everything was translated into the present, and given with many homely, natural touches; and in
the early days at least the plays were naïvely pious and devout.

*The plays leave the altar.* With the enlargement and elaboration of the play, the chancel of the church proved too small

for its production; also the plays became too long to be incorporated into the service of the Mass. Consequently, about the twelfth century the performance was moved out to a platform before the church door, or perhaps onto the steps, or even into the street. Lay actors began to take part, and the common speech soon crowded Latin out of the lines. The performance was still under the control of the priests; but in spite of this its tone began to deteriorate. Gradually, the simplicity and sincerity of the earlier days was replaced by an effort to entertain at any cost, or to afford a thrilling spectacle. Coarse and vulgar scenes crept in, serious passages were made ridiculous by the comic antics of Vice, devils and imps; and often the whole purpose of the play was forgotten for the sake of providing some novel feature. The taste of the people was corrupted by the presentation of scenes of torture, bloodshed, and violence.

*The Martyrdoms of the Apostles* became the subject of performances so realistic that the life of the actor was often in danger. In one play, the executioner kills all twelve of the apostles. Fools and hunchbacks, blind men, lame men, and jesters made cheap diversions for the thoughtless mob. As the part of the fool was seldom written down, he had the license of his genius, whatever it might be, and could prolong his clownish part as long as he could get applause. Jugglers and conjurers held an important place, working their wonders before the eyes of an ignorant populace. The wife of Noah became the stock figure of the stubborn shrew, who had to be coaxed, cajoled, and finally driven into the Ark. The comicalities connected with Hell's Mouth, as its victims were thrown into its red-hot cavern, were practically inexhaustible. Sometimes the imps and victims were actually in danger of being scorched as they were thrown too near the tongues of flame. Taking freedom with what might be called the paraphernalia of the Church may have caused some loosening of authority; and eventually the players did not hesitate to scoff at the weaknesses of kings, priests, and wealthy and important people, who were uniformly represented as stupid, vicious or greedy.

*The later medieval stage.* One plan of production on the continent seems to have been to erect a long, wide platform in the public square or in front of the cathedral. Along the back of this platform were ranged the stations (or mansions) necessary for the play. There were no footlights, front curtains or wings; but in the flourishing days sometimes a splendidly decorated curtain was hung at the back of the platform. An illustrated copy of a *Mystery of the Passion of our Lord,* given in Valenciennes about the middle of the sixteenth century, represents the stage settings as follows: at the extreme left of the spectators is the throne of heaven, elevated, and perhaps furnished with a half-curtain so that only the head and shoulders of God should be visible. Proceeding from left to right are Nazareth, the Temple at Jerusalem, the City itself; the palace of Pilate, the house of the High Priest; the Sea of Gennesaret; and finally, at the spectator's extreme right, Hell's Mouth. The devices used to indicate the mansions were of the simplest sort, such as a high door in the wall for a temple, or a small tank of water for the Sea. They often exhibited amusing anachronisms and childish ideas. There was no attempt at historical truth, and not the least desire to deceive,—only to make the story clear. Different mansions were of course necessary for different plays; but Heaven and Hell were nearly always in demand and were, in fact, too popular to omit.

Upon this stage were ranged the different groups of actors, who stood or sat at the rear when not taking part in the performance. God, with gilded face, sat upon Heaven's throne. The devil and his imps belonged naturally at the other end. There was usually a Prologue, recited by a herald or one of the banner bearers, in which the theme of the play was announced, the audience complimented, and an attempt made to secure silence. Possibly the herald, in order to gain some degree of attention, would attempt a joke, saying, "It is quite easy to be silent. You have only your own tongue to hold!" There must have been great differences in the manner and excellence of production in different places, according to the wealth or zeal of the townspeople. Since the priests no longer participated and professional actors did not exist, even

Mystery-stage in the 16th Century

the most difficult parts had to be entrusted to people whose ordinary business in life was buying, selling, or working at some trade. Only occasionally were women allowed to take part; more often their places were filled by beardless youths whose voices had not yet changed.

As the festivals became more popular and frequent, and the productions themselves more splendid, the task of financing and preparing them was of great importance, especially after they had passed out of the hands of the clergy. In Paris a brotherhood, called the Fraternity of the Bazoche, in 1303 acquired the right to conduct religious festival plays. This brotherhood was made up of the clerks of Parliament and of the palace. Their privilege lasted for about a century, when another company, called the Brotherhood of the Passion, took over the right to present the mysteries and miracles, while the Bazoche continued the moralities and other secular plays. Even where such organizations existed, important men of the parish took part in the festival play and helped to finance it. Members of the cast took pride in their rôles, and the whole community had a share in the glory and prestige of the performance. Aside from the festivals of the Church, there were also performances for the entertainment of visiting royalties, and for the celebration of royal marriages and birthdays. When the kings of France and England entered Paris on the first day of December, 1420, the *Mystery of the Passion* was performed "on a raised scaffolding 100 paces long."

The groups indicated by the terms *mystery* and *miracle* often overlap; but in general, on the continent after the fifteenth century, the term *mystery* applies to biblical plays, *miracle* to those founded upon the stories of the saints. The *Mary Magdalen* plays, of which there are many, partake of the nature of both groups. The mysteries, which began about the ninth century and lasted until nearly the end of the sixteenth, reached their most flourishing period in the fourteenth and fifteenth centuries. The vogue of the *Mary* plays was highest during the thirteenth and fourteenth centuries. The description of performances in France probably applies fairly well to other continental countries; but since playhouses, stages, properties, and directions for actors and managers have all disappeared, an accurate knowledge of details is well-nigh impossible.

*In Italy.* The taste for theatrical entertainment in Italy was met in two ways: first, by plays similar to those just described; and, second, by spectacular processions *(trionfo)* which in time grew to such proportions as to astonish the world. One of the earliest representations in the first group was a *Bethlehem* play at a Christmas celebration in Umbria in 1223. A *ludus Christi* was performed at Cividale in 1298, and again in 1303. Like most of the sacred pieces, these plays were in verse, some of which was sung. Symonds relates that an inventory of the Perugian confraternity of Saint Domenico, made in 1339, includes "wings and crowns for 68 angels, masks for devils, a star for the Magi, a crimson robe for Christ, black veils for the Marys, two lay figures of thieves, a dove, and a coat of mail." By the year 1375 performances in churches in Italy were common, either before or after the sermon. "The audience assembled in the nave, and a scaffold was erected along the screen which divided the nave and transepts from the choir. Here the brethren played their pieces, while the preacher at appropriate intervals addressed the people, explaining what they were about to see." [2]

*Italian nomenclature.* The plays of the Old Testament were first called *figuri,* and those of the New Testament *vangeli.* By the fifteenth century, however, all plays of a sacred nature were known as *sacre rappresentazione.* Other names, rather loosely applied, were *festa, funzione, storia, divozione, mistero, Passione, miraculo,* or *esemple.* As everywhere else, the earliest plays were extemporaneous. In 1264 a *Societa del Gonfalone* was established at Rome for the express purpose of representing the *Passion of our Lord.* One of the earliest written Italian plays, composed by Feo Belcari in 1449, in the vernacular, tells the story of *Isaac and Jacob.* The scholarly octave verse was used, however, and there was an attempt to make the work polished and elegant. In this and other Italian plays dramatic force was not so much considered as neatness in epi-

[2] John Addington Symonds, *The Renaissance in Italy.*

gram and elegance of phrase. The *sacre rappresentazione* were at their highest point of development during the fifty years from 1470 to 1520. Fraternities were formed to give them at their own expense, and they set an example of pomp and splendor. The actors were usually boys, and the performances often took place in the oratory or refectory of a monastery. The *festa* were also given, free of cost, in the public squares. In Florence the great Lorenzo di Medici set the fashion of writing sacred plays.

*The Italian triumphs* (*trionfo*). The second group of entertainments, the spectacular processions, must be noted as indicating the popular appetite for semi-histrionic display; for these spectacles undoubtedly distracted the genius and the attention of the people from true drama. They were heralded long in advance, and enormous sums of money were expended upon them. The most eminent artists were engaged to provide the decorations, the music, the costumes and dances. In many cases the purpose was merely to provide something to excite the wonder of the crowd; but in certain instances the producers, in their desire for a thrilling spectacle, descended to almost unheard-of brutalities. Sismondi relates that on the occasion of a great public demonstration near the end of the thirteenth century, there was arranged a triumphal procession and spectacular pageant called *The Torments of the Damned*. In this play the river Arno was turned aside (at enormous public cost) and the cave thus exposed was made to represent hell. Into this hell living actors were cast, and real tortures were perpetrated upon them, so that their groans and cries should render the portrayal of the torments more horrible and lifelike. These activities, however, have little to do with drama, except to show how easily, especially in Italy, the theater was debauched into the circus.

*In Germany.* The sacred play, called *Spiel,* in Germany developed with far more seriousness along the lines of true drama. The Easter plays were generally of a joyous, hopeful nature, offering opportunity for the admixture of comedy, while in the *Passion* plays a more serious tone prevailed. *The Play of the Ten Virgins* was performed at Eisenach in 1322 before the Landgraf Friedrich. Tradition says that the play so impressed him with its severity that he fell into a melancholy mood, suffered an apoplectic stroke and soon died. When the biblical stories, the miracles of the saints, the Virgin and the apostles had all been worn threadbare, the playwrights turned to folk-lore and history. By the fifteenth century the sacred play was somewhat associated with the more literary output of the Mastersingers; and in the sixteenth century it was often used as a means of attacking the papacy, especially in Switzerland. A play called *The Prodigal Son,* written in 1527 by a Hessian named Waldis, was much admired for its rough force and wit. It was divided into two acts, with a portion of the Psalms used as a chorus. In it there is an allusion to Terence, though the play itself is in Low German. The opponents of the Reformation of course were not slow in utilizing the same means of forwarding their doctrines.

The earliest German biblical play which shows a striving both for artistic effect and dramatic force is *Susanna,* written by Paul Rebhun, a clergyman, and performed in 1535. It has five acts, a prologue, epilogue, and chorus. The verse is carefully written, with cadences and length of line varying to avoid monotony and to suit the changes of scene. The religious play remained in vogue in Germany until long after Luther and the Reformation.

*In Spain.* From the twelfth century the sacred plays formed one of the popular amusements; but the extant fragments belong, at the earliest, to the thirteenth and fourteenth centuries. The Spanish name was *auto,* or *auto sacramentale* (sacrificial act). All the larger cities had their appointed festivals which began with a procession, headed by banner-bearers and musicians. After the procession came various entertainments, the whole ceremony ending with the *auto sacramentale,* which taught some lesson of religion. In the fifteenth and sixteenth centuries the *auto* continued to be an important national amusement, and was carried on by the greatest of the Spanish dramatists.

*Stage machinery.* No adequate idea of medieval sacred drama can be complete without a knowledge of the extraordinary mechanical devices which these amateur play-actors had at their command. The plays of the sixteenth century were often far-famed for their wonders.[3] At a *Passion* play in Vienna in 1510 there were eight masters of machinery who had charge of the conjuring tricks. In the *Acts of the Apostles,* performed at Bruges, there appeared artificial dromedaries and camels; a vessel full of all kinds of animals, which descended from heaven and ascended; devils flying through the air and spitting fire; tigers which came up from the earth and were converted into sheep; a fire-spitting serpent creeping up an oak tree; angels flying about singing, and irradiated with a lovely light. Other wonders caused blood to come out of bodies, water was changed into wine, the staff of Moses bloomed, the sun was eclipsed, and earthquakes rent the earth. When Saint Paul was decapitated, the head made three bounds, and at each place where the head rested a spring started flowing with milk, blood and water. All this shows mainly that the simple play, meant to teach the stories of the Bible and the principles of religion, soon became transformed into a means of displaying cheap tricks and magic before an ignorant and gaping populace.

[3] Described at length in the *History of the Theatrical Art* (Vol. II), by Karl Mantzius.

## CHAPTER XV

# MYSTERIES AND PAGEANTS IN ENGLAND

The religious mysteries were designed for the edification of youth, their piety too often hypocritical, and their extravagant monastic morality in glaring opposition to the ethics of society.— J. ADDINGTON SYMONDS, *The Renaissance in Italy.*

It is probable that the sacred play was brought to England from France after the Norman conquest. Throughout the fourteenth, fifteenth, and sixteenth centuries there was a constant supply of mysteries and miracles. More than one hundred English towns, some of them very small, are known to have been provided with these entertainments, which in some places were given every year. Usually, however, an interval of a few years elapsed between productions. Corpus Christi day, which falls in early June, was the most popular time, though Whitsuntide and occasionally other Church festal days were marked by performances. On one occasion the Parish Clerks gave a pageant which lasted for three days, and again one lasting for eight days. The boy choristers of Saint Paul's in London became celebrated for their histrionic ability, and in 1378 they begged Parliament to issue an injunction against "unskilled performers." In 1416 Henry V entertained the Emperor Sigismund at Windsor with a play on the subject of Saint George; and in the following year the English bishops who were delegated to the Council of Constance—the same Council which promised safe conduct to John Huss and then burned him at the stake—entertained their hosts with a Christmas play in three parts, the *Nativity,* the *Visit of the Magi,* and the *Slaughter of the Innocents.* Two performances were given, one for their fellow councillors and themselves, the other for the burghers of the town.

*Some of the extant manuscripts.* The usual name for these

plays in England was *miracle,* or the Latin *ludus,* or sometimes the word *history.* The name *mystery* is said to have
been first applied, in England, in the early eighteenth century
by Dodsley, the editor of a volume of old plays. Of the extant
manuscripts, the earliest is probably the *Harrowing of Hell,*
in three versions, all of which were probably taken from the
French. It is simply a dramatic dialogue in verse, in which
Christ and Satan argue over the ownership of the souls in
hell; and it belongs naturally with the Easter group of plays.
Two plays have been discovered within the present century, one
on the subject of *Abraham and Isaac;* the other, belonging to
the lost Newcastle Cycle, on the *Building of the Ark,* both
probably surviving from the fourteenth century.

*The Cycles.* The greater part of the important manuscripts
of biblical drama belongs to the cycles—a medieval product
in a sense peculiar to England—which attempted to cover the
history of Man from his creation to the Day of Judgment.
In these cycles there appeared, almost unconsciously, something like the principle of unity: first came the creation, then
the fall of Man, which necessitated his redemption. This
redemption, after being foretold by the prophets, was accomplished by the birth and passion of Christ, with his resurrection. The series, taken as a whole, formed a true dramatic
sequence, in which the soul of Man was the hero.

There are commonly counted four important English cycles:
Chester, York, Coventry, and Towneley (also called Wakefield). Cycles are also known to have been produced at Newcastle, Canterbury, and Lincoln. Of those that survive, the
Chester cycle is probably the earliest. Of the Newcastle cycle
but one play remains, *The Building of the Ark,* in which there
are five characters, and Noah's wife is represented as a vixen.
Such is her stubborn temper that Noah is constrained to say
to her,

> "The devil of hell thee speed
> To ship when thou shalt go!"

The cycles vary in quality, and the plays are not always the
work of one hand, nor even of one century. The manuscripts,

as we have them, have been revised, edited, and arranged, probably from several earlier models, possibly in some cases from the French. In the different cycles there is naturally great similarity both in subject matter and in the sequence of plays; but there are also interesting differences of treatment.

*The Pageant.* Doubtless biblical plays were often given in England in the continental manner, on a stationary platform with the "mansions" arranged in proper order. Gradually, however, the pageant became specially associated with the English play. The word first meant the movable scaffolding upon which the play was given, but was afterward applied to the play itself. Reduced to its simplest elements, the pageant was a play on wheels. This of course was not a new thing. Tradition assigns a cart to Thespis; there were "carriage plays" in Spain; and traveling shows in Japan. In England, as a rule, each play of the cycle had its own carriage, and all moved along in procession, each wagon giving its play in turn at each stopping place. Usually the pageant began very early in the morning. In the proclamation of the York performances in 1415, it was announced that the plays would begin between four and five o'clock in the morning.

All our knowledge concerning the method of presenting the pageant comes from a report left by one Archdeacon Rogers, who wrote of it in quaint English about the year 1517. He said that each carriage had a higher and a lower room, the lower "where they appareled themselves," and the higher where they played. Temporary stands were built for spectators, and good seats sold for high prices. Sometimes the action of the play called for horsemen, in which case obviously the action would spread out beyond the limits of the stage. The celebration opened with a procession, and after its close there was an orderly round-up by the councilmen and mayor. One writer says:

"To a medieval town the performance of a mystery was an event of immense interest. . . . The magistrates ordered all the shops to be closed, and forbade all noisy work. The streets were empty, the houses locked up, and none but solitary armed watchmen, specially engaged for the occasion, were seen about the residences. All were gathered in the public square." [1]

*The Guilds.* We have seen how in France the production of plays, once having left the hands of the clergy, passed into the care of certain Brotherhoods. In England the production was managed by the tradesmen's guilds. Each play was arranged, acted, costumed, and financed by its own guild. A study of the distribution of the plays among the guilds forms one of the diverting features of this medieval carnival. In the York cycle the tinners began with *God Creating Heaven;* the plasterers followed with *God Creating the Earth;* and then came the card-makers, with *God Creating Man.* Of course the ship-builders and seamen played *Noah and the Ark,* while the goldsmiths enacted the *Three Kings,* because they could furnish gold crowns. The guilds took pride in making a good showing, being inspired doubtless both by the spirit of good workmanship and the desire to advertise their wares. The smiths had the task of affixing the body of Christ to the cross. A dialogue between the torturers in one of the Towneley plays indicates how one holds down his knees, while the other is cautioned to draw down the limbs with all his might. They then congratulate themselves that neither "lewde man ne clerke nothing better shuld."

*Scenery, costumes, and finance.* In the larger towns considerable time and care were spent in preparation for the pageants. The scenery and stage appliances must have been somewhat scant, if all were accommodated in a rolling greenroom and stage combined. The splendor of the costumes perhaps made up for anything that was lacking in the setting. It was the custom for God to wear a white coat and have his face gilded. Herod, and miscreants generally, were dressed as Saracens, they being the stage villains of the Middle Ages. The expenses, which were often large, were sometimes partly met by a nobleman or other public spirited benefactor; but in general the citizens or guilds financed the production. A collection was taken up at the time of the procession; and, in

[1] Karl Mantzius, *History of the Theatrical Art.*

addition, a tax, ranging from a penny to fourpence and called pageant silver, was imposed upon each member of the guilds. It was paid over to the pageant master, who was elected each year. Today he would be called the business manager, or impresario. The actors and "drawers" were paid for their services; but there was a fine for bad acting or undue forgetfulness of the parts, also fines for guilds which were slow in handing over their pageant silver.

The most impressive of all the mysteries was the *Passion of Christ;* and this was, as we have seen, also the earliest to be dramatized. In England it took shape about the fourteenth century, gradually showing the conflict between the spiritual strength of Jesus, on the one hand, and on the other the combined forces of the Jewish and Roman worlds. Of all the ecclesiastical plays, this alone can still be seen enacted in modern times.[2]

*Lack of artistic quality in the biblical plays.* Theoretically, the escape of the liturgical plays from the control of the Church, the extension of subjects and the possibility of greater freedom of treatment, ought to have enabled the dramatists to produce at least one masterpiece; but none such exists. Here and there are passages of such sturdy simplicity, so sincere and pleasing, that they for a moment seem to lift the play out of a dull and commonplace atmosphere into one of life and reality; but there is not one genius of the first rank, not one play of the quality of *Macbeth* or the *Œdipus* in all the enormous output of the Middle Ages. One mystery is just about as good, and just about as dull, as another. So poor did the plays become that a celebrated French writer, Du Bellay, publicly advocated the importation of Greek and Roman tragedy to take the place of the native mysteries. There was none of that struggling with the problems of life and destiny which marks the tragedy of the Greeks; no attainment of an artificial but beautiful conventional form, such as appeared in the *No* plays of the Japanese; only an occasional naïve touch, interesting because of its spontaneous simplicity.

*The decline and disappearance of the biblical play.* The

[2] At Oberammergau, every tenth year.

Jesus and the Apostles
From the Oberammergau Passion Play

next phase of the sacred play is just what might be expected, namely, its condemnation by the Church under whose protection it had risen. It was condemned, however, not only by the Church. The time came when the hollowness, the absence of all religious feeling, made the performance a disgrace and a scandal. A pious habit had became a conventionalized and empty show. Both Romanists and Protestants ultimately frowned upon the mysteries, and denounced them for their childishness and coarseness. The guilds, which had once gladly given time and money for their preparation, now felt the yearly tax a burden. The cycle of sacred drama had run its course. In France, performances were forbidden during the latter part of the sixteenth century. In Spain and in Catholic Germany, as well as in Italy, they persisted somewhat longer. In England they were forbidden by Henry VIII, but were restored again for a brief time under Mary. There were few performances after 1600. The last York play was in 1597, the last Newcastle play in 1589. The Chester plays died out with the sixteenth century. The most important result of all this dramatic activity was perhaps the fostering of a love for the theater, and the shaping of native material into rough dramatic form.

## CHAPTER XVI

# MORALITIES, INTERLUDES AND FARCES OF THE MIDDLE AGES

Twelfth-night had come and gone, and life next morning seemed a trifle flat and purposeless. But yester-eve and the mummers were here! They had come striding into the old kitchen, powdering the red brick floor with snow from their barbaric bedizenments; and stamping, and crossing, and declaiming, till all was riot and shout.—KENNETH GRAHAME, *The Golden Age.*

The sacred plays of the Middle Ages often contained farcical, irreverent, and even lewd situations, while the so-called secular plays frequently carried with them some degree of sermonizing. The distinction between comedy and tragedy, so marked in classical plays, was forgotten. In the day of Hans Sachs if a play had a fight in it, it was tragedy. No fight, no tragedy.

*The morality.* The play nearest to the mystery in manner of production, costumes, and general tone was the morality, which might almost be classed as a religious play. In the age-long attempt to portray the dual nature of Man, in whom good and evil perpetually fight for supremacy, the playwrights lighted on the allegorical method. They conceived the different desires and appetites of Man as personalities, named them Greed, Pride, Vanity, Good Will, Patience, and the like, and caused them to weave their plots so as to capture the soul of the hero, who was called Everyman, Humanum Genus, or Man. Besides the personified desires, there were also in most plays other characters such as the Doctor, the Priest, or a public officer. God and the Devil were usually present.

The first English morality of which there is record was on the subject of the Lord's Prayer, and was given at York sometime during the fourteenth century. It is now lost, but it made so profound an impression upon the spectators that a company was immediately formed for the purpose of providing frequent and regular performances. At the end of the fourteenth century the company numbered one hundred members and their wives.

The earliest extant morality in English is *The Castle of Perseverance*, which belongs to the fifteenth century. In it the whole life of Man, called Humanum Genus, is portrayed from birth to death. There are two other very early English moralities, one entitled *Spirit, Will and Understanding*, the other *Humanity*. By their very nature, the moralities were all obliged to use the same or similar abstractions for their allegories; but a French writer, Nicolas de la Chesnaye, was inventive enough to make a slight variation. His play is called *The Condemnation of Banquets*, and is nothing less than a tract on temperance in both eating and drinking. It is very long, having more than 3,600 lines and employing thirty-nine characters. By far the most interesting extant morality is *Everyman*, ascribed by many scholars to the Dutch Dorlandus. It appeared in English translation four times between 1493 and 1530, and opens with these lines: "Here beginneth a treatise how the High Father of Heaven sendeth Death to summon every creature to come and give an account of their lives in this world, and is in manner of a moral play."[1]

Even from the first, the morality was nearly always sprawling in construction and long-winded. Moreover, all advance in dramatic conception has been towards the concrete rather than the abstract; so it would seem that the allegorical manner was a turn in the wrong direction. On the other hand, such fables were popular and quickly understood; and the abstract qualities, personified by living actors, took upon themselves something of the nature of reality. Furthermore, the moralities mark the end of the biblical cycle of drama, and, with the interludes, form the link between the medieval and the modern play. In them can be recognized the seeds of the romantic and

---

[1] *Everyman* was produced in London and New York early in this century, the chief part being acted with extraordinary skill and perfection by Miss Edith Wynne Mathison.

later schools. The habit of using qualities for names is a stock device of comedy, and has long persisted, the Mrs. Sneerwell and Mrs. Backbite of Sheridan being a direct continuation of the tribe of Greed and Vanity.

*Varieties of medieval secular plays.* Coexistent with biblical plays and the moralities, there grew up during the late Middle Ages several kinds of plays of a more or less secular nature. In a rough classification we discover the following branches:

> Carnival or Shrovetide plays
> Interludes
> Farces
> Puppet shows
> "Feasts" of various sorts, being travesties
> of Church rituals.

Some of these types are as ancient as the sacred play, while others developed from it. There are naturally no hard and fast lines between the groups; but the existence of such a variety of forms proves anew the enormous appetite for theatrical entertainment in the late Middle Ages.

In these secular plays there were, generally speaking, four classes of performers: strolling players (successors of the ancient mimes and pantomimic actors); roystering citizens out for revel; the Fool companies; and people connected with the schools and universities. The first of these were what might be called professional performers. They belonged to the lowest stratum of society and were classed as vagabonds. Besides keeping alive the ancient Roman skits, they probably picked up for their own use such contemporaneous pieces as served their purpose. They were often jugglers, acrobats, minstrels and magicians as well as actors. No doubt it is due to this class that certain stock comic situations and "business" have been handed down in an unbroken tradition from early Roman days.

The second group of actors was composed of ordinary citizens, merchants, petty officers, journeymen and the like, who banded themselves together during carnival season for purposes of revelry and mumming. The third class, the Fool companies, consisted of bands of youths—a sort of underground clique—sometimes organized under a secret code, whose chief business it was to play gross comedies and to execute nonsensical and often ribald travesties on the Mass. These companies existed all over Europe and England, and gained immunity for their ribaldry by their popularity, their anonymity, and their audacity. Mantzius says: "They satirized the Mass, turned the church into a ballroom, and the altar into a bar." These boisterous "Feasts" antedate most of the mysteries, and may have been reverent in their origin. Remnants of pagan ceremonies seem to be embedded in their rites. Theophylact, Patriarch of Constantinople in 990, ordered the *Feast of Fools* and the *Feast of the Ass,* with other "religious farces," to be played in the Greek Church. In France one group of these youthful mummers was called *Enfants sans souci,* another the *Société des Sottes,* still another *La Bazoche du Palais.* The fourth group was composed of school and choir boys, with an admixture of university men. These would naturally give their attention to plays of a more scholarly nature, imitations of Seneca and Terence, dramatic exercises in Latin, and adaptations more closely allied to the classic stage.

*Shrovetide plays.* It is likely that the Shrovetide or carnival mummers were in many cases the same people who participated in the mysteries. Sometimes the same stage was used both for the sacred play and the farce, which were often given in immediate succession, with the same audience sitting through both performances. The Shrovetide plays—also called *interludes, sotties, Fastnachtsspiele*—for some centuries made a specialty not only of the comic, but of the indecent aspects of society. The fables, found upon the lips of the Crusaders and Spanish Moors, in the pages of French *fabliaux,* in the *novelle* of the Italian Renaissance—had become current throughout Europe. We must allow, of course, for a difference of standard in language and manners; but even granting all that, one can but grimace at the nastiness of many of these so-called comic plays.

Sex and digestion were the two subjects which particularly excited the mirth of these lovers of medieval farces. In plays on the first topic, the joke usually turned on the deceived husband, who, to the medieval mind, was always a ludicrous object. The other unfailing source of comedy was even more intimate—the vicissitudes, distresses, and experiences accompanying digestion. Mantzius says that the subject of sex was peculiarly Gallic, while that pertaining to digestion was typically Teutonic. Both themes were bandied about all over Europe to the last shred of vulgarity.

At its best, however, the humor of the secular plays is naïve and diverting. The farce of *Mak the Sheep Stealer* may have been taken from the French; but as we have it, it forms an interlude in the second Shepherd play of the Towneley cycle. The French farce of *The Wash Tub* introduces the henpecked husband whose wit, combined with his wife's misfortunes, restores him to his masculine prestige. The most famous of all the medieval farces, *Pierre Pathelin,* is entirely innocent, without vulgarity of any sort, and has a well rounded plot. It is fairly long, consisting of about 1600 lines; and like all medieval pieces was played through without intermission. Its author is unknown; but it is of French origin, and was played by the Fraternity of the Bazoche in 1480. It was immensely popular in its day, going through six different editions in the fifteenth century, and no less than twenty-four in the sixteenth. In the eighteenth century it was adapted for use in the repertory of the Théâtre Français, and restored to a form much nearer the original in 1872. It was also used as the libretto for a comic opera by Bazin.

These farces picture authentic types of character, and have comedy situations which were native to the participants, not borrowed from Greece or Rome. They smack of the soil and carry on the true dramatic tradition. The Brotherhood of the Passion gave a play in the fifteenth century on the subject of Griselda, a story which came through the Moors from Spain, was part of the Italian stock of tales, and was used by Chaucer and Spenser. An English sixteenth century play is still in existence, with Friar Tuck, Little John, and all the other characters of the immortal Robin Hood legend. The story goes that Bishop Latimer's own church was closed on a festal day, because all the congregation had gone to see *Robin Hood*.

*Hans Sachs.* 1494-1576. The name of Hans Sachs should be placed in an honorable niche with the writers of early secular plays. He touched upon more subjects, had more wit and charm, and developed a better technique than any other play-maker of his time. He lived as an honored and distinquished citizen of Nuremberg, following the trade of shoemaker and at the same time producing plays, songs, poems and other works to the number of more than six thousand separate pieces. Of these, about two hundred are in dramatic form—tragedies, comedies, Shrovetide pieces, or simple dialogues to which he gave no name. He was at his best in the Shrovetide piece which, under his hand, changed from a formless dialogue to an entertaining, well constructed, merry and wholesome little play. It was seldom more than four hundred lines, and nearly always inculcated some lesson in morals or manners.

*The interlude.*[2] The interlude was usually a short, humorous piece, suited for two or three, scarcely ever more than four, actors; and it was, *par excellence,* the banquet entertainment. Occasionally it was used as a comic diversion between the more serious parts of a sacred play; or as one of the features of medieval vaudeville in a program of juggling acts, necromancy, and wrestling. Gradually the interlude acquired a courtly character; but it was also employed, during the period of religious strife, as a means of propaganda. It was essentially witty and full of action. A fragment of a very early interlude exists, called *Interlude de Clerico et Puella,* probably belonging to the reign of the first Edward. It is written in dialect, and requires three actors and a puppy. There is no prologue or explanation; but the characters begin at once, Clericus making immediate love to Puella. In the fourteenth century the Society of Parish Clerks, which enjoyed considerable renown in medieval London, played interludes before King Richard, his queen and court. Nicholas Udall and John

[2] The interlude is more fully treated in Chapter XXI.

Bale, both of whom belong to the sixteenth century, wrote religious and political interludes. The most famous of all the writers of this species of play is John Heywood (1497-1580) under whose hand the form became satirical and entertaining. He discarded rustic and biblical subjects, also subjects of controversy, and turned towards Chaucer and the French fables for his themes. With him the medieval secular play changed almost imperceptibly into the English realistic comedy of the Elizabethan age.

*Historical, legendary, and puppet plays.* There are a few extant plays, generally called mysteries, which are based on non-biblical stories. Two of these are French and have for themes, respectively, the Fall of Troy and the story of Joan of Arc. They were evidently meant for gigantic spectacles, and seem to foreshadow the chronicle play. It is recorded that, in these plays, from three hundred to five hundred people were on the stage at one time.

The puppet show (also called "motions") developed in its humble way side by side with the more pretentious types of drama. *Dumb shows,* which were pantomimic performances with either living actors or puppets, were performed in Florence early in the fourteenth century, and spread over Europe and into England in the fifteenth. Old stories of cheating merchants, devils in disguise, and of Noah's Ark were standbys in the way of fables. A letter from Bath, mentioned in the *Tatler,* relates the appearance of a puppet show featuring Alexander the Great as hero. At Bartholomew Fair in the reign of Queen Anne, a performance of the *Creation and Flood* was followed by a puppet show called *Punch and Sir John Spendall.* In it Punch beat his wife, insulted the priest, was frightened by a ghost and was finally carried off to hell.

# SECTION  FIVE
## THE  GROWTH  OF  NATIONAL  DRAMA

## CHAPTER XVII

# NATIONAL DRAMA: ITALY TO 1700

Benvenuto Cellini, in his autobiography, presents a graphic picture of the times. . . . He and the Italians of his century killed their rivals in the streets by day; they girded on their daggers when they went into a court of justice; they sickened to the death with disappointed vengeance or unhappy love; they dragged a faithless mistress by the hair about their rooms; they murdered an adulterous wife with their own hands, and hired assassins to pursue her paramour; lying for months in prison, unaccused or uncondemned, in daily dread of poison, they read the Bible and the sermons of Savonarola, and made their dungeons echo with psalm singing. . . . The wildest passions, the grossest superstitions, the most fervent faith, the coldest cynicism, the gravest learning, the darkest lust, the most delicate sense of beauty, met in the same persons, and were fused into one glittering humanity.—J. Addington Symonds, *The Renaissance in Italy*.

The national dramas of Europe grew upon the ashes of the miracles and mysteries. As the biblical plays lost their hold upon the public and gradually disappeared, there swept over Europe that liberating movement called the Renaissance, whose most vigorous phases fell in the fourteenth and fifteenth centuries. One of its features was the rediscovery of the ancient literatures, which brought to light the plays of the Greeks and Romans. While there was probably no century during the so-called Dark Ages in which an ancient play was not read and possibly imitated, nevertheless it is not more than truth to say that the literary treasures of the antique world had practically been lost. Many of them were actually lost, for all time. Manuscripts that were known were not easy of access, owing to the difficulties of travel and the vicissitudes of war. Few scholars knew the Greek language. It seems as if, indeed, all intellectual curiosity concerning the past had lain quiescent for centuries.

*The rediscovery of the ancient plays.* When men at last turned to the writings of the ancients, it happened that, among the dramatists, Plautus, Terence and Seneca were the first to be recovered; and the recovery was made in Italy. It was natural, therefore, that the "new" drama should begin there. The plays of Seneca were studied and imitated by the historian Mussato of Padua in 1300; and though his compositions were dry and dull, yet they encouraged among scholars the fashion of imitating the ancients. In 1427 twelve "lost" plays of Plautus were found through the efforts of the famous Bracciolini Poggio, who recovered many classic works which had been hidden and forgotten in the monasteries. Gradually there was established a practice of giving the ancient plays, first in Latin, later in translation. In 1486 the *Menœchmi* of Plautus was given at Ferrara, and again in 1502 at the Vatican. At the marriage of Lucrezia Borgia and the Duke of Ferrara there was a five-day festival, the chief feature of each evening being the presentation of one of the Plautine comedies. One of the actors of the time gained the nickname of Phædra by his brilliant acting of that rôle in the *Hippolytus* of Seneca.

Italy, artistically in advance of other sections of the continent, was a whole century ahead of England in respect to the stage. By the time the last mystery had been given at Canterbury, there was a well established drama of another sort in the southern peninsula, where the Roman plays took precedence over the Greek, and were regarded as models of excellence in all things pertaining to the theater. In contrast to the unpolished biblical plays, they indeed represented design, scholarship, and the pomp of courtly settings. The practices of Terence and Seneca were elevated into rules. The law of the three unities was revived, and the mythological subjects brought forth again for rejuvenation, together with other paraphernalia of the classic drama—chorus, fate motives, long speeches, Messenger and all.

*Tragedy.* The domination of the antique models was most apparent in the Italian tragedies, which were at first written in

Latin. When the playwrights were at length forced to turn
to the vernacular, they used the *octave* (eight-line stanza) or
*terza rima* [1] forms of verse, neither of which lends itself successfully to dialogue. A great advance, however, was made
by Gian Giorgio Trissino, who had the good luck to live in
the first half of the sixteenth century during the pontificate
of Leo X, a prelate who loved splendid and costly theatricals.
Trissino was influenced not only by Seneca, but also by Euripides and Sophocles. In a tragedy called *Sofonisba* he discarded the *terza rima* for blank verse, kept the chorus and used
it to divide the action, as in the ancient manner. The story,[2]
found in Livy, was well constructed and rather an advance
upon the Italian products of the time. Other writers followed
the example of Trissino and sought their material in classic
pages. A tragedy on the subject of *Orestes* was written by
Rucellai in imitation of the *Iphigenia in Tauris* by Euripides;
and another writer, Alemanni, made a brilliant translation of
the *Antigone* of Sophocles.

These plays and others similar to them were produced in a
spectacular and costly style before dukes, princes and car-
dinals, with special scenery and music. Their composers, however, leaned too heavily towards the pompous, the rhetorical,
and the stilted. The works exhibited nearly every possible
dramatic fault: long monologues, confidential talks for the
obvious purpose of informing the audience about something
that ought to have been displayed by means of action; dry sermons from the chorus; off-stage action, and passages full of
windy elocution. They had the classic form and labored with
the classic subjects; but they lacked the classic inspiration.

*Comedy.* There was a much more luxuriant growth of
comedy than of tragedy after the rediscovery of the ancient
drama. The polished and witty courts were eager for entertainment, and under their patronage there developed an
enormous body of social comedy as polished and witty as
themselves. A few years before the appearance of *Sofonisba*

---

[1] The rhyme-scheme of the *terza rima* is a b a, b c b, c d c, etc.
[2] Used frequently by subsequent playwrights and librettists.

a writer named Dovizio produced a farcical comedy, founded upon the *Menœchmi* of Plautus, called *Calandra*. Though fairly obscene, it was brilliant and dramatically effective. While keeping to the general outlines of the Plautine play, the author instilled into it a contemporary life and spirit which immediately appealed to his audience. The male twins were changed under the Italian hand into a boy and girl, thus adding to the piquancy and subtracting from the modesty of the scenes. The play was produced in turn in all the courts of Italy, and was especially enjoyed by Pope Leo X. The author was thenceforth known as Cardinal Bibbiena.

The success of *Calandra* was equalled many times during the following two hundred years. Nearly five thousand plays from the sixteenth and seventeenth centuries are known to scholars. They are similar to one another, devoted to trivialities, indecencies, and delineations of illicit love intrigues. To us they are as monotonous as the second class musical comedies of our own day, and far more appalling in their depravity. The love theme which starts the action is never the romantic love which carries youth, and sometimes middle age, off its feet and fills it with generous and poetic enthusiasms; it was rather the commercial connection, of a routine sort, with which fashionable young men were accustomed to occupy their time.

*Stock situations and characters.* The Italian playwright took over, in a way, both the situations and the characters of Roman comedy, changing them superficially to suit the conditions of Florentine, Neapolitan, or Venetian circumstances. The central figure, the chief young lover, is usually poor or in debt, and wishes to advance his fortune either by a rich marriage, or by seducing the wife of a rich neighbor. Or perhaps, in his need for money, he blackmails some one with whose indiscretions he is acquainted; or, again, he is married to two women at the same time and needs the services of a rascally parasite or slave to get him out of his trouble. There are no heroines or heroes: none who risk danger for a worthy or generous purpose, such as had appeared in the classic drama, and were to appear so abundantly in the later romantic plays of Europe. There are only central characters, and there is always a disagreeable joke on somebody: either a deceived husband, a rustic or simpleton, an unsuspecting father or master, or the old love being displaced by the new. The scheming, plotting and rascality which constitute the action are the work of the comic servant, who has license, audacity, and the spot-light.

*Machiavelli.* 1469-1527. The most famous names of this period are Machiavelli, Ariosto, and Aretino. Machiavelli left two comedies, *Mandragola* and *Clizia,* both founded on plots from Plautus, with strongly conceived characters, amusing dialogue, and effective scenes. If any doubt about the truth of Cellini's description of Italian society should rise, a reading of *Mandragola, Clizia,* or *Calandra* would dispel it. However, the deep-seated depravity of *Mandragola* is far removed from the coarse, hearty ribaldry of the medieval plays. The whole tissue of society, as Machiavelli and others of his school conceived it, was a network of selfishness, vice, and greed. The assumption was that all men and women are mean and full of vicious desires, which they will gratify at any cost of truth, honor, or kindness; the only difference in people is the finesse and cunning with which they are endowed.

Concerning the women of these plays Symonds says:

". . . the girls were corrupted by nurses, exposed to the contaminating influences of the convent, courted by grooms and servants in their father's household, tampered with by infamous duennas, betrayed by their own mothers. They accept the first husband that is proposed to them, confident in the hope of continuing clandestine intrigues with the neighbor's son who has seduced them. . . ."

He gives no less scathing a description of the male youth; and he adds significantly: "From the innumerable scenes devoted to these elegant and witty scapegraces, it would be difficult to glean a single sentence expressive of conscience, remorse, sense of loyalty, or generous feeling."

*Ariosto.* 1474-1533. Five comedies remain from Ariosto, four of which turn on the rascally tricks of a servant who is trying to get money for his master's love intrigues. The fifth is concerned with the devices by which this same servant manages to keep his master in favor with two wives at the same time. These plays show a deal of invention, and are written in brilliant style. The *Suppositi*,[3] built upon the *Menœchmi*, became in turn the basis for the *Comedy of Errors* of Shakespeare. It is said that Pope Leo built a new theater in Rome, seating two thousand people, for the express purpose of producing the *Suppositi*. The scenery was painted by Raphael. On the day of the performance, Leo sat at the entrance and gave his blessing to all whom he thought worthy of witnessing it.

*Aretino.* 1492-1556. The list of comedy writers from this period embraces some of the most celebrated names of that brilliant but decadent time. There are Ficenzuila, Cecchi, Gelli, Ambra, Il Lasca, Doni, Dolce. In Peter Aretino the type reached its most shining and most disgraceful example. He made a boast of his immorality and profligacy, and these traits were amply reflected in his work. He flattered kings and princes, attacked his enemies with caustic indecency, and also wrote with great unction upon devotional subjects. He had wit and audacity, combined with a low mind, and the sneaking courage of a back-stairs adventurer. For his scurrilous attacks a nobleman tried to kill him with a stiletto, and lamed him for life; another vowed to kill him in bed, and actually kept him for months a prisoner in his house; and Tintoretto, one of the most famous painters of his time, pretended ignorance, got him to sit for his portrait, and then faced him with a pistol. In spite of all this, he was the favored darling of his time, the friend of two popes, of Charles V and Francis I, and at his death was about to become a cardinal of the Church.

*The kidnapping school of comedy.* One of the ever present features of Italian comedy was a child kidnapped by the Turks, and restored to its home just at the fall of the curtain. The parents, generally wealthy and noble, recognized their

[3] Literally, *The Substitutions*, sometimes incorrectly called *The Supposes*.

offspring by a necklace, ring, or birthmark. This fable, of course, goes back to early folk lore, was used by the Greek comedy writers, and by Plautus, as well as by the Italians.

Even while these comedies were flourishing, during the sixteenth century, there were not lacking critics who began to scoff at such childish theatrical tricks. Il Lasca (whose real name was Grazzini), a dramatist of some note, was sincere in his scorn. In his Prologue to *The Jealous One,* he says:

"All the comedies which have been exhibited in Florence since the siege end in discoveries of lost relatives. This has become so irksome to the audience that, when they hear in the argument how, at the taking of this city or the sack of that, children have been lost or kidnapped, they know only too well what is coming, and would fain leave the room. . . . They lay their scenes in modern cities and depict the manners of today, but foist in obsolete customs and habits of remote antiquity. They excuse themselves by saying Plautus did this, and this was Menander's way and Terence's; never perceiving that in Florence, Pisa and Lucca people do not live as they did in Rome or Athens. For heaven's sake, let these fellows take to translation, if they have no vein of invention, but leave off cobbling and spoiling the property of others and their own. . . ."

*The Commedia dell' Arte.* The title, Comedy of Art, means unwritten or improvised drama, and applies rather to the manner of performance than to the subject matter of a play. This peculiar species had a long life in Italy, probably of about four hundred years (from the fourteenth to the eighteenth century); but it flourished especially in the sixteenth and seventeenth centuries. Of course in actual practice the play was not, in any sense, the result of the moment's inspiration. The subject was chosen, the characters conceived and named, their relations to one another determined, and the situations clearly outlined, all beforehand. The material was divided into acts and scenes, with a prologue. The situations were made clear, together with the turn of action and the outcome of each scene. When this general outline (called also scenario, or canvas) was satisfactorily filled out there was left an opportunity for actors to heighten, vary, and embellish their parts as their genius might suggest. The necessity for smoothness, constant surprise, clearness, and wit called forth histrionic abilities which had been unknown to the medieval stage. "The actors had to find the proper words to make the tears flow or the laughter ring; they had to catch the sallies of their fellow-actors on the wing, and return them with prompt repartee. The dialogue must go like a merry game of ball or spirited sword-play, with ease and without a pause." [4] Such parts required actors able to make a serious study of their parts; actors who took pride in their achievements, and were willing to accept the discipline which all professional art demands. These comedians changed forever the standards of acting. The best of them stamped their parts with individuality, freshness and brilliance, and gave value to pieces which, often enough, were otherwise worthless. The Comedy of Art introduced the professional actor into Europe.

*Subjects of the Comedy of Art.* Like the court comedies of Ariosto and Machiavelli, the Comedy of Art was concerned mostly with disgraceful love intrigues, clever tricks to get money or to outwit some simpleton. There were the same long-lost children stolen by the Turks, the same plotting maids, bragging captains, aged fathers and wily widows. Each gentleman had his parasite, each woman her confidante. There was considerable diversity of incident, such as night scenes, in which the hero was mistaken for the villain; cases where father and son fall in love with the same girl; and risqué situations—the representation of fire, shipwreck, and the like which served as a pretext for allowing actresses to appear naked on the stage.

*Comic relief.* An important part of every play, given always to the most expert and popular actors, were the humorous interruptions, called *lazzi,* which often had nothing to do with the play itself. It might be clever pantomimic acting, acrobatic feats, juggling, or wrestling. For example, three characters meet at a cook shop, where they hear of an accident which has befallen the wife of one of them. While they express their dismay at the affliction, they fall to eating greedily from a

[4] Mantzius, *History of the Theatrical Art.*

huge dish of macaroni; and as they eat, tears stream down their faces. Or again, a servant, disgusted at an order his master has given him, delays carrying it out until he has turned a complete somersault. One famous actor could execute this trick having a full glass of wine in his hand, without spilling a drop. Another was able, in his eighty-third year, to box the ear of a fellow servant with his foot. Elaborate imitations of women taking off their stays, false hair, and crinolines were always acceptable, together with many pantomimic diversions of a less innocent character. These are examples of the *lazzi* of the Comedy of Art.

*The masks.* In the course of the development of the Comedy of Art, there grew up certain traditions which held fast for many years. The rascally servant, the old man, the lady's maid, and the like—stock characters which appeared in every play—always wore a conventional dress, with masks. In general these masks may be classed under four or five groups: Pantalone and the Doctor, both old men; the Captain, a young man of adventure; the valet or jester, usually called Zanni; the hunchback Punchinello; and another old man, somewhat different from the first two.

Pantalone was usually a shop-keeper from Vienna, somewhat stupid, fond of food and of pretty women, talkative, gullible, full of temper, the butt of all the jokes—some of them very indecent—yet forgiving in the end. His business was to get deceived by his young wife, or his son, or his servant. The second old man, the Doctor, filled the part of a lawyer, an astrologer, or perhaps a philosopher from Bologna. Sometimes he represented an absent-minded pedant, quoting Latin at inappropriate times, and enormously conceited. The bragging Captain, a boasting, swashbuckling officer, often Spanish, dressed-to-kill in cape, feathered hat, high boots, with sword in belt, was always a prime favorite. He told extraordinary tales about how he beat a whole army of Turks and carried off the beard of the Sultan, but when there was a hint of real danger he was the first to run away. He made love to the none-too-innocent servant maid, and got thrashed by her Harlequin lover. This character, of course, is none other than the

Miles Gloriosus of Plautus, called in Italy *Il Capitano Spavento della Valle Inferno,* or simply Spavento. In time he gained a choice variety of bombastic names in different countries: Capitano Metamoros, Capitaine Fracasse, Captain Horribilicribilifax, Ralph Roister Doister, and Bobadil.

Zanni, the scoundrelly valet or jester, resembled the Greek slave of the Middle and New Comedy. Most plays contained several valets: one each for the Doctor, Pantalone, and the *primo amoroso.* All were variations of the type of which Pierrot and Harlequin are the most celebrated. They were generally indolent and knavish, sometimes cunning and cruel; always stupid in their own way, first deceiving others and then being duped themselves. All made love to the servants, and often imitated the love scenes of their masters in ridiculous parody. Punchinello was a hunchback with a long crimson nose, dressed in a dark cloak and wearing a three-cornered cap. He too was a great rascal, but dry and less talkative than Pantalone.

All these characters had costumes, stock gestures and stage business which could be reckoned upon to create a laugh and put the audience in tune for the knavery that was to follow. In course of time there crystallized about each mask an entire code or repertory of phrases, exclamations, curses, exits, epigrammatic sayings and soliloquies appropriate to the rôle, which could be memorized and made to fill in the blank when the actor's wit could find nothing better. The *primo amoroso,* the female lover, and the maid servant were not masked, though they were thoroughly conventionalized. The male lover was a perfumed scapegrace; while the girl, rarely well individualized, stood simply as the helpless or ignorant foil for the intrigue. The hero became known as Flavio, Leandro or Valerio; the woman as Isabella, Lucinda, Leonora or Ardelia; while the maid servant was generally Columbine. The importance of these typical stage characters, which enjoyed at least four centuries of popularity on the European boards, lies in the influence which they exerted upon the superior dramatists of a later time. Already one can catch a breath of the Shakespearean comedies in the names of the heroes; and one can see that Molière, both as actor and author, learned much from this branch of Italian art. Its influence passed through Holberg into Denmark, where it became a powerful factor in shaping the romantic drama of a later age.

*Pastoral drama.* For some time during the late Middle Ages, pastoral poems, eclogues, and stories of an ideal life in some impossible country had a mild vogue. Niccola da Corregio appeared with a play in which the chief characters were a shepherd and shepherdess named Corydon and Thyrsis. A writer named Beccari followed his example and improved upon it; and in 1573 a pastoral play was written which not only had pretty music and costumes, but also great literary beauty. This play was *Aminta,* written by Torquato Tasso. It has little action, and is too rhetorical and effeminate for the passion which makes effective stage action; but it is a beautiful poem, graceful, delicate, and sympathetic. Such fine qualities, appearing at the right moment, were destined to create a school.

One of the first followers of the celebrated Tasso was Guarini, who in 1590 produced another pastoral play called *Pastor Fido.* Obviously an imitation of Tasso, it was nevertheless good enough to stand on its own merits. It is less beautiful than *Aminta,* but has more life. There is an elaborate plot, with an intrigue, a mysterious prophecy, and a case of mistaken identity. The dialogue and characterizations are vigorous. One scene begins with music and dancing, which suggests the later development of opera. *Pastor Fido* had the honor of being performed at Turin at the wedding ceremonies of the Prince of Savoy.

*Arcadia, the home of the pastoral play.* Arcadia is the realm of Art and Song, undisturbed by the troubles which visit the ordinary homes of earth. There Love is master, and the laws which rule are those of nature. Laws of society and of man-made realms must be set aside if they conflict with the laws of love. In this remote, imaginary pasture of beauty lovers can live free from the cares and excitements of the gay world. The shepherds are gifted with grace, faithfulness, gaiety and song; the shepherdesses blessed with a corresponding degree of loveliness, charm, and grace. Lyrics and lutes, running streams, panniered costumes and picnics *de luxe* abound, while the tiresome laws, duties, and responsibilities of the world are forgotten. Such are the illusions which the pastoral plays, at their best, create.

The production of Aminta, however, might almost be considered one of the minor catastrophes in the history of literature, for the cult of the pastoral spread through the fashionable circles of Europe like a pestilence. *Aminta* and *Pastor Fido* were the only plays of note that the Italian school produced; but the romantic contagion went from court to court into Spain, France, England. The Arcadian idea seemed to be the formula for a universal saccharine concoction, whose delicate and cloying beauty for a time drove nearly everything else from the stage. The plays grew more and more insipid until they became almost a curse. In the endeavor to keep them going, the playwriters enlivened the monotonous rustic scenes with sly allusions to contemporary affairs: the shepherdess became a local duchess or countess, but thinly disguised; and the shepherds were none too subtle replicas of actual princes and courtiers. Fortunately, even the worst of plagues must have an end; and the whole Arcadian species in time degenerated into foolishness and burlesque.

*Changing conditions.* With the new types of plays, the performers began to go under cover, into the halls of palaces or monasteries. Nobles began to build theaters in their own houses. In Nuremberg, Hans Sachs and his company gave plays in the town hall. Moreover, at this time (the sixteenth century), professional actors, practically for the first time in European history, organized themselves into companies. Here and there women actors appeared upon the stage. With the establishment of professional companies there came a great change in the conduct of the performances: for it followed as a matter of course that they would sooner or later have houses of their own, and would play, not for a certain stated festival, but as often as they could secure patronage. Thus the production of plays came in the course of time to be a private, money-making enterprise.

## CHAPTER XVIII

# NATIONAL DRAMA: SPAIN TO 1700

In Spain the dramatic revival declared itself earlier than in any other country, with the possible exception of Italy; and declared itself unequivocally in the form of romance. . . . In no people had chivalry taken so firm a root; the point of honor was the very life blood of the Spaniard; his very instincts had taken the ply of fantasy and romance.—C. E. Vaughn, *Types of Tragic Drama.*

By the year 1500 Spain had come to the end of the long contest with the Moors, which had lasted for more than seven centuries. The enemy, leaving the country, bequeathed to the Spanish a wealth of learning and culture. Though there was no comedy, tragedy, pastoral play or farce among their literary relics, yet there were many tales of magic, of passionate love, and of oriental splendor. From the north came ideals of chivalry and knighthood to mix with these oriental influences. Troubadours from Provence crossed the Pyrenees, bringing with them stories of tournaments, or of allegiance to some difficult trust, and of a holy Cup which was the quest of many a knight. In her own right Spain was also rich in ballads, which seem to flourish wherever drama is found. Good ballads have concentration, directness of action, sharp characterization, and often a terse and pithy dialogue—all of which offer a good basis for a play. Out of this blend of oriental fancy, chivalric ideals, and gift of balladry came the remarkable period of the romantic Spanish drama.

*Classicism in Spain.* Naturally the Italian influence towards classicism was felt. A few pastoral and satiric plays in the Italian style made their appearance; and one tragedy, *Celestine, or the Tragedy of Callisto and Melibœa,* had a brilliant success as a piece of literature in the later fifteenth century. It could scarcely have been enacted on any stage. It dealt with

witches, love potions, and the like—elements which later were
to become the stock in trade of the romanticists. Spain's
greatest genius, Cervantes, was for a time on the side of the
classicists. Following the example of Trissino in Italy, he
produced in 1583 a drama called *Numancia*, in classical dress;
and this play was succeeded by nearly a score of others in the
same manner.

The classic ideal, however, was not destined to dominate the
Spanish stage. About the middle of the sixteenth century a
gold-beater of Seville, named Lope de Rueda, became chief
actor, playwright and manager of a small band of strolling
players. He seems to have been much the same type of man
as Hans Sachs of Nuremberg, full of homely sense, humor,
gaiety, and possessed of a natural, easy style. In his plays he
pictured the people he knew, hitting them off with good-natured
shrewdness. Cervantes regarded Rueda as the real founder
of the national drama in Spain.

*Lope de Vega.* 1562-1635. When Cervantes produced his
pseudo-classical tragedy, *Numancia,* Lope de Vega was twenty-
three years old. He was born two years before Shakespeare,
in the family of a poverty-stricken nobleman, and lived to be
seventy-three years old, devoting most of his mature life to
the writing of poetry and drama. Both as a writer and as a
citizen, he received extraordinary honors. His plays brought
him wealth and renown; admiring crowds followed him whenever he left his house. He was called the Spanish Phœnix,
and Prodigy of Nature. Good days and good women were
called Lope days and Lope women. When he died, only the
memory of his pomp and generosity towards the poor was
left; there was no vestige of his large fortune. His funeral
was observed like that of a king, with three bishops to officiate,
and a three-day period of mourning for the city.

The phenomenon of Lope's dramatic output remains one of
the wonders of literary history. He wrote twenty-two hundred
plays, besides a sufficient number of poems to fill twenty-one
volumes quarto. It is said that he could write a play, full of
captivating incident, fresh versification and humor, in a day,
and that no amanuensis could keep up with his dictation. So

eager were the managers, that he was allowed no time for correction or revision. His plays are of many sorts: love stories, plays of adventure, farces, scenes from society, moralizing pieces, tragedies, and sacred plays (*autos sacramentales*). He was not, of course, uniformly good in all these species of writing; two of his plays are notorious as being the worst tragedies ever written.

*Lope's plays.* For convenience, four classes of plays may be indicated. First, there are the "dramas of the cloak and sword," dealing with a high-spirited gallant who goes through many adventures in order to win the lady of his love. This type of play usually contains an underplot carried on by servants and other minor characters. A second class, similar to the first, is occupied with historical or semi-historical figures of a more heroic cast than those of the first group. These plays too are full of intrigues and adventures, with underplots which parody the principal one. Whatever the main theme, there is sure to be much ado about the "point of honor," with jealous quarrels, misunderstandings, and tempers on the trigger. A few dramas of social life constitute a third class. They portray rather intimately the manners, customs and thoughts of the time, but are not concerned exclusively with polite society, as are the contemporaneous Italian works.

These three groups would probably have included all of Lope's dramatic writings had not Philip II, on his death-bed, forbidden the representation of all secular plays for an indefinite time within his kingdom. The order remained in force two or three years. During that time Lope turned his attention to the *autos,* investing them with the same glamour as that which had surrounded his secular plays. The pious deeds performed by one of his saints became as interesting as the adventures of one of his buccaneers or swashbucklers. His sacred plays were a mixture of the grotesque, of fine poetic fervor, lively images, entertaining incidents, sincere Catholic piety, and a good knowledge of character. They were played on the street on Corpus Christi day, being preceded by a farce. They became famous throughout the country, and were performed by actors before taking the sacrament.

*Characteristics of Lope's work.*  Of all European countries, Spain was least influenced by the Renaissance and most deeply averse to any reforms in religion; and Lope was, in a peculiar sense, representative of his country. His was nearest the medieval mind, farthest from that of reawakening Europe. At the same time, his plays give us the first important examples of what is known as romantic drama. He was either unconscious of, or ignored, the classic tradition; he had no interest in the three unities, no use for the Messenger, for long soliloquies, for the exalted personages so dear to the classic dramatist, or for the carefully designed plot. He built his plays out of Spanish material, using folk lore, ballads, history or legend, always with native characters. His genius was many-sided; with immense fertility he unfolded scenes of lively action, invented countless entertaining and thoroughly dramatic situations; he was master of brisk dialogue, pleasant versification, humor and vivacity. He adopted outlaws as heroes, mixed together the sacred and farcical, and cared little for probabilities or for historical accuracy; but his energy and contagious vitality carried all before him.

It was Lope de Vega who, above all others, gave the shape and stamp to modern European drama. His tendency was to emphasize the individual, to exhibit strange phases of passion, ambition, or hatred. If we do not today read or see Lope's plays in their original dress, we nevertheless have seen their descendants; for the European world has for four centuries enjoyed many an entertainment based upon situations that came from his brain. The Italians of the seventeenth century, the French writers preceding and including Voltaire, the early Elizabethans, and that great pair, Shakespeare and Molière—all borrowed and learned from him. Professor Matthews says: ". . . the dramatists of every modern language are greatly indebted to the models set by Lope de Vega,—and none the less because most of these later writers are unconscious of their obligation. Nowhere has modern dramatic craftsmanship been carried to a higher pitch of perfection than in France; and it must never be forgotten that 'The Cid,' the first of French tragedies, and 'The Liar,' the first of French comedies, were both of them borrowed by Corneille from Spanish plays written by contemporary disciples of Lope de Vega."

*Influence of Lope de Vega outside of Spain.* It would be difficult to enumerate all the instances in which dramatists of other countries drew either upon Lope de Vega or upon one of his followers, but here are a few examples:

| Spanish author | Play | Borrowing author | Play |
|---|---|---|---|
| Agustin Moreto | El valiente justiciero | Molière | L'École des maris |
| Agustin de Zarate | (two plays) | Molière | Les femmes savantes |
| | | | Les précieuses ridicules |
| Tirso de Molina | | Molière | Don Juan |
| Fernando de Rojas | | Rotrou | Venceslas |
| Fernando de Rojas | Celestina | Corneille | Don Bertram de Cigarral |
| Juan Ruiz de Alarcón y Mendoza | La Verdad sospechosa | Corneille | Le Menteur |
| Lope de Vega | El Acero de Madrid | Molière | Le Médicin malgré lui |
| Guillén de Castro | Las Mocedades del Cid | Corneille | Le Cid |
| Lope de Vega | El Conquista d'Arauco | Voltaire | Alzire |
| Lope de Vega | El Palacio confuso | Corneille | Don Sanche d'Aragon |

The enumeration of the indebtedness of these non-Spanish writers to Lope and his school is in no sense a deprecation of the borrowers; all dramatists everywhere have used old material; it is meant only as an indication of the extraordinary fertility of the genius of Lope de Vega. When he began to write, the drama was an insignificant and vulgar art, with but two poor playhouses in the city of Madrid; when he died, the theater had become an important institution. Less than fifty years after his death there were forty playhouses in the capital, and the conduct of the drama was a subject not only of royal but of national consideration. At least thirty talented Spanish playwrights flourished during his time or immediately after. The love of the theater spread rapidly until almost every little town had its playhouse. The skill of professional actors increased, buildings improved, scenery appeared on the stage, and mechanical devices for working wonders were invented or rediscovered.

*Calderón de la Barca.* 1600-1681. We have now come to the beginning of a period when the dramatist did not hesitate to attempt both comedy and tragedy. Calderón, the second of the two outstanding figures in the Spanish drama, was a writer of both species, but was far greater in tragedy than in comedy. Like Lope, he wrought with native literary material and for the most part disregarded classical models. He did not create new forms, or make any striking departure from the style and standards set by Lope. He was hazy in regard to history and geography. In his youth he was counted a prodigy of talent; and upon the death of Lope, which occurred when Calderón was thirty-five years of age, he was officially appointed the writer of dramas for the royal theaters and for the Church. He became formally attached to the court, somewhat in the position of a poet laureate. After some years he withdrew from the court and entered a religious brotherhood; but he continued throughout his life to write for the theater.

*The plays of Calderón.* Of the many pieces which were at one time or another attributed to Calderón, one hundred and eight dramas and seventy-three *autos sacramentales* are authentic. The dramas are of many varieties, though always romantic. He threw his sword-and-cloak heroes into one difficulty after another, handled supernatural and ghostly themes in a masterly fashion, and was also able to write scenes of grim humor. His plots are unfailingly interesting, even though, to the modern mind, some of them are absurd. He was thoroughly medieval and devoutly Catholic in his point of view.

*The Devotion to the Cross,* written when the author was nineteen, portrays the instantaneous redemption of a revolting criminal through his death-bed appeal to the Cross. His plots are often highly theatrical, affording thrilling moments, scenes of tenderness and beauty, and surprising climaxes. After his appointment as court poet he produced a spectacle called *Circe* near the lake at Buen Retiro. During its course there were represented mountains, forests, with trees fashioned in human form, waterfalls with concealed lights, and an immense car plated with silver and drawn by two fishes, out of whose mouths flowed sparkling fountains. The man of genius had turned showman; and no doubt Calderón himself was deeply conscious of the emptiness of such spectacles, in comparison to the thoughtfulness and poetic beauty of such a play, for example, as *Life is a Dream* (*La Vida Es Sueno*), which is indeed not one of his best plots, yet is one of his most appealing tragedies.

There is in Calderón something splendid, ethical, intense. Like all writers, he was limited by the peculiarities of his age and country. He must have understood and felt something of the spirit of the Renaissance and of the stirrings within the Church; but he gives no sign. He never emerged into the world of modern thought. His greatness reveals itself in a certain depth and richness of nature, a poetic quality, and an attitude of large tolerance and sympathy for the vagaries of the human heart. He made an extraordinary appeal to his contemporaries, sometimes as mystic, sometimes as lover, and always as the seeker after truth. With him a new tone came into the drama—a tone of questioning, of ironical patience mingled with bitterness.

*Excellences and weaknesses of Spanish drama.* With the complete establishment of the romantic type, certain weaknesses inevitably showed themselves. Only such geniuses as Lope and Calderón could triumphantly overcome the frequent excess of passion, extravagances of plot, and childishness of intellect. Moreover, the writers were bound by the restrictions both of the court and of the Church, which limited all kinds of art. Nevertheless the Spanish drama of the sixteenth

and seventeenth centuries stands with the Greek and Elizabethan as one of the supreme monuments of national genius.
There was in it abundance of invention, poetry, revelation of
human nature, and that undercurrent of philosophy which indicates the struggle of the mind with the problems of existence.

When Calderón passed from the stage, the influence of the
Italians and French became more pronounced, and the neo-
classic style came into fashion. The supposed rules of the
antique stage little by little smothered the native spontaneity;
and for more than a century there were indeed many plays,
but little of dramatic worth. Not until near the close of the
eighteenth century did Lope and Calderón come into their own,
through a revival of interest in the romantic type of play.

## CHAPTER XIX

# TRAGEDY IN FRANCE BEFORE 1700

The French followed the bent of their own genius, just as the Spanish had done, and the English; and this led them in time to a drama not so energetic as the English, and not so full of surprises as the Spanish, but surpassing them both in the symmetry of its structure and in the logic with which the action was conducted.— BRANDER MATTHEWS, *The Development of the Drama.*

The year 1500 marks the beginning of the decline of the sacred drama in France. The mysteries held out for nearly half a century longer, but the life had gone out of them. They were despised alike by the Church, by men of letters, and by men of fashion. On the other hand, the lure of the ancient literatures was growing stronger. From the beginning of the sixteenth century, the study of Greek and Latin became the fashion in cultured circles. Gray-haired men went to school for the purpose of acquiring these languages, people copied the antique mode in dress and manners, and sought in numberless ways to revive the pagan ideals. The elegant translations of Amyot, a professor of Latin and Greek at the University of Paris, had a great vogue. While Greek was occasionally studied and mastered, yet it was Latin, on the whole, which caught the attention of men of the Renaissance. The playwrights did not go back to the great tragic poets and comic writers of Greece; it was Seneca, Plautus and Terence whom they studied and imitated. Roman heroes, and Greek heroes as presented by the Latins, were destined to be the favorite subjects of French dramatists for a period of more than two hundred years.

In this phase, the activities of colleges and schools had considerable importance. The plays of Seneca, with the *Sofonisba* of Trissino, supplied the model; but the first products were only declamatory dialogues and recitations. The names of more than a dozen of these translators and imitators remain, and the titles of their work tell the same old story that was heard in Italy: Dido, Medea, Agamemnon, and so on. The leader of this group was Jodelle, whose most important play, *Cleopatra,* was produced in 1552. Some of the writers attempted religious subjects, but few of the plays have been found interesting enough to suggest any modern reprint. The works of Robert Garnier, however, were collected and reprinted in the latter part of the last century. Garnier wrote tragedies on both Greek and Latin subjects: Portia, Cornelia, Antigone, The Trojans, Hippolytus, which are scarcely more than pleasing conversations interspersed with lyric passages. The action is described, not shown, and seldom leads to anything like a climax. Nevertheless, Garnier was popular in his day. An edition of his tragedies was reprinted every year for forty years.

*Protest against the classic type.* In the midst of this boom of the classics, certain voices were raised in protest, among them that of Alexander Hardy,[1] who had written plays for the Brotherhood of the Passion before the performance of the mysteries was forbidden. Hardy was familiar with the practical workings of the stage, and was also a born playwright. He produced pastorals, tragedies, and tragi-comedies, taking his subjects from ancient history, through Plutarch and other writers. His tragedies were built in five acts, according to the Senecan model; but the characters were his contemporaries, and the ideas were those of his time and nation. The honesty of his workmanship and his avoidance of indecency drew the interest of men of influence to the theater, which soon began to be recognized as an æsthetic institution. Women of refinement found they could attend performances, where hitherto they had been kept away by the indecorous nature of the plays. The tennis-court stage of the Hotel de Bourgogne became more and more respectable and influential, until in time Richelieu took it under his powerful patronage. As theater audiences grew in numbers, a second playhouse was estab-

[1] Alexander Hardy, 1560-1631. Court poet to Henry IV.

lished—the Marais, which soon became a rival to the Hotel de Bourgogne.

The influence of Hardy was of a mixed sort. He was much nearer the romantic than the classic school, so far as his own nature was concerned; but he was not powerful enough as a writer to mould and shape, once for all, the dramatic taste of his time, as Lope had done in Spain. Hardy's immediate followers, less inventive and less gifted than himself, imitated his habit of borrowing the classic subjects without being able to endow them with fresh life. As the vogue of the theater increased, they not only borrowed plots wholesale, but imported from Italy the pseudo-classical rules for tragedy. The idea of logical procedure, order, and a fixed design, so congenial to the French mind, laid its stranglehold upon the drama. In addition to this, the influence of the famous salons and literary societies was strongly away from contemporary and national, towards foreign and antique standards. It is time now to examine the nature of these celebrated French salons.

*The Blue-stockings of the Renaissance.* Shortly after the death of Hardy the cause of art and learning in France received a powerful impetus through the sudden popularity of literary clubs. The most famous of these was the group of young men of fashion, writers, statesmen and clever women who convened at the salon of the brilliant Marquise de Rambouillet, an accomplished, witty hostess who seems to have set the fashion for women, as well as men, to be acquainted with literary and political affairs. Mlle de Scudéry, who had a turn for story writing, composed romances in which were portrayed her companions of the salon, and they in turn tried to live up to the exotic picture she had made. Their speech, at first simply polite and cultured, began quickly to be affected and artificial. They got into the habit of using absurd circumlocutions, catchwords, and pompous roundabout phrases in order to avoid mentioning anything common or vulgar. Often these euphemisms were unintelligible to everybody except members of the group. The young men composed stilted verses in praise of the ladies, attributing to them virtues as well as impossible perfections. With all this interchange of compliments, there was a strict standard of decorum. The exalted refinement of the ladies and the pedantic gallantry of the men allowed no familiarity, nor anything so vulgar as a flirtation; but between themselves the ladies used terms of endearment such as *ma chère, ma précieuse.* From this custom they received the name *les précieuses,* and from that time till the present any stilted, highly artificial form of artistic work has been called "précieuse."

A list of the people who frequented the Hotel de Rambouillet reads like a political and literary *Who's Who* for Paris of the early seventeenth century: Mlle de Scudéry, Mme de Sévigné, Mme de la Fayette, Duchesse de Longueville, Duchesse de Chevreuse, Mme Deshoulière, the earlier Balzac, Voiture, Bossuet, Costart. It was their purpose to forward the cause of culture and to direct their thoughts towards the things of the mind rather than towards things of the body. They made literature and the arts of at least equal importance with eating, drinking, and hunting; moreover, they set their seal upon the movement towards better ideals for the stage. Their appreciation encouraged young unknown writers, and their criticism and discussions must have done much to keep alive an interest in arts and letters. Brunetière asserts that the drama of Corneille is "a lasting testimony to the nobility, loftiness and generosity of the artistic ideals of the *précieuses.*" There is no doubt, however, that the activities of this coterie of learning became in time absurd and foolish, and perhaps they merited the ridicule which Molière heaped upon them. The affectation of their speech, their leaning towards sentimentality, the over-niceness of their tastes, all tended towards falseness and superficiality, not to say sham.

*Pierre Corneille.* 1606-1684. At this stage, when the classical ideal had not yet become unalterably fixed, Corneille appeared. His first works were comedies, and none too good; but when, at the age of thirty-one, he produced the *Cid,* there was erected an important landmark in the history of drama. The *Cid,* it will be remembered, was a Spanish hero of the twelfth century. His deeds were celebrated in many ballads and poems, and had been made the subject of a play by the

Spanish Guillén de Castro. Corneille, conscious of the classic bent of French taste, adhered pretty closely to the so-called Aristotelian rules, yet contrived to produce a tragedy which, in depth of passion, poetic fervor and vigor, far surpassed anything that had so far been seen on the Parisian stage. Thus the first important French tragedy had for its subject a medieval though foreign fable, and was a compromise between the romantic and classic schools. Its spontaneousness and boldness were romantic in character; while the conduct of the struggle of the hero between love and duty, with the subordination of all other incidents, was decidedly in the classic spirit. The play was in many respects technically faulty; yet it stood, and still stands, the one practical test of a good play: it acts well.

In 1635, two years before the appearance of the *Cid,* a group of literary friends, accustomed to meet regularly for the purpose of discussion, had been officially recognized by Cardinal Richelieu and elevated into a national institution under the name of the French Academy. This body of men, inspired by the great Cardinal, reproached Corneille for too close an observance of the classic rules; for "sinning against nature in his anxiety not to sin against the rules of art." This oddity in historic criticism could not have crushed Corneille completely, however, for the *Cid* had a great success. It had been put on in the theater in the Marais, which was filled; and seats were placed on the stage after the English custom. The merits of the play were the subject of much discussion, and its author almost immediately acquired the position, which he occupied for many years, of the leading dramatist of his country.

*Corneille's workmanship.* French drama is indebted to Corneille not only for its first important tragedy, but also for its first important comedy, *The Liar* (*Le Menteur*). Although as a writer of comedy he exhibited undoubted genius, yet his greatest work, both in bulk and in quality, was in tragedy. He wrote thirty plays, choosing a great many historical subjects, several of which had often been used before, such as *Sofonisba, Attila, Œdipus.* He avowed his allegiance to the so-called classical rules, and for a part of the time he adhered to them.  His theory was that the subject of a tragedy should be remote and improbable, with as many striking and extraordinary situations as were compatible with unity of action. His plays succeeded in spite of his theories.  As an artist he had boldness, spontaneity, and a love of the marvellous.  He was impatient of the austere restraints which the classic spirit imposes upon its followers, and his complicated plots did not easily fall into the mould required by the unities.  But he was anxious for the favor of the literary circles, especially for that of the *précieuses*, and was almost forced to submit to the fashion for classic styles.

Corneille carried on the work, begun by Hardy, of purifying and refining the stage.  He claimed with pride that women need no longer be offended by the vulgar license of former times.  He was fond of political plays, but made little of the passion of love.  When he used that theme, he was apt to become frigid and artificial.  He reigned on the French stage like an autocrat, though not without criticism and opposition. Sixteen years before his death the work of the younger poet Racine displaced that of Corneille, whose decline was as rapid as his rise.  Fontenelle, his nephew, wrote: "The fall of the great Corneille may be reckoned as among the most remarkable examples of the vicissitudes of human affairs; even that of Belisarius asking alms is not more striking."  Nevertheless, Corneille justly ranks as a great figure in French drama.  He had much skill in unfolding an intricate plot; and, as a poet, his verse is marked by imaginative power and tenderness.

*Jean Racine.* 1639-1699.  The second representative of French classical tragedy was born two years after the appearance of Corneille's *Cid*.  Racine was well educated at the school of a religious brotherhood at Port Royal, and, unlike most of the dramatists of the age, he knew Greek as well as Latin.  His first pieces were failures, and called forth from the great Corneille the advice not to attempt any more tragedies.  The young man was ungrateful enough not to take this advice.  His *Andromaque* (1667) was highly successful.  It made the greater impression because already there was apparent in it a principle of composition which differed fundamentally from that of Corneille. This difference (to be explained presently) was the cause of a long and bitter literary warfare. There rose in Paris two cliques, one represented by Racine, Boileau and Molière, the other by Corneille and his followers. In 1670 Racine and Corneille were asked to write a play on the subject of Bérénice, though each was kept ignorant of the fact that the other was attempting the same theme. Corneille's play was coldly received, while that of Racine proved a triumphant success. Corneille's popularity, already waning, received a death blow, and the supremacy of Racine was established.

Racine, however, was far from being satisfied. The court and literary circles were full of intrigue, which turned him against the world; and he was beset by religious doubts concerning the morality of the theater. Soon after his success with Bérénice he abandoned his career as a dramatist, and accepted an appointment as historiographer to Louis XIV. For twelve years he wrote nothing for the stage; then at the request of Madame de Maintenon he produced *Esther* and *Athalie* for the pupils of Saint Cyr, a girls' school under royal patronage. *Esther* was presented with great success, but *Athalie,* though published, was never enacted until after the author's death.

In his later life, Racine developed an attitude very different from that of the self-confident youth who so boldly withstood the criticisms of Corneille. He became conscientious almost to the point of morbidity, and looked with distaste upon his own writings. New editions failed to interest him. "For a long time past," he said, "God has graciously permitted that the good or evil that may be said of my tragedies scarcely moves me, and I am only troubled by the account of them I shall one day have to render to Him." Racine was accomplished as a prose writer as well as a poet, and produced histories of value. He died April 21, 1699.

*Racine's plays.* Eleven tragedies and one comedy remain from the pen of Racine. Nine of his tragedies are based upon historical subjects of the ancient world, and two upon biblical subjects. The story of Esther had already been treated six times by French dramatists, but a comparison of Racine's method with that of other writers, even of his own school, reveals a wide difference. Racine reduced the action to its bare bones,—no underplots, no digressions, episodes, or characters extraneous to the main action. Instead of the extravagant sensational incidents such as Corneille delighted in, Racine worked with probabilities, everyday events, characters nearer to the commonplace. His object was to depict the possibilities of passion implicit in the common experiences of man, the living reality instead of the exceptional situation. Corneille had declared it a law that the subject of a fine tragedy ought not to be probable; to which Racine answered that nothing but what is probable should ever be used in tragedy.

Racine's genius, however, was something far beyond the mere negative virtue of avoiding intricate and improbable plots. Not only did he simplify the action of his plays, but he formed an austere and elegant style appropriate to such simplicity. He avoided windy, rhetorical declamations and "purple patches," and expressed complex things with ease and beauty. His was an authentic voice, not an echo. Given a simple situation, he sought to go deeper into it, to throw upon it the searchlight of understanding combined with a passionate sympathy. As Corneille was more concerned with events, so Racine was more concerned with character; and he gave more importance to the passion of love than any previous dramatist had ever done. He said that as love is the most universal of passions, so it is therefore capable of being the most tragic; that love best displays the peculiarities, the fickleness, the weaknesses and strength of character; and that while there are few ways of showing such a passion as avarice, for example, there are many ways of being in love.

*Racine and the critics.* Racine did not escape criticism even from the men who followed in his footsteps. Voltaire sneered about the similarity of his heroes; and the Encyclopædists of the next generation disparaged what they termed the access of sensibility into the drama. The disposition towards sensibility, they said, accompanies weakness, and results from a motion of the diaphragm. It is a disposition which inclines us to admire, to sympathize, to be thrilled; but it is also one which inclines us

to lose our reason, to be mad, to have no exact idea of the
true, the good, and the beautiful.  Inept as this criticism seems
when applied to Racine, yet it was in accordance with the
movement, fostered by the Encyclopædists, which sought to
make practical use of everything.  This attitude was expressed
by Newton when he spoke of poetry as ingenious fiddle-faddle.
Boileau considered that Racine stood at the head of the art
of his time.  It may be said, in passing, that Boileau was the
Horace of the late seventeenth century, a man of extraordinary
good sense and taste, trying, in his criticisms, to point out
reasons for admiration or condemnation—reasons which could
be justified by nature and experience.  His main idea was that
the models of the ancients should be used to restrain the too
exuberant outpourings of undisciplined talent.  To him, naturally, the work of Racine appeared to be more in accordance
with the canons of good taste than that of Corneille.

Many of the modern critics have found Racine somewhat
cold and formal.  It cannot be denied that to the reader of
today, accustomed to the greater diversity and richness of the
romanticists, his concentration and simplicity seem occasionally bare and frigid.  Professor Erskine, in comparing the ancient with the French classic play, says: "The Greek type of
life is made clear by wonder and love; the Racine type is life
set in order by rule."  Saint-Beuve comments: "His style as a
rule borders on prose, except as regards the invariable elegance of its form."  Even single lines bear evidence of this
elegance and concentration.  Professor Vaughn, in his study of
types of tragic drama, has summed up as follows:

"These then are the supreme qualities of Racine: his deep
knowledge of human character, so far as it bears directly upon
action; his power of directing the action so as to grip the given
characters at close quarters, to wake the energies of their soul to
the utmost intensity, to call forth the strongest instincts of the
heart.  The two plays in which these qualities reveal themselves
most clearly are probably *Andromaque* and *Phèdre*." [2]

[2] *Phèdre* is based on the story of Hippolytus, used by both Euripides
and Seneca.

Mr. Arthur Symons, of our own day, said of Phèdre that it is the greatest rôle in the whole repertory of poetic drama, and that it alone reveals Racine as one of the most passionate of poets.

It must be generally admitted that among the writers of the French classical school, Racine stands preeminent. He had the singleness of purpose which characterized the ancients at their best. The strength of the neo-classic school lay in its depth of understanding, its clear simple beauty, and in the poetry with which the author was able to envelop his theme.

## CHAPTER XX

# COMEDY IN FRANCE BEFORE 1700

Molière: Surely of all the wits none was ever so good a man, none ever made life so rich with humor and friendship.—ANDREW LANG, *Letters to Dead Authors.*

He took the side of simple dignity, of human nature against all the narrowing vices, whether of avarice, licentiousness, self-righteousness or preciosity. He has written the smiling poetry of our sins.—ROBERT LYND.

The broad and often vulgar humor of the Middle Ages was not the foundation upon which the comedy of Molière and the seventeenth century was built. *The Farce of Pierre Pathelin* and other comic pieces continued to live; but the dramatists turned away from such naïve material and sought their plots in the tales, *novelle,* and plays of Italy and Spain. It has already been noted that Italy in the late Middle Ages was the home of learning and the nursery of aristocratic amusements. Both social comedy and the Commedia dell' Arte were flourishing there in the sixteenth century; and in 1571 a company of Italian comedians, called the Gelosi, came to Paris, became very popular and remained for six years.

*Early writers of comedy.* Pierre de Larrivey, a Frenchman of Italian ancestry who belongs to the latter half of the sixteenth century, left nine comedies, all of which were either translations or adaptations from the Italian. They are in prose, with the typical Italian intrigues, stock characters, misunderstandings and recognitions. The plots generally hinge on the rascally valet, conniving either for money or for an illicit love affair for his master. Besides Larrivey, there were Jean Godard and Odet de Turnèbe, each of whom contributed a little in the way of Italian adaptations or imitations. In the early seventeenth century we have the names of Thomas Corneille, Quinault, and Scarron, who for the most part turned to Spain for their models.

Although there was no outstanding comic genius, yet during the century following the visit of the Gelosi some advance was made in naturalness and in construction. In the years between 1640 and 1658 more than two hundred French comedies were produced. They were generally of a romantic turn, often extravagant, with fantastic or stock characters. The plots, however, never reached that stage of elegant and cynical depravity achieved by the Italian writers of comedy. Certain playwrights, influenced by the Spanish mode, dealt in disguises, trap doors, dark lanterns and mysterious happenings. Whether following the Spanish or Italian style, however, the plays generally portrayed type-characters, such as the miser, the doctor, the parasite, or the shrewd servant. Few are of interest today except as they mark the steps in the progress which was to culminate in the work of Molière.

*Jean Baptiste de Poquelin de Molière.* 1621-1673. The life of Molière is a story of struggle, hard work, domestic unhappiness, death and burial in obscurity and almost in shame. In time, he belongs between Corneille and Racine, but he died before either of them. His birth is obscure. At school he seems to have become acquainted with many Latin, Spanish, and Italian comedies. In his poverty he associated with low companions, and at one time he acted as valet in the household of the king. At about the age of twenty-two he became an actor and manager; but for a time he was wholly unsuccessful. One theatrical enterprise after another failed, and in 1645 he was imprisoned for debt. After being released, he gathered together a group of actors and left Paris for a tour of the provinces—a tour which lasted about ten years.

In 1658 Molière brought his company of actors to Paris and played for the first time in the presence of the king, Louis XIV, in the guard room of the old Louvre. The pieces presented were Corneille's *Nicomède,* and *Docteur Amoureux,* by Molière himself. Fortunately, on this return to the capital Molière's sense of humor was tickled by the absurdities of the salons and the literary ladies whose chief aim in life was to promote culture; and the production of *Les précieuses ridi-cules* in 1659 proved the turning point in his career. It was his first attempt to handle real life as it was in the Paris of his own day. Madame de Rambouillet was dead; but the literary cult which she had established was still very much the fashion. Molière seized upon the affected speech, the elegant gallantries and the learned sentimentality of the *précieuses* and caricatured them with infinite skill. Even the blue-stockings and the gallants were obliged to laugh at themselves. *Les précieuses ridicules* was an immediate success, and encouraged its author to believe that contemporary life was his true field.

From that time on Molière gradually perfected his style, though as manager he continued to produce the plays of intrigue and roystering adventure which were characteristic of the older school. In his own plays he created a new *genre,* attacking not only the sentimental blue-stockings and vapid swains of the salon, but nobles, actors, priests, doctors, Corneille and the high-flown writers of his class together with the plays of the rival theater—anybody and everybody afforded a target for his laughter-provoking shafts. He was not only dramatist but also chief actor in his company, and as comedian he must have had extraordinary gifts. While acting in his last play, *Le malade imaginaire,* in 1673, he was seized with an attack of coughing which proved to be the forerunner of his death. He was denied the sacrament of the Church, and grudgingly allowed Christian burial. During the following century his bust was placed in the Academy, and a monument erected over his grave.

*The plays of Molière.* There are in all more than a score of plays from the hand of this genius. They are written in verse of a rather prosaic sort, and divided sometimes into three, sometimes into five acts. He attempted many different methods in the handling of comedy, and in almost every one he succeeded brilliantly. Professor Matthews has listed plays which belong respectively to the comedy of manners, the comedy of character, romantic comedy, tragi-comedy, comedy ballet, criticism in dialogue, satiric interlude, legendary drama, and a sort of philosophic comedy which sometimes turned to farce, and sometimes developed into serious drama. Molière took his plots from whatever source pleased his fancy. Some came from Lope de Vega and other Spanish playwrights; others from Italian originals which had been brought to France by Larrivey. He was familiar with the methods of the Italian Commedia dell' Arte. It is neither in his plots nor in his situations that the greatness of Molière lies, but in his understanding and revelation of character. He could pick up the trifling, intimate details of a man's daily habit and turn them to dramatic uses with marvellous dexterity. His style was well adapted to speech, his wit almost unfailing. While borrowing freely from Spanish and Italian sources, yet he had small interest in the childish devices of trap doors, lost children, abductions and strawberry-mark recognitions. What interested him was the way a man could act when vanity, conceit, hypocrisy or greed gained control. He set forth his story and brought the action to a climax without the use of confidants, asides, soliloquies, or clumsy explanations; and all the time he kept his audience laughing. In the language of George Meredith, he was "both precise and voluble," regarding nothing as sacred, nothing beyond the reach of his wit. With all this, however, there was in his mind a positive belief in the goodness of human nature and in the saving power of common sense. He himself was kind, sincere, honest, with a hatred of hypocrisy and cant, of sham and humbug. He loved youth and all things that are hearty and wholesome; and he was never bigoted, malicious or mean.

*Molière and the critics.* Nearly all of Molière's work was done with too much haste. He has been accused of not having a consistent, organic style, of using faulty grammar, of mixing his metaphors, and of using unnecessary words for the purpose of filling out his lines. All these things are occasionally true, but they are trifles in comparison to the wealth of character he portrayed, to his brilliancy of wit, and to the resourcefulness of his technique. He was wary of sensibility or pathos; but in place of pathos he had "melancholy—a puissant and searching melancholy, which strangely sustains his inexhaustible mirth and his triumphant gaiety." [1]

[1] Brander Matthews, *The Development of the Drama.*

Both the comic and the serious drama were powerfully affected by the work of Molière, not only in his own age and country but everywhere and up to the present time. Every dramatist who has lived since his time is indebted to him. Fielding and Sheridan in England, and Regnard in France learned their technique from him, and sometimes borrowed his situations outright. The general structure of his plays has never been improved. Professor Matthews says:

"The plays of Sophocles and of Shakespeare cannot be shown on the stage of today without many suppressions and modifications; but the plays of Molière can be performed now anywhere without change or excision, absolutely as they were acted by their author and his comrades nearly two hundred and fifty years ago. So far as the external form of their dramas is concerned, Sophocles is ancient, Shakespeare is medieval, Molière is modern; and the large framework of his ampler comedies has supplied a model for the dramatists of every living language."

*Mode of giving seventeenth century plays.* The "tennis court" of the Hotel de Bourgogne and other French theaters was a long narrow auditorium with a shallow stage at one end, set as in a picture frame. It sometimes had a curtain, and was lighted by candles. Plays were given by companies of professional actors, and spectators paid to see them. The medieval and ancient plan of periodic festivals, outdoor performances, amateur actors, and a general community interest in the production had definitely given place to public theaters open at regular and stated times, and managed for the most part by private enterprise for gain. Playwrights had turned from poetry to prose, scenery was growing more and more important, and music and dancing, which in the beginning had been of quite as much importance as the play itself, were almost entirely eliminated.

## CHAPTER XXI

# THE KINDS OF ENGLISH DRAMA BEFORE 1700

For the English people, it (the drama in London) was the mirror of the sixteenth century, the compendium of all that the Renaissance had brought to light. . . . It meant for England the recovery of Greek and Latin culture, the emancipation of the mind from medieval bondage, the emergence of the human spirit in its freedom. It meant awakening continents beyond Atlantic seas. . . .
—J. A. SYMONDS, *Shakspere's Predecessors in the English Drama.*

The Tudor family, who came to the throne in 1483, not only patronized but enjoyed the theater and music,—the only forms of art flourishing in England at that time. As compared with Italy or France, England was crude and unsophisticated. Cellini, who has given us a vivid description of Italian society in 1500, openly regarded the English of his day as savages. Erasmus the Dutch *savant,* half of whose life extended into the sixteenth century, visited England several times, and gave lectures on Greek literature at Cambridge. He commented on the filth of the houses and the diseases in the cities due to defective sanitation, poor ventilation and other unhygienic conditions. The whipping post, pillory and stocks were in every township, and an execution block on Tower Hill in London. With harsh civil laws, there existed also coarse and irreverent festivals such as the *Feast of the Ass,* the *Feast of Fools,* and the *Boy Bishop,* during which the revelry was carried into the church and up to the altar. Nobles and riffraff together, in the vile smelling bull and bear pits, witnessed cruel sports. Old women were burnt as witches. Men of letters who discoursed of Aristotle and philosophy relished the disgusting obscenities of jesters and fools; and people who dressed in velvet had personal habits and table manners which today would disgrace a tramp.

*The pursuit of learning.* There is another side to the picture, however. Contemporaneous with the gallants and fine ladies who led merely a life of pleasure, there existed also a group of people devoted in their way to the pursuit of literature and the arts. The study of Greek had been instituted in the fifteenth century both at Oxford and Cambridge. Erasmus had found scholars as brilliant as any in Europe. Men and women of high birth often spent considerable time in study, following the example of Queen Elizabeth in learning the ancient languages. The royal family and the nobility imported humanists from the continent for the education of their children. With the increasing interest in things of the mind, moreover, there remained a certain sturdy manliness characteristic of the race. The English had so far escaped the cynicism and sophisticated vice represented by Machiavelli and Aretino in Italy, and betrayed none of the fatigued and insolent indifference to moral standards that characterized so many popular writers of the south.

*Forces that shaped the Elizabethan drama.* Against such a background rose the theater that was to produce Shakespeare and his fellow-craftsmen. With the decline of the mysteries and miracles, other types of plays quickly took shape, and many playwrights sprang up. The love of the theater extended to all classes. The dramatic instinct of the people had been fostered by the circulation of ballads and romances of chivalry, notably by the *Morte d'Arthur* of Malory. The printing press of William Caxton, set up in 1474, began to put forth works of various sorts, sixty-four books being printed during the first twenty years of its existence. There ensued for the drama, even before the advent of the greater Elizabethans, a germinating, experimenting, and fertile period in which at least a dozen species began to flourish, each influenced, though in different degrees, by three forces: (1) the existing native drama; (2) romantic literature; and (3) the classic models. We shall now make a brief study of the more important of these species, beginning with the interlude, which was the link between native medieval drama and that of the Elizabethans.

## I. THE INTERLUDE

The interlude, which grew out of the morality, was intended, as its name implies, to be used more as a filler than as the main part of an entertainment. At its best it was short, witty, simple in plot, suited for the diversion of guests at a banquet, or for the relaxation of the audience between the divisions of a serious play. Unlike the pageants, it was essentially an indoors performance, and generally of an aristocratic nature. In its development it tended always towards greater refinement and concentration. At first the flavor of the morality clung to it, as is seen by such titles as *The Four Elements,* or *The World and the Child.* In the early part of the sixteenth century political subjects began to be used, and public officials were satirized under allegorical names. It will be remembered that this was the century of Luther and much dissension in the Church; and religion was often criticised under cover of the interlude. Cardinal Wolsey imprisoned an author, John Roo, and an actor, for alleged satire against himself in a play called *Lord Governance and Lady Public Weal,* presented at Gray's Inn at Christmas time, 1525 or 1527. The author pleaded that the play had been "compyled for the moste part" twenty years before, at a time when the Cardinal had not yet come to any position of authority; consequently the culprits were released. In a Latin play given before the king and the French ambassador in 1527 unflattering portraits of "Lewter" and his wife were presented, other characters in the piece being Religion, Veritas, Heresy, and False Interpretation. In the Protestant camp John Bale, author of *God's Merciful Promises* and other interludes, was one of the strongest of the anti-popish writers.

The best of the interludes, however, were not those used for the purpose of propaganda. As the species developed, abstract characters gave place to recognizable human beings, didacticism disappeared, and a spirit of genuine comedy emerged. Life was no longer like the morality, a battlefield between Virtue and Vice, with the betting chances strongly in favor of Vice, but an opportunity for amusing and diversified experiences.

The engaging quality which characterizes Chaucer and Piers Plowman was little by little transferred to the stage, partly at least through the interlude.

*John Heywood.* Conjectural dates 1497-1580. The most important writer of interludes, at the period when they were merging into comedy, was John Heywood, choir boy at the Chapel Royal in London, and at one time connected with the production of plays at the court of Henry VII. He was a loyal Catholic; and after the death of Mary, being out of sympathy with the strong Protestant movement of the day, he journeyed to the continent and died there. Although entirely faithful to his Church, Heywood did not hesitate to criticise its weaknesses. In his plays he broke away from the conventional tone and allegorical manner of the morality, and treated his themes in an ironical, good-humored style. His titles alone are diverting. *The Merry Play between Johan the Husband, Tyb his Wife, and Sir John the Priest* is a farce showing how Tyb and the Priest discipline the Husband by making him sit by, fasting, while they devour the pie which has been cooked for dinner. *The Play of the Pardoner and the Friar* is a lively debate between two churchmen each of whom tries to out-argue and out-preach the other. The most famous of Heywood's interludes is the comic piece *The Four P's,* written about 1530.[1] It is in racy verse, has excellent dialogue, a witty situation, and no ulterior purpose, unless it be to expose in an amusing manner the weaknesses both of religionists and medicine men. There is nothing strikingly original in the plot, and long passages were taken bodily from Chaucer; but it offers a good illustration of the extraordinary advance the interlude had made since the days of *Everyman* and *The Castle of Perseverance.*

*Extension of subjects.* The taste of the public led the writers of interludes ever more and more towards greater realism, more blood-curdling scenes, and increasing excitement in plot,

---

[1] As given in the Athenæum Press Series, *Specimens of the Pre-Shaksperean Drama,* edited by John M. Manly, the title reads: *The playe called the foure PP. A newe and a very mery enterlude of A Palmer, A Pardoner, A Potycary, A Pedler. Made by John Heewood.*

together with a wider range of subjects. Bale's *King John* illustrates the use of English history, while an unknown author presents Roman history in *Appius and Virginia*. Greek legend appears in the *Interlude of Vice concerning Horestes*, by Pikering; a medieval tale in the *Commodye of pacient and meeke Grissill* by John Phillips; and an oriental subject in Preston's *Lamentable Tragedy mixed full of pleasant mirth, conteyning the life of Cambyses King of Percia*. These plays belong to the sixth decade of the sixteenth century, and keep the general tone of the interlude. They are written in rhymed verse, without division into acts or scenes; and the historical matter is interspersed with gags, horse play and general buffoonery. The stock figure of Vice appears under various names: Ambidexter in *Cambyses*, Sedition in *King John*, Haphazard in *Appius and Virginia*. The existence of these somewhat sensational plays indicates the growing taste on the part of the public for heavy-handed passions, lurid scenes, and vivid action. The interludes were thoroughly English, both in characterization and humor, and were not overcome either by the classic or the Hispano-romantic influences. They present abundant evidence of the native sense, good humor, and energy of mind which became so important a part of the work of the great Elizabethans.

## II. The Earliest Comedies

It was upon native material such as *The Four P's* and similar interludes that English comedy was built. It is plain, however, that there was need of design, or form, which would enable writers to shape the story material more effectively. This element of design was supplied in England, as elsewhere, by the classic models. While there was not much first-hand acquaintance with the Greek plays in England, yet there is record of the *Plutus* of Aristophanes being given in the original before Queen Elizabeth. Latin, however, both as a language and literature, was more familiar. Scholars of the universities read Terence and Seneca for the purity of their style, and often enacted their plays, giving them in Latin. When the twelve lost plays of Plautus were restored to the world, they were immediately added to the repertory of the academies and universities. *The Girl of Andros,* by Terence, appeared in an English translation late in the fifteenth century, and was reprinted three times during the sixteenth. Translations of the Seneca plays began to be issued about 1560, and of the Plautine plays a little later.

Nicholas Udall, author of the first native comedy, prepared from Terence a book of Latin recitations designed to be used as a reader; and about the middle of the sixteenth century an unknown writer produced *Jack Juggler,* a one-act piece "for children to act," which was avowedly an imitation of the first act of the *Amphitruo* of Plautus. Though in structure this piece was an imitation, yet the people as well as the scenes are Elizabethan English.

Classic influences, however, came not only from a study of the originals, but also through European imitations, especially those of Italy. The fashionable youth of England went to Italy for culture and finish. To almost every department of Italian literature great names had been added—names which were nowhere else paralleled; and the works of these authors were almost immediately put upon the market in England. The drama of Italy, as has already been pointed out, was a peculiar blend of Seneca, Terence, Horace, and Aristotle. It is not surprising, therefore, that by imitation and adaptation a powerful classical school of drama rose in England. One of its first representatives was George Gascoigne, who made two translations of Italian plays: Ariosto's *Suppositi* (incorrectly called *The Supposes*) and the *Jocasta* of Dolce, produced in 1566 by the Gentlemen of Gray's Inn, a group to which Gascoigne belonged. The first of these, so far as main plot and characters are concerned, is founded on *The Captives* of Plautus.

*Nicholas Udall.* Born about 1505. The name of Udall is famous as the author of the first English comedy. He was a Protestant, a student at Oxford, headmaster at Eton, and later at Westminster School. While at Eton he encouraged the production of plays in Latin, and without doubt he mastered the details of plot construction by studying Plautus and Terence. It will be remembered that in *Miles Gloriosus,* by Plautus, the chief character is the bragging soldier who told amazing tales of his exploits in foreign lands, made love to every pretty woman, freely offered to fight when there was no one to take him up, and fled when there was any sign of danger. It was a reincarnation of Miles Gloriosus whom Udall introduced to the English stage about 1535 in *Ralph Roister Doister,* the first comedy in the English language. Like the classic plays, it was arranged in the five-act form, with the proper preparation, climax, and close. The air of restraint, order, and intellectual grasp of the material is classic, but the style is homely and original. The time is limited to one day, the scene is the usual Roman comedy scene of a street running before several houses; but the characterizations, the brand of humor, and the general attitude toward life and affairs is English to the core. Doister has a parasitic and unscrupulous companion, Matthew Merigreek, who is in part the scoundrelly valet of the Italian Comedy of Art, and in part the Vice of the medieval stage. The old nurse, Margery Mumblecrust, stands not only as a somewhat new character, but as the progenitor of a long series, the most famous of which is the Nurse of Juliet. Symonds comments upon this play as follows: "In *Ralph Roister Doister* we emerge from medieval grotesquery and allegory into the clear light of actual life, into an agreeable atmosphere of urbanity and natural delineation."

*Gammer Gurton's Needle.* The second example of pure native comedy is no less interesting than Schoolmaster Udall's play, though for a different reason. *Gammer Gurton's Needle* was performed at Christ's College, Cambridge, about 1566, and is attributed variously to Dr. John Still, Dr. John Bridges, and William Stevenson. Like *Ralph,* it is in five acts; the action takes place within one day, and the scene is the conventional street with houses. Beyond these details, *Gammer* owes nothing to the classic model. It is a lusty farce, with very little plot. Gammer Gurton has lost her needle, and Diccon the Bedlam, who has been loafing about the cottage, accuses a neighbor, Dame Chat, of stealing it. With this incident begins a scandalous village row, in which the parson, the bailie, the constable and most of the neighbors one by one become entangled. The original trouble is lost sight of in the revival of old quarrels and hidden grudges. The neighbors come to blows, and confusion seems to reign, when a diversion is created by Dame Chat's finding the needle in the seat of the breeches of Hodge, the farmhand.

*Gammer* is often coarse and vulgar, with buffoonery of the slapstick variety, with no polish or intricacy of plot to tempt the intellect. It would be a morose person, however, who in good health could entirely withstand its fun. The characters belong to the English soil and have English blood in their veins. Diccon of Bedlam, who is in reality the cause of the whole fuss, is a new figure on the stage. When, under Henry VIII, the monasteries were broken up, there were left without home or patrons many poor, often half-witted people who had been accustomed to live on the bounty of the religious houses. These people became professional beggars and vagabonds, sometimes pretending to be mad in order to be taken care of. They were called Bedlam Beggars, Abraham Men, or Poor Toms. It will be recalled that Shakespeare used one of this class with considerable tragic effect in *King Lear*.

### III. EARLY TRAGEDIES PATTERNED AFTER THE CLASSIC SCHOOL

The influences coming from the revival of classic learning were more openly manifest in tragedy than in comedy. The publication and study of ancient plays, both in translation and in the original, has been noted. The *Sofonisba* of Trissino, appearing in Milan in 1515, traveled over Italy and France, came to England, and, to some extent at least, set the style for tragedy. The characteristic marks of the neo-classic form—the observance of the five-act structure and the unities, the use of the messenger, and absence of death scenes—have already become a truism; but it is to be noted that the farther the dramatists were from the true classics, the more afraid they were of presenting action. By the time the so-called classic school arrived in England, it had become a school of talk and quietism instead of passion and action.

Just before the advent of the Elizabethans, namely in the middle years of the sixteenth century, the giving of classic tragedies in Latin was one of the aristocratic and scholarly pastimes. Members of the royal family and court circles were often bidden to performances given in the universities, or by members of amateur societies such as the Gentlemen of Gray's Inn and Gentlemen of the Inner Temple. In 1546 there was a *Jephtha* dedicated to Henry VIII; and in 1564 a performance of a drama based upon the story of Dido was given at Cambridge before Queen Elizabeth. Another *Dido* was presented at Oxford in 1583 for the benefit of a visiting Polish prince, and a play called *Roxana* a few years later. These were examples of classic imitations, given in Latin by schoolmen and amateurs.

*Gorboduc.* The first distinctly English tragedy, performed before Queen Elizabeth in 1561 by the Gentlemen of the Inner Temple, was published under the title of *The Tragedie of Gorboduc.* Later it was reissued under the name of *Ferrex and Porrex.* The first three acts were written by Thomas Norton, a learned barrister, the remainder by Thomas Sackville, afterward Earl of Dorset. The subject is taken from Geoffrey of Monmouth's *Historia Britonum:* that is, from ancient English, not classic, fables. Nothing of a more grisly nature could well be found. The *Argument* to the first edition reads thus:

"Gorboduc, King of Britain, divided his realm in his lifetime to his two sons, Ferrex and Porrex. The sons fell to division and dissension. The younger killed the elder. The mother, that more dearly loved the elder, for revenge killed the younger. The people, moved with the cruelty of the act, rose in rebellion and slew both father and mother. The nobility assembled and most terribly destroyed the rebels. And afterward, for want of issue of the Prince, whereby the succession of the crown became uncertain, they fell to civil war, in which both they and many of their issues were slain, and the land for a long time most desolate and miserably wasted."

This tragedy is worthy of some notice, not only because it is the first play of its kind in English with an English subject, but on account of its obvious attempt at blending the medieval and classic elements. In form it is classic, with five acts, a chorus, an observance of at least two of the unities, and a style that is solemn and declamatory. The action occurs off-stage and is reported by a Messenger. Noblemen and privy councillors, with the King and Queen, deliver set orations, each in turn, but nothing is seen to happen. Each act ends with a chorus consisting of "four ancient and sage men of Britain." Preceding each act was a dumb show, or panto-mime, which gave as in a series of tableaux the gist of the scenes about to follow. Even with the help of the dumb shows, however, *Gorboduc* must have been incredibly dull. It lacks almost everything a drama needs,—characterization, conflict, triumph of will over circumstances, climax, tenderness. Chief of all it lacks life. The cultured minds of the period, obsessed by the Senecan-Italian-French ideas of tragedy, admired it.

*First use of blank verse.* One feature connected with *Gorboduc* was of supreme importance to English drama: it was written in blank verse. Hitherto tragedies had been written either in stanzaic forms or in rhymed alexandrines, both of which are undramatic and unsuited to dialogue. *Gorboduc* was the first English play written in blank verse. The form was Italian, and had previously been used by Surrey in his translation of two books of the *Æneid*. As used by Norton and Sackville in *Gorboduc* it was monotonous and lacking in flexibility; but it was musical, adapted to dialogue, and far better suited to dramatic scenes than any vehicle hitherto known to the English stage.

*French influence.* In the meantime, while English scholars were engaged in studying and imitating the classic models, the French were holding Robert Garnier up as an example superior to Trissino or even to Seneca. Garnier illustrated nearly all the faults and few of the virtues of the classic cult. Action, in his eyes, was too vulgar to treat at first hand. This point of view met with cordial approval in London, especially in the more learned circles such as that presided over by the Countess of Pembroke, sister to Sir Philip Sidney. This lady made an attempt to domesticate Garnier on the English stage by translating his *Antony;* and four years later Thomas Kyd made a rendering of the same author's *Cornelia,* dedicating it to the Countess of Sussex. The *Cornelia* is a masterpiece of undramatic writing. There is no plot, the action is off-stage and several years in the past, the chorus is hard-worked but not the actors. These defects in dramatic quality were not at the time perceived, and Kyd took more pride in having achieved this classic imitation than in *The Spanish Tragedy* which, seven years earlier, had made a profound appeal to the popular taste.

*The Misfortunes of Arthur.* Twenty-six years after the first appearance of *Gorboduc* (which brings us to the year 1587), the Gentlemen of Gray's Inn enacted before Queen Elizabeth a play in English called *The Misfortunes of Arthur,* based upon the legend of the House of Pendragon and treated, presumably, in much the same manner as the Greeks dealt with the legend of the House of Atreus. It was mainly by Thomas Hughes, but he was assisted by seven other members of the Inn as collaborators, among whom was Francis Bacon, then in his twenty-third year. The result of the combined efforts was an exceedingly hateful panorama of murders, incest, adultery and parricide. The spectators should have been thankful, on this one occasion at least, for the Messenger, who doubtless saved them from nerve-racking scenes. Each act opens with a dumb show and ends with a chorus as in *Gorboduc.* One character, the Ghost, who appears early in the first act crying for revenge, was destined to become a popular and brilliant addition to the Elizabethan stage. At the close of the fifth act the Ghost again comes on with a prophecy of the glorious reign of Queen Elizabeth.

*Other tragedies in classic form.* The poet Samuel Daniel made an avowed and conscious effort to overcome what he considered the vulgarity of the non-classical plays. He produced two tragedies, *Philotas* and *Cleopatra,* which were strikingly similar to the work of Garnier, being in rhymed verse, conforming to the unities, and making free use of the Messenger, even to relating the events connected with the asp and the last moments of the heroine. Thus it will be seen that the foremost men of letters, wits, and scholars attempted, for more than thirty years, to support a type of drama exactly contrary to the genius of the nation. They sought in all sincerity to impose the classic model upon the English play, and the wonder is they did not succeed. In the end, their method was repudiated by the theater-loving public; yet it was through these followers of classicism that the lessons of design and regularity were handed down from "Seneca his style." The drama was compelled to discard the crudities inherited from the medieval sacred plays, and assume a greater dignity, coloring and beauty. In the words of Symonds: "Their efforts forced . . . principles of careful composition, gravity of diction, and harmonious construction, on the attention of contemporaneous playwrights." They showed the young romantic geniuses of the drama that something was of importance besides the telling of a story by imitation; that it mattered supremely *how* the story was told. Furthermore, we must again remind ourselves that it was through these neo-classicists that the characteristic vehicle of the romantic drama, blank verse, was domesticated into the language.

## IV. TRAGEDY OF BLOOD

In spite of the gruesome nature of the themes of *Gorboduc* and other tragedies written by the pseudo-classical school, the plays themselves were far too pale and feeble for the public taste. The classic characters talked blood but gave rhetoric, satisfying nobody but the so-called intelligentsia of the time. The common people, whose tastes had been formed by the native interludes, farces and miracles, demanded more swordplay and action. Their sensibilities were coarse and tough. They went to the play to be thrilled, to laugh loudly, to shiver and to wonder. Therefore they would have little to do with the classical school of tragedy, but flocked instead to the roystering comedies or to the bear-baiting spectacles, leaving the enjoyment of such plays as *The Misfortunes of Arthur* to more aristocratic circles. About fifteen years before the end of the sixteenth century, however, the popular demand for thrilling plays began to be understood. Playwrights appeared who combined the good points of the classic school with fresher, more romantic themes. They sought out lurid stories, reorganized the material in such a way as to fit it into the Senecan form, grasped the importance of the element of horror, and combined the whole in a sensational sort of play called the tragedy of blood, which is in fact scarcely more than the pseudo-classical tragedy with the undramatic features left out.

*Locrine.* The first attempt at this combination was seen in a play called *Locrine,* whose author is not known with certainty, though some scholars consider it to be George Peele. It probably was written before 1587, and the subject was taken from the English chronicles. The general form is that of Seneca, although the unities of time and place are disregarded. The ghost is introduced, and the dumb show is utilized, while the chorus plays a not very important part. Most significant of all, however, the author gives the Messenger little to do. Cruelties and atrocities and torments are not reported but presented before the eyes of the spectators, and emphasized by all the devices known to the European stage. Unlike both the ancient and the pseudo-classic tragedy, *Locrine* has considerable comic relief, with the humor inherent in the action of the play, not inserted as in the case of the mysteries. It is scarcely a play to admire; but it is at least founded on the true dramatic idea that the essential part of a play is action.

*The Spanish Tragedy.* The outstanding example of the new type was *The Spanish Tragedy,* written by Thomas Kyd and produced about 1587. Little is known of the life of Kyd, but it may be inferred that he was university bred since he showed an understanding of classical mythology and used Latin verses. The events preceding the opening of *The Spanish Tragedy* were revealed in a play called *The First Part of Jeronimo, With the Warre of Portugall, and the life and death of Don Andrea.* This play has been considered by some commentators as simply a first part of *The Spanish Tragedy,* also written by

Kyd; but others think that some theatrical hack writer of the time dressed up the story and passed it off as the work of Kyd. Portions of *The Spanish Tragedy* have been supposed, on the authority of certain items in the *Diary* of Henslowe, to have been additions made by Ben Jonson. The question of the authenticity of these passages is at this time a puzzle.

Kyd's play created a sensation. The more artistic spectators and playwrights laughed at it, but the commoners delighted in it. A melodramatic school rose producing plays founded on material of the wildest character, usually taken from some medieval chronicle, and intertwined with a comic theme and a love story. It was not the object of the playwright to emphasize or even consider the moral or ethical aspects of the case, nor even to delineate character. The first importance was given to the unfolding of the sensational story, showing as many as possible of its cruel, mysterious, or blood-curdling features. All this was developed within the Senecan framework.

The extraordinary thing about *The Spanish Tragedy* was that it exposed, as in a show window, all the wares belonging to the school: the ghost, the romantic lovers, the fine figure of the old man whose reason seems always on the point of slipping; the beautiful but unhappy woman; poison; threats and blows; crazy soliloquies; dirges, death-bed repentances, suicide, murder, insanity. It is a harrowing list; but it is the virtue of melodrama to be melodramatic. Its avowed program is exaggeration, unbelievable incident, indifference to characterization, and insistence upon horrors that glut the stage. In good melodrama these elements should be thrown out with a kind of passionate bravado; and this is precisely the quality of Kyd's masterpiece, which rendered it then, as now, the subject of merriment or disgust to the cultured spectator or reader, and the cause of excitement and thrills to the crowd. Many of the elements mentioned above became stock features of the Elizabethan drama. The half-crazy father, the romantic lovers, the motive of revenge for a father or a son, the insinuating villain, and the play within the play,—all these are familiar today through the work of the greater Elizabethans.

Other examples of the tragedy of blood followed closely upon the success of *The Spanish Tragedy*. *Soliman and Perseda*, possibly by Kyd, is a five-act elaboration of the short tragic piece interpolated in *The Spanish Tragedy*. Marlowe followed the type in *The Jew of Malta*, besides which there were *Titus Andronicus*, thought by many scholars to be the work of an amateur touched up by Shakespeare; *Lust's Dominion*, ascribed to Marlowe, also to Dekker, Haughton and Day; *Alphonsus of Germany*, by an unknown writer; *Hoffman*, by Henry Chettle; and the first *Hamlet*, author unknown, the manuscript of which is lost. All these plays are, to a greater or less extent, embodiments of the tragedy of blood.

## V. Domestic Tragedy

Another sort of thriller, dealing with notorious criminal cases, appeared on the English stage near the end of the sixteenth century. There were of course no newspapers. When a crime was committed, it was often made the subject of pamphlets, sermons, and speeches; and it was set down by such chroniclers as Holinshed and Stow. Not infrequently it became the theme of a popular ballad. Curiosity concerning the details of celebrated murder cases was as high then as now. Henslowe [2] kept a few "play carpenters" in his employ; and, when the vogue of the domestic tragedy was at its height, these workers took all available details of a contemporaneous murder case and out of them built up a theatrical shocker. This species flourished especially between 1592 and 1608. Out of the great number that must have been produced, the titles of nine, and the text of a still smaller number, have been preserved.

Two examples of the domestic tragedy, *Arden of Faversham* and *A Warning for Fair Women*, have been attributed to Shakespeare, probably without sufficient evidence. The manuscript of *A Yorkshire Tragedy* has the words "Written by W. Shakespeare" across its title page. Scholars, however, do not accept it as the work of Shakespeare, in spite of sundry bril-

[2] See note, page 236.

liant passages; and the assumption is that it was ascribed to him by an unscrupulous publisher. Two other plays may be mentioned, one by Heywood called *A Woman Killed with Kindness,* and *Two Tragedies in One,* the author of which is supposed to be Robert Yarington—a person seemingly difficult to identify.

Of these plays, the most powerful is *Arden of Faversham,* whose story was taken from Holinshed's *Chronicles* and follows the original source faithfully. The subtitle reads:

"The Lamentable and True Tragedye of Master Faversham in Kent. Who was most wickedlye murdered, by the means of his disloyall and wanton wyfe, who for the love she bare to one Mosbie, hyred two desperat ruffins, Black Will and Shakbag, to kill him. Wherin is showed the great mallice and discimulation of a wicked woman, the unsatiable desire of filthie lust and the shamefull end of all murderers."

Thus the details of the plot are entirely set forth at the beginning of the play. The murder actually occurred in 1552. The play was given in 1592, was published anonymously, and reprinted in 1770 by Edward Jacob, who made the suggestion that it might have been written by Shakespeare in his 'prentice days. Tieck, who translated it into German in 1823, and Goethe both considered this the true explanation of its authorship. Among English critics, Swinburne was the warmest supporter of this view; but doubt persists among modern Shakespearean scholars.

The most noticeable feature in *Arden* is the rough, uncouth, wild vigor of Arden's wife Alice. She is a woman crazed, almost hypnotized by her unworthy lover, but valiant, defiant, and sincere to the end. She cries out the justification of her love; seizes the dagger when the others bungle over it; calls the servant a fool for his fears; and when forced to look upon her husband's corpse, falls into quite as sincere a repentance. It needs no clairvoyant vision to detect in these details a close relationship to some of the greatest scenes in Othello and Macbeth.

The last notorious crime which served as a basis for this

type of play was that of Walter Calverley, who murdered two of his children, stabbed his wife, and started for his third child with murderous intent. He was condemned and executed at the Castle of York in 1605. This horrible incident was used as the basis for two plays, *A Yorkshire Tragedy,* and *The Miseries of an Enforced Marriage.* Before the end of the first decade of the seventeenth century, however, the vogue of the domestic tragedy abruptly ceased. The style had its uses, however. Hitherto, much of the action in the English plays had been in a sort of standardized world, not belonging to any locality or time. Now we begin to see the creation of local types, and the portrayal of customs which belong to a certain class. The dumb show, the chorus, and the frigid atmosphere of the earlier works have disappeared, and the play jumps right into the action at the first scene. The attention of playwrights was now drawn to contemporaneous events and characters, and the field of their observation enlarged.

## VI. Chronicle and History Play

In England, the chronicle play seems suddenly to have risen into vogue during the last decade of the sixteenth century. At first it was more like an epic poem than a dramatic composition, loosely constructed, covering the entire life of a king or hero, with not even a long distance acquaintance with the unities. Minor events were often invented, but in the more important happenings the authors usually made an attempt to follow history. Three plays on the subject of King John illustrate the three stages of its development: the morality *King John,* by John Bale, written sometime before the accession of Mary in 1553; a second play called *The Troublesome Reign of King John,* written between 1587 and 1591; and a third completely developed tragedy in the romantic style, the *King John* of Shakespeare. The second of these pieces is a genuine example of the chronicle play. It is written in crude blank verse and contains a satirical episode concerning the monastic system of the period. There is also an early *True Tragedie of Richard Third* which contains allegorical figures representing Truth and Poetry, is written mostly in rhymed couplets, and has the pseudo-classic Induction in which the ghost of Clarence walks up and down the stage crying "Vindicta!" Another play on the same subject, *Ricardus Tertius,* was written in Latin by a certain Dr. Legge. Two dramas of this earlier time, *The Famous Victories of Henry Fifth* and *The Contention of the Two Famous Houses of York and Lancaster,* formed the basis of Shakespeare's *Henry Fifth,* and the second and third parts of *Henry Sixth* respectively. An early play called *Edward Third* was ascribed to Shakespeare by Edward Capell more than a century and a half after Shakespeare's death; though critical opinion of to-day has not endorsed his judgment.

*The chronicle play becomes drama.* In the midst of these efforts, while the chronicle play was still in its inferior stage, it was suddenly lifted into a position of distinction by the production of Marlowe's *Edward Second.* Its appearance was an epoch-making event. For the first time the English history play was pulled up into the tenseness of true drama. The characters are bold and vivid, conceived amply as taking part in the sweep of history. Here too is something of the power of Marlowe's "mighty line," and the skill which can portray a great figure overborne by the consequences of his own folly. *Edward Second* is the first fine historical drama in the English language, and aside from the Shakespearean tragedies the best in existence.

A long list of historical plays can be made, showing how great was the interest of the public in the presentation of drama dealing with the national chronicles. If the plays mentioned, together with the English historical plays of Shakespeare, *Edward First,* by Peele, *Edward Fourth* by Heywood, and perhaps half a dozen others which were popular in their time,— if these plays be taken in the chronological order of their subjects, the reader will have an almost continuous story of England's rulers, with the wars in which the country was engaged, the plots which threatened the safety of the sovereigns, the parasites, women, generals, royal children and court jesters who made up the pageant of four centuries, from the reign of "Kynge Johan" to the time of Elizabeth herself.

*Plays about popular heroes. Sir Thomas More* and *The Life and Death of Thomas Lord Cromwell* are examples of plays built upon the biography of national statesmen. It is interesting to note that these two celebrated men, both of whom were beheaded by order of Henry VIII, were taken as the subjects of heroic tragedy within the century of their death, and during the reign of Henry's daughter. There were also, in this period, plays founded upon the adventures of pirates and travelers. Sir Thomas Stukeley was one of these adventurers, and his actual career would make almost any melodrama seem pale. Several plays were written around his history, one of which, *The Battle of Alcazar,* by Peele, contains an account of his death. Stukeley was an imposing figure in his time, mentioned frequently in pamphlets and ballads, one reference classing him with the "proud tragedians, Mahomet, Tamburlaine, and Charlemagne."

A third group of half biographical, half legendary plays is represented by the Robin Hood pieces, whose story is related by Stow. At least three of some merit were produced on this subject: *The Downfall of Robert Earl of Huntington,* by Anthony Munday; *The Death of Robert Earl of Huntington,* by Munday and Chettle; and *George a Greene, Pinner of Wakefield,* by an unknown author. Considering the lively and dramatic nature of both the Stukeley and Robin Hood stories, we find these plays not at all extraordinary, though there are passages of real vigor and power. The picture of woodland life, in which Robin tempts Marion to go away with him, has more than a touch of Elizabethan delicacy and charm.

There remain the plays founded on famous characters or events of other countries. First of these, not only in time but also in importance, stands Marlowe's *Tamburlaine,* in two parts, produced at Newington Butts Playhouse before 1587, when its author was twenty-three years of age or younger. It was this play which gave the impetus to the great choir of singers and playwrights who filled the years up to and into the seventeenth century; and it went far towards fixing the type of English historical tragedy. There is, however, in its monstrous and elemental plan, power enough to generate a dozen ordinary tragedies. There are touches of bombast and absurdity, but the play as a whole is neither bombastic nor absurd. It was not only the delight of the Elizabethan public, but in a sense it became a standard according to which the work of subsequent years was measured, and to which every playwright was more or less indebted.

## VII. ROMANTIC COMEDIES AND PASTORALS

There is naturally no sharp dividing line between the romantic comedy and the pastoral. In both species the conflict is likely to be of slight interest. The important elements are the happy adventures, the atmosphere of gaiety and romance, the play of wit and humor. In them Youth is glorified and celebrated. Romantic comedy is well illustrated in the woodland scenes of Greene's *Friar Bacon and Friar Bungay,* in *As You Like It* and *Twelfth Night* by Shakespeare. Greene also wrote *The Pleasant Comedie of Fair Em, the Miller's Daughter of Manchester; with the love of William the Conqueror,* produced in 1589 and 1591. According to Professor Brooke, this play is "an inartistic medley of two plots in the two most popular current styles." Anthony Munday also composed a piece somewhat in imitation of the Greene comedy called *John a Kent and John a Cumber.* Munday was able to construct good plots, but was quite lacking in the ability to envelop his plays with the atmosphere of charm and romance which is so marked in the work of Greene and Shakespeare. The best romantic comedy, outside of Shakespeare, is an anonymous piece called *The Merry Devil of Edmonton,* published in 1607.

Greene supplied the early models both for romantic and pastoral comedy. The *Aminta* of Tasso and *Pastor Fido* of Guarini had appeared in book form in Italy as early as 1590 and had been promptly brought to England, where they had attracted the attention of the courtly and aristocratic clans. The most gifted writer of this group was Samuel Daniel, author of the two court pastorals produced in the early years of the seventeenth century. The pastoral play, however, never flourished in England as it had in Italy. *The Faithful Shepherdess,* by Fletcher, and the unfinished *Sad Shepherd,* by Ben Jonson, are the most notable pieces of their kind. The influence of the species is apparent, however, not only in the minor comedies, but especially in the pleasant garden and rural scenes which enliven the comedies of the greatest of the Elizabethans.

## VIII. COURT COMEDIES AND MASQUES

There were two groups of plays which belonged neither to the democratic, popular class, nor to the pseudo-classical species fostered by the academic circles. One of these was the court comedy, designed especially as a compliment to the queen; the other was the masque, in which the aristocracy and royalty itself took part as actors. The court comedy was in a sense a variation, or a specialization, of the pastoral, brought into England from Italy chiefly by John Lyly, the author of *Euphues, the Anatomy of Wit,* and *Euphues, His England.* Lyly produced a series of court comedies in which allegorical and classical stories were made to veil complimentary allusions to the queen and her court. There are eight plays which most scholars accept as authentic, six of which were first played by the Children of the Chapel Royal. Four of them are based on classic subjects, with the allegory so contrived as to constitute one colossal hymn of adulation to the queen. Elizabeth had already become the "Virgin Queen" to her subjects, and she had been styled Cynthia by Spenser. Lyly used the fable of Endymion as the vehicle for one of his early panegyrics. The sleeping Endymion was Leicester, the queen's favorite. Out of pity, charity, and queenly goodness she rouses him from his entranced slumber with a kiss. Never before have her lips been touched, nor would they ever again be soiled by such condescension. Throughout the play the queen is gracious, charming, and always queenly. Other characters in the allegory could easily be identified by the coterie of spectators, and not all of the *dramatis personæ* were pictured with as kind a pen as that which had drawn the lovely Cynthia. The adulation is unmistakable, though never vulgar. The play has little plot, but is imbued with high spirits, delicacy of taste, and graceful poetry. Hazlitt and Keats both praised *Endimion* extravagantly.

The successful *Endimion* was followed by similar plays, and the figure of Lyly seemed for a time to dominate English drama. All but one of his comedies are in prose. They show no suspicion of struggle or passion, but they are imbued with an atmosphere of sunshine and classical purity. It was Lyly who popularized a peculiar type of gay but innocent dialogue, used the device of putting his play into a dream setting, made the disguise of girls as boys an amusing and harmless feature, and still proved that such spiceless diversions could stand the test of public performance. All these devices are familiar to us in the work of Shakespeare, Fletcher, and Ben Jonson. Lyly's importance lies in the fact that he practically created the English court comedy—a type which has no exact parallel in any other language.

*The court masque.* One of the most spectacular entertainments of the nobility was the masque, introduced into England from Italy by Henry VIII as early as 1512. The first requisite for the masque was a pleasant and entertaining story in verse, preferably with mythological or allegorical characters. There was of course some dialogue and declamation, but these matters were relatively unimportant. Far more significant were the tableaux, music, the ballet, the elaborate settings, the gorgeous costumes and scenery, stage appliances, and surprises in mechanical effects. The actors were members of the aristocracy, sometimes of the royal family. They wore masks, spent huge sums upon their costumes, and lent their halls and treasures of art to enrich the scenes. Little else was required of them, as actors, but to look beautiful and stately. The success of the masque depended upon the architect, the scene painter, decorator, and ballet master. In the course of time considerable importance was given also to singing and instrumental music.

The cost of these accessories was too great to permit masque production in the public theaters, even supposing they had been acceptable to the taste of the populace; and during the reigns of Henry VIII and Elizabeth, royal ideas of economy forbade the lavish display which had characterized the masque in Italy. With the accession of the Stuarts, however, this form of theatrical display took on a new importance. James I and his son Charles were willing to spend a good deal of the country's money upon them. Among the poets engaged to write masque librettos were Jonson, Beaumont, Fletcher, and most of the other talented writers of the day. Ben Jonson was first of all, not only in point of time but in genius. He became poet laureate, and devoted his amazing learning, his theatrical sense, and his gift for charming lyrics to the work of perfecting the masque. With him, as manager and stage director, worked the artist, Inigo Jones; also a director of chorus, a dance master, and a composer for instruments. The court musicians numbered as many as fifty-eight persons, and neither time nor expense was spared in their training. Not only the court, but noblemen wishing to compliment royalty, arranged for these entertainments. The courts of the Inner Temple, Gray's Inn, and such societies, vied with each other in the lavishness of their productions. The king and queen, each, provided a masque at Christmas. There remain more than thirty examples of this sort of play written during the reigns of James I and Charles I. In 1634 there was given at Whitehall, in the royal banquet room, by the members of the various Inns of Court, a masque called *The Triumph of Peace,* designed by Inigo Jones and written by Shirley, for which the cost amounted to more than one hundred thousand dollars. This was but fourteen years before the tragic end of Charles and the abolition of such extravagant gaieties.

## IX. THE ATTITUDE OF THE CRITICS

By the last quarter of the sixteenth century the theater was within reach of nearly all classes; and, in the end, it was the public, not the court, which set the fashion. The Elizabethan public liked strong colors, passions torn to tatters, and mouth-filling, passionate lines.  More and more the classic models were disregarded, while the romantic spirit took the lead with extravagant situations, a riot of action, a wealth of fancy. According to Collier's published list of the minutes of the Court Revels between 1568 and 1580, fifty-two plays were given, not one of which is now in existence, so far as is known. They were written by authors who could not or would not afford the luxury of having their work printed.  Among the lost manuscripts is the first stage version of *Romeo and Juliet,* made before 1562; a dramatization of Boccaccio's *Tancred and Gismunda,* made as early as 1563; and an English version of a play by the Italian Cinthio, *Promos and Cassandra,* made by George Whetstone.  The latter play was used in part by Shakespeare in *Measure for Measure.*

It is instructive to note the attitude of critics towards the "new" departure in drama.  Stephen Gosson, critic and actor, asserted that "immoral comedies of Latin, French, Spanish and Italian had been wransacked to furnish the playhouses of London."  He charged the playwrights with distorting history in order to show forth exciting scenes: "So was the history of Cæsar and Pompey, and the play of the Fabii at the Theater, both amplified there where the drums might walk or the pen ruffle."  In short, Gosson accused the playwrights of treating the ancient subjects in the romantic manner.  Whetstone, in his preface to *Promos and Cassandra,* played in 1578, held up the classical model and compared contemporary plays with it, much to the disadvantage of the new species.  He said also that the Italian writers of comedies were so lascivious as to make honest people grieve; that the French and Spanish authors followed in the steps of the Italian; that the German plays were too serious and "holy"; and that English writers for the stage took any liberties they liked, provided only they got a laugh.

Among all the critics of the time, however, the most famous was Sir Philip Sidney, who died in 1586.  His pamphlet, *A Defence of Poesy,* was printed in 1595, though probably written a dozen years earlier.  He said that *Gorboduc* was the model for all tragedy, saving only in the one particular that it did not conform to the unities of time and place; but that it was well-nigh perfect in spite of this defect. All other plays of the time were full of vulgar errors: discrepancies of plot, absurd changes of scene, and an impossible prolongation of time. He called attention to the manner in which Euripides had handled dramatic situations, beginning with the last culminating incident; whereas the writers of his own day must needs start *ab ovo* and recount the whole long series of events. How much better, said Sidney, to use the Messenger, as the ancients did! "The dullest wit may conceive it!" He went on to complain that the plays of his own day mixed up comic and tragic matter, associated kings with clowns, "so that we have nothing but scurrility, unworthy of our chaste ears; or some extreme of doltishness, indeed fit to lift up a loud laughter, and nothing else; where the whole tract of a comedy should be full of delight, as the tragedy should be still maintained in well raised admiration." These criticisms were all written before Shakespeare or Marlowe had become known; and they show, if anything, not that educated opinion is always wrong, but that it is constitutionally timid and conservative.

## CHAPTER XXII

# ELIZABETHAN PLAYHOUSES, ACTORS, AND AUDIENCES

This populace that watched with joy the cruel torment of a bear or the execution of a Catholic, also delighted in the romantic comedies of Shakespeare. This people, so appallingly credulous and ignorant, so brutal, childish, so mercurial compared with Englishmen of today, yet set the standard of national greatness. This absurdly decorated gallant could stab a rival in the back, or write a penitential lyric. Each man presented strange, almost inexplicable, contrasts in character, as Bacon or Raleigh, or Elizabeth herself. The drama mingles its sentiment and fancy with horrors and bloodshed; and no wonder, for poetry was no occupation of the cloister. Read the lives of the poets—Surrey, Wyatt, Sidney, Spenser, Raleigh, Marlowe, Jonson—and of these, only Spenser and Jonson died in their beds, and Ben had killed his man in a duel. . . . Crime, meanness, and sexual depravity often appear in the closest juxtaposition with imaginative idealism, intellectual freedom, and moral grandeur. . . .—NEILSON and THORNDIKE, *Facts About Shakespeare.*

The theater as a public amusement was an innovation in the social life of the Elizabethans, and it immediately took the general fancy. Like that of Greece or Spain, it developed with amazing rapidity. London's first theater was built when Shakespeare was about twelve years old; and the whole system of the Elizabethan theatrical world came into being during his lifetime. The great popularity of plays of all sorts led to the building of playhouses both public and private, to the organization of innumerable companies of players both amateur and professional, and to countless difficulties connected with the authorship and licensing of plays. Companies of actors were kept at the big baronial estates of Lord Oxford, Lord Buckingham and others. Many strolling troupes went about the country playing wherever they could find welcome. They commonly consisted of three, or at most four men and a boy, the latter to take the women's parts. They gave their plays in pageants, in the open squares of the town, in the halls of noblemen and other gentry, or in the courtyards of inns.

*Regulation and licensing of plays.* The control of these various companies soon became a problem to the community. Some of the troupes, which had the impudence to call themselves "Servants" of this or that lord, were composed of low characters, little better than vagabonds, causing much trouble to worthy citizens. The sovereign attempted to regulate matters by granting licenses to the aristocracy for the maintenance of troupes of players, who might at any time be required to show their credentials. For a time it was also a rule that these performers should appear only in the halls of their patrons; but this requirement, together with many other regulations, was constantly ignored. The playwrights of both the Roman and the Protestant faith used the stage as a sort of forum for the dissemination of their opinions; and it was natural that such practices should often result in quarrels and disturbances. During the reign of Mary, the rules were strict, especially those relating to the production of such plays as *The Four P's,* on the ground that they encouraged too much freedom of thought and criticism of public affairs. On the other hand, during this period the performance of the mysteries was urged, as being one of the means of teaching true religion.

Elizabeth granted the first royal patent to the Servants of the Earl of Leicester in 1574. These "Servants" were James Burbage and four partners; and they were empowered to play "comedies, tragedies, interludes, stage-plays and other suchlike" in London and in all other towns and boroughs in the realm of England; except that no representation could be given during the time for Common Prayer, or during a time of "great and common Plague in our said city of London." Under Elizabeth political and religious subjects were forbidden on the stage.

*Objections to playhouses.* In the meantime, respectable people and officers of the Church frequently made complaint of the growing number of play-actors and shows. They said that the plays were often lewd and profane, that play-actors were mostly vagrant, irresponsible, and immoral people; that taverns and disreputable houses were always found in the neighborhood of the theaters, and that the theater itself was a public danger in the way of spreading disease. The streets were overcrowded after performances; beggars and loafers infested the theater section, crimes occurred in the crowd, and 'prentices played truant in order to go to the play. These and other charges were constantly being renewed, and in a measure they were all justly founded. Elizabeth's policy was to compromise. She regulated the abuses, but allowed the players to thrive. One order for the year 1576 prohibited all theatrical performances within the city boundaries; but it was not strictly enforced. The London Corporation generally stood against the players; but the favor of the queen and nobility, added to the popular taste, in the end proved too much for the Corporation. Players were forbidden to establish themselves in the city, but could not be prevented from building their playhouses just across the river, outside the jurisdiction of the Corporation and yet within easy reach of the play-going public.

This compromise, however, did not end the criticism of the public. Regulations and restrictions were constantly being imposed or renewed; and, no doubt, as constantly broken. In the end this intermittent hostility to the theater acted as a sort of beneficent censorship. The more unprincipled of the actors and playwrights were held in check by the fear of losing what privileges they had, while the men of ability and genius found no real hindrance to their activity. Whatever the reason, the English stage was far purer and more wholesome than either the French or Italian stage in the corresponding era of development. However much in practice the laws were evaded or broken, the drama maintained a comparatively manly and decent standard. There was no *Calandra,* no Aretino or Machiavelli of the Elizabethan stage.

*Companies of actors.* In 1578 six companies were granted permission by special order of the queen to perform plays. They were the Children of the Chapel Royal, Children of

Saint Paul's, the Servants of the Lord Chamberlain, Servants of Lords Warwick, Leicester, and Essex. The building of playhouses outside the city had already begun in 1576. One of the popular catches of the day runs:

> List unto my ditty!
> Alas, the more the pity,
> From Troynovant's old city
> The Aldermen and Mayor
> Have driven each poor player.

This banishment was not a misfortune, but one of the causes of immediate growth. There was room for as many theaters as the people desired; a healthy rivalry was possible. In Shoreditch were built the Theater and the Curtain. At Blackfriars the Servants of Lord Leicester had their house, modeled roughly after the courtyard of an inn, and built of wood. Twenty years later it was rebuilt by a company which numbered Shakespeare among its members. In the meantime, the professional actor gained something in the public esteem, and occasionally became a recognized and solid member of society. Theatrical companies were gradually transformed from irregular associations of men dependent on the favor of a lord, to stable business organizations; and in time the professional actor and the organized company triumphed completely over the stroller and the amateur.

*Playhouses.* The number of playhouses steadily increased. Besides the three already mentioned, there were in Southwark the Hope, the Rose, the Swan, and Newington Butts, on whose stage *The Jew of Malta,* the first *Hamlet, The Taming of the Shrew,* and *Tamburlaine* had their premières. At the Red Bull some of John Heywood's plays appeared. Most famous of all were the Globe, built in 1598 by Richard Burbage, and the Fortune, built in 1599. The Globe was hexagonal without, circular within, a roof extending over the stage only. The audience stood in the yard, or pit, or sat in the boxes built around the walls. Sometimes the young gallants sat on the stage. The first Globe was burned in 1613 and rebuilt by King James and some of his noblemen. It was this theater which, in the latter part of their career, was used by Shakespeare and Burbage in summer. In winter they used the Blackfriars in the city. At the end of the reign of Elizabeth there were eleven theaters in London, including public and private houses. Various members of the royal family were the ostensible patrons of the new companies. The boys of the choirs and Church schools were trained in acting; and sometimes they did better than their elders.

*Composition and ownership of plays.* Scholars and critics have inherited an almost endless number of literary puzzles from the Elizabethan age. A play might be written, handed over to the manager of a company of actors, and produced with or without the author's name. In many instances the author forgot or ignored all subsequent affairs connected with it. If changes were required, perhaps it would be given to some well known playwright to be "doctored" before the next production. Henslowe, who had an interest in several London theaters, continuously employed playwrights, famous and otherwise, in working out new, promising material for his actors. Most dramatists of the time served an apprenticeship, in which they did anything they were asked to do. Sometimes they made the first draft of a piece which would be finished by a more experienced hand; sometimes they collaborated with another writer; or they gave the finishing touches to a new play; or revamped a Spanish, French, or Italian piece in an attempt to make it more suitable for the London public.

The plays were the property, not of the author, but of the acting companies. Aside from the costly costumes, they formed the most valuable part of the company's capital. The parts were learned by the actors, and the manuscript locked up. If the piece became popular, rival managers often stole it by sending to the performance a clerk who took down the lines in shorthand. Neither authors nor managers had any protection from pirate publishers, who frequently issued copies of successful plays without the consent of either. Many cases of missing or mutilated scenes, faulty lines or confused grammar may be laid to the doors of these copy brigands. In addition to this, after the play had had a London success, it was cut

down, both in length and in the number of parts, for the use
of strolling players,—a fact which of course increased the
chances of mutilation.

*Performances.* Public performances generally took place
in the afternoon, beginning about three o'clock and lasting perhaps two hours. Candles were used when daylight began to
fade. The beginning of the play was announced by the hoist-
ing of a flag and the blowing of a trumpet. There were playbills, those for tragedy being printed in red. Often after a
serious piece a short farce was also given; and at the close of
the play the actors, on their knees, recited an address to the
king or queen. The price of entrance varied with the theater,
the play, and the actors; but it was roughly a penny to sixpence
for the pit, up to half a crown (about sixty cents) for a box.
A three-legged stool on the stage at first cost sixpence extra;
but this price was later doubled.

The house itself was not unlike a circus, with a good deal
of noise and dirt. Servants, grooms, 'prentices and mechanics
jostled each other in the pit, while more or less gay companies
filled the boxes. Women of respectability were few, yet sometimes they did attend; and if they were very careful of their
reputations they wore masks. On the stage, which ran far
out into the auditorium, would be seated a few of the early
gallants, playing cards, smoking, waited upon by their pages;
and sometimes eating nuts or apples and throwing things out
among the crowd. At first there was little music, but soon
players of instruments were added to the company. The stage
was covered with straw or rushes. There may have been a
painted wall with trees and hedges, or a castle interior with
practicable furniture. A placard announced the scene. Stage
machinery seems never to have been out of use, though in the
early Elizabethan days it was probably primitive. The audience was near and could view the stage from three sides, so
that no "picture" was possible, as in the tennis-court stage of
Paris. Whatever effects were gained were the result of the
·gorgeous and costly costumes of the actors, together with the
art and skill with which they were able to invest their rôles.
The inn-court type of stage required a bold, declamatory

method in acting and speaking; and these requirements were no doubt speedily reflected in the style of the playwrights.

England was the last of the European countries to accept women on the stage. In the year 1629 a visiting company of French players gave performances at Blackfriars, with actresses. An English writer of the time called these women "monsters"; and the audience would have none of them. They were hissed and "pippin-pelted" from the stage. Boy actors were immensely popular, and the schools were actually the training ground for many well known comedians and tragedians. The stigma of dishonor rested, however, upon the whole profession, playwrights, players, and on the theater itself. The company in the pit was rough, likely to smell of garlic and to indulge in rude jests. The plays were often coarse and boisterous, closely associated with bear-baiting and cock-fighting. Playwrights and actors belonged to a bohemian, half lawless class. The gallants who frequented the play led fast lives, and were constantly charged with the corruption of innocence.

Comparison between an Elizabethan and an Athenian performance affords interesting contrasts and similarities. The Athenian festival was part of an important religious service, for which men of affairs gave their time and money. Every sort of governmental support was at its disposal, and manuscripts were piously preserved. All this was contrary to the practice of the Elizabethans, who tried to suppress the shows, lost many of their most precious manuscripts, and banished the plays to a place outside the city walls. In both countries, however, the audiences were made up of all classes of people who freely expressed their liking or disapproval. In each country the period of dramatic activity followed close upon the heels of great military and naval victories; and the plays of both countries reflect the civic and national pride.

## CHAPTER XXIII

# THE SCHOLAR POETS

The romantic, as opposed to the classical, school of dramatists, were right in their perception that not ethical wisdom and not description, but action, was the one thing needful to their art. They saw that the drama . . . must present human life in all its possible fullness, vigour and variety; must portray and develop character; must combine events into a single movement with a climax and a catastrophe.—J. A. SYMONDS, *Shakspere's Predecessors in the English Drama.*

Grouped together, the various kinds of plays which existed in England in the last quarter of the sixteenth century form a remarkable body of stage literature. It is both brilliant and vigorous. Emerson said that "the rude, warm blood of the living England circulated" in the Elizabethan plays. When Shakespeare came to London, probably about 1585 or 1586, the field of dramatic writing was occupied by men of considerable education, who called themselves "gentlemen" according to English caste and birth. They were also gifted as poets. The members of this group have been variously styled the Bohemians, the early Elizabethans, the University Wits, the Scholar Poets.

*Lyly, 1552-1601, Kyd and Lodge.* The first of the scholar poets to come to London to try his fortune was John Lyly, the author of *Euphues,* noted in an earlier chapter as inaugurating a new fashion both in language and in plays. He stands a little apart from the main group of University Wits in that he was essentially a courtier, with an orderly habit of life and mind. His plays were presented before the queen and her circle, not on the public stage. He was fastidious, a dilettante in the arts, with a talent exactly suited to the demands of the polite world in and near the royal court.

Kyd and Lodge also stand a little apart, in temperament and in education, from the main company of scholar poets. The rampant and lurid genius of Thomas Kyd was often coupled with that of Marlowe, but he was probably not a university man. He was born in London in 1558, was a fellow student at the Merchant Taylor's School with Spenser and Lodge, and died in London in poverty about eight years after the success of his *Spanish Tragedy*. Thomas Lodge, the son of a baronet (always a little ashamed of his profession), collaborated with Greene in *The Wounds of Civil War,* and also wrote romances after the Spanish style. After considerable travel he settled in London, studied medicine and became a reputable doctor of physic, living until 1625. All the other members of the bohemian group died before the end of the sixteenth century either in youth or in early middle life.

*Robert Greene.* 1561-1592. The four friends, Marlowe, Greene, Peele and Nash were closely connected by ties of friendship and companionship in work. All but Marlowe were well born; all were highly educated and gifted as poets. Together they led a life defiantly unconventional, passionate and roystering, of the sort which has since been named "bohemian." Greene was the first of the four to come to London, and was in a sense the center of the group. He was Master of Arts from Cambridge, possibly a clergyman of the Anglican Church, and first became popular through his prose romances adapted or imitated from the Italian. On one of these tales, *Pandosto,* Shakespeare later founded his *Winter's Tale.* In his way Greene was an innovator. He was extraordinarily quick in sensing the popular tendency and turning it to account in his plays. Many of his works perished in the London fire of 1666. His extant plays were all written after the appearance of Marlowe's *Tamburlaine,* and show the influence both of Marlowe and of Lyly. He first attempted heroic pieces in the manner of Marlowe. *The Comicall Historie of Alphonsus, King of Arragon,* had some success, but is of little dramatic merit. He versified the *Orlando Furioso* of Ariosto, and with Lodge wrote *The Miseries of Civil War, a History of Marius and Sylla,* and *A Looking Glass for London.* The latter, under cover of the story of Jonah and Nineveh, satirizes the local morals and customs. In *James the Fourth, King of Scotland,* Greene made use of the device, already ancient, of putting a person to sleep and making the play appear like a dream. A variation of this scheme was the encountering of some magic adventure in a wood, or meeting a conjuror who called forth strange happenings. These devices had already been used by Lyly, by Heywood, and by the unknown author of the first version of *The Taming of the Shrew.*

Greene's most attractive gift was in the field of romantic and pastoral comedy. In *Friar Bacon and Friar Bungay* he dramatized in part an old English legend of a necromancer-friar, combined it with a love story, and showed himself at his best. Up to 1589 all his plays had been written in rhymed verse, and he publicly announced himself as disapproving of the "unscholarly" blank verse. Later, seeing the sudden and overwhelming popularity of this form, he adopted it. Although he could write clear and flowing English both in prose and verse, his language was sometimes pompous and bombastic, sometimes in Lyly's euphuistic style. He had, however, an authentic gift of poetry; and he showed considerable skill in contriving incidents full of humor, variety and interest.

Greene left a number of autobiographical writings, which reveal not only the miserable and degraded existence he himself led, but also the unenviable position of men of letters of his time. He declared, with a kind of disjointed, passionate sincerity, that he lived a "lewd life and practiced such villany as is abominable to declare." He said he learned all the villanies under heaven in Italy, where "gluttony with drunkenness was my only delight." He was not above petty thievery, he abandoned his wife and child, contracted a disgraceful disease and died a disgraceful death, in debt to his landlady and at war with society in general. Nevertheless, he was careful to insist upon his birth as a "gentleman" and his standing as a University Master of Arts. In his last days he taunted Shakespeare not only with plagiarism but also with his lack of birth and education. On his deathbed he called his friends about him—Marlowe, "famous gracer of tragedians", Nash "that biting satirist", and Peele "in nothing inferior" to the other two—and urged them to abandon the theater. He said to them, in effect, that though he and they, gentlemen and scholars, had founded the English drama and had hitherto enjoyed almost a monopoly in writing for it, yet now others, who had no right to do so, had imitated them and driven them out. He scoffed at actors as puppets, grooms, peasants, painted monsters. Famous as he had been and still was, he was out of tune with his world. He could turn out a play or a pamphlet almost overnight, and was much in demand by both theater managers and publishers, who paid him well. Yet he was so far outdone by his immediate followers in sincerity, earnestness and intensity of thought, that to-day, in comparison with Marlowe, Shakespeare and Ben Jonson, he seems thin and strangely unreal.

*George Peele.* 1558-1598. In 1579 George Peele was graduated from Oxford, where he had come into notice through his arrangements of pageants. In 1584, the year which saw the production of Lyly's *Alexander and Campaspe,* Peele appeared in London with a pastoral play for the court which he called *The Arraignment of Paris.* In this piece Peele is probably at his best; and although it is in the vein of Lyly, yet it is in no wise an imitation. The allegorical, complimentary style was in the air, and authors often found such writings an easy road to success. Under the superficial design there are evidences of dignity, a feeling for harmony and graceful power. In *Edward First* Peele attempted the chronicle play; and in it he was guilty of slandering Queen Eleanor, the wife of "Longshanks." In *The Battle of Alcazar* he essayed the tragedy of blood, but produced little more than a bombastic melodrama. Hamet, a character in *Alcazar,* gives an epitome of the lust for murder, which characterized this type of play. He says:

> Sith they begin to bathe in blood,
> Such slaughter with my weapon will I make,
> As through the stream and bloody channels deep
> Our moors shall sail in ships and pinnaces,
> From Tangire shores unto the gates of Fez.

The dumb show [1] was used, also the Presenter, who appeared on the stage preceding each act, and explained what was coming. In the last act of *Alcazar* the figure of Thomas Stukeley appears, giving an opportunity for flag-waving and the expression of national hero worship. In *The Old Wives' Tale* there was a rather delicate satire on the conventional idea of chivalry and generosity in love—ideas which had been freely used in the pastoral plays and were becoming threadbare. In *David and Bathsabe,* written in euphuistic language, Peele used the Jewish theme of the sins of the fathers being visited upon the children. The play is filled with oriental imagery, but it is essentially a morality surviving out of season.

*Thomas Nash.* 1567-1601. Another of Greene's immediate circle, Nash, was of more importance as a lampoonist and writer of pamphlets than as a dramatist. As a satirist, he vanquished his opponents by ridicule and abuse rather than by argument. He was called Juvenal, the English Aretino, and "railing Nash." Tradition says that he was one of the company at the carouse which suddenly ended Marlowe's life. He defended his friend's reputation after death against learned and powerful enemies. His fame as a dramatist rests upon three plays. The first, never published, is a political satire called *The Isle of Dogs,* and caused its author to be put into jail. The second is *Queen Dido,* written with Marlowe; and the third *Summer's Last Will and Testament,* a sort of court pastoral, embodying an elaborate play upon the word Summer. It contains a long parody of euphuism, besides a masquerading show passing in procession before the queen, upon which the court fool makes witty comments. As was the universal custom, in *Summer's Last Will* the queen is extravagantly praised:

"Unto Eliza, that most sacred name,
Whom none but saints and angels ought to name."

*Christopher Marlowe.* 1564-1593. The greatest of this group was Marlowe, the immediate forerunner of Shakespeare, and the only one of the company who bears comparison with

[1] A pantomimic rehearsal of the action which was to follow.

him. "Kit" Marlowe was the son of a shoemaker of Canterbury, born a few weeks before Shakespeare. He became a pensioner in Benet College, Cambridge, where he took his Master's degree in 1587, before which time his *Tamburlaine* had been presented in London. Coming to the city, he gained immediate fame as a dramatist and poet, writing for the Admiral's company. Even in those easy times he was declared an atheist and looked upon as one who lived a life of debauchery, though he seems never to have sunk so low as Greene. He was killed in a quarrel over a love affair in a tavern at Deptford in 1593.

Various traditions portray Marlowe as mild and kindhearted. The book-seller Thorpe, in the dedication of a translation of Lucan, wrote: "To the memory of that pure, elemental wit, Chr. Marlowe." Stopford Brooke wrote of him: "Marlowe lived and died an irreligious, imaginative, tenderhearted, licentious poet." Of all the characterizations that have been made of him, none seems so full of the genius of intuition as that of Swinburne, who said that Marlowe came up to London to seek his fortune "a boy in years, a man in genius, a god in ambition." The line

"Who ever loved, that loved not at first sight?"
from Marlowe's poem *Hero and Leander* is quoted by Shakespeare; and again, in *As You Like It,* Marlowe is addressed in the lines beginning "Dead Shepherd." The youthful roysterer was remarkably prolific. In six years he produced six tragedies, the poem *Hero and Leander,*[2] and one unfinished play. *Tamburlaine,* in two parts, belongs to the group of chronicles. After *Tamburlaine* there followed *Doctor Faustus, The Massacre of Paris, The Jew of Malta,* and *Edward Second.* The unfinished tragedy, on the subject of Queen Dido, was completed by Nash.

*The Faust legend.* The Faustiad, or Faust legend, is one of the few folk tales which can be traced from its first appearance through almost every stage of its development. The idea of a man's selling his soul to the devil for some immediate pleasure had appeared during the Middle Ages in more than

[2] Incomplete, later finished by Chapman.

one mystery, notably in the *Miracle of Theophilus*. The Faust story, however, has for its historical basis the career of a quack doctor or necromancer who lived in Suabia in the fifteenth century. This Doctor Faustus gained notoriety as a professor of magic. It is probable that the history of the celebrated Paracelsus, mystic, philosopher, and experimenter in the occult sciences in the early sixteenth century, may have been combined or confused with that of the original Doctor Faustus.

The earliest known story of Faust dates from 1587. It was written in German by an unknown author who made no pretense to literary skill. According to this version, Doctor Faust is a sensualist who prefers twenty-four years of happiness now to the uncertain joys of a future world. He is benighted, credulous, well acquainted with the demonological lore of the age, though he scoffs at the reality of a hell. Nevertheless, given the opportunity, he makes his bargain, enjoys his twenty-four years of earthly happiness, and then goes to hell, according to agreement.

Even in the unliterary form in which it was first told, the story must have had a sinister glamour. Faust is represented as "taking eagles' wings to himself and proposing to fathom all the depths of earth and heaven." To the dullest imagination he is something of a lordly sinner. The story became so popular that in the space of eleven years five different editions were published in Germany, and a continuation called the *Wagnerbuch* was added to it. As early as 1588 it had traveled to England, where a Faust ballad appeared. Marlowe's tragedy, *Doctor Faustus*, was completed either in 1589 or 1590, and went back to Germany, where it held the stage all through the seventeenth and up to the middle of the eighteenth century. No copy of this German version has been preserved; but from contemporary accounts it appears to have been well supplied with devils, striking scenes of necromancy and magic, and thrilling lines. As it lost its attraction for living actors, it was transferred to the puppet show. Even in this form, the story had some power. Lessing, the greatest critic of the eighteenth century, commented upon its dramatic possibilities; and it was through a puppet show that the story first became known to the youthful Goethe.

*Marlowe's Doctor Faustus.* Marlowe followed the Faust book closely in its surface arrangement. His play is not divided into acts or scenes; it has no female characters, no dumb show. The serious incidents are varied with passages of somewhat childish drolleries and buffoonery. The theme, as Marlowe conceived it, was the revolt of man against the limitations of human knowledge and power. There are many features closely akin to the morality. The struggle between the good and the bad angels is similar, but the arena had broadened to include man's intellectual and spiritual life, the realms of science, the history of thought, and the possibilities of man's power. Rupert Brooke expressed it: "Faust is but Everyman with a name and a university degree."

*Characteristics of Marlowe's work.* Each one of Marlowe's plays is, in a sense, a *tour de force,* a special creation. *The Jew of Malta, Dido,* and *The Massacre of Paris,* though abounding in passages of strength yet do not fulfill the requirements the author himself had set up. *The Jew,* however, was very popular, being performed thirty-six times in four years, which in those days was an unusual record. Marlowe's first and most important service to drama was the improvement of blank verse. Greene had condemned its use as being unscholarly; Sackville and Norton had used it, but were not able to lift it above the commonplace. In their work, it usually consisted of isolated lines, one following another, with no grouping according to thought. All the verses were made after one rhythmic pattern, with the same number of feet and the cæsura always in the same place. Marlowe invented numberless variations while still keeping the satisfying rhythm within a recurring pattern. Sometimes he left a redundant syllable, or left the line one syllable short, or moved the position of the cæsura. He grouped his lines according to the thought and adapted his various rhythms to the ideas. Thus blank verse became a living organism, plastic, brilliant, and finished.

Marlowe's second-best gift to drama was his conception of

the heroic tragedy built on a grand scale, with the three-fold unity of character, impression, and interest, instead of the artificial unities of time and place. Before his time tragedies were built either according to the loose style of the chronicle, or within the mechanical framework of the Senecan model; but in either case the dramatic unity attained by the Greeks was lacking. Marlowe and Shakespeare, with their disregard of the so-called classic rules, were in fact much nearer the spirit of Æschylus and Sophocles than the slavish followers of the pseudo-classic schools. Marlowe painted gigantic ambitions, desires for impossible things, longings for a beauty beyond earthly conception, and sovereigns destroyed by the very powers which had raised them to their thrones. Tamburlaine, Faust, Barabbas are the personifications of arrogance, ambition and greed. There is sometimes a touch of the extravagant or bombastic, or even of the puerile in his plays, for he had no sense of humor; nor had he the ability to portray a woman. He wrote no drama on the subject of love. Furthermore, his world is not altogether our world, but a remote field of the imagination. Mr. Cabell has remarked that "in Marlowe's superb verse there is very little to indicate that the writer had ever encountered any human beings." [3] In spite of this, he was great, both as dramatist and poet. His short life, the haste of his work, the irregularities of his habits,—these things combined to keep him from perfecting the creations of his imagination. Taken together, his plays imposed a standard upon all succeeding theatrical compositions. Before him, in England, there was no play of great importance; but after him, and based upon his work as a model, rose the greatest drama of English history.

[3] James Branch Cabell, *Beyond Life.*

## CHAPTER XXIV

## SHAKESPEARE

The tragedies: They are no mere poems. We could imagine we were standing before the gigantic Book of Fate, through which the hurricane of life was raging, and violently blowing the leaves to and fro.—GOETHE.

Shakespeare, by his freedom and spontaneity and resource, has succeeded, perhaps better than any other writer, in giving a voice and a body to those elusive moments of thought and feeling which are the life of humanity . . . the generations who have come after him, and have read his book, and have loved him with an unalterable personal affection, must each, as they pass the way that he went, pay him their tribute of praise. His living brood have survived him, to be the companions and friends of men and women as yet unborn.—SIR WALTER RALEIGH.

To any English speaking person, at least, Shakespeare must stand as the climax and peak of historical drama. His thoughts, phrases and people have permeated our thoughts and language, until we are no longer always conscious of his presence. Everybody knows something of Shylock, of Portia, of Hamlet and of Macbeth. We have only to remember how commonplace and banal some of the joke-phrases are: What's in a name? A rose by any other name would smell as sweet; Lay on, Macduff! Sweet are the uses of adversity; To be or not to be; Can honor set a leg? A poor thing, but mine own,— and a hundred other common sayings, to realize how their author has stamped himself upon English speech and thought. The plays, taken as a whole, have grown into a kind of Scripture, a Book, whose various chapters are all about one subject, human nature. The very universality of Shakespearean catchwords makes the poet seem unreal and impersonal. It is only by going to the plays and finding in them the amusing, instructive, or appealing story, that we can make him seem real, living, and human. We come, little by little, to see that this man of myriad fancies was a struggling, often puzzled, often weary human being, like ourselves. We learn to know that he was a hard worker in his profession, that he was thrown by destiny into an environment full of rivalries, disappointments, and difficulties. Out of these he made his Book.

*William Shakespeare.* 1564-1616. The known facts of Shakespeare's life, few as they are, are yet rather more numerous than those concerning most of the other playwrights of his time. Stratford-on-Avon, at the time of Shakespeare's birth, was a village of about two thousand inhabitants, somewhat off the main routes of travel, eighty miles from London. John Shakespeare, father of William and resident of Stratford, is reported to have been at one time a farmer doing business in hides and meats. His wife was Mary Arden, rather an heiress for her time, who brought into the family a house and fifty acres of land. Two girls were born and died in infancy. William, the third child, was baptized the twenty-sixth of April, 1564. The day of his birth is unknown, but is usually reckoned as three days earlier than his baptism. Five other children were born to John and Mary Shakespeare, and for a time the family prospered. When William was about four years old the father became bailiff, or mayor, of Stratford, and seems to have occupied other positions of prominence in the community. In all probability William went to the free grammar school of the town; but when he was about thirteen years old the father got into financial difficulties, and William, apparently, was taken out of school and put to work at home. In 1582 the license for the marriage of William Shakespeare and Anne Hathaway was entered in the town records. Three children, Susanna, the eldest, and twins, Hamnet and Judith, were born to the couple. Hamnet lived only about eleven years, but the two daughters survived their father.

After the birth of the twins, there follows a long gap in the authentic records. There is ground, however, for believing that William, leaving his family at Stratford, went up to London about 1586. At that time Queen Elizabeth had already reigned twenty-eight years, and London had grown rich and prosperous. The city spread loosely along the north side of the Thames, and had about two hundred thousand inhabitants. Wealthy merchants had built fine houses to the west and south; but the fields at the north and the precincts across the river were rather disreputable. It was in those sections that the first theaters—The Theater, the Curtain, and the remodeled house known as Newington Butts—had been built ten years earlier.

Shakespeare at first took jobs as a man-of-all-work about the theaters. The tradition is that he held horses at the door, and employed boys for this service, so that for a long time these servitors were called "Shakespeare's boys." At that time the Scholar Poets belonging to Greene's circle were in practical possession of the stage, so far as authorship was concerned. About 1587 Greene was somewhat eclipsed by Marlowe and Kyd, whose *Tamburlaine* and *The Spanish Tragedy,* respectively, appeared that year. During the years immediately following, Shakespeare must have gained a foothold, both as actor and playwright. The evidence for this conclusion lies principally in an unfinished pamphlet, called *A Groatsworth o' Wit,* left by Greene at his death in 1592, in which he warns his friends, Nash, Peele, and Lodge, against the injustices and difficulties of the theatrical profession, and incidentally refers to one "Shakescene" as an impudent upstart of an actor and a plagiarizing author. In this skit Greene parodied a line, "Tiger's heart wrapped in a woman's hide," which occurs in what is now considered Shakespeare's first play, the first part of *Henry VI.* The probabilities, therefore, are strong that Greene referred to Shakespeare; thus establishing the fact that the younger playwright had already become something of a rival to the university set.

In the early 1590's Shakespeare's activities as a theater man were well begun. He was summoned to act at court with Burbage, Heminge, Condell and others, and he received a salary as actor, a share of the profits of the enterprise, and certain sums for each play he wrote. In 1599 the Shakespeare family was granted a coat-of-arms; and "William Shakespeare" became "William Shakespeare, Gent." He purchased New Place, the largest house in Stratford, for sixty pounds; and thereafter he frequently added to his property in land and houses, not only in Stratford, but also in London. He was involved in several cases of litigation concerning mortgages and the recovery of sums of money. A recent investigator, Professor G. M. Wallace, has discovered that for a time Shakespeare lodged in the house of one Christopher Mountjoy, a wig-maker living near Cripplegate. In 1601 John Shakespeare died; the widow, Mary, lived until 1608. In 1607 Susanna married a physician named John Hall and went to live at New Place, the mother remaining, for the remainder of her life, in a small cottage in Henley Street.

During the following years it is probable that Shakespeare detached himself gradually from his London associations, and finally, three or four years before his death, made Stratford his home again. He made his will early in 1616, about the time his daughter Judith married Thomas Quiney; and on the twenty-third day of April, the same day of the same month in which he is supposed to have been born, he died. Two days later he was buried in the chancel of the Church of the Holy Trinity at Stratford, where, on the now famous grave, are carved the lines:

> Good friend, for Jesus' sake forbeare
> To dig the dust enclosed here;
> Blest be the man that spares these stones,
> And curst be he that moves my bones.

The inscription on the monument in the church at Stratford reads:

> Judico Pylium, genio Socratem, arte Maronem
> Terra tegit, populus maeret, Olympus habet.

> Stay passenger, why goest thou by so fast?
> Read, if thou canst, whom envious death hath plast
> Within this monument: Shakespeare with whome
> Quick nature dide; whose name doth deck ys tombe
> Far more than cost; sith all yt he hath writt
> Leaves living art but page to serve his witt.

> Obiit ano. doi 1616. Aetatis 53, Die 23 Ap.

*The four periods.* The earliest recognition of Shakespeare as a man of letters followed the publication, in 1593-4, of the poems, *Venus and Adonis* and *Lucrece,* dedicated to the Earl of Southampton. Many of the Sonnets were written in the poet's youth and circulated privately among his friends, but they were not published until 1609. In regard to the plays, it has been the custom among critics to divide Shakespeare's working life into four periods. The first, ending about 1593, covers his experimental stage, includes the comedies *Love's Labour's Lost, Two Gentlemen of Verona,* and *The Comedy of Errors,* together with *Titus Andronicus* and five of the chronicle plays. From that time to 1601 constitutes the second period, marked especially by the production of seven of the romantic comedies. There are also four histories and two tragedies. The third period, covering the first ten years of the seventeenth century, saw the completion of seven of the more important tragedies, including *Hamlet, Othello, Macbeth* and *Lear.* In the fourth and last period there are the *Winter's Tale, Cymbeline,* and the incomparable *Tempest,* together with the work Shakespeare did probably in collaboration with Fletcher. Professor Dowden has named these four periods respectively, "In the Workshop," "In the World," "In the Depths," and "On the Heights." Such a designation marks fairly well the distinction in temper between the different periods; and it also indicates, no doubt, that the mood of the public was subject to changes, and that Shakespeare knew how to meet them. He experimented with all the types of plays—tragedies, tragedies of blood, chronicles, comedies, and histories—and in them all he proved himself a dramatist of power.

Not a single Shakespearean manuscript has survived. It was not the custom, as we know, for playwrights to have their work published. It was only when the plays began to be stolen and printed from imperfect manuscripts that the dramatists found it important to attend to the matter of publication. Even then there was no copyright protection from pirated editions. Shakespeare attended to the publication of his poems, but seems never to have done as much for the dramas.

*The quartos.* The first appearance of the plays in print was in the quartos—small pamphlets, each containing one play and selling probably for sixpence. Sixteen of the plays were thus issued during Shakespeare's lifetime, and one other, *Othello,* five years after his death. Seven of these first quartos were probably stolen and published from shorthand notes; the remaining ten were apparently printed from manuscript copies such as were used in the theater. The first quarto, *Henry VI, Part II,* came out in 1594. After this time quartos, either original or reprinted, appeared almost every year up to 1622, when *Othello* was issued for the first time, and *Richard III* and the first part of *Henry VI* for the sixth time.

*The First Folio.* In 1623, seven years after the poet's death, two of Shakespeare's friends and associates in the theater, John Heminge and Henry Condell, collected and published the plays in the edition which is now called the *First Folio.* This book was entitled:

The Workes of William Shakespeare, containing all his Comedies, Histories, and Tragedies; truely set forth according to their first Originall.

It contains thirty-seven of the plays now accredited to Shakespeare. It lacked only one, *Pericles,* which modern scholarship has assigned to him. In this Folio there were twenty plays which had not before appeared in print. The book is dedicated to the Earls of Pembroke and Montgomery, who, in the words of the dedication,

"have been pleased to thinke these trifles some-thing, heeretofore; and have prosequuted both them, and their Authour living, with so much favour."

To the general reader the editors made an appeal to buy and read, since

"these playes have had their triall alreadie, and stood out all appeales."

Moreover, the editors claimed that former plays, which had been "maimed and deformed by the frauds and stealthes of injurious imposters," had now been "cured and made perfect in their limbes"; and they added modestly, concerning the author, that as he was a "happie imitator of Nature, was a most gentle expresser of it."

In the introduction to the *First Folio* occurs the justly famous eulogy of Ben Jonson. It is entitled, "To the Memory of my Beloved, the Author, Mr. William Shakespeare: and what he hath left us." In it are the lines,

> "Soule of the age!
> The applause! delight! the wonder
> of the stage!"

and "He was not of an age, but for all time." Three other poetic eulogies stand at the beginning of the volume; and also a list of the principal actors in the plays. The volume numbered 908 pages. It is not known how many copies of it were published; but somewhat more than one hundred and fifty are now known to be in existence.

During the seventeenth century there were published the *Second, Third,* and *Fourth Folios.* Two reprints of the *Third Folio* were made, and in the second reprint, 1664, *Pericles* and six other plays (the latter now considered spurious), were added to the Shakespeare canon. Among other plays these additions included *The Yorkshire Tragedy* and *Locrine.* The *Fourth Folio* followed the *Third* in keeping the enlarged list. The texts of the different *Folios* were not identical; and within each Folio the plays differed in external form. A few only were supplied with a list of characters; the division into scenes and acts was wholly lacking in six plays, and partly lacking in others; the spelling was archaic, and inconsistent with itself; exits and entrances were often missing, and the verse was disarranged.

All these difficulties connected with typographical form were supplemented by the confusion caused by piratical publishers and shorthand copies. However expert the shorthand copyist might have been, he was certain to commit many errors as to the order of the verse. Sometimes whole passages were omitted, words were mistaken, and the sense was garbled. The actors occasionally forgot their lines and omitted them, or improvised new ones. The result of these conditions is that Shakespeare students must ask many questions, some of which are: By what company of actors was the piece first played? Is there any internal evidence of the date? Any external evidence? How does the blank verse compare with that of Marlowe, Webster, Dekker, or with the writings of other poets? Are the characterizations of such a temper and quality as to suggest date or author? What references are there to books, pamphlets, or current local events? These are only a few of the most obvious questions whose answers would throw light on the date or authorship of a given play. The time has come when any fact concerning Shakespeare's life, or even the smallest light upon any one of the Shakespeare lines, is counted a discovery of the first magnitude.

*The editors.* The world owes a debt of gratitude to the scholars who have devoted their services to the restoration of the Shakespeare texts. Outside of the Bible and the Greek tragic poets, no other writer has ever received such loving attention from poets and learned men as has the English bard. Nicholas Rowe, poet laureate to Queen Anne, was the first person, after Heminge and Condell, to study the plays with a view to establishing a correct text. He traced and corrected many errors which had persisted or crept into the *Folios.* In 1709 he published an edition of the plays in six volumes with a memoir of the author, and brought comparative order out of the chaotic condition. He completed the division into acts and scenes, listed the characters, rearranged the verse of many passages, and used much good sense in the correction of obvious faults. Some of the things he did were wrong, and he left much still to be done; but he opened the way in a spirit of scholarship, sympathy and sense. Fourteen years later came Pope's edition. Probably the most important service rendered by Pope was the rejection of the seven plays which had been added to the *Third* and *Fourth Folios.* Modern criticism has agreed with him concerning six of the questioned plays, but has restored *Pericles* to the Shakespearean canon. This drama, with the thirty-seven plays printed in the *First Folio*, make up the list now included in every edition.

Other Shakespeare lovers, more painstaking than Pope, quickly found errors in the edition printed under his name; and from that time to this, revisions, emendations, and new interpretations have never ceased. Theobald, a learned, brilliant and sympathetic critic, showed up Pope's carelessness and ignorance, and in turn was spitefully pilloried by Pope in the *Dunciad*. Hamner was not so important as Theobald, but still achieved notable results. Men of letters have worked *con amore* for a better understanding of one whom they tacitly acknowledge as master of all scholars. The eighteenth century produced Doctor Johnson, Edward Capell, and others; and the distinguished list goes on with the names of Knight, Malone, Coleridge, Lamb, Halliwell-Phillips, Dyce, up to the Americans—White, Rolfe, Furness, Thorndike and Neilson. The Germans Schlegel, Schiller, Goethe and Herder have also added much in the way of critical and explanatory material.

*Sources of plots.* It has already become a truism that tradition and folk lore have been much more important in the making of plays than invention. Shakespeare's two early comedies, *Love's Labour's Lost* and *The Merry Wives of Windsor,* seem to have been original plots; but they are the exceptions in the long list of plays. The career of the *Romeo and Juliet* fable fairly illustrates the history of many of the stories. The groundwork of *Romeo* was a medieval romance in prose (usually ascribed to Xenophon of Ephesus), translated in the Middle Ages into Italian, perhaps by Da Porto. In the fifteenth century a part of the story appeared in a novel by Masuccio. Then Bandello, another Italian, made a poetic version of it, and before 1562 it had appeared as a play in England. From this play Arthur Brooke made a poem, creating the characters of Mercutio and the Nurse. In each of these versions doubtless fresh touches or new characters were added to heighten the interest. In 1567 another prose version was published by Paynter in *The Palace of Pleasure*. It is probable that Shakespeare took the story from Brooke's version, producing his *Romeo and Juliet* in 1594. Upon it are many marks of his youthful style. In the verse are rhyme endings, internal rhymes, and sonnet forms mixed with the blank verse; here and there are echoes of the ranting, high-flown rhetoric of Kyd or Marlowe. The play belongs to the school of *The Spanish Tragedy*, for it is passion and not reason which determines the action and final result. The century-long family feud is, in a way, a fate-motive which overwhelms alike the innocent and the guilty. The story, sordid and depressing in its original form, was transformed by Shakespeare into a thing of beauty, the consummate eulogy of Youth and Love.

Shakespeare based many other plays upon fables which had enjoyed a long and sometimes brilliant career before he touched them. *Hamlet* came to him *via* the Saxö Chronicle, Bandello, a French version by Belleforest, and an early play in English, probably by Kyd. *Othello* is from a novel by Cinthio, *Lear* from an earlier play based upon the chronicle of Geoffrey of Monmouth. *Macbeth* is from Holinshed, and treats the same subject as a lost Latin play acted before James First at Oxford. Shakespeare was a devoted reader of Plutarch, probably in the English version of Sir Thomas North; and from him he took the idea of *Coriolanus* and the other Roman plays. *Timon of Athens* is founded partly on Plutarch and partly on a tale from *The Palace of Pleasure*. A part of *Measure for Measure* came from Cinthio by way of Greene's *Pandosto*. The casket scene in *The Merchant of Venice* is found in the *Gesta Romanorum* and in the *Decameron;* and from the latter also came the love story in *Cymbeline* and the plot of *All's Well*. And so on through the list.

In spite of the fact that Shakespeare did not once in his plays enter upon the political or religious controversies of his day, yet he was intensely of his time. Carlyle called him an epitome of the era of Elizabeth. He had an interest in strange countries, as had all the Elizabethans; was acquainted with law and the terms of legal procedure; knew the current superstitions and witch-lore; and like his generation he was fascinated by Italian books, music and amusements. He reflects all the characteristics of the London gentleman of his time, who was fond of fencing bouts, wrestling matches, duels, dances and

Estelle Winwood, as Katharine, and Rollo Peters, as Petruchio, in
*The Taming of the Shrew*

love stories. He was familiar with all sorts of plays—those of his own day and the day preceding, of Lope de Vega and Calderón. His language is full of the catchwords, proverbs, and tags of current speech; and he, like the dramatists of all ages, was easily caught in the net of the supernatural. He exalts his England, just as the Athenian playwrights exalted their beautiful city. In his verse there are puns, curious conceits which overload the sense, and an occasional childish play upon words, crowded imagery and improbable stories.

Even from the first, however, Shakespeare showed himself able to produce radiant passages and portrayals of character far outweighing any weaknesses. He worked with a great variety of subjects, could delineate subtleties of emotion and desire, was a master of gorgeous poetry, and showed a profound understanding of the sources of human happiness. The tragedy of blood, hitherto full of ranting fury, became in his hands a *Hamlet;* the domestic tragedy, founded on some revolting murder case, an *Othello.* The history plays were transformed from the cold, dull *Gorboduc* to the warmth and reality of a *Julius Cæsar* or *Richard III.* Perhaps his most important service to drama lay in his incomparable adaptability to the stage.

"His stories are so vividly told, that even people who dislike plays and who do not care for poetry delight in them. . . . Shakespeare's plays visualize themselves. Each character is, as it were, costumed in his own language. Erase the names of the speakers, and the text keeps them in place. Destroy the stage directions, remove the stage from under their feet, and pull down the theater, and yet the play goes forward: everything is expressed in the lines themselves. . . . You cannot keep Shakespeare off the stage. The plays veer towards the boards as ducks veer towards the water when passing a pond; and this lurch is felt, not only in the whole drift and action of a play, but in its scenes and incidents, its decorative passages, its dumb show. These dramas excite the dramatic ambition of every reader, they create good actors, and they have maddened the bad ones in all ages. Little scenes cut out of them are thrilling if properly done; and the great speeches, soliloquies, and harangues are the best monologues in existence. No actor has ever given a final interpretation of any one of the great rôles. Even when they are murdered by bad actors, they come to life again, as true creatures of the stage should do." [1]

Shakespeare may be measured by many tests; but this measurement can only be done, finally, by each reader for himself. It is only by letting the characters speak to you that the real Shakespeare can be revealed. In his Book you may see what he admired, what he laughed at, what he loved and handled tenderly. What did he like in women? Not only beauty and modesty, like all poets, but the clear brain of a Portia, the gay spirits of a Rosalind, the womanly dignity and kindness of Olivia; women who were not squeamish or clinging, but courageous and gallant. His heroes are men of character, though often beset by some demon which temporarily perverts them; they are not cads or rakes. In spite of the occasional coarseness of his words, common in his time, he was essentially clean-minded. Sincerity, faithfulness in friendship, dependability, loyalty—these are the qualities which he constantly elevates, and whose infringement he punishes. He scoffs merrily at conceit, bombast, vanity, and worldly folly. What emerges more and more, as one reads and thinks, is the wisdom and knowledge of the man combined with his gift of poetry. These qualities have lifted him into eminence. He could make words mean more than they logically mean, and express such commonplace emotions as young love, sorrow, despair, and ambition, in a radiant kind of language so that these experiences seem not commonplace, but the very essence of romance, adventure, pathos.

[1] John Jay Chapman, *A Glance Towards Shakespeare.*

## CHAPTER XXV

# THE FIRST HALF OF THE SEVENTEENTH CENTURY IN ENGLAND

During the last phase. . . . English drama is no longer what it had been. It has forfeited all claim to consideration as a moral and ethical force, has accepted the brand of vagabondage, and is content to make its appeal to moral outcasts. It was for this reason that Stuart drama faded and decayed. . . . The form is there in almost undiminished splendor; it is the healthy spirit, the sane and comprehensive grasp of life, which is missing.—C. E. TUCKER BROOKE, *The Tudor Drama.*

The first decade of the seventeenth century must be called, on the whole, the most glorious period in English dramatic history. After that time, the remarkable genius which had so enriched the stage began to wane. The younger men, writing contemporaneously with Shakespeare, brought to their work perhaps more technical skill and scarcely less richness of imagination; but they began to use abnormal and repulsive subjects, to delineate trickery and chicanery for its own sake, and to depend upon rhetoric instead of creative imagination,—all marks of overripeness and decadence. At the same time they broadened the field, pictured many contemporary types, and indeed invented new kinds of plays, such as the "comedy of humours," the mixed comedy, and the dramatic romance.

*Ben Jonson.* 1574-1637. In the group of playwrights immediately surrounding Shakespeare, who with him were perhaps accustomed to gather in the Mermaid Tavern, were Ben Jonson, Webster, Ford, Beaumont and Fletcher, Chapman, Marston, and Dekker. Among these Jonson was easily first, both in the quality of his genius and the amount of his work. He was a man of enormous learning, poet laureate, a soldier in

Flanders, an actor, and hack writer for Henslowe.[1]  He appeared first as playwright in the late years of the sixteenth century, at the moment when Shakespeare and the romantic comedies were at the height of their popularity.  To some extent he was obliged to conform to the prevailing taste; but his natural inclination was toward the classic and regular style rather than toward the romantic; and his "humour" was satirical rather than sentimental.

Jonson's plays fall roughly into three groups: the realistic comedies, the tragedies, and the masques.  As a contribution to drama the realistic comedies are most important.  Even in his 'prentice work, the two plays *The Case is Altered* and *The Tale of a Tub,* it is evident that he was influenced more by classic models than by contemporary fashion.  *The Case Is Altered* is based upon two plays of Plautus and the old familiar theme of the abduction of infants.  The action is completed in one place and covers but a single day.  Jonson's importance, however, is not owing to this return to the classical form, but to his keenness in portraying contemporaneous types. He took from the Plautine plays some of the most successful stock characters such as Miles Gloriosus (whom he named Captain Bobadil), the spendthrift son, the jealous husband, and so transformed them that they stand forth revived and recreated, as true comic figures belonging to Elizabethan London.

The play *Every Man in His Humour* (1598) inaugurated the school of realistic comedy, unlike anything which had hitherto appeared on the English stage.  It deals not with the passions, but with the follies, the "humours" of mankind.  The scene is laid in London, and different sorts of city characters are pictured to the life.  The play was the sensation of the

---

[1] Philip Henslowe (died 1616) was the first famous theatrical manager.  He built the Rose Theater in 1591, and with the actor Edward Alleyn built the Fortune in 1599 (1600 O. S.).  In 1592 he began a *Diary* in which he entered many facts of interest, including the dates of the production of new plays, the amounts he paid for them, and the names of writers whom he employed.  The *Diary* was edited for the Shakespeare Society in 1841.

hour, and was enacted before the queen by the company to which Shakespeare belonged, and in which he at one time acted.

Jonson was brilliant, but apparently neither genial nor lovable,—indeed he had the reputation of being pompous and arrogant. Though manly and honorable, he seems to have been lacking in sympathy. As a dramatist, he was resourceful in the creation of character and in the invention of comic situations. While for the most part he confined himself to laughing at the more obvious, surface absurdities of society, yet his wit was so keen and his humor so robust as to make a lasting impression upon English drama. He influenced nearly all the writers of the seventeenth century, and his peculiar type of play has persisted on the English speaking stage to the present time.

*Francis Beaumont,* 1584-1616. *John Fletcher,* 1579-1625. Collaboration between playwrights was common enough in Elizabethan times, but the remarkably successful partnership between Beaumont and Fletcher was unique even for that day. Both men came from the upper class, Beaumont being the son of a chief justice, and Fletcher the son of a clergyman who later became Lord Bishop of London. The former was educated at Oxford, the latter at Cambridge. From about 1608 until the marriage of Beaumont in 1613 the two friends lived together near the Globe Theater in Southwark, sharing everything in the closest intimacy. They belonged to the Mermaid Tavern group and were friends of Jonson and Shakespeare. Poets have commented on the manliness and "lordly aspect" of these two men. They enjoyed great popularity, and their plays kept the stage until long after the Restoration. In 1616, a few weeks before the death of Shakespeare, Beaumont died and was buried in Westminster Abbey. Nine years later Fletcher died of the plague and was buried at Saint Saviour's in Southwark.

As Jonson best represents the classic play of this period, so Beaumont and Fletcher best represent the romantic. The plays written together reach a higher point of excellence than anything either one wrote alone. In their combined work there is sureness of touch, humor, pathos, intensity. Students of every generation have wondered at the completeness of the fusion of the two talents. It was said that Fletcher was the more brilliant of the two, with the ability to turn off witty, graceful dialogue; while tragic intensity and genial humor were the special gifts of Beaumont. In their joint plays their talents are so organically combined, so completely merged into one, that the hand of Beaumont cannot be clearly distinguished from that of Fletcher.

*The joint plays of Beaumont and Fletcher.* The *Cambridge History of English Literature* attributes seven plays to the collaboration of the two friends. More than fifty are listed as written either by one or by both, and at least six have been lost. The first piece announced as coming from them was *Philaster, or Love Lies a-Bleeding.* It is partly in verse and partly in prose, and has many marks of the prevailing romantic school, such as the disinherited prince, a lord from foreign parts who comes to court the king's daughter, the high-born girl disguised as a page, and the intrigues of courtiers. The play has the true Elizabethan ring. The sentiment of the pastorals, too often mawkish, is here introduced with happy results. When Philaster, the inheritor of the kingdom, tells the shepherd boy that he does not realize what it is to die, the boy answers:

> "Yes, I do know, my lord:
> 'Tis less than to be born, a lasting sleep;
> A quiet resting from all jealousy
> A thing we all pursue; I know, besides,
> 'Tis but a giving over of a game
> That must be lost. . . ."

And again,

> "Alas, my lord, my life is not a thing
> Worthy your noble thoughts! 'tis not a life,
> 'Tis but a piece of childhood thrown away."

So the poetry goes, full of rich fancy, delicacy and technical virtuosity. It is often full of vehemence, too, as though winged by genuine emotion. The facts of the story may not always be within the realm of reality, yet the passion rings true, and the poetry has the lift which is the mark of genius.

The Fletcher and Beaumont plays show how luxuriant and forceful, even outside Shakespeare, was the romantic Elizabethan style, and how brilliant were some of his contemporaries.

"Their best heroes are earlier Hernanis, bred in the ideals of Castilian honor; even their villains—and monstrous villains some of them are—utter very noble sentiments. You feel that such persons never existed, and yet you know the thoughts to be true, and you cannot resist the fascination, the glamour, if you will, of ideals borrowed from the age of chivalry. There is, in Beaumont and Fletcher, a 'constant recognition of gentility,' as Emerson has remarked; this, and their picturesque descriptions, their genuine sentiment, and their occasional flashes of imagination revealing intense passion, constitute their chief merits, and interfuse through their dramas the spirit of romance." [2]

After the death of Beaumont, Fletcher collaborated with Massinger, Shirley, Jonson, Field, and perhaps others. In two plays, *Henry VIII* and *The Two Noble Kinsmen,* it is supposed that Fletcher and Shakespeare worked together. Some of the plays often attributed to Fletcher have no less than three or four authors; or they were revised so many times, by different hands, that they became as it were a composite of the wit and skill of the times. Nobody tried very hard to be "original" in the sense of inventing the fables; the tales of Boccaccio (coming to England probably by way of Chaucer), Cinthio, Tasso, Guarini, Cervantes and Lope de Vega were a constant source of supply for plots.

*General importance of Beaumont and Fletcher.* Both of these men were poets of a high order, and their work was superior in invention, scholarship, and charm to anything else in the Elizabethan age except the best of Shakespeare. Webster equalled them in powerful expression of passion and tragic despair. Massinger, and perhaps Marston, achieved passages which were comparable in beauty; but for volume, sustained

[2] William Roscoe Thayer, in his *Preface* to a collection of Elizabethan plays.

energy, and poetic power the names of Beaumont and Fletcher stand above them all. These two possessed luxuriance of fancy and eagerness for new ideas combined with a scholarly conservatism towards upstart modes; they had, occasionally, the licentiousness and coarseness characteristic of their times. Their command of phrase was unsurpassed; they avoided foolish conceits and violent metaphors, at the same time achieving a sort of gorgeousness of language. Not only for their influence on language, but also for their singular modernity of spirit should they be remembered. They seem already far away from Shakespeare, as if speaking almost in the tongue of today.

*Thomas Dekker.* 1570-cir. 1637. As in the reign of Elizabeth, so in the time of James the stage continued to draw the most brilliant men of letters. Thomas Dekker did not belong to the "gentle" class, and he appears not to have been a university man. Versatile and talented but often careless, he lived the life of the real bohemian. Once he was for nearly three years in prison for debt; and he had a thorough knowledge of the hardships of life. Yet in spite of all, his temper was sweet and to him life was good. His name is frequently mentioned in Henslowe's *Diary,* which means that as a hack writer he made himself useful; and he is known as the author of various pamphlets. He left a vivid account of the plague in 1603; also, in *The Gull's Horn Book,* a lively record of the loose manners and morals of the fashionable London gallants. He wrote charming songs, and a series of fine prayers. All in all, Dekker must be counted as one of the most manly and attractive of this group of playwrights.

Dekker's *Shoemaker's Holiday* is one of the most delightful of comedies, full of fun and hearty enjoyment of life. Another Dekker comedy, *Old Fortunatus,* was based on a well known story which had appeared in Italian, German, and French versions. Hans Sachs and others had already used it before Dekker, who wrote his play probably in 1600. Dekker collaborated with nearly all of the Henslowe group of playwrights, and was one of the principal contestants in the famous War of the Theaters, which occurred towards the end of the sixteenth century. The causes of this trouble are somewhat obscure, but it is generally thought that Marston, Dekker and others, on the public stage and under the slightest of disguises, had made sport of Jonson as being conceited and arrogant. In an attempt at punishment, Jonson claimed that he had given Marston a beating and taken his pistol from him. Evidently the sport continued, however; and in 1601 Jonson retaliated in another way. He produced a play called *The Poetaster,* in which he ridiculed both Marston and Dekker. The next move was the production by Dekker of a burlesque tragedy called *Satiromastix,* which was full of good-humored mockery of Jonson. The quarrel was patched up and apparently forgotten, for, in the same year, Marston and Jonson collaborated in *Love's Martir;* and shortly afterward the three writers, Marston, Dekker and Jonson together produced *Eastward Hoe,* a lively play with the plot taken from the *Decameron* but the characters from contemporaneous London life. Professor Brooke thinks the War of the Theaters was partly caused not so much by personal animosity as by rivalry between different theatrical companies. Jonson's plays were given by the Children of the Royal Chapel, while Dekker and Marston could be seen at the Globe and the Fortune.

*George Chapman.* 1559-1634. Unlike most of his literary contemporaries, Chapman did not in early youth turn to playwriting. He was born five years before Shakespeare, and is best known for his translation of Homer, which inspired the famous sonnet by Keats. Like Jonson he was a learned man, with an elevated style and considerable gift for epigram. One of his plots, *The World Runs on Wheels,* was taken from Terence, another, *The Widdower's Tears,* from Petronius. In his two most successful tragedies, *Bussy D'Ambois* and *The Revenge of Bussy D'Ambois,* he drew his fable from recent French history. He was never entirely at home in the dramatic field, and never achieved a really good plot.

*John Marston.* 1575-1634. The history of Marston is a singular one. He was a graduate of Oxford and for about eight years a prominent figure in the theatrical world of London. His thinly veiled ridicule of Ben Jonson occurs in the play called *Histriomastix;* and it was probably this piece which involved him, with Dekker, in the prolonged quarrel known as the War of the Theaters. Besides his collaborations with Dekker and Jonson, Marston also dramatized the well worn story of Sophonisba, told originally by Livy, used by Trissino in Italy, by Corneille in France, and by other writers in England and Germany. Marston's success, however, lay primarily in comedy, in such pieces as *Eastward Hoe* and *What You Will.* By the year 1606 he was an outstanding playwright; but in the following year he suddenly retired from everything pertaining to the stage and took orders in the Church.

*Thomas Middleton.* 1570-1627. The scene of Middleton's plays is always London, and his plots are based upon experiences of men of the world. To be sure, his world was made up of taverns and less reputable places; but so far as it went, it was the veritable universe in which the gallants of the age lived. His titles alone, *A Trick to Catch the Old One,* and *A Mad World, My Masters,* are diverting. Mr. Arthur Symons calls the comedy of Middleton "light, rancid, and entertaining, irresponsible rather than immoral." During this period English drama was becoming increasingly dominated by sex; and the more realistic it grew, the farther it strayed from the world of imagination in which it had dwelt with the earlier dramatists. Some of the most brilliant writers of the younger group followed Jonson's lead in the "comedy of humours," and although Shakespeare, Marlowe and the others were still to be seen on the boards, yet they were already regarded as belonging to the older and more conservative school. The modern note was becoming clearer.

*John Webster.* 1580-cir. 1625. The few plays left by Webster are of commanding quality. Little is known of his life. In the early years of the seventeenth century he collaborated with Dekker, Middleton, and Marston. Between 1610 and 1614 he produced the tragedies *The White Devil* and *The Duchess of Malfy,* both based on the theme of revenge. *The White Devil,* afterwards put on the stage as *Vittoria Corombona,* portrays historical events which occurred in Italy during Webster's own lifetime. In it the author cuts loose from

tutorship and shows his own genius, which was sombre, powerful, and full of grandiose poetic fury. *The Duchess of Malfy*
also comes from an Italian source and has a plot which was
used as the basis of a play by Lope de Vega. Other dramas
ascribed to Webster are, for us, of slight importance. He
never attained the authoritative position of Jonson, nor the
popularity of Fletcher; but many recent critics have accorded
him a higher place than either. He is occasionally crude and
a trifle obscure; but in spite of a few such lapses, his plays
have the touch of greatness. Professor Vaughn places him
nearer to the author of *Hamlet* than any other of the group.
Even a short excerpt reveals the swing and energy of his
genius:

> "I know death hath ten thousand several doors
> For men to take their exits;
> Yet stay: heaven's gates are not so highly arched
> As princes' palaces; they that enter there
> Must go upon their knees." [3]

*Philip Massinger.* 1583-1640. Massinger went to Oxford
without taking a degree, and came to London in 1606. He was
one of the numerous writers occasionally befriended by the
manager Henslowe. It was Fletcher, however, who became his
teacher and fellow worker. Though the early editions of the
work of Fletcher make no reference to Massinger as collaborator, yet it is now thought that he was joint author in no less
than twenty of the so-called Fletcher plays. The two authors
seem always to have been on friendly terms; and Massinger,
probably at his own request, was buried in Fletcher's grave.[4]
Massinger collaborated also with Dekker in *The Virgin Martir,*
and later with Nathaniel Field in *The Fatall Dowry.* Sixteen
plays survive to which Massinger's name alone was attached;
and the titles of twelve lost works are known. Three of the
surviving dramas are tragedies, the others either comedies or
serious pieces ending without bloodshed. The highly successful comedy, *A New Way to Pay Old Debts,* kept the stage

[3] *The Duchess of Malfy.*
[4] Cambridge History of English Literature, Vol. VI, p. 161.

almost up to the present day. The plot was borrowed from Middleton.

Massinger was expert in dramatic construction, well able to write effective stage scenes and to portray character. He transplanted Jewish, Spanish, or English stories to Italy, which was the conventional *locus* of the comedies of his day. His women are frequently licentious and coarse, and he was satiric about Englishmen, picturing them as hard drinkers and gross feeders, all too ready to ape the fashions of the French. Haste in work, and perhaps too little earnestness, prevented him from reaching the highest level. He could not throw his whole weight into the business in hand, but repeated himself, used superficial and hackneyed terms, and abounded in coarseness.

*John Ford.* 1586-1640. Like so many other playwrights of his day, Ford is thought to have studied at Oxford. He collaborated with Dekker in *The Sun's Darling,* and wrote the first act of *The Witch of Edmonton,* Dekker probably writing the remainder. Ford was almost the only member of this group who did not borrow his plots. Like Webster, his spirit was gloomy and sombre, "weaving the spell of genius around strange sins." He has been called the dramatist of broken hearts. With no gift for comedy, he appeared at his best in plays of eccentric action, where his polished and measured verse conveys an impression of resentment and suffering. His poetry is far removed from the eager and passionate lines of Marlowe and the Scholar Poets. "With Ford, the sun-born radiance of the noblest Elizabethan drama fades from the stage." [5]

*Tourneur and Shirley.* Among the minor writers of the Stuart period belong Cyril Tourneur and James Shirley. Tourneur is not an important figure, but he is generally considered the author of two existing pieces, *The Atheist's Tragedy* and *The Revenger's Tragedy.* One tragi-comedy, *The Nobleman,* which was performed at court, is now lost. Shirley has far greater weight than Tourneur. He was a student both at Oxford and Cambridge, and took orders in the Church of England about 1619. Shortly afterward he became a convert to

[5] F. C. Gummere, *The Elizabethan Stage.*

the Church of Rome and changed in profession from dramatist to school teacher; then again he returned to the work of dramatist and was chosen to write a court play, *The Triumph of Peace* (1634). Residing in Ireland for a time, he wrote plays for the Dublin theater; but at the outbreak of the civil war he enlisted as a soldier. After his military service he returned to London and resumed his old profession of teaching. A contemporary writer says that he and his wife were overcome in the great London fire (1666), that they both died on the same day and were buried in the same grave. Shirley's work is for the most part in comedy and tragi-comedy, with scenes laid in London, and the action belonging to the author's own time. As in so many other plays of the period, there are ladies disguised as page boys, farcical underplots, satirical passages, and considerable liveliness. In general, Shirley is not so coarse as his contemporaries. Among some forty or fifty surviving dramas *The Cardinall* and *The Traytor* are perhaps the best.

*General characteristics.* Like the Greek, the Elizabethan period of dramatic greatness was short. The sudden growth of wealth, the political changes caused by the victory over the Spanish Armada, religious enfranchisement, the exploration of new continents,—these and similar agencies brought about a liberation of genius which has never been duplicated. The playwrights were often impatient of discipline, crude but opulent, coarse but not vicious. They were not fatigued with life. The note of cynicism, of disillusion, of indifference was seldom heard. The rich legacy which they left was largely formed of three elements: the vital remnants of the medieval drama, the corrective influence of the classic models, and the folk lore of the Middle Ages. While French and Italian playwrights turned towards classicism, those of Spain and England were unmistakably romantic, ignoring the unities of time and place, abandoning the chorus, presenting violent and passionate types of characters, with crime, melancholy, insanity and death as familiar companions. Revenge was a popular theme; and so frequent was the appearance of the ghost that the anonymous writer of the Prologue to *A Warning for Fair Women* (1599) expressed himself as follows:

"Then, too, a filthy whining ghost,
  Lapt in some foul sheet, or a leather pilch,
  Comes screaming like a pig half stuck'd
  And cries, Vindicta! Revenge, revenge!
  With that a little rosin flasheth forth,
  Like smoke out of a tobacco pipe, or a boy's squib."

*Causes of the condemnation of the theater.* We come again to a period when the influence of the Church was arrayed against the theater; and this time its efforts towards its suppression were markedly successful. It is perhaps unnecessary to recall to the reader that the London Corporation, during the greater part of the sixteenth century, had been in a chronic state of resentment on account of play-actors and playhouses. The reasons for their complaints were, for the most part, sound enough: opportunities for lawlessness and violence, congestion of traffic, encouragement of disreputable taverns, and danger of the spread of the plague. As time went on, other arguments, somewhat less reasonable, came to light. Some people contended that it was sacrilegious for men to dress up in clothes belonging to the other sex.[6] One clergyman, not a Puritan but a Churchman, issued a pamphlet in which he stated that the stage was the cause of the visitations of the plague: when it was not present the ungodliness of the plays brought it on as a curse from heaven; and when it was present, the gathering in the playhouse caused it to spread.

About the time Shakespeare arrived in London there was an outbreak against the theater which was especially violent. An earthquake had occurred in 1580, and in the following year there was a recurrence of the plague. At a bear-baiting show, given on a Sunday, a wooden scaffolding had given way, killing several people and injuring others. A few years later, a brawl outside the theater caused serious disturbance. To many of the good people of London, all these things were signs of

[6] No women were as yet on the English stage. Women's parts were taken by boys.

the wrath of heaven against the play-acting profession, and arguments for its extermination. When it was recognized that play-acting, not long before, had been utilized as a means of teaching the lessons of the Church, the argument against it was that it was popish. At the very time when England was making the greatest single contribution that any modern nation has ever made to the literature of the stage, preachers both Puritan and Anglican, pamphleteers, and politicians were loud in their denunciations.

*Royal protection.* Fortunately, the stage had a powerful friend in Queen Elizabeth. Since companies of actors "belonged" to the queen and were under the protection of the highest nobles of the land, the fight over the theaters resolved itself mainly into a struggle on the part of the queen's agents, or counsel, to outwit the decrees of the city Corporation. One method was to regard the giving of a play as a "rehearsal" for a royal production. Of course these "rehearsals" could be as numerous as the manager wished; and the public could be, and was, admitted. This practice brought on a bitter quarrel in which professors of Oxford and Cambridge were involved. One wise man at Oxford condemned the public plays, but defended those of the universities. "As an occasional recreation for learned gentlemen, acting received his highest praise; as a regular means of livelihood, it was regarded with scorn." [7] In all this contention, however, the astute Elizabeth managed to have her own way. The stage and its players were kept alive.

After the death of Elizabeth the condition of playing companies was changed. The privilege of licensing and protecting them was gradually withdrawn from the nobles and taken over by the king. The London theater was thereby strengthened, but dramatic activity in general received a blow. It became more fashionable to attend public performances; and the court masques brought to the city many people of talent—painters, musicians, designers, actors and playwrights. Plays became more polished, less coarse, but often more indecent. Protected by the play-loving monarchs, actors were less apprehensive of the law, and did not scruple to ridicule their enemies. As the

[7] Cambridge History of English Literature.

seventeenth century wore on, no doubt politics had as much to do with the feeling against the theaters as religion; for playwrights and actors inevitably were classed among the supporters of the crown. The scandal was increased by the licentiousness of the court, where so many attractive theater people found protection, and by the extravagances connected with the masques. Actors grew bold and began to insult the pious-minded, especially the Puritans.

As the difficulties between the crown and Parliament increased, there were circulated numerous pamphlets and petitions in which the stage was attacked for its immorality, indecency and extravagance. All the old arguments, which had preceded the building of the playhouses in the sixteenth century, were revived. The annual attacks of the plague in the years following 1630 were exceptionally violent. In 1642 Parliament issued an ordinance suppressing all stage plays; and five years later even a stricter law was passed. Finally, in 1648 all playhouses were ordered to be pulled down, all players to be seized and whipped, and every one caught attending a play to be fined five shillings. Of course, no such ordinance, in such a city as London, could be completely enforced; but the playhouses, in effect, were practically closed from 1642 until the Restoration in 1660.

## CHAPTER XXVI

# THE RESTORATION DRAMATISTS

Then came the gallant protest of the Restoration, when Wycherley and his successors in drama commenced to write of contemporary life in much the spirit of modern musical comedy. . . . A new style of comedy was improvised, which, for lack of a better term, we may agree to call the comedy of Gallantry, and which Etherege, Shadwell, and Davenant, and Crowne, and Wycherley, and divers others, labored painstakingly to perfect. They probably exercised to the full reach of their powers when they hammered into grossness their too fine witticisms just smuggled out of France, mixed them with additional breaches of decorum, and divided the result into five acts. For Gallantry, it must be repeated, was yet in its crude youth. . . . For Wycherley and his confreres were the first Englishmen to depict mankind as leading an existence with no moral outcome. It was their sorry distinction to be the first of English authors to present a world of unscrupulous persons who entertained no special prejudices, one way or the other, as touched ethical matters.—JAMES BRANCH CABELL, *Beyond Life*.

From 1642 onward for eighteen years, the theaters of England remained nominally closed. There was of course evasion of the law; but whatever performances were offered had to be given in secrecy, before small companies in private houses, or in taverns located three or four miles out of town. No actor or spectator was safe, especially during the earlier days of the Puritan rule. Least of all was there any inspiration for dramatists. In 1660 the Stuart dynasty was restored to the throne of England. Charles II, the king, had been in France during the greater part of the Protectorate, together with many of the royalist party, all of whom were familiar with Paris and its fashions. Thus it was natural, upon the return of the court, that French influence should be felt, particularly in the theater.

In August, 1660, Charles issued patents for two companies of players, and performances immediately began. Certain writers, in the field before the civil war, survived the period of theatrical eclipse, and now had their chance. Among these were Thomas Killigrew and William Davenant, who were quickly provided with fine playhouses.

*Appearance of women on the English stage.* It will be remembered that great indignation was aroused among the English by the appearance of French actresses in 1629. London must soon have learned to accept this innovation, however, for in one of the semi-private entertainments given during the Protectorate at Rutland House, the actress Mrs. Coleman took the principal part. *The Siege of Rhodes,* a huge spectacle designed by Davenant in 1656 (arranged in part with a view of evading the restrictions against theatrical plays) is generally noted as marking the entrance of women upon the English stage. It is also remembered for its use of movable machinery, which was something of an innovation. The panorama of *The Siege* offered five changes of scene, presenting "the fleet of Solyman the Magnificent, his army, the Island of Rhodes, and the varieties attending the siege of the city."

*Disappearance of national types.* By the time the theaters were reopened in England, Corneille and Racine in France had established the neo-classic standard for tragedy, and Molière was in the full tide of his success. These playwrights, with Quinault and others, for a time supplied the English with plots. The first French opera, *Cadmus and Hermione,* by Lully and Quinault, performed in Paris in 1673, crossed the channel almost immediately, influencing Dryden in his attempts at opera. The romantic, semi-historical romances of Madame Scudéry and the Countess de la Fayette afforded a second supply of story material, while Spanish plays and tales opened up still another. Sometimes the plots of Calderón or Lope de Vega came to the English at second-hand through French versions. Whatever the case, it was now evident that the national type of play had ceased to be written. From this time on every European nation was influenced by, and exerted an influence upon, the drama of every other nation. Characters, situation, plots, themes,—these things traveled from country to country, always modifying and sometimes supplanting the home product.

*Persistence of Elizabethan plays.* With this influx of foreign drama, there was still a steady production of the masterpieces of the Elizabethan and Jacobean periods. The diarist Samuel Pepys, an ardent lover of the theater, relates that during the first three years after the opening of the playhouses he saw *Othello, Henry IV, A Midsummer Night's Dream,* two plays by Ben Jonson, and others by Beaumont, Fletcher, Middleton, Shirley, and Massinger. It must have been about this time that the practice of "improving" Shakespeare was begun, and his plays were often altered so as to be almost beyond recognition. From the time of the Restoration actors and managers, also dramatists, were good royalists; and new pieces, or refurbished old ones, were likely to acquire a political slant. The Puritans were satirized, the monarch and his wishes were flattered, and the royal order thoroughly supported by the people of the stage.

Richard Boyle, Earl of Orrery (1621-1679), seems to have the doubtful glory of re-introducing the use of rhymed verse. Boyle was a statesman, as well as a soldier and a dramatist. During the ten years or so following the Restoration, he wrote at least four tragedies on historical or legendary subjects, using the ten-syllabled rhymed couplet which (at the moment) he borrowed from France. It runs like this:

> "Reason's a staff for age, when nature's gone;
> But youth is strong enough to walk alone."

No more stilted sort of verse could well be contrived for dialogue. Monotonous as well as prosy, it was well suited to Orrery's plots. He took a semi-historical story, filled it with bombastic sentiments and strutting figures, producing what was known as "heroic drama." Dryden, who identified himself with this type of play, described it as concerned not with probabilities but with love and valor. A good heroic play is exciting, with perpetual bustle and commotion. The characters are extricated out of their amazing situations only by violence.

Deaths are numerous. The more remote and unfamiliar the setting the better; and the speech should be suited to the action: hence the "heroic couplet." Pepys saw *Guzman,* by Orrery, and with his engaging frankness said it was as mean a thing as had been seen on the stage for a great while.

*John Dryden.* 1631-1700. In the history of the drama Dryden occupies a peculiar place. He had no great genius for the theater, and yet he imposed his ideas upon the English play-going world. He was that unusual product, a politician with a poetical mind. For a time he was attached to the Puritans, and wrote an ode on the death of Cromwell; but, on the accession of Charles, he found no difficulty in transferring his muse to the royalist party. Towards the end of his stormy life he became a Roman Catholic. Soon after the accession of William and Mary, the queen, as a mark of honor to the poet, ordered a performance of *The Spanish Fryar,* one of his best comedies. Among his last writings is rather an apologetic answer to Jeremy Collier's attack upon the stage. He died in May, 1700, and was buried in Westminster Abbey in the grave of Chaucer. He bequeathed his "dramatic laurels" to William Congreve.

*Dryden's plays.* Although Dryden began his career as playwright with the production of two or three comedies, yet it was in heroic drama that he achieved his great popularity. A brother-in-law, Sir Robert Howard, wrote a play called *The Indian Queen,* which had an absurd plot with a picturesque setting. Dryden assisted in its revision; and its success was such as to encourage him to write a sequel, *The Indian Emperor, or the Conquest of Mexico by the Spaniards,* which took the stage by storm. Later came *The Conquest of Granada,* in two parts with five acts each, the scene laid in unknown regions, and the story full of intrigues, battles, bull fights, revenge, ghosts and murders. Three distinct love affairs are threaded together. Another piece of this type, *Tyrannick Love,* has for its subject the persecution of the Christians by the Emperor Maximin and the sufferings of Saint Catherine.

Dryden tried his hand at opera, one of his efforts being the arrangement of Milton's *Paradise Lost* for a musical setting.

Some of this work was composed by the celebrated Englishman, Henry Purcell. Dryden and Davenant together re-wrote *The Tempest,* giving Caliban and Ariel each a sister for some unknown reason. *Romeo and Juliet,* revised by Dryden and his brother-in-law James Howard, had a happy ending, and was performed on alternate nights with the original play. In *All for Love, or the World Well Lost,* a revision of Shakespeare's *Antony and Cleopatra,* Dryden abandoned the heroic couplet and used blank verse; he also reconstructed the original play in such a way as to make it conform to the three unities. About 1678 he gave up the use of the heroic couplet altogether. His version of *Œdipus,* in collaboration with Nathaniel Lee, has already been referred to as being too ghastly and horrible for stage production, even in those days of strong nerves.

Dryden's influence was greater than would be thought possible from a study of any one of his dramas. As a playwright he did not consider himself wholly a success, and expressed his dislike and contempt of the stage more than once. Of certain of his plays he said, "I knew they were bad enough to please, even when I wrote them." He had no sense of the ridiculous, nor any conception of a natural, sincere portrayal of human nature. Ranting and absurd imagery often lie beside passages of real beauty. Dr. Johnson described his style as a "false magnificence." One comedy, *The Spanish Fryar,* and one tragedy, *All for Love,* deserve to be remembered. Far more interesting than the plays, however, are Dryden's discussions of dramatic questions. Like Mr. Shaw of the present day, he had the habit of writing long prefaces and comments as an accompaniment to the text. In these dissertations are to be found many sound principles, including the idea that dramatic rules should be deduced from a study of plays rather than from abstract speculation.

*Parody of heroic drama.* Other writers, Davenant, Etherege, and Sir Robert Howard, had also produced specimens of heroic plays, and by the time *The Conquest of Granada* reached the stage these clever gentlemen had grown tired of the species. Compared to Dryden they were nobodies in the literary world; but among them they contrived a hilarious burlesque called *The Rehearsal*,[1] in which these showy but shallow productions were smartly ridiculed. Dryden is represented as Bayes (in reference to his position as poet laureate), and his peculiarities of speech and plot are amusingly derided. Though *The Rehearsal* was condemned as "scurrilous and ill-bred," yet it served a useful turn in puncturing an empty and overblown style.

*Thomas Otway*. 1652-1685. As an intellectual force Dryden towered above his generation, yet there were other writers, such as Thomas Otway, who had far more dramatic power. Otway was a scholar, and first tried his fortunes as an actor without much success. He translated plays from the French, wrote several half-successful pieces, and at length made a name for himself in 1680 with a tragedy in blank verse called *The Orphan*. So great was the praise lavished on this drama that its author was called the English Euripides. In later years Dr. Johnson said that Otway "conceived forcibly, and drew originally, by consulting nature in his own breast." *The Orphan* kept the boards well into the nineteenth century, and famous actresses like Mrs. Barry and Miss O'Neill were renowned for their pathetic presentation of the part of the heroine. The second play on which the fame of Otway rests is *Venice Preserved*, produced in 1682. Even today it seems a good play, with fluency, imaginative wit and tragic power, such as inevitably holds the attention. The verse runs with ease and has an accent of sincerity. In the following extract the dying Pierre prays for his wife:

> "Then hear me, bounteous heaven!
> Pour down your blessings on this beauteous head,
> Where everlasting sweets are always springing,
> With a continual giving hand; let peace
> Honor and safety always hover round her,
> Feed her with plenty, let her eyes ne'er see
> A sight of sorrow, nor her heart know mourning. . . ."

Otway's life, which lasted only thirty-four years, was passed in poverty and desperate circumstances. His fame did not bring him to affluence. In one of his prefaces he says that he

[1] The same theme was used later by Sheridan in *The Critic*.

was "rescued from want" by the Duchess of Portsmouth. Some idea of the compensation received by dramatists in Otway's time may be gained from the fact that *The Orphan* and *Venice Preserved* each sold for one hundred pounds.

*Writers of comedy. Sir George Etherege.* 1634-1691. It is a relief to turn from the artificial and ponderous tragedies of the Restoration period to its comedies, which perhaps are not less artificial but certainly are not ponderous. Several influences—French comedy, the gay life of the court, the reaction from Puritan domination, and the participation of beautiful and talented actresses—combined to create a new type of comedy which was brilliant, superficial, and often quite indecent. The earliest writer of this sort was Sir George Etherege, whose works form a bridge between the comedy of humours of Elizabethan days and the comedy of manners as perfected by Congreve. One of Etherege's stage characters, Sir Fopling Flutter, is a Restoration type, and somewhat different from the stock types of preceding periods. Etherege's plays are rather poor in construction, and are surpassed in wit by those that followed; but they have the genuine Restoration-comedy flavor—frothiness and grace, mixed with the spice of naughtiness. After Etherege came four writers—Wycherley, Congreve, Farquhar and Vanbrugh—who stand for all that is glittering and frivolous in the comedy of the period.

*William Wycherley.* 1640-1715. The father of William Wycherley sent him to school in France, where he embraced the Roman Catholic faith. Upon coming to London he left the Roman Church (temporarily, as it turned out), entered the Temple as a student of law, and later became tutor to one of the more obscure members of the royal family. Four comedies, including *The Country Wife* and *The Plain Dealer,* came from his pen between 1670 and 1680. He offended the king, however, by a secret marriage and was thrown into prison for debt, where he remained for several years. Charles's successor, James, on witnessing a performance of *The Plain Dealer,* was so impressed with the genius of the author that he paid Wycherley's debts and gave him a pension of two hundred pounds a year. Prosperity, however, did not support his genius; for he produced no more witty plays. He returned to the Roman Church, received sundry comfortable appointments and lived to the age of seventy-five as a fashionable man of the city.

*William Congreve.* 1670-1729. Congreve, the most celebrated writer of this group, was the son of an English officer living in Ireland, and was educated at Trinity, Dublin. His first play, *The Old Bachelor,* written at the age of twenty-three, was a great success. *The Double Dealer,* following almost immediately, brought forth the praise of Dryden, the autocrat of English letters. At the age of twenty-seven Congreve had gained a prestige scarcely less in importance than that of Dryden himself. Not only as a comic wit, but as a writer of noble tragedy was he esteemed. He promised his hopeful managers to write a play a year, but the promise was not kept. *Love for Love* appeared in 1695, followed by *The Mourning Bride* two years later. After one more comedy, *The Way of the World,* which seems to have been something of a failure on the boards, Congreve, at the age of thirty, gave up writing for the stage. He affected to despise the profession of dramatist. Voltaire visited him, Dryden praised him, and Pope dedicated to him his translation of the *Iliad.* Swift, Steele, Lord Halifax, Mrs. Bracegirdle, and all the other fashionable blades and ladies of the time were his friends; and he had the honor of being buried in Westminster Abbey. In his praise it should be said that, for almost the first time in England, he brought to the service of the stage a *painstaking* art. He cared much about the way a sentence was built, about balance, and getting the right shade of meaning. His diction is exactly fitted for oral use; and his pictures of the world of wealth and fashion are diverting. Congreve is perhaps the only English writer who can at all be compared with Molière.

Sir John Vanbrugh (1664-1726) and George Farquhar (1678-1707), with Congreve and Wycherley, make up the celebrated quartet of Restoration wits, the creators of the drama of gallantry. Vanbrugh was of Flemish ancestry, and attained an eminent position as architect. His comedies were highly successful, showing careful craftsmanship, a genuine comic gift, and a constant flow of animal vigor. Farquhar was more sympathetic and human than Vanbrugh, but was likewise noisy and full of mirth.

The heroes of the Restoration comedies were lively gentlemen of the city, profligates and loose livers, with a strong tendency to make love to their neighbors' wives. Husbands and fathers were dull, stupid creatures. The heroines, for the most part, were lovely and pert, too frail for any purpose beyond the glittering tinsel in which they were clothed. Their companions were busybodies and gossips, amorous widows or jealous wives. The intrigues which occupy them are not, on the whole, of so low a nature as those depicted in the Italian court comedies; but still they are sufficiently coarse. Over all the action is the gloss of superficial good breeding and social ease. Only rarely do these creatures betray the traits of sympathy, faithfulness, kindness, honesty, or loyalty. They follow a life of pleasure, bored, but yawning behind a delicate fan or a kerchief of lace. Millamant and Mirabell, in Congreve's *Way of the World,* are among the most charming of these Watteau figures.

*Nature of Restoration comedy.* In almost every important respect, Restoration drama was far inferior to the Elizabethan. Where the earlier playwrights created powerful and original characters, the Restoration writers were content to portray repeatedly a few artificial types; where the former were imaginative, the latter were clever and ingenious. The Elizabethan dramatists were steeped in poetry, the later ones in the sophistication of the fashionable world. The drama of Wycherley and Congreve was the reflection of a small section of life, and it was like life in the same sense that the mirage is like the oasis. It had polish, an edge, a perfection in its own field; but both its perfection and its naughtiness now seem unreal.

Everywhere in the Restoration plays are traces of European influence. *The Plain Dealer* of Wycherley was an English version of *The Misanthrope* of Molière; and there are many admirable qualities in the French play which are lacking in the English. *The Double Dealer* recalls scenes from *The Learned Ladies* (*Les femmes savantes*); and Mr. Bluffe, in *The Old*

*Bachelor,* is none other than our old friend Miles Gloriosus, who has traveled through Latin, Italian and French comedy. The national taste was coming into harmony, to a considerable extent, with the standards of Europe. Eccentricities were curbed; ideas, characters, and story material were interchanged. The plays, however, were not often mere imitations; in the majority of them there is original observation and independence of thought. It was this drama that kept the doors of the theater open and the love of the theater alive in the face of great public opposition.

*Women playwrights.* Soon after the Restoration women began to appear as writers of drama. Mrs. Aphra Behn (1640-1689) was one of the first and most industrious of English women playwrights. Her family name was Amis (some writers say Johnson). As the wife of a wealthy Dutch merchant she lived for some time in Surinam (British Guiana). Her novel, *Oroonooko,* furnished Southerne with the plot for a play of the same name. After the death of her husband, Mrs. Behn was for a time employed by the British government in a political capacity. She was the author of eighteen plays, most of them highly successful and fully as indecent as any by Wycherley or Vanbrugh. Mrs. Manly and Mrs. Susannah Centlivre, both of whom lived until well into the eighteenth century, also achieved success as playwrights. The adaptations from the French, made by Mrs. Centlivre, were very popular and kept the stage for nearly a century.

*Collier's attack on the stage.* Although the Puritans had lost their dominance as a political power, yet they had not lost courage in abusing the stage. The most violent attack was made by the clergyman Jeremy Collier in 1698, in a pamphlet called *A Short View of the Immorality and Profaneness of the English Stage,* in which he denounced not only Congreve and Vanbrugh, but Shakespeare and most of the Elizabethans. Three points especially drew forth his denunciations: the so-called lewdness of the plays, the frequent references to the Bible and biblical characters, and the criticism, slander and abuse flung from the stage upon the clergy. He would not have any Desdemona, however chaste, show her love before the footlights;

he would allow no reference in a comedy to anything connected with the Church or religion; and especially would he prohibit any portrayal of the clergy. Next to the men in holy orders, Collier had a tender heart for the nobility. He said in effect that if any ridicule or satire were to be indulged in, it should be against persons of low quality. To call a duke a rascal on the stage was far worse than to apply such an epithet to plain Hodge, almost as libellous as to represent a clergyman as a hypocrite. Collier made the curiously stupid error of accusing the playwrights of glorifying all the sins, passions, or peculiarities which they portrayed in their characters. He had no understanding of the point of view of the literary artist, nor any desire to understand it.

Collier's attack, unjust as it was, and foolish as certain phases of it appear today, yet made an impression. The king, James II, was so wrought up over it that he issued a solemn proclamation "against vice and profaneness." Congreve and Vanbrugh, together with other writers, were prosecuted, and fines were imposed upon some of the most popular actors and actresses. Dryden, Congreve and Vanbrugh made an attempt at a justification of the stage, but it did little good. D'Urfey, Dennis, and others entered the controversy, which raged for many years. The public buzzed with the scandal set forth in *The Short View,* but did not stay away altogether from the playhouses. The poets answered the attack not by reformation, but by new plays in which the laughter, the satire, and the ridicule were turned upon their enemies.

## CHAPTER XXVII

# THE EIGHTEENTH CENTURY IN ENGLAND

The period . . . is distinguished by certain well-marked characteristics from any other in European literature. In none has the flame of poetry sunk so low; in none has the play of intelligence been more lively; in none has there been a more bountiful supply of sheer cleverness.—J. H. MILLAR, *The Mid-Eighteenth Century.*

In England in the eighteenth century only two writers, Goldsmith and Sheridan, were distinguished in drama. Men of brilliant minds were directing their efforts to other enterprises,—history, science, philosophy, or prose fiction. The status of the stage was shifting. The actor and playwright were no longer mainly dependent for protection and support upon the favor of royalty or some member of the nobility. Play-producing had become a business. The two companies, under Davenant and Killigrew respectively, which had received royal patents immediately after the Restoration, in the eighteenth century united and gave their performances at Drury Lane Theater. Somewhat earlier a license had been granted to another company which played at first in Lincoln's Inn Fields, but in 1733 settled at Covent Garden. In 1705 Vanbrugh the playwright built a theater at Haymarket.

Drury Lane Theater, which was under the management of Colley Cibber during the earlier part of the eighteenth century, afterwards came into the hands of David Garrick, who managed it for nearly thirty years. From him it fell to Sheridan. The century was marked by the appearance of great actors and actresses. Mrs. Oldfield, Mrs. Siddons, Mrs. Woffington, Charles Macklin, and David Garrick could lend distinction even to a mediocre play. There was a steady demand for the Elizabethans,—Shakespeare, Ben Jonson, Beaumont and Fletcher.  Shakespeare was revised, adapted, moralized and bowdlerized until very little of the original remained. Translations of Corneille and Racine were given, also the tragedies of Voltaire,—Alzire, Zaïre, Mérope.  In theory at least, the influence of critics was against the romantic temper of the Elizabethans and in favor of the more formal practices of the French.

*Addison's Cato.*  1713.  Early in the century the neo-classic influence was given a great boom by the triumph of Addison's *Cato,* in which the three unities are observed and the characters clothed in what was supposed to be antique dignity and grandeur.  The theme is Cato's stand for liberty against the suspected domination of Cæsar, and his choice of death rather than submission.  The verse flows with ponderous strength and has many quotable passages; but to most readers of today the play as a whole is monotonous and dull.  The London audience, however, greeted it with enthusiasm, and for a month it was played to crowded houses.[1]  The sentiments of liberty, put into the mouth of Cato, could easily be translated into political opinions of 1713.  Dr. Johnson reported that the Whigs applauded every line in which liberty was mentioned, and that the Tories likewise applauded to show that they were not to be outdone in admiration of freedom.  Voltaire, with easy assurance, called *Cato* the "first reasonable English tragedy."

*The vogue of classicism.*  In the years that followed, the weight of authority was largely on the side of the classic form, while the popular instinct steadily turned away from it.  Men of learning like Johnson, or men of curious genius like Smollett, came to London in considerable numbers, each carrying a play in his pocket; and that play was sure to be in the classic style of *Cato.*  John Home's *Douglas* (1756) was the only tragedy of its time that could compete in popularity, even for a short period, with Shakespeare and the pantomimes.  It was written in verse and is remembered today, when remembered at all, for its once-familiar school recitation piece, "My name is Norval." Of the score of classic pieces written scarcely one showed the flair for the theater or the human sympathy which covers all

[1] A month was a long run in the eighteenth century.

sins. English tragedy had lost its glory. *Cato* had killed the species.

*Ballad-opera, Italian opera and pantomime.* Meanwhile, there appeared during the century a number of sub-varieties of entertainment, such as the ballad-opera, which consists of a light, romantic story, partly spoken and partly sung, with pretty costumes and scenery, catchy music, and a fable which taxes the intellect but slightly. Interest in the ballad-opera was suddenly aroused by the success of *The Beggar's Opera,* written by John Gay and produced in 1728. The piece is of the mock-heroic type, the characters being pickpockets, informers and constables, and the plot full of diverting incidents. Under the apparently innocent story spectators could detect a sly satire upon the political and party leaders of the day. For weeks all London talked of the new opera, not only on account of its satire, but also because of its charm and gaiety. Gay wrote a sequel called *Polly,* but the Lord Chancellor refused to license its production, and it was brought out in book form by subscription.

Gay had many imitators, but there was no one in his immediate following who achieved an equal success. The style of the ballad-opera, however, has persisted and is one of the popular species of the stage of today. There were also in eighteenth century London successful productions of Italian opera. Regular producers, like Colley Cibber, resented this invasion of a foreign type of amusement; and Steele called it "an insult to the English stage," a mark of vulgar taste, and a sign of the decadence of the times. Even worse, in the estimation of these judges, was the revival of interest in the pantomime—a kind of play-acting which, as we know, is almost as old as man himself.

*Influence of Lillo and Moore.* There were two eighteenth century tragedies which deserve attention not so much because of intrinsic merit as on account of their influence upon European drama. The first of these is *The London Merchant, or The History of George Barnwell,* written by George Lillo and produced in 1731. The title indicates the play's chief claim to attention: namely, the hero is a tradesman and not a prince or a warrior. Even to an indulgent reader the piece is full of bad writing, tiresome characters and absurdities of situation; nevertheless it was a great success. Twenty-two years later, in 1753, appeared another and a better play, *The Gamester* by Edward Moore, which illustrated the same revolutionary ideas as to subject, theme and construction as did *Barnwell*. The notable thing about these plays is that their fame went abroad. Up to this time the English had imported, but scarcely ever exported their theatrical pieces. In France Diderot and Jean Jacques Rousseau were delighted with *Barnwell*, and Diderot used it as an illustration of his revolutionary ideas concerning the drama. His theory was that subjects should be taken from common life, that prose should be used, the unities abandoned, and much greater freedom allowed both in theme and form. In Germany the young Lessing was formulating similar principles in opposition to Voltaire and his classical dogma. The success of *Barnwell* and *The Gamester* gave these rebels the encouragement they needed.

*Minor writers and stock themes.* Among the irreverent scoffers who looked upon the current theatrical offerings with an ironical eye was Henry Fielding (1707-1754), whose genius, despite its undoubted greatness, never brought him to the front rank as dramatist. He experimented with comedy, burlesque, and adaptations from the French comic writers. The tone of good-humored satire, first heard in *The Beggar's Opera,* was carried much further by Fielding in his ridicule of politicians and plays. He became so brutal and indecent in his attacks, however, that the government was forced to interfere. In 1737 Parliament passed the Licensing Act, which amounted to an active censorship, through which the stage was freed from the worst forms of coarseness. Fielding was one of the earliest discoverers of the value of the "Little Theater" for plays which did not find a welcome on the commercial stage.

During this period of mediocrity there were many writers of comedy, though none of the first rank. *The Liar* and *The Minor,* by Samuel Foote, are still entertaining. Foote's fun lay chiefly in tags of current slang and local hits. Isaac Bickerstaff turned out librettos for comic operas. The stock themes of comedy constantly reappeared: the gullible and betrayed husband, the illicit amours of the city gallant, the conflict between town and country. Adaptations and translations were made wholesale from the French theater, while at the same time Shakespeare and the other Elizabethans were revamped and produced in extraordinary guise. George Colman the elder, well known both as manager and playwright, produced *King Lear* with a "happy" ending, made translations of Terence, and excelled most of his contemporaries in the charm and originality of his own pieces. As manager Colman had the distinction of producing Goldsmith's first comedy, *The Good Natured Man;* and he also wrote the Epilogue to Sheridan's *School for Scandal.* Two comedies held the stage for many years: *High Life Below Stairs* (1759), by James Townley, and *The Man of the World,* by Macklin, an actor-playwright who lived a full century. Richard Cumberland, whose best work was *The Wheel of Fortune,* wrote thirty-seven plays and created at least one memorable character in Sir Fretful Plagiary.

*Sentimental comedy.* Meantime English drama did not escape a kind of disease which had spread over Europe,—a disease illustrated most clearly by the "tearful comedy" (*comédie larmoyante*) of France. In general tearful comedy depicted innocence in distress, goodness pursued by evil, and modesty just at the point of being outraged by the rough and rude blatherskites of the world. The point of the play, of course, consisted in the triumph of virtue and the discomfiture of the bold bad man. The whole school was enveloped in an atmosphere of affectation and false delicacy—which, by the way, was the title of a play by Kelly. The structure of plot was in general better than the dialogue. Colley Cibber, manager, actor, and poet laureate, was inclined toward this type, as were also Kelly, Whitehead, and Arthur Murphy. As tragedy had committed suicide through *Cato,* so comedy expired "in the embraces of an artificial sweetness."

*Oliver Goldsmith.* 1728-1774. The dramatic dullness was at last broken by the appearance of Oliver Goldsmith, who was born in Ireland, educated partly at Trinity, partly in Edinburgh and on the continent. Having been apprenticed in his early youth to an apothecary, he actually attained a professional position as a doctor of medicine, and followed it at different times during his life. He was also an usher in a school, a writer of magazine articles, a poet and a playwright.

Goldsmith came to London in 1756; but it was not until about twelve years later that he produced *The Good Natured Man,* a play which made genial fun of tearful comedy, that is, of humbug and affectation in affairs of gallantry. Like every reform in art, that of Goldsmith heralded a return to nature. It was in no sense, however, a return to the indecent and sordid side of nature, but a bid for laughter and good sense instead of tears and sighs. A second play, *She Stoops to Conquer, or The Mistakes of a Night,* produced in 1773, was even better than the first. From a technical point of view it has faults of construction, inconsistencies and lapses; but beneath all these trifling defects are indestructible gaiety, a healthy tone, and the accent of genuine character. After the wantonness of Dryden, the indecencies of Vanbrugh, or the cloying sentiment of Hugh Kelly or Murphy, the penetrating, gentle humor of Goldsmith comes like a breath of mountain air on a sultry day. The plays have an ingratiating charm which disarms criticism and almost defies analysis. Doctor Johnson, whose judgments were seldom too lenient, bequeathed the famous remark about Goldsmith: "He left almost no kind of writing untouched, and touched nothing that he did not adorn."

*Richard Brinsley Sheridan.* 1751-1816. During the greater part of the eighteenth century the theater in Ireland had a brilliant history, and many celebrated people were connected with it. Macklin, Mrs. Barry, Mrs. Woffington, Congreve, Farquhar, and Sheridan were all Irish either by birth or education. Sheridan was born in Dublin of English parents, his mother being the author of a novel called *Sidney Buddulph.* She recommended her son to the headmaster at Harrow by telling him that Richard was a dunce. (One suspects that this was merely a literary gesture.) At the age of twenty-one Richard made a romantic elopement with Elizabeth Linley, one of the famous "nest of nightingales," and the couple came to London.

All of Sheridan's important work was produced between 1775 and 1779. Upon the retirement of Garrick, he became owner and manager of Drury Lane Theater, and so stepped at once into a position of influence. With occasional brilliant ventures as exceptions, he proved himself a rather careless and reckless man of business. He went into Parliament as Whig member and came quickly into notice as an orator, particularly at the trial of Warren Hastings. For twenty years or more he lived in London as man of fashion, professional wit and wastrel, and companion of dissolute princes. At his death Lord Byron said that Sheridan had written the best play (meaning *The School*), the best opera (meaning *The Duenna*), and had made the best oration of the times (the one in defense of Hastings). He closed his rather inflated eulogium by saying that with his death "Nature broke the die."

Although Sheridan was twenty-three years younger than Goldsmith, yet his period of productivity fell within the same decade as that which witnessed the hilarities of *The Good Natured Man* and *She Stoops to Conquer*. Sheridan took up the crusade against sentimental comedy at the point where Goldsmith dropped it, but he was not a prolific writer. He revamped a play of Vanbrugh's (*A Trip to Scarborough*), wrote one farce, one comic opera, one dull tragedy, and three comedies. He was a master of smart repartee, lively dialogue, and easy playfulness. His plots are somewhat better defined and more clearly constructed than those of Goldsmith; but he lacks the sunny, human quality that made the older man so lovable.

Even the least friendly critic would probably admit that *The School for Scandal* is the best eighteenth century play. It has entertaining turns of action and a steady flow of sparkling dialogue. Technically it is not quite so well constructed as *The Rivals,* and the famous screen scene was borrowed from Molière. The main plot and the under-plot do not dovetail very well, and the action often waits while the scandalmongers destroy the reputations of their friends; but the characters are alive, the plot is entertaining, and minor blemishes are easily forgotten. Charles Lamb said it was some compensation for growing old, to have seen *The School* in its

Mrs. Fiske, as Mrs. Malaprop, in Sheridan's *The Rivals*

glory, meaning not only the play but also the fine troupe of actors originally cast for its performance. It is said to have been the favorite stage piece of Washington. Hazlitt called it "the most finished and faultless comedy we have," and Henry James commented on its "literary atmosphere and tone of society."

One of Sheridan's excellences was his oral style, perfectly adapted to the tongue. This quality is marked in *The School* and *The Rivals,* which have long outlasted his other works. *The Duenna,* however, was remarkably successful in its time, running for seventy consecutive nights at Drury Lane, and holding the stage more or less for fifty years. *The Critic* belongs to high-class farce, and is rated as a masterpiece by no less a judge than Mr. George Saintsbury. It is a burlesque on the high-flown style of tragedy, and bears some resemblance to *The Rehearsal* (written mainly by George Villiers), in which the heroic dramas of Dryden were ridiculed. In *The Critic* the author showed great theatrical skill in managing the interplay between the mock actors, the manager, the critics and the author. Sheridan himself said that he valued the first act of *The Critic* more than anything else he ever wrote.

It is only too evident that in the progress of the eighteenth century English drama fell upon evil days. One realizes with difficulty the wealth of imagination and prodigality of genius which marked the drama of the Elizabethans. All its rich qualities had now disappeared. Sheridan and Goldsmith flared up like meteors. They produced the last of the English plays, previous to our time, which were both readable and actable. Mr. John Drinkwater, in commenting upon them, said: "After their death, the drama in England rapidly dropped into the gutter, and was not drawn out of it again until a hundred years had passed."

## CHAPTER XXVIII

# THE EIGHTEENTH CENTURY IN FRANCE, ITALY AND SPAIN

It was an age of reason, of severe literary discipline, which gave attention to the externals of technic more than to the mystery of life; and on its worst side ran to dead formula and meaningless phrase.—JOHN ERSKINE.

## FRANCE

At the beginning of the eighteenth century the prestige of France in all matters relating to literature and art was unquestioned. The great reign of Louis XIV had brought the country into the foremost place as a center of culture and learning. Peace had been relatively secure, and men of letters had been encouraged. Molière, Corneille, and Racine had all died within the last twenty-seven years of the seventeenth century, but the splendor of their achievement had not yet waned. Encouraged by their success and by the establishment of permanent theaters, playwrights increased in number, and new types of plays began to appear. One of these new types was called, rather inappropriately, *drame,* meaning a serious work not quite in the class with conventional tragedy. In this group were included the *tragédie bourgeoise,* dealing with commonplace people and often ending in comparative happiness; also the sad or tearful pieces (*comédie larmoyante*) which, transplanted to England, became the sentimental comedy of Murphy or Kelly. There was also the comedietta, a short piece, sometimes with music, resembling the "one-acter" of the modern vaudeville.

The writers who bridge the gap between the neo-classicists and Voltaire were often men of considerable talent, but there was no first-rate genius among them. Fontenelle, nephew of the great Corneille, was a writer of comedies, who broke away from the habit of writing in verse. Seven of his eight plays are in prose. Regnard sought to imitate Molière, but lacked the depth and earnestness which make an artist important. Dufresny, who collaborated with Regnard, consciously disengaged himself from the influence of Molière and attempted new themes and situations. Dancourt was an actor whose prose plays definitely enlarged the field of comedy. He portrayed the world of business, the demi-monde, and the common occupations; and at the same time he revived the old, yet ever new, conflicts between the sour guardian and youth, pictured the rogue entrapped in his own roguery, and the wise man caught in his weaknesses. The ideas of Dancourt were in the right line, but his equipment as dramatist was not sufficient to give much weight to his work.

There were likewise writers of tragedy, well thought of and fairly successful in their day, who have left little trace in dramatic history. The most distinguished of these was Crébillon the Elder, whose *Idoménée* (1703) and *Rhadamiste et Zénobie* (1711) were far above the level of the majority of the dramatic offerings of his time. There were Pompignan, who again brought Dido from the dead; Saurin who wrote about Spartacus; and Belloy who, among other themes, dramatized the triumphs of Titus. It is evident that the genius of modern classicism had passed the peak of its development; the decline had set in. Before the low-water mark was reached, however, there rose a man of energy and intellect—Voltaire—who achieved a somewhat hectic career as a dramatist and gave his name to a period.

*François Marie Arouet (Voltaire).* 1694-1778. The young writer Arouet, who is said to have written his famous tragedy, *Œdipe,* at the age of nineteen, adopted the name Voltaire after the successful production of that play in 1718. He was born in Paris of a middle-class family and educated by Jesuit priests. From his earliest youth he seems to have breathed skepticism and a spirit of rebellion against intolerance. Twice he was imprisoned in the Bastille, and more than once he was forced to leave France. One of his periods of exile (1726-

1728) was spent in England, where he shrewdly observed many contrasts to the customs in his own country. It was during this period that he sought out Congreve, who affected to disdain his visitor's admiration of him as a dramatist, saying he was but a "gentleman of the world." Voltaire promptly replied, "If you were but that, then I should not care to see you."

Voltaire's writings gained friends for him among the most distinguished people of Europe. In 1745 he became a member of the French Academy and was ennobled. Catherine of Russia corresponded with him, and Frederick of Prussia invited him to Berlin, where he remained for some years. The last twenty years of his life were spent on his estate at Ferney, near Geneva in Switzerland. When in 1778 he visited Paris again after a long absence, he was welcomed by throngs of the populace with an enthusiasm that spread throughout the city. Few kings or emperors were ever so honored. Voltaire, however, was then in his eighty-fourth year, and the presentations, visits, and ceremonies proved to be too great a strain on his health. He died in Paris, May 30, 1778.

*Voltaire's plays.* With the success of *Œdipe,* Voltaire won almost immediately the first place among living French dramatists. He continued to write for the stage for more than fifty years, producing something like twenty tragedies and a dozen comedies. He came near absolute failure in the latter species; but one of his pieces, *L'Enfant prodigue,* is still remembered. Such genius as he had for the stage lay in tragedy. *Zaïre* (1732) and *Mérope* (1743) are among the best of his plays. He obtained plot material from sources which before his time had never been touched, such as China, South America, and Mexico. Unfamiliar countries and ages attracted him; nevertheless, he did not overlook the conventional sources of supply. In *Mérope* he borrowed from the Italian Maffei; and Corneille, Calderón and Shakespeare all furnished him with ideas. He had the supreme theatrical gift of portraying a sharp conflict: between patriotism and love, as in *Brutus;* between love and religious duty, as in *Zaïre;* between love and filial obedience, as in *Alzire* and *Tancrède.* In the play *L'Orphelin de*

*Chine,* taken from an ancient Chinese story, the conflict between parental love and patriotic duty takes unusual turn. If a love interest were not present, he nearly always borrowed or invented one, *Oreste* being the only drama in which it is absent. In the best of his work the action is carried on with spirit and vigor; and if the original plot were not sufficiently striking, he created something to make it so.

Voltaire was greatly influenced by English drama, and in early life he expressed his admiration for Shakespeare. As he gained an authoritative position among men of letters in Europe, however, he became satirical about the practices of the English, calling Shakespeare "a savage with some imagination," and "a Corneille at London, elsewhere a great fool." He was annoyed by the English disregard for formality, by the exuberance of fancy, the mixture of comic and tragic elements in the same piece, the absence of the unities, and carelessness as to poetic form. Gradually he evolved what he considered to be a correct formula: namely, the use of the alexandrine rhymed verse, the observance of the unities, the differentiation between tragedy and comedy, and the presentation of people of importance as heroes. Sophocles, and after him Racine, were the true models. Addison's *Cato* was truly great, the only fine tragedy in English!

Superficially it would seem that Voltaire was attached to the classic mode; and in *Oreste,* it must be admitted, he actually followed his own theories to some extent, abolishing the love interest, the confidants, and other features which had been injected by Renaissance writers. The majority of his plays, however, reveal the fact that he was in practice very little troubled by rules classical or otherwise. Whenever the observance of the unities embarrassed him, he disregarded them; or, observing them, he caused an absurd foreshortening of events into an impossibly brief period of time. Only the shell of classicism—pseudo-classicism—was kept; its austere and noble tone, its reliance upon the deepest springs of human sympathy, its wholesome lessons of courage and endurance "purging the soul through pity and terror,"—these things were forgotten in the desire to be sensational at any cost. Nevertheless, Voltaire as dramatist stands head and shoulders above his fellow craftsmen. Writing of the eighteenth century, Saintsbury says: "Were it not for the prodigious genius of Voltaire, not a single tragedy of the age would have much chance of being read, still less of being performed; and were it not for that genius, and the unequal but still remarkable talent of Crébillon the Elder, not a single tragedy of the age would be worth reading."

In a peculiar way Voltaire was representative of his age. Skepticism, ardor for new things, rashness, zeal, keen sensibilities with comparatively little depth,—these were his characteristics. He was the crack journalist of his time. His great virtue was his courage in a fight; and his whole life was a battle for intellectual liberty, religious tolerance, and freedom of speech. The modern world would be infinitely poorer, more enslaved, had it not been for his courageous and lifelong rebellion against every sort of tyranny. Often he inserted his teachings of independence into his plays. Lacking in the gift of poetry and an understanding of the human heart, he was unable to give his dialogue the accent of real life and passion; but he was able to dramatize a thrilling story and at the same time preach a sermon. Voltaire as dramatist was merely the greatest in a poverty-stricken age; but Voltaire, the banner-bearer of intellectual and personal liberty, is still marching on.

*Production of Shakespeare in France.* Although in his later years Voltaire scoffed at Shakespeare, yet he was instrumental in introducing the English dramatist into France; and many strange "adaptations" were seen. In making these changes, the adapters were influenced by the older classical writers, such as Racine. Characters which in the original performed bloody and hair-raising deeds on the open stage, in the Gallic version were sent behind the scenes, and their crimes were related by that pest, the Messenger. Hamlet was changed into a dutiful son; *Lear, Macbeth,* and *Romeo* were provided with happy endings. As to *Lear,* there was grave doubt about the propriety of introducing a king as crazy as he upon the Parisian stage, whatever his end might be. Shakespeare, however, survived the indiscretions of friends and enemies alike, and gained a firm foothold, six of his plays being translated by the writer Ducis alone.

*Comedy in France.* The eighteenth century produced no Molière, but there were writers of acceptable comedy—LeSage, Piron, Destouches, and a few others. LeSage, in his prose comedy *Turcaret* (1709), satirized the corruption of financiers, the loose morals of the nobility, the absurdities of provincial pride, and the mean ways of shopkeepers. Destouches left at least seventeen comedies, among them *Le philosophe marié* (1727) and *Le glorieux* (1732), both worthy of being remembered. Piron is said to have accomplished the difficult feat of composing a comic opera and using but a single actor.

*Pierre Carlet de Chamberlain de Marivaux.* 1688-1763. More than thirty comedies remain from this romantic writer, who gave his name to a special style of language, *marivaudage,* meaning a delicate but affected expression of emotion. Marivaux avoided violence, but displayed a wealth of wit, surprise, and entertainment. He gave the first place to the heart rather than to the intellect, and so insinuated a romantic interest into plots which had very little action. His plays enjoyed great popularity, and are even now known on the stage. The characters are more natural than those created by earlier writers; and at the same time they are sophisticated and elegant. The theme is always love; and the "big" scenes always portray the crisis of some *affaire du cœur.*

*Pierre Claude de la Chaussée.* 1692-1754. It has been said that the chief business of La Chaussée was to afford the public the luxury of tears. His name is inseparably connected with the *comédie larmoyante.* He had imbibed some of the philosophy of Rousseau, and his plays can often be reduced to the thesis: Whatever is sanctioned by love is right; unrestrained actions are a sign of force of character; the heart and its passions must rule. Unfortunately, La Chaussée had not sufficient genius to prove his thesis. His plays were popular without being very highly regarded. Voltaire made fun of them; and other critics complained of their unreality and lack of strength. They are written in verse in which may be found many improving sentiments.

*Denis Diderot.* 1713-1784. One of the important intellectual leaders of the eighteenth century was Diderot, who had definite ideas concerning the reformation of the drama. He was not an admirer of the high-riding style of Voltaire; but he was greatly interested in English plays such as *The London Merchant* and *The Gamester,* which took for their chief characters people of the middle class. Diderot claimed that the theater had been too remote from real life, that it should be used as an educational medium, that prose was the more natural vehicle, and that the fable should illustrate the duties, temptations and peculiarities of the special class of society in which the hero finds himself. In other words, the stage should be used to teach men how to conduct themselves in their own sphere. Diderot's two principal plays, *Le fils naturel* and *Le père de famille,* written soon after the middle of the century, are dull and rather priggish, but the theories they set forth found a response. The *drame bourgeois,* which may be said to begin with the appearance of *Le fils naturel,* has not yet ended its course. The actions of kings and mythological heroes became, at last, of less importance than the experiences of Tom, Dick and Harry, who represent the common man. Followers of Diderot's theory wrote pieces no less concerned with bourgeois virtues, but better suited to the stage than those of their master. Sedaine, La Harpe, and Mercier continued the use of common themes in plays which now seem dreary and absurd, but were stirring for their time. The French stage then, as for the century previous, was far cleaner and more decent than the English stage of the corresponding period. Wives, sisters, and mothers could witness the *drame bourgeois* not only without injury to their modesty, but with benefit to their education. The air of the theater became a bit heavy and oppressive with its domesticity, but at least it was "near to the people."

*Pierre Augustin Caron (Beaumarchais).* 1732-1799. As Sheridan and Goldsmith afforded a brilliant exit for eighteenth century English drama, so Beaumarchais in France relieved the general dramatic stodginess of the dying century. The career of Beaumarchais is sufficiently remarkable in itself to afford a theme for a playwright. As an inventive genius he devised a new escapement for timepieces, and became "clock-maker to the king," Louis XV. He took the name Beaumarchais from the wealthy widow whom he married. After her death he was appointed instructor in music to the daughters of the sovereign; and after a second marriage and widowhood, he was again made some sort of court official. He was involved in lawsuits, and made and lost a fortune in speculation. During the American Revolution he financed the shipping of supplies and ammunition to the colonists, sending out his own cruiser, named "Le fier Roderique," in the D'Estang fleet. During the reign of terror he resided in Holland, and upon returning found that his mansion had been destroyed. He died the same year as Washington, with his claims against the United States government still unsettled.

At about the age of thirty-five Beaumarchais became interested in Diderot's ideas of drama, and sought to touch a pathetic vein in the tragedy *Eugénie* (1767), which treats of everyday events in the life of common people. The play was a failure; but in 1775 he won an extraordinary success with *The Barber of Seville;* only, however, after an initial failure and a revision of the first text. The play is in five acts, in prose, and the chief character, Figaro, is the lying, intriguing servant familiar to us since the time of Plautus. The plot, though simple, is full of surprising and amusing turns, the wit flows, and the character study gives excellent opportunity for the actor.

Nine years after his first success Beaumarchais wrote *The Marriage of Figaro,* which was so permeated with revolutionary ideas that public performance was forbidden. The author had to content himself with reading it in private houses. When in 1784 its presentation was permitted, the crowd at the Théâtre Français was so great that three people were crushed to death. Strangely enough, this "seditious" play in time became popular even with royalty. Enacted by amateurs of the court of Louis XV, the chief woman character was impersonated by Marie Antoinette. It is very amusing, even now. *The Barber* and *The Marriage of Figaro* are widely known

and accepted as the most famous French comedies of the eighteenth century, and among the celebrated comedies of the world.
They found a new sort of immortality in opera, *The Barber*
being composed by Rossini, *The Marriage* by Mozart.

## ITALY

For Italy, as for other sections of Europe, the seventeenth
century was a period of political and military strife, with the
art of the stage in a precarious condition. By the beginning of
the eighteenth century the *commedia dell' arte,* or improvised
comedy, had begun to decline. The stock types represented by
the masks and the conventional comic situations, however, continued to hold the stage. So firmly were they entrenched in the
popular favor that talented new writers could but with difficulty dislodge them. The low farcical entertainments consti-
tuted the most disreputable rival to regular comedy; but the
new art of opera, which had developed with surprising rapidity, was the most powerful rival of all.

*Carlo Goldoni.* 1707-1793. Regular comedy in Italy was
apparently about to expire when Goldoni appeared to bring it
back to life. He was a native of Venice, and began his career
by writing opera librettos. Gaining in experience and in technical skill, he cautiously attempted to replace the empty and
pornographic entertainments, which too often passed for comic
drama, by plays of innocent action representing contemporary
events and characters. One hundred and sixty comedies remain from his pen, twenty of which are in verse, the remainder
in prose, either of the Venetian dialect or the national language.
He is said to have written as many as sixteen pieces in one
year. His invention was remarkably fertile, and his sense of
comedy sprang from his understanding of the human emotions,
as real comedy always does. He was not profound, but he was
charming, witty, true to nature, with buoyant spirits and an
inexhaustible humor.

Another attempt at the purification of the stage was made
on quite a different principle by Carlo Gozzi (1722-1806),
who introduced the fantastic and remote. He dramatized the

familiar fairy tales, such as *Bluebeard* and *The Sleeping Beauty,* provided them with magnificent settings, and gave them to the public with considerable pomp and ceremony. Gozzi disliked the *bourgeois* style and parodied the comedies of Goldoni.

The writers of tragedy continued to treat the well known plots in the same old way, growing more and more stale with each repetition. Near the end of the seventeenth century the Academy of Arcadians had been instituted at Rome. This organization attempted to inject new life into tragedy, to broaden the field, and to abolish the old-time stage trappings. Among the few names which deserve to be remembered is that of Scipione Maffei (1675-1775), who possessed undisputed talent combined with sincere feeling. His tragedy *Merope* (1713) not only won great success, but aroused the admiration of Voltaire, and inspired the English John Home with the idea of *Douglas.* It is the last good play of the older Italian school. Metastasio (1698-1782) was educated as a musician under the Neapolitan composer Porpora, but won fame through his librettos. The earliest of these, *Dido abandonata* (1724), like almost all the work of Metastasio, is well constructed and entertaining on the stage even without the adjunct of music. He stands out, among the writers of the world in any language, as excelling in pure and harmonious lyric verse. In the later years of his life Metastasio held the post of court poet at Vienna.

*Vittorio Alfieri.* 1749-1803. The name of Alfieri is one of the greatest among Italian playwrights. He was of a wealthy and noble family, and, like Voltaire, was born with a passion for liberalizing the human spirit. He believed that the drama of his country could be purified most effectively through a re-introduction of the classic modes—(familiar words!)—and he therefore followed in the footsteps of Racine, taking up one, and only one, thread of action, discarding underplots and "relief," and concentrating on the advancement of the plot. The personages in his plays do not grow, but remain the same from the beginning to the end. He was attracted by horrible crimes and abnormal passions, was sombre in temperament and inclined to be somewhat violent in his expressions, but possessed of a kind of flaming intensity. Despising sentimentality and the merely pretty adjuncts of drama, he was able to infuse into his tragedies a kind of dark wisdom and sublimity. In almost every play he revealed his detestation of tyranny (which he considered identical with royalty), and his passion for liberty, which he regarded as the dearest thing in life. In five of his nineteen dramas the theme is the struggle for freedom, and one of them is dedicated to Washington, *"Liberator dell' America."* He pictured the degradation of Florence under the rule of the Medici, and deeply resented the condition of Italy in his own time.

## SPAIN

During the early part of the eighteenth century Spain was very little troubled by any ideas of progress in literature or the arts. The drama was at its lowest ebb. Only the more vulgar plays had survived from the previous century, and their presentation was often accompanied by coarse and brutalizing features. Even the language of Lope de Vega and Calderón had gone under eclipse, French being used at court and in smart society. Fashionable people patronized Italian opera or the occasional performance of a French play. Boileau's theories concerning poetry and the drama were translated into Spanish in 1737, but it was not until the latter half of the century, under the sovereignty of Charles III, that men of letters were encouraged. About that time some of the more severe restrictions of the Church were removed, and there rose the school of Salamanca, whose purpose was to revive interest in the literature of earlier days and in the rich drama of Lope and Calderón. Jovellanos, belonging to this school, left one good comedy, *The Honest Criminal,* but his powers, for the greater part of his life, were applied to politics rather than to literature.

Another group of writers during the eighteenth century sought to foster French drama. The leaders of this movement, one of whom was the elder Moratin, attacked the *autos,* representing them as too degrading and blasphemous to be tolerated by civilized people. Moratin wrote the first Spanish play modeled upon the French pattern, *The Female Coxcomb (Petimetra)* published in 1762. Moratin's son, Leandro, followed his father's ideas concerning the superiority of French importations, and as dramatist was even more celebrated. He gained the title of the "Spanish Molière," and his works are still admired. The condemnation of the elder Moratin was so effective that in 1768 the performance of the old sacred mysteries was forbidden. The most successful writer for the stage during the century was Ramon de la Cruz, who left upward of three hundred dramatic compositions, based mostly upon the everyday experiences of the middle and lower classes, and faithfully exhibiting national types of character. La Cruz attempted almost every species of stage entertainment, but was most capable in his farces, which display a rough and ready wit and considerable invention.

## CHAPTER XXIX

# THE EIGHTEENTH CENTURY IN GERMANY AND SCANDINAVIA

> Conceived in godhead, born beside the altars, slain in the brothel and born again in the soul of man—endlessly repeating in its own person the story of its immortal and rejuvenate god, Dionysus—the theater has lived the whole history of Europe. No art has spanned such range of time and forms and morals. No art has so changed and so remained the same.—KENNETH MACGOWAN, *The Theater of Tomorrow.*

## GERMANY

In the two hundred years from the death of Hans Sachs in 1576 to the debut of Lessing in the last quarter of the eighteenth century, Germany had not much dramatic literature to her credit. The devastating wars of the seventeenth century, with the necessarily long periods of recovery, delayed the development of all the arts. As in other countries, however, there was also in Germany first, a spasmodic interest in university productions of scholarly plays; and, secondly, a constant supply of popular and vulgar farce. In regard to the first class, the imitations of Latin comedies and the performance of the originals, we have considerable evidence. Luther had no objection to the theater, and regarded two of the apocryphal books, *Judith* and *Tobit,* as dramas, the first a tragedy, the latter a comedy. Some of Luther's followers used the stage for purposes of Protestant propaganda; and one of them, Paul Rebhun, introduced the custom of dividing plays into five acts and ending each act with a chorus. Zwingli, at Zürich, inspired a performance of *Plutus* by Aristophanes as early as 1531. Thomas Naogeorg and J. C. Hofteufel were good Latin scholars, able to make pleasing imitations of the Plautine comedies. Nicodemus Frischlin, who flourished at Tübingen in the last quarter of the sixteenth century, not only wrote plays in Latin (which were performed before the court at Stuttgart), but also in the vernacular. Under the veil of a biblical story he ridiculed contemporaneous characters, such as sly lawyers and extortionate innkeepers. Frischlin was generally regarded as too much of an innovator, especially by his learned colleagues; but early in the seventeenth century, at the Academy Theater at Strassburg, his plays with those of Naogeorg were performed with much success.

In 1587 appeared the earliest German *Faust* in story form; and in the same year a traveling company of English comedians became very popular in Germany. They visited Berlin, Dresden, Cologne and many other cities; and a little later we hear of the Duke of Brunswick and the Duke of Hesse keeping a troupe of English players at their courts. The Landgrave of Cassel, to whom is due the honor of building the first court theater, engaged English comedians who brought with them Shakespeare's *Hamlet, Lear, Romeo and Juliet,* and Marlowe's drama, *Doctor Faustus.* Whatever native products held the stage were mostly melodramatic horrors or pieces of coarse buffoonery, with Hans Wurst, the German clown, as the chief performer. The entertainments often included processions, fireworks and wrestling matches. An Italian troupe of players, coming in 1670, of course introduced Harlequin to the public, and his antics soon gained great popularity, especially in Vienna. Transposed into the German type, Harlequin became a composite of all the low comic characters of European stages, such as Hans Wurst, Eulenspiegel, the Fool, Vice or Devil of medieval days, or the sly servant, conjuror, or parasite of still earlier times. He was sometimes called Pickleherring (Pickelhäring), and his appearance was always associated with filthy jests. Sensational scenes could be contrived by means of flying machines, trap doors leading into the infernal regions, and transformation devices. Marionette plays were common; and persons in control of the stage strove to keep themselves independent of men of learning by doing without the written play. On the whole, at the beginning of the last half of the eighteenth century, civilized drama in Germany may be considered as being nearly at zero.

*The Leipzig School.* One of the first effective protests against the existing state of affairs came from a woman, Frederike Karoline Neuber (1697-1760), the director of a company of actors at Leipzig, and herself an actress of no small prestige. Madame Neuber found a supporter in Johann Christoph Gottsched (1700-1766), professor of philosophy and poetry at the local University. These two reformers attempted first to abolish Hans Wurst and his coarseness; second, to present definite forms of comedy and tragedy, instead of the slapstick variety show; and, third, to encourage the writing of new plays. Gottsched persuaded Madame Neuber to adopt the French classical school as a model, and published an essay on *The Art of Poetry,* based chiefly upon Horace and Boileau. A stage was installed like that of the Théâtre Français, and the dramas of Corneille and Racine were given. One of Gottsched's own plays, called *The Dying Cato (Der sterbende Cato)* was rather a feeble imitation of Addison. Neither Gottsched nor Madame Neuber saw any promise in the national traditions, nor did they attempt to portray national characters. They performed an inestimable service to the German stage, however, in deposing the vulgar clown and in clearing the way for the talent of a later time.

*The Storm and Stress School.*[1] Other critics who resented the degradation of the stage were in favor of the English school rather than the French. Young writers appeared, turning their eager attention to the stage and emphasizing the need of imagination and vigor, rather than formal rules. They wanted life, variety and color; and they were of course opposed to Gottsched and the Leipzig school. About 1760 this new movement became well defined in what is known as the Storm and Stress period. Among the young writers was Christian Gellert (1715-1769), who had considerable success with sentimental comedy. He was admired by Frederick the Great and enjoyed for a time the position of leader of a

[1] The name was derived from a play, *Sturm und Drang,* written by Friedrich von Klinger, performed in 1775.

"nationalist" school. Of far greater influence, however, was Martin Wieland (1733-1813), whose main service was the translation of twenty-two of Shakespeare's plays, thus inaugurating a study and appreciation of the English dramatist which has ever since been characteristic of German scholarship. Wieland also translated portions of the Greek tragedies, and was himself a composer of light opera.

*Gotthold Ephraim Lessing.* 1729-1781. Lessing's name belongs in the very first rank among writers for and about the theater. He was born in a Lutheran clergyman's family, and began very early to show his interest in the stage, having written a comedy before he was seventeen. He came under the notice of Voltaire, who employed him in making translations. During several years Lessing was one of the contributors to Madame Neuber's Leipzig theater; but his dramatic principles, as they defined themselves, became more and more opposed both to those of Voltaire and the Leipzig school. His first important play, *Miss Sara Sampson* (1755) was not at all suited to the tastes of the pseudo-classicists. In 1767 Lessing became associated with a group of actors in Hamburg, at which place he wrote the justly celebrated *Hamburg Dramaturgy,* in which he explained to the world the principles underlying the art of the theater. The great event of the year 1767, however, was the production of his *Minna von Barnhelm,* the first good comedy in the German language. During the next ten years two other dramas came from his pen; but he was slandered and misrepresented by Voltaire and his followers, and he suffered the usual fate of the man who is in advance of his age. The essays on dramaturgy were pirated, with the result that when he left Hamburg he was still poor, though famous. He became court librarian at Wolfenbüttel, and died in 1781.

*Lessing's plays.* Voltaire had warned his young translator against anything so banal as the *tragédie bourgeois* of certain of his contemporaries; but *Miss Sara Sampson,* Lessing's first mature play, is concerned with middle-class people, is written in prose, and was in general a challenge to the Voltairean school. Although *Miss Sara* is seldom read or acted today, yet in its time it was effective enough to popularize the new type, and became the center from which all modern German drama sprang. In *Minna von Barnhelm* the scene is laid in Berlin, the characters are easily recognized, the plot natural and quietly unfolded. Goethe praised it, and its influence was not only far reaching, but of a healthy and fertilizing nature. In 1772 Lessing wrote the tragedy *Emilia Galotti,* whose central situation is the same as that in the story of Virginia and Appius Claudius. The scene is transferred to contemporary times and the writing is in prose. In the powerful drama called *Nathan the Wise* (1777), the author turned to verse again. The Sultan Saladin in his palace at Jerusalem, at the time of the Second Crusade, is in need of money and other help. He sends for Nathan, a rich Jew, and tries to entrap him by asking which religion is best, Jewish, Mohammedan, or Christian. The astute Nathan does not reply directly, but relates the *Story of the Three Rings,* which causes the Sultan to exercise his own judgment. Certain features in *Nathan* were taken from Boccaccio.

*Lessing's theory of drama.* Interesting as are the plays of Lessing, especially *Minna von Barnhelm* and *Nathan,* yet it is by reason of his constructive criticism that he holds his high place. First, he did a much needed piece of work when he attacked the French theories of tragedy. Instead of merely denying their validity, he analyzed and explained genuine Greek classicism, and pointed out the differences between it and French classicism. He recognized the genius of Shakespeare, showing that only a perverted interpretation of Aristotle would exclude the English poet from the ranks of the great dramatists. Secondly, he pointed out that drama should aim at giving a first-hand representation of life; that tragic elements should flow from the character concerned, and should induce sympathy as well as surprise. And thirdly, he proved with his own work that vital stage creations should reflect all grades of common life and experience; that stilted, borrowed forms should be discarded, and that sincerity is of all things the first requisite. His own plays are well contrived and theatrical, in the good sense. His characters have the speech and motions of real men and women; they are interesting and vigorous.

Schiller considered Lessing the clearest and most liberal thinker concerning questions of dramatic art; and men of learning in every country today recognize him as the first reasonable European writer upon the principles and conditions which govern the modern stage. As a man, he can scarcely be too highly praised. What he taught, as the true basis of art, he incorporated into his own work and life. He was admirable not only in courage, but in patient tenacity of will, clever, cultured, unselfish. In his search for truth he was tireless, and remained charitable in the face of almost constant abuse and misunderstanding.

*Slow progress of reforms.* The improvements advocated by Lessing made their way but slowly. Coarse entertainments still held the stage, and many of the newer playwrights preferred to follow the well recognized path. Lessing's immediate follower, in the popular esteem, was August Friedrich Kotzebue, an official in the Prussian foreign service. He left about two hundred plays, and during his lifetime enjoyed a phenomenal popularity which extended over Europe and even to America. Sheridan took one of his pieces, *Die Spanier in Peru,* and adapted it for the English stage under the title *Pizzaro.* Another work called *Menschenhass und Reue,* translated into English and entitled *The Stranger,* held the boards for many years and afforded the English actor John Kemble opportunity for one of his most admired rôles. Kotzebue's strength lay in his expert stagecraft and his knowledge of the public taste, which was not high; but his work is noteworthy mainly as an index of the times. The next steps in dramatic progress were taken by Goethe and Schiller, whose work formed the logical and happy fulfilment of the purposes of Lessing.

*Johann Wolfgang von Goethe.* 1749-1832. The man who is best known as the creator of Faust was born into the family of a wealthy merchant of Frankfort, Germany, the eldest of six children. The mother was sympathetic, intelligent, and delightful, while the father entertained unusually advanced ideas concerning his son's education. Wolfgang entered the university at Leipzig while Gottsched and the French influence were still paramount; but illness caused him to leave Leipzig and later he went to Strassburg, where he became interested in Shakespeare and the so-called romantic school. During the years that followed he worked with great intensity in many fields—science, philosophy, mystic lore, history—and came to be looked upon as the greatest scholar of Europe. In 1791 he was appointed director of the Court Theater at Weimar, and remained in that position until 1817. During that time the German stage gained a prestige which it has never since entirely lost. The year 1794 saw the beginning of the friendship between Goethe and Schiller—a friendship which lasted until the latter's death. After Goethe's retirement from the management of the theater, he continued to live at Weimar, occupying himself with the completion of Faust, which he had begun in early life, until his death in 1832.

*Goethe's plays.* At the age of twenty-four Goethe threw himself into the thick of the fight raging between French classicism and the Shakespearean-romantic school, by producing *Götz von Berlichingen,* a prose tragedy of medieval chivalry obviously written under the influence of Shakespeare. In it the irregularities of the romantics were carried to an extreme: the plot carelessly constructed, the unities ignored, comic scenes interwoven with tragic. For the first time a German hero was used for the central figure in a tragedy; (only once before, in Lessing's *Minna,* had a German principal figure been used in comedy). The performance of *Götz* was in a sense the proclamation of a new day for the German stage; and its success, moderate as it was, was still sufficient to inaugurate a long period of popularity for plays dealing with knighthood and chivalry. Moreover, in this drama Goethe gave evidence of having taken up the work so courageously begun by Lessing in Hamburg, and avowed himself on the side of nationalism and freedom from French formula.

Besides a large number of pieces covering almost every type of stage production—masques, operettas, satirical dramas and comedies—Goethe wrote nine tragedies. *Clavigo* is said to be based upon certain events in the life of Beaumarchais, and, with *Stella,* belongs to domestic tragedy. Both plays are written in prose. *Egmont* is historical, while *Iphigenia in Tauris* was built upon the true classic principle. "*Iphigenia* is the noblest restoration of antique drama which the eighteenth century has to show. . . . It is a splendid illustration of the blending of the new humanity, born of the Renaissance, with the oldest humanity of all, that of the Greeks." [2] Although *Torquato Tasso* was not classic in subject, yet in the treatment of the plot Goethe here also adopted the Hellenic principles. These two dramas mark the culmination of classical achievements in Germany.

*Faust.* Several versions of the Faust tale appeared in the sixteenth century,[3] one of which was translated into English. In 1589 there came upon the London stage Marlowe's *Doctor Faustus,* which followed the German legend closely. From its nature, the story was susceptible of much spectacular elaboration, in the way of tricks of magic, transformations, and diabolical appearances. Marlowe's play, brought back to Germany by English comedians, enjoyed great popularity and finally became a puppet show, in which form it was seen by the child Wolfgang. In later years both Lessing and Goethe conceived the idea of writing a drama upon the subject, but Lessing never got any farther than notes for its construction. Goethe actually began work upon the poem in 1773 (the same year in which *Götz von Berlichingen* was written), working on it from time to time, brooding over it, and leaving it untouched for long periods. The complete poem, in two parts, was finished about two years before his death, fifty-seven years after its beginning, when the author was eighty-one years old.

The legendary material connected with Faust, the necromancer, was but the nucleus around which Goethe's poem grew. The final work far transcends its source, as it also far surpasses Marlowe's play. *Doctor Faustus* is a morality illustrating sin and its punishment; the German *Faust* is a drama of redemption. A great literature has accumulated around it, and there are many differences of opinion as to the finer subtleties of its interpretation; but the main point is clear: salvation

[2] Robertson, *The Literature of Germany.*
[3] See Chapter XXIII, *Marlowe.*

for men lies, first, in beneficent action rather than in penitential brooding; and, secondly, in the spiritualizing power of beauty and art. With Goethe, beauty and art are personified in the Greek Helen, through whom the soul is redeemed.

*Faust* can scarcely be criticised adequately by the same canons which apply to *Macbeth, Lear,* or *Phèdre.* As a whole, the poem is far more than a play; it is the vehicle of a philosophy, the poetic interpretation of the intellectual history of an entire life. A small portion only of the poem is ordinarily known to the playgoer,—that which deals with the wooing of Marguerite and the tragic experience of her love. This portion, arranged for the stage, has been translated into many languages, and was used as the basis of an opera by Gounod. Even this single episode shows the power of the author's genius. The simple, affectionate nature of Marguerite, the relation between Faust and Mephisto, the realism of the village life,—these features explain and justify the perennial charm and seductiveness of the drama.

*Goethe and the Weimar stage.* Besides opening the way for writers of his own country, Goethe made a practice of presenting foreign dramas on the stage at Weimar. In the six years from 1798 to 1804 there were given under his direction seven of the dramas of Schiller, Lessing's *Nathan,* and other German plays; also the tragedies of Racine and Corneille, and works of Shakespeare, Calderón, Terence, Plautus and Sophocles. Such a record is almost without parallel in the history of the theater. Following the example of Weimar, many other theatrical centers raised the standard of their productions; distinction and freedom of expression, which had been so discouragingly fought for by Lessing, became the inheritance of the next generation.

*Johann Friedrich von Schiller.* 1759-1805. Schiller was thirty years younger than Lessing, ten years younger than Goethe, and very nearly contemporaneous with Sheridan in England. He began his career as playwright with *The Robbers,* one of the many extravagant pieces dealing with knights and chivalry in imitation of *Götz von Berlichingen.* *The*

Firmin Gemier, as Mephistopheles, in *Faust*

*Robbers* was produced at Mannheim, the very year of Lessing's death, when the author was but twenty-three years old. As one might expect, it shows many of the faults of youth and of the school to which it belongs. Even Goethe was not pleased with the success of a piece which seemed to him full of false rhetoric and sensational appeal. The next play of Schiller's proved a failure; but *Love and Intrigue (Kabale und Liebe)* was an immediate success. It is the story of an unhappy marriage between people of different stations in life, and is genuinely national in its character portrayal. In 1787 came *Don Carlos,* which not only won admiring audiences in Germany, but carried Schiller's name far beyond its borders.

Twelve years elapsed between the appearance of *Don Carlos* and the next play, during which time the author married, studied the Greek tragic poets, and became immersed in the history of his own country. Most important of all, about 1794 began his friendship with Goethe. Five years later the three *Wallenstein* dramas, in verse, were given at Weimar under the management of Goethe, with a success that has rarely been equalled on any stage. From that time, his dramatic trend was determined. Turning definitely to history for his subjects, he displayed, with each succeeding work, an extraordinary technical skill, an ability to appeal tenderly to the heart, and a genuine talent for the theater. His weakness lay in a tendency to over-idealize his characters, to indulge in declamation at the expense of concentration.

When *The Maid of Orleans* was first performed in 1801 at Leipzig, the occasion was one of unparalleled triumph for the author. As he left the theater he found the audience outside, standing silent, with bared heads, waiting to do him honor, while parents lifted their children high so they might see him. In *The Bride of Messina* Schiller used the classic theme of Nemesis following wrong-doing, and employed the Greek chorus. *Wilhelm Tell,* his last play, is in many respects his best. The portrayal of the mountain scene and the conflict is brilliant, and the lines ring with manliness and true independence. Its splendid poetry and the note of national struggle stirred the hearts of all Germany.

## SCANDINAVIA

As education and culture spread over Europe, theaters began to be established in countries not heretofore heard from in matters connected with the dramatic art. Norway and Denmark, united politically until 1814, had a common language and a single intellectual center, Copenhagen, where a playhouse was opened in 1720. From time to time companies of foreign players visited the city, giving the works of Molière, Racine, and other French writers. The king, Frederick IV, was not greatly pleased with these foreign offerings, and invited Ludwig Holberg (1684-1754), a native of Bergen, Norway, to try his hand at a drama. Holberg had settled at Copenhagen after having filled various positions as tutor, college professor, and preacher. His first attempts at comedy were so successful that he continued to write for the Copenhagen stage, providing no less than twenty-eight plays in five years. For a time, during the reign of Christian VI, all theaters were closed; but about the middle of the eighteenth century they were again opened under the patronage of a new king, Frederick V. Again Holberg supplied the demand for plays, writing at least six more comedies.

Among the works of Holberg is a *Plutus,* an imitation of Aristophanes, and *Melampe,* a parody of the high-stepping French tragedy. For the most part, however, his plays are prose comedies of social life, concerned with the affairs of common people. In a series of six pieces each one has for its subject a popular superstition, such as witchcraft, alchemy, and the like. Another group is devoted to portraying the "humours" of mankind, somewhat in the vein of Ben Jonson; still another is concerned with intrigue and satire. In *The Political Pewterer* ridicule is turned on an ignorant upstart who claims to know all about public policies and methods of government. Holberg, like many another playwright, found his subjects for satire in such universal types as the snob, the bragging soldier, the dandy just returned from France, and he portrays them with humorous insight and close observation. He had the good sense to take national life as the basis of his work, winning the title of "Father of Danish literature." His comedies have also been much admired in Germany and in other parts of Europe. Schlegel said of him: "His pictures of manners possess great local truth; his exhibitions of depravity, folly, and stupidity are searching and complete; in strength of comic motives he is not defective; only he does not show much invention in his intrigues." Perhaps his most important service was in helping to restore saneness and reality to a stage which had become partially demented through Voltaire and the ravings of the pseudo-classicists.

The Prussian poet Klopstock, who visited Denmark in 1751 by invitation of the king, Frederick V, attracted pupils and followers, one of whom, Johannes Ewald (1743-1781), turned his attention to the theater. He based the plot of one of his tragedies on a Danish legend found in the Saxö Chronicle, and thus made a beginning of a truly national type of drama. A satirical piece by Ewald called *The Brutal Applauders* dramatized the conflict between the supporters and opponents of foreign plays. Ewald had an unhappy life, with wretched poverty, until shortly before his death, when he was pensioned by the government.

Another writer, Johan Herman Wessel (1742-1785) won considerable success with a parody of French tragedy called *Love Without Stockings*. It was written in alexandrine verse, showed an absurd regard for the unities, and was altogether so clever and amusing that it materially helped to drive the worst type of imitations from the Danish stage.

## CHAPTER XXX

# FRANCE: 1800-1875

The qualities of writing best fitted for eager reception are either such as startle the world into attention by their audacity and extravagance; or they are chiefly of a superficial kind lying upon the surfaces of manners; or arising out of a selection and arrangements of incidents, by which the mind is kept upon the stretch of curiosity and the fancy amused without the trouble of thought . . . there never has been a period, and perhaps never will be, in which vicious poetry, of some kind or another, has not been far more generally read than good.—WILLIAM WORDSWORTH, *Supplement to the Preface to Lyrical Ballads.*

The "well-made play" of Scribe, and later of Sardou, with the pseudo-psychology of Dumas *fils,* held the European stage. . . . —STORM JAMESON, *Modern Drama in Europe.*

The outstanding literary commotion of the late eighteenth and early nineteenth centuries was of course the romantic movement, most evident in Germany but assimilated by each country according to its bent. Romanticism, reduced to brief terms, inculcated first the importance and dignity of man as an individual; and, secondly, the power of nature as a solace and an inspiration. Trailing along in the wake of these two main ideas were a renewed interest in local legends, medieval history, many half-forgotten heroes, and what has been called a "renascence of wonder." Somewhere Mr. Gilbert Chesterton has suggested that the true romantic regards life and the cosmos as an adventure rather than a scheme. Looked at from the vantage point of distance, the romantic movement, like most other literary reforms, was simply a protest against dullness, pedantry and rules that had lost their efficacy.

For three-quarters of the nineteenth century, France alone

produced a drama not of the first rank indeed, but interesting enough to achieve European popularity. There were three groups which gradually replaced the pseudo-classic Voltairean play: melodrama (which had practically merged with the *drame bourgeois*); secondly, the romantic play (really a literary variation of the melodrama), which flourished roughly from 1830 to 1840; and thirdly, the social drama, which evolved from the vaudeville sketch through the hand of Scribe.

*Melodrama.* The germ of melodrama, doubtless latent in several types of play, was conspicuously present in the *drame bourgeois,* which must present "a slice of life," and emphasize those features which would make the audience hold its breath and curse the villain; and it proved to be only a step from the serious study of middle-class life to the sensational claptrap in which thrills occur in every scene, characterizations are in black and white, and the *dramatis personæ* always the same, namely, the noble hero, the distressed heroine, the villain, and the "comic." Guilbert de Pixérecourt (1773-1844), one of the prolific writers of the early nineteenth century and sometimes called the "Corneille of the boulevards," wrote as many as one hundred and twenty plays, a full half of them belonging to the lurid school. By the end of the first quarter of the century, melodrama had become so popular that many French theaters were kept open by this type of play alone, and more than a score of writers were employed in supplying their needs. The very nature of this species, however, is such that the thriller of yesterday becomes the commonplace of today; and thus there is ever a need for greater and greater sensation. Frederick Soulié (1800-1847) went practically to the extreme of violence in picturing murders, extraordinary escapes, burning buildings and maniacal villains.

## ROMANTICISM

Translated to the stage, romanticism seems at this distance to be no more than a glorified phase of melodrama; yet the romantic play in general offered better verse, a higher literary quality, comedy of a more refined type, and characters more humanly conceived. The drama of romanticism was excellent to read as well as to act.

*Alexander Dumas the Elder.* 1803-1870. The first successful play of Dumas the Elder, *Henry III et sa cour* (1829), was the logical sequence of melodrama and the link between it and the later romantic school. The action of *Henry III* is set in the sixteenth century; and its theme, adultery, became from that time the theme *par excellence* of the French stage. The action of *Antony* (1830), laid in modern times, also deals in seduction, murder, and melancholy resentment against the social code. Dumas collaborated with many men of letters; and as his popularity as novelist and playwright increased, managers often attached his name to plays which he had not written. In an edition of his works published in 1863 the dramas, written either wholly or in part by Dumas, fill fifteen volumes. He used many historical themes and organized the *Théâtre historique* for the production of his special type of play. *Le tour de Nesle* (1832) contains perhaps the essence of his genius and best illustrates his style. It is a historical piece with "gloomy medieval towers, postern gates, secret panels, ambushes, a criminal queen, corpses flung into the river, flashes of lightning in the storm, curses. . . . Now his medieval horrors are tawdry, and his heroes make us laugh. In his own day, they swept all before them." [1]

*Victor Hugo.* 1802-1885. Although it was Dumas who lit the torch, yet it was Hugo whose magnificent windmills fanned the romantic blaze into a conflagration. Hugo's father was an officer in the French army, and Victor's childhood was spent in various parts of Europe—Corsica, Spain, Elba, Italy. His education, necessarily irregular, was carried on at the *Lycée Louis le Grand* at Paris, where at the age of sixteen he took prizes for poems and wrote his first tragedy, *Inez de Castro.* Among the trappings for *Inez* were a tomb, a hall with a throne, a scaffold, executioners with torches, and a ghost. These appurtenances would be of no consequence were it not for the fact that they reappear in *Hernani* almost to an item. During the next few years, Hugo worked out a set of prin-

[1] Wright, *History of French Literature.*

ciples for the stage, which he set forth in his preface to *Cromwell* (1827). The chief feature of the "new" theory was the necessity of getting away from the conventional formalities of classicism *à la Voltaire*. In Hugo's opinion the unities of time and place were non-essential, action was of supreme importance, the style though poetic should be "natural," and the couplets which had so long been embedded in tragic verse should be discarded. The grotesque should be mingled with the terrible, as was illustrated in the comedy of the Greeks, in Dante, and in Shakespeare, Molière and Goethe.

*Cromwell*, Hugo's first published play, illustrated several of these principles; but it was not a first-rate piece of work, even for melodrama. In 1830, however, with the production of *Hernani*, Hugo's creed was trumpeted to the world. The plot turns upon a point of Castilian honor which required Hernani, at the moment when his happiness seemed assured, to take his own life in fulfilment of a vow made to a brother rebel. The first night of *Hernani*, February 25, 1830, was one of the notable performances in the history of the stage. The adherents of the old school and the adherents of romanticism met at the theater and, as the play progressed, fought their battle scene by scene with hissing, shouting, cane-rappings and hand-clappings. The struggle continued to some extent during succeeding performances, and even spread to outlying cities. It would seem that in the end the classicists were routed. *Hernani*, extravagant as it seems today under a cold analysis, and unreal as are its characters, is yet an amazingly interesting play, with passages of fine lyric poetry, picturesque settings and stirring incidents. Robert Louis Stevenson has described his almost feverish absorption, sitting up all night to read it; and Wright, the historian of French literature, notes that "yet, eighty years after it was written, *Hernani* can still make an audience at the Théâtre Français weep."

Hugo's next play, *Le roi s'amuse*, another illustration of its author's dramatic principles, was somewhat of a failure at its first performance; and a second appearance was forbidden by the government on account of the character attributed to the king, Francis I. The story, based upon the tragedy of the court jester, Rigoletto, who murders his own daughter under the supposition that he is killing the king, her seducer, is familiar to the world through Verdi's opera. In three plays, *Lucrèce Borgia, Marie Tudor,* and *Angelo,* written between 1832 and 1835, Hugo employed prose, while otherwise adhering to his romantic principles. Robbed of the splendor of his verse, these plays show plainly as melodramas, clever, but empty of serious meaning. In *Ruy Blas* (1838), the author returned to poetry, and created an amusing comedy, which many critics regard as the crowning piece of his dramatic work. With *Les Burgraves* (1843), in which the legend of the sleeping Barbarossa was used, his instinct for the stage deserted him. The characters are grandly conceived but have no breath of life. Its career on the stage was brief, and never again, during life, did Hugo offer a play to the public. *Les jumeaux* and *Torquemada* were performed after his death.

By the end of the third decade of the nineteenth century the fever of romanticism was dying down. Critics were finding out its weaknesses, and comic playwrights were parodying its extravagances. As a school the movement passed out of sight and new types won the popular favor. Goethe, looking back in later life on his period of romanticism, judged its principles unsound. All Europe lived through a similar period, and, when the vitality of the movement was spent, turned to modes of expression more closely associated with contemporary life, one of which we have called social drama.

## Social Drama

*Eugène Scribe.* 1791-1861. The form of dramatic composition known as vaudeville was a short sketch in verse, either recited or sung, used at country fairs and other popular but mediocre resorts. It might sometimes be a parody of a more pretentious play, or the dramatization of a short, lively anecdote. One of its features was the insertion of couplets to mark a climax, or the point of a jest, or a special piece of witticism. In 1816 Eugène Scribe, after making no less than fourteen failures, wrote a vaudeville called *Une nuit de garde nationale,* which was brisk and dramatic and gained an immediate success. Starting with this modest form, Scribe enlarged its scope and strengthened its structure until, in his hands, the *comédie-vaudeville* developed into a full-fledged play. His vogue suddenly became so great that in 1820 the manager of the Gymnase Théâtre contracted for all Scribe's writings for a period of ten years. Collaborators were secured, and in the decade beginning with 1820 he brought out something like one hundred and fifty pieces, all more or less after the enlarged vaudeville pattern. His first "regular" play, *Valérie*, in three acts, was performed at the Comédie Française. Scribe is generally called the inventor of the *comédie-vaudeville*,—a form which has considerable intrigue, lively dialogue, and unfailing movement. The formula may be turned to farce, sentimental comedy, mystery play, or domestic drama,—in each it is stage-proof. As examples of a sort of mechanical perfection, with links of action neatly joined, ingenious incidents, and promptness of come-back, Scribe's plays were a complete success. Occasionally too a character escaped the workshop and emerged into the world of reality. Professor Matthews asserts that no other maker of plays, either before or since Scribe, was ever so uniformly successful, and over so wide an area. His period of activity covered nearly the first half of the century, during which time he wrote about four hundred dramatic pieces, twenty being produced in a single year. His enormous output is comparable only to that of Lope de Vega, Hans Sachs, or the elder Dumas. His plays brought him not only a princely income, but secured for him the honor of a seat among the forty immortals of the French Academy.

*Émile Augier.* 1820-1889. By the time Augier had arrived as a dramatist, the strife between the romantic and classical school had abated. The group to which he belonged tried to avoid both the dullness of the neo-classicists and the absurdities of the romanticists. Augier's career began in 1844 with the performance at the Odéon of a comedy in two acts, written in alexandrine verse and entitled *The Hemlock* (Ciguë). The play ran three months and was subsequently taken into the repertory of the Comédie Française. In this first piece the author displayed the characteristics which marked all his work,—a sure technique, a knowledge of stage effects, understanding of human nature and an absence of sentimentalism. The next six dramas were also in verse. *Gabrielle* (1849) was notably successful, placing its author in a commanding position. Even with the prestige of these seven works, Augier had not yet come to the maturity of his powers. In 1853 he began writing in prose and collaborated with various men of letters, producing a coolly satirical type of comedy not quite like anything the European stage had heretofore seen. *Le gendre de Monsieur Poirier* (1854), by Augier and Jules Sandeau, was his first masterpiece in collaboration. It is in four acts and has for its theme the clash between a rich, middle-class father-in-law and a spendthrift, worthless but aristocratic son-in-law. It is dramatic and sincere, and is universally considered one of the best, if not the very best, comedy of manners of the nineteenth century. Two other plays, *Aventurière* (in verse) and *Le fils de Giboyer* (in prose) reached the high-water mark of success in their class.

For a period covering the entire third quarter of the century Augier continued, often with collaborators, to produce excellent dramas, not all of which were immediately successful on the boards. His partners included Sandeau, Alfred de Musset, Labiche, Edouard Foussier, and others of high ability. Sandeau, Musset, and himself were members of the Academy. The plays were generally satirical, attacking false emotionalism and sickly taste; and so effectively was it done that active resentment was aroused amongst editors, clergymen and politicians. One of Augier's greatest services, however, was proving to the public that French social drama need not always be salacious. Even before his time, the grip of the courtesan had been sufficiently strong; and Dumas the younger, whose career was contemporaneous with that of Augier, had as it were completed the glorification of the harlot. Scribe, Sardou, and other less gifted writers—taking perhaps from romanticism the idea that the claims of passion are superior to those of loyalty or faithfulness—had brought upon the French stage the reproach of looseness and immorality. A reading of the mid-century social dramas would almost convince a stranger to France that the only respectable, kind people in the country were the demi-mondaines. Augier in 1855, in *Mariage d'Olympe,* treating a theme similar to *La Dame aux camélias* by Dumas, answered, in a measure, the false sentimentalism about the life of the courtesan with an unsparingly truthful picture of the essential tawdriness of such an existence. Augier's challenge was not primarily a demand for conventional respectability, but a demand for honesty. He believed in the dignity and sacredness of the home when built upon faithfulness and honor. He threw the searchlight upon what seemed discreditable in the ideas of Dumas, and so stands as a positive force in the shaping of nineteenth century drama. In his own work he achieved simplicity and directness without falling into the dull pedantry of the pseudo-classicists; and he made his plays interesting without the excesses of romanticism.

*Alexandre Dumas the younger.* 1824-1895. At the beginning of the last quarter of the nineteenth century three men, Augier, Dumas the younger, and Victorien Sardou were considered the leaders of dramatic activity in France. The influence of Strindberg and Ibsen, never at any time so powerful in France as elsewhere in Europe, had not yet even begun to make itself felt. Alexandre Dumas, son of the exuberant creator of *Monte Cristo* and *The Three Musketeers,* was the author of a dozen or more important plays which had appeared between 1850 and 1875. *La dame aux camélias,* a dramatization of a novel by the young Dumas, had to wait three years for a stage performance, which was finally obtained in 1852. Its immediate success, not only in France but in other parts of Europe and in America, was one more indication that the theater-going public was eager to sentimentalize over the sorrows of the professional light sister. Hugo's Marion Delorme had been one of the earliest presentations of this class, as Nana, Zaza, Marguerite Gautier and others were among the later types. *La dame aux camélias,* while essentially vulgar and melodramatic, yet bears marks of imaginative and theatrical power.

Dumas's second play, *Diane de Lys,* had the same subject as the first; while the third and in many respects the best of all his plays, *Le Demi-monde,* varied the theme slightly by depicting the attempts of a clever but socially discredited woman to reestablish herself in respectable society. It is regarded by certain critics and playwrights as the model nineteenth century comedy. Though his skill in construction sometimes failed him, yet Dumas always had a brilliant, diamond-like edge. He created genuine comic characters, also charming young women of the world, though many of his dramas have thoroughly disagreeable subjects. In his later works he regarded himself as a moral teacher, meanwhile asserting that the stage, by its very nature, is immoral. His theories, as stated in his prefaces and dramatic essays, seem contradictory and puzzling; and his obsession with sex amounted almost to mania. In eleven plays, written before 1880, the subject of illicit love was the theme. All his genius, undoubtedly of a marked character, was turned towards the contemplation and analysis of seduction, adultery, and the passions which oftenest conflict with honor and faithfulness.

*Victorien Sardou.* 1831-1908. Perhaps no French author is better known in England and America than Sardou, the author of *Les pattes de mouche, Théodora, Divorçons, La Tosca,* and other plays to the number of at least two score. Sardou was a member of the Academy and gained a fortune through his dramatic works. His first piece was a failure, and he had some years of obscurity. In the five years from 1860 to 1865 he wrote comedies, farces, and opera librettos. Of these, *Les pattes de mouche* and *Nos intimes* have been adapted, translated, and performed in several different versions in England and America. His successes, slight in comedietta and farce, reached their highest peak in social comedy, such as the amusing but indecent *Divorçons.* Sardou's merit lay in his gift for shaping every situation, almost every human experience, to the requirements of the acted scene,—a cleverness which seems to have excelled that of almost every other playwright in the whole history of the drama. He was deficient, however, in his understanding of the more serious and nobler passions of men and women, and he also lacked the sincerity required in artists of the first rank.

In France during the nineteenth century the habit of collaboration flourished. Halévy and Meilhac were notably successful in their literary partnership from about 1869 to 1881, writing society dramas, comic operas, and librettos for grand opera. Bizet's *Carmen* is the work of their hands, also the popular comedy *Froufrou*. Octave Feuillet (1821-1890) followed the example of his more distinguished contemporaries and gained considerable fame as a delineator of frail women. His heroes are weak and the tone of his plays is unhealthy. Alfred de Vigny and Alfred de Musset, both men of genius, made contributions to the stage, but gained their finest laurels in the field of poetry rather than in drama.

## CHAPTER XXXI

# THE VICTORIANS AND THEIR PREDECESSORS

Stories invented for the stage are more compact and elegant, and more as we should wish them to be, than true stories out of history.—FRANCIS BACON.

In England the romantic movement, so far as drama was concerned, was not so much a failure as an anti-climax. A race of play-goers nourished on *The Spanish Tragedy* and *Arden of Faversham,* for example, could not goad themselves into a riot over such a play as *Hernani.* Moreover, the art of the theater in England, during the greater part of the nineteenth century, was undergoing an eclipse. In a previous chapter it has been noted how the German Kotzebue, a third-rate writer of the romantic school, for a time took possession of the stage. In five years, from 1796 to 1801, twenty of his plays were translated into English and some of them appeared in several versions. Sheridan, who occupied the important position of manager of Drury Lane Theater, twenty years before (1779), had parodied the absurdities of the romantic style; nevertheless he not only produced some of Kotzebue's works but adapted *Die Spanier in Peru* for his London stage under the title of *Pizzaro,* which in a year ran through twenty editions and was translated back again into German. With the conservatism and lethargy which is characteristic of the stage in all but its rare creative periods, the English theater continued to exploit the Kotzebue-Sheridan type of play long after the life had gone from it.

Matthew Gregory (Monk) Lewis (1775-1818), with his *Castle Spectre* and other plays, had a sensational though transitory success. He depicted a fantastic world of knights, bandits, ghosts, melodramatic horrors and impossible events. Even Lewis was outdone, however, by Charles Robert Maturin

(1782-1824), who wrote *Bertram, or the Castle of St. Aldo-
brand,* brought out by Sheridan at Drury Lane. Mrs. Oliphant, in her *Literary History of England,* describes *Bertram*
as a "play of the most wildly Satanic character, dealing with
crimes of primitive magnitude, with terrific storms and equally
terrific bloodshed, to appall the terrified reader," and says that
it is difficult to imagine how it could have been put on the
stage at all. Sir Walter Scott praised it, though somewhat con-
servatively. Byron was enthusiastic over it, and the public
flocked to it. The result, for the author, was a momentary
notoriety and the handsome sum of a thousand pounds. Other
plays by Maturin followed in a similar vein; but at the second
one even Byron gave up, calling it Maturin's Bedlam and a
nightmare.

In the midst of this riot of melodrama appeared Joanna
Baillie (1762-1851), who conceived the stage, as it had so often
been conceived before, as a means of education and instruc-
tion. She wrote three volumes of *Plays on the Passions,* the
first of which came out before the end of the eighteenth century, the second in 1802, and the third two years later. Miss
Baillie's idea was, first, to revive poetic drama; secondly, to
restore the Shakespearean type of character to the stage; and,
thirdly, to make each of the powerful human passions the subject of study and analysis. In following out the last-named
purpose she used each sin, as avarice for example, as the subject of both a comedy and a tragedy. In the preface to her
first volume she explained that the *Plays on the Passions* re-
sponded to "the universal desire in the human mind to behold
man in every situation, putting forth his strength against the
currents of adversity, scorning all bodily anguish, or struggling
with those feelings of nature which, like a boiling stream, will
often burst through the barriers of pride." After this grandiloquence, it is surprising to find that the *Plays on the Passions*
were not, after all, bad enough to be popular. The stream of
Miss Baillie's genius did not "boil" hard enough. She admitted that she set little value upon plots and incidents, nor
were passion and feeling paramount. Her sole aim was to
illustrate some high moral purpose. Jeffrey, editor of the

*Edinburgh Review,* was ungallant enough to criticise these principles, saying that the end of drama is the entertainment of the audience, and that Joanna's theory was not suited to the stage; and he also hinted that she plagiarized Shakespeare. Wilson (Christopher North) was much impressed by her talents, and Scott called her the "new Shakespeare." Her tragedy *De Montfort,* with John Kemble and Mrs. Siddons in the cast, was successful, running eleven nights at Drury Lane; but this was the exception in the long list of her "worthy" plays.

George Colman the younger (1762-1836) inherited much of his father's cleverness, without his manly, genial, and highly intelligent character. Early in the nineteenth century he produced several plays, the most interesting of which seems to be *The Heir at Law* (1808). In this and other compositions Colman followed a warranted-to-please pattern, with hard landlords, spendthrift sons, lily-handed maidens and extravagantly noble gentlemen. He attracted the favor of George IV, who made him examiner of plays for the crown.

A relative of Sheridan, James Sheridan Knowles (1784-1862) was somewhat more talented than either Miss Baillie or the younger Colman. Like the earnest Joanna, Knowles had a desire to restore poetic drama after the Elizabethan style. Acquiring in early life a practical knowledge of the theater, he soon came into prominence as a writer of both historical tragedy and domestic plays of a serious type. His *Caius Gracchus* was performed in 1815, *Virginius* in 1820. After several more historical pieces, in 1832 he wrote *The Hunchback,* which immediately made him the most admired of living playwrights.

After Knowles, the outstanding writer in the mid-years of the nineteenth century was Edward Bulwer, the first Lord Lytton (1803-1873), three of whose plays, *The Lady of Lyons, Richelieu,* and *Money,* held the stage for many years. The works of Lytton, though easy and brilliant, show a kind of "false fervor" which, as a style, has happily passed into limbo. As the nineteenth century progressed, the art of the drama became less and less interesting, *qua drama.* The period produced a number of playwrights who, though not of the first rank yet were often clever, ingenious, and popular; but in the course of three-quarters of a century there was no one to bring a copious, invigorating life to the stage. As the playwrights declined, however, the number of great actors and actresses increased; and these artists, with their talents, were able to make commonplace pieces effective. Also, the public press in general was too kind to poor shows, often giving far more importance to the personality of the actor than to the quality of the play.

About the middle of the century James Madison Morton (1811-1891) appeared with a fresh, abundant sense of humor and the ability to create characters which stood up well before the footlights. In *Speed the Plough* he introduced Mrs. Grundy to an appreciative public. In 1864 Thomas Robertson successfully dramatized a story in which David Garrick was the principal figure and later wrote several other comedies of some merit, including *Caste* and *Society*. Tom Taylor (1817-1880), editor of *Punch* for several years, was one of the numerous playwrights who had originally prepared for the practice of law. He adapted many plays from the French, among them *The Ticket-of-Leave Man* (1863) from *Leonard* by Edouard Brisbarre and Eugène Nus. Among more than a hundred dramas his *Still Waters Run Deep*, also adapted from the French, has been regularly offered on the English-speaking stage until recent years.

*Popularity of French Plays*. The demand for theatrical entertainment far outran the supply offered by the few native writers, and was filled, for a large part of the century, by importations from Paris. The prestige of French technique, and the financial profits to be had by utilizing works which cost little or nothing in translation, were among the causes making for the sterility of the English drama. There were two chief types of imported plays: first, melodramas, represented by the work of Pixérecourt, Soulié, and others; and, secondly, the "well-made play," represented by the works of Scribe, Augier, and Sardou. There was an almost inexhaustible supply of comedies of the light, intriguing, usually risqué sort. As romanticism glorified the bandit and the outlaw, so the well-made play glorified the harlot and the domestic triangle of husband, wife, and lover; and it in turn became as mechanical in structure and as hackneyed in its stock figures as the more humble Punch-and-Judy shows. Such a play as *Les pattes de mouche* or *La dame aux camélias,* interesting enough for a season or two, left much to be desired as models for a score of writers in half a dozen different countries: for, as patterns, they produced nothing but a succession of neat, crackling society plays with sex and the domestic triangle nauseatingly present. As a consequence, at the end of the third quarter of the century the theater in England seemed infinitely removed from reality, intellect, or sincerity. It was, in fact, almost at its lowest ebb.

*Literary or "closet" drama.* The record of this period would be incomplete without a glance at the so-called closet plays which the age produced. From the beginning to the very end of the century almost every man of letters undertook to write poetic drama. Sheridan has the distinction of having refused plays by both Wordsworth and Coleridge; between 1817 and 1822 Byron wrote at least five dramas, and Shelley at least two. Walter Savage Landor, Richard H. Horne, George Darley, Thomas L. Beddoes, and Sidney Dobell all contributed to the species; also Matthew Arnold and William Morris, the latter offering a sort of modern morality called *Love Is Enough.* All these writers, many of them distinguished in the world of letters, wrote in verse, often using eminently "stagey" themes, yet achieving plays which were generally not actable. In our own day Thomas Hardy has written a monumental dramatic poem, *The Dynasts,* which perhaps was not intended for stage production.[1] Doubtless these writers, in most cases, desired to utilize the opportunities for revelation of character and feeling offered by dialogue, yet found it difficult to conform to the exacting conditions of actual performance.

The three most celebrated writers of the unactable poetic drama of this period, however, are Browning, Tennyson and Swinburne. Browning was eager to produce plays which could be acted, and, in certain single scenes, he proved himself

[1] It has actually been produced by Mr. Granville Barker.

capable of doing so. *Strafford* (1837), his most pretentious dramatic effort, is filled with off-stage action and is written in a style poorly adapted to speech. *In a Balcony,* in spite of many poignant and effective passages, does not quite *act,* even with skilful performers, but remains a story told by talk rather than by action. Browning's gift, while certainly dramatic, was not disciplined to the conditions of the stage. Tennyson likewise possessed an ambition to write actable plays; and at least one piece, *Becket,* as presented by Sir Henry Irving, gave pleasure to theater-goers for many years. Tennyson, however, like Browning and the others, failed in the oral style, the telling situation, the surprising turn of action, which the stage requires. He remains the poet of the library rather than of the playhouse. Swinburne was still further from the dramatic tradition. Although he wrote nine long tragedies, full of splendid verse, on subjects which in the hands of an Elizabethan would have become stage thrillers, yet it is doubtful if any one of his plays ever has been, or could be, acted. Such a judgment does not mean, however, that these works, even as drama, are wholly negligible. We have seen how in the unacted plays of Seneca the seeds of the art remained, to germinate and flourish unexpectedly after the writer had long been dead. In the closet drama of the nineteenth century lie buried many excellent plots and characters which possibly, in the hands of future poets, may rise and take on new life.

*Sir Arthur Wing Pinero.* Born 1855. The leading English playwright in what might be called the pre-Ibsen manner was Sir Arthur Pinero, who, before the last decade of the century had brought out at least twenty-seven works and was the reigning favorite of the stage. Such plays as *The Magistrate, The Cabinet Minister,* and *Sweet Lavender* found ready acceptance both with managers and play-goers. They were constructed mainly after the excellent French model, with crisp and ready dialogue, a plentiful sprinkling of smart society doings, and occasionally just enough of the risqué element to promote piquancy without seriously offending "chaperone" standards of taste. This tea-table drama was so firmly established in the popular favor that when Ibsen with his devastating ideas finally crossed the Channel, he was at considerable disadvantage as compared with Pinero. However, finally the Victorians were in a discreet measure affected by the robust Norwegian. After a few bouts with the drama of ideas, represented by *Ghosts* and *The Pillars of Society,* even timid managers were emboldened to open their stages to a careful mixture of social criticism, intrigue, and pessimism, provided it were sufficiently well-bred. In 1893 Sir Arthur Pinero wrote *The Second Mrs. Tanqueray,* called by Miss Storm Jameson "his great drawing-room version of Ibsen." *Mrs. Tanqueray* was received with considerable acclaim, held the stage for some time, was sent to the English provinces, to America, and finally to continental capitals, and had the honor of providing Eleanora Duse and Mrs. Patrick Campbell with a stellar rôle. Since *Mrs. Tanqueray* nearly a score of plays have come from Pinero's pen, some of them, such as *Iris* and *Midchannel,* plainly showing a change of method on the part of the author. The plots are more tightly constructed, the anterior action is implied and woven skilfully into the scene, theories of heredity, predestined guilt, and a sort of social redemption are hinted at. No one is a greater master than Pinero in depicting the nuances of the fashionable drawing-room and boudoir, or in forging an effective climax.

Henry Arthur Jones (born 1851) offered his first play, *A Clerical Error,* in 1879. Like Pinero, Mr. Jones learned his technique from the French. In 1884 he adapted Ibsen's *Doll's House* for the English public under the title *Breaking a Butterfly.* Perhaps no more eloquent revelation could be made of the difference in the dramatic world between the spirit of today and of forty-three years ago. It would be a bold person now who would offer any "adaptation" whatever of Ibsen, and with such a title! At the time, however, adaptations were in order, and Ibsen was then only another European playwright, not a prophet. Mr. Jones continued his work with domestic comedy and social pieces, including *The Masqueraders* and *The Bauble Shop.* In 1896 he wrote *Michael and His Lost Angel,* generally considered his strongest drama. It is a study of small-town people, concerned with the expiation of guilt. It is both sentimental and romantic, with the solemn attitude towards sexual irregularity which generally characterized the Victorian writer. Mr. Jones, however, has shown a kind of evangelistic spirit in regard to the stage: a perception of its possible nobility and truth, and a desire to contribute to its ethical and moral value.

**CHAPTER XXXII**

# GERMANY, AUSTRIA, ITALY AND SCANDINAVIA:
## 1800-1875

The drama must, then, go on treating over and over emotions the same in kind. Real novelty comes in presenting them as they affect men and women who are in ideas, habits, costume, speech, and environment distinctly of their time. Their expression of the old elemental emotions brings novelty.—GEORGE PIERCE BAKER, *Dramatic Technique*.

The most notable result of the romantic movement in its later years in Germany was the production of a group of talented young writers whose passionate souls seemed born to endure morbid sufferings. The sorrows of Werther were repeated and intensified in such men as Heinrich von Kleist (1777-1811) who, in the space of thirty-four years, served as soldier, a minor government official, a newspaper writer, story writer, and dramatist. His brief and stormy life ended in suicide. In his first play, *The Schroffenstein Family* (1803), written in Switzerland whither the author had gone with the intention of becoming a *Bauer*, or small farmer, he used a theme similar to that of *Romeo and Juliet*. The play is both extravagant and powerful. Six tragedies and one comedy followed from the pen of Kleist; and though they were marked by rich talent—imagination, humor, good dialogue, and excellent character portrayal—yet they won little or no recognition during the author's lifetime. He never saw one of his plays performed on the stage. In later days, however, he was ranked as one of the best of Prussian dramatists, and the only good playwright among the romanticists of his period. In *The Prinz von Homburg* Kleist produced his last and best play.

*Franz Grillparzer.* 1791-1872. The most distinguished name in the dramatic history of Austria in the nineteenth century is that of Grillparzer, who was trained in law, entered government service in 1813, and remained at the official desk for forty-three years. He was a born dramatist; and, in spite of his treadmill occupation, produced a considerable body of literary work. His first drama, *The Ancestress* (*Die Ahnfrau*, 1817), a fate tragedy, was written in three weeks of intense concentration, and brought him immediate recognition. It is a gloomy piece, comparable only to the horror tales of Poe, artificial to twentieth-century taste but considered powerful in its time. There followed nine tragedies and one comedy; and in two of these works the author used native historical material. In a trilogy called *The Golden Fleece* he took an ancient theme which has fascinated many dramatists. It includes the tragedy of *Medea*, which the author sought to interpret in terms of modern ideas of faithfulness and honor. In *Dream Is a Life* he reversed the Calderón play (*La Vida es Sueño*), using the device of the dream to foreshadow coming events in the life of the hero. He was able to write good dialogue and to construct a sound plot, with charming, heroic, or passionate characters. His plays have been popular on the European stage until recently, and he still has an honored place among the "old masters."

*Minor German playwrights.* There are few names in the nineteenth century worthy to rank with those of Kleist and Grillparzer. Christian Grabbe (1801-1836), an extravagantly ambitious youth, began his career with two pessimistic, blood-curdling plays, *The Duke of Gothland* and *Don Juan and Faust,* following them with a number of historical pieces well conceived and executed. Count von Platen's special gift was for satire, *The Fatal Fork* and *Romantic Œdipus* being clever parodies on the pseudo-classic fate tragedy. One of the few instances of the use of a modern historical theme was in a tragedy called *The Death of Danton* (1835), by Georg Büchner, who died at the age of twenty-four. The middle years of the century witnessed a change in the tone of the drama from extravagant action and romantic types of character to discussion,—*Tendenz-Drama.* The stage again began to be used, as in all its history it has periodically been used, for the presentation of political and religious ideas. One of the writers of *Tendenz-Drama* was Karl Gutzkow (1811-1878), whose first prose tragedy, *Richard Savage* (1839), though somewhat confused and unreal, yet expressed thoughts and longings which had not hitherto appeared in German plays. In a long succession of tragedies, some in prose, others in blank verse, he remains for the most part the preacher and pamphleteer rather than the dramatist. His best known work, *Uriel Acosta* (1847), is based upon a historical incident of seventeenth-century Amsterdam, and has for its theme the liberation of the Jews from religious oppression. It is skilfully constructed and effective both as literature and as drama.

*Friedrich Hebbel.* 1813-1863. The best German dramatist of the middle years of the century was Hebbel who, at the age of twenty-six, composed a prose tragedy called *Judith.* Its success procured its author a pension from the Danish government. Being thus enabled to travel and study, Hebbel evolved a theory of the stage which in some respects anticipated that of Ibsen. He disapproved of the play of discussion (*Tendenz-Drama*), also of the cult of beauty or entertainment for its own sake. He claimed that characters, to be convincing, should live out on the stage their most intense and vital experiences; and that the drama, if used as a pulpit, should teach through action rather than by discussion. Though his theories were sound, yet his plays are mostly a bit under standard and depressingly realistic. *Genoveva* and *Gyges and His Ring* illustrate his attempt to throw new light upon old themes.

Otto Ludwig (1813-1865), like Hebbel, believed that the drama should be brought back to life and reality, and in *The Hereditary Forrester* (1840) achieved a play which did to some extent lift the stage out of its insignificance. Gustav Freytag (1816-1895) was more celebrated for his novels than for his three or four dramas, though they were popular in their time. His most important service was his analysis and explanation of the principles of drama, which he set forth in 1863. This was practically the first time since Aristotle that the technique of playwriting had been seriously considered and formulated by a European writer.

## ITALY

In his *Contemporary Drama of Italy* Professor Landor Mac-Clintock has pointed out that the Italians are a histrionic rather than a dramatic people, and that in all their history they have no name to compare with Shakespeare, Marlowe, or Jonson. The eighteenth century had produced Goldoni in comedy and Alfieri in tragedy,—the former a sane, good-humored fun-maker, the latter a writer of high moral purpose, a follower of the classic mode, and a passionate advocate of social and political freedom. During the greater part of the nineteenth century the country was engaged in great struggles,—with Napoleon and Austria from without, and with warring political and religious factions from within. As in every other European country, except perhaps Russia, the stage was largely supplied by importations from Paris; and native writers were followers of the French schools. Therefore the forms which flourished in France, reappeared in Italy.

*Melodrama.* The best of the writers of melodrama was Pietro Giacometti (1816-1882), who, according to his own account, by reading Victor Hugo and Dumas, was led to the belief that "by dint of creating seduced ladies, . . . poisons, daggers, assassinations, strugglings, ghosts, butchers and grave-diggers, one could become a dramatic author,—that is to say, with some new and original ideas scattered here and there." Giacometti wrote nearly a hundred plays, most of which are characterized by clever craftsmanship. Among the best are *Marie Antoinette, Queen of France,* and *Civil Death.* The latter, a reform drama dealing with political imprisonment, was praised by Zola. The celebrated actor Salvini performed the principal rôle in England and the United States within the memory of men now living.

*Romanticism.* The chief representative of the romantic school in the early part of the century was Alessandro Manzoni (1785-1873) who, like Alfieri, was a powerful advocate of freedom. His nature, however, was warmer and more sympathetic than that of the earlier writer. Manzoni strove to make a compromise between the romantic and the pseudo-classic styles, keeping the chorus and the long declamatory speeches, but otherwise throwing off the bonds of formalism. He strove for "unity of impression," effective scenes, and appealing characters; but in some cases his plays seem to be merely a succession of incidents instead of drama. *The Countess of Carmagnola* (1819) and *Adelchi* (1822) are important as illustrations of the revolt from the tradition of Alfieri, and also on account of their fiery patriotism.

*Historical drama.* There were in Italy few studies of contemporary social life such as had appeared in other countries; but there was a revival of interest in national history. Giovanni Niccolini (1782-1861) began his career with poetic tragedies of the pseudo-classic type, using historical or semi-historical themes. *Antonio Foscarini, Giovanni da Procida,* and *Rosamunda d'Ingliterra* are among his titles; but they, like most of his other plays, are better suited for reading than for acting. In Niccolini, as in Alfieri and Manzoni, there was an active fire of patriotism and love of freedom, which found expression in his work. *Arnoldo di Brescia* is considered his best drama. For the most part, the writers leaned toward the romantic style. Leopoldo Marenco (1831-1899), in *The Falconer of Pietro Ardena,* made use of a medieval tale. Angelo de Gubernatis (1840-1913) treated oriental themes; and Pietro Cossa (1834-1881), who is called "the first genuine man of the theater in the nineteenth century," wrote in verse on the subject of *Nero, Messaline, Cleopatra,* and *Plautus and His Century.* Cossa was not a distinguished poet, but he was stronger and more rugged in his characterizations than many of his countrymen. Giovanni Bovio (1841-1903) chose religious subjects in *Saint Paul* and *Christ at the Feast of Purim.* There were also talented imitators of Shakespeare, such as the brothers Pindemonte, who belong to the early years of the century.

Although the romanticists of this period seem to have produced no masterpiece, yet through them the deadening conventionalities of the older schools were in a measure dissipated, the minds of spectators and readers were turned towards patriotic and humanitarian subjects, and contemporaneous social conditions were brought to light. The link between the old and the new schools was Giacosa, whose work will be considered in a succeeding chapter.

## DENMARK

The most prominent figure in Danish literature during the early part of the nineteenth century was Adam Öhlenschläger (1779-1850), who was born in Copenhagen of German parentage. In 1805 he wrote *The Legend of Aladdin,* counted one of the masterpieces of European literature. On his travels he visited Goethe and other literary celebrities, and while living in Germany he composed *Earl Haakon,* his finest tragedy. Our chief interest in Öhlenschläger centers in the fact that he was one of the first, if not the very first, to conceive of using the figures of Norse mythology in his plots. His plays attained a sort of recognition among the learned; but the legends of Siegfried and Brunhild were then too unfamiliar to the public to permit of any general or immediate popularity.

Hans Christian Andersen (1805-1875), known to the world through his fairy tales far better than through his dramas, was a somewhat successful writer for the stage. His first piece, a satire on the excesses of the school of chivalry and romance, was followed by fairy plays, comedies and romantic dramas. His work now seems to be lacking in backbone and sinew. During the mid-years of the century many minor playwrights flourished, the most important of whom was Johan Ludwig Heiberg (1791-1860), the son of Peter Heiberg, exiled in the eighteenth century for his "radical" plays. Johan was a close student and admirer of Calderón, and at the age of twenty-five he brought out two plays which won instant recognition. The lure of the Parisian theater, however, was greater than his desire for originality. He introduced into Denmark the French vaudevilles, just then at the height of their success, and followed their pattern to some extent in his own works, which were full of delightful humor, catchy melodies, and ingratiating characters. Though scoffed at generally by the critics, they were applauded by the people. *A Soul After Death* is a satire on contemporaneous fads, somewhat after the manner of Aristophanes. He used fairy tales, legendary themes, or current social fashions, and made a success with them all. With the work of Heiberg and other native writers, the Danish theater made remarkable progress, producing poetical dramas, historical tragedies, and comedies. Taken all in all, during the second and third quarters of the century it was probably better served than any other European stage except that of France.

## Norway

After the political separation of Norway and Denmark in 1814, it was but natural that a desire for literary independence should rise. The first national dramatist of Norway to attain European fame was Björnstjerne Björnson (born 1832) who, in his first play, declared his belief in the use of national subjects, in simple and unaffected dialogue, and in the exclusion of long, declamatory speeches. After several unsuccessful plays he aroused great enthusiasm with a tragedy called *Maria Stuart in Scotland*. Any play on this subject would of course challenge comparison not only with Schiller's fine work, but also with that of many other excellent craftsmen. Critics have remarked that while Björnson portrayed a picturesque and seductive heroine, yet through a weak ending the drama falls far short of being a masterpiece. During a period of about fifty years Björnson produced, besides a large amount of other literary work, more than a score of plays, using themes from the Norse sagas, from contemporaneous and ancient history, and from modern social life. Björnson belongs to the group of notable writers who in the nineteenth century fought for liberalism in government, in religion, and for the redress of social wrongs. He has the keen eye for injustice that characterized Ibsen; but his methods of regeneration seem more humane and genial.

## CHAPTER XXXIII

# IBSEN, STRINDBERG, AND THE DRAMATIC AWAKENING

Ibsen replaces the old formula with a new, vital one—Truth at all hazards. . . . This Ibsen of the over-arching poetic power, is a man disdainful of our praise or blame, knowing, with the subtle prevision of genius, that one day the world will go to him for the consolations of his austere art.—JAMES HUNEKER, *Iconoclasts*.

Looking back over the mid-years of the nineteenth century, one can see that there were numerous quiet but unmistakable signs of the coming of a change in the dramatic world. As early as 1844 Hebbel in Germany had protested against the clever but artificial plays that formed the chief attraction of the European stage. He made scathing comment upon the emptiness and monotony of the themes, upon the use of asides, soliloquies, mechanical plots and puppet-like characters. In his tragedy *Mary Magdalene* he illustrated his ideas concerning sincerity in the treatment of theme and character, and antici-pated in a measure the theories set forth by Ibsen. Zola, fa-mous as an exponent of naturalism in fiction, wrote a pamphlet on the necessity of naturalism in the theater; and, with char-acteristic eloquence, he made a plea for new life, greater vigor, and action more in accord with actual experience. These men, with others whose voices were more timidly raised, were the heralds of a new day; or perhaps prophets foretelling the break-up of the old régime.

*Henrik Ibsen.* 1828-1906. In the entire history of litera-ture, there are few figures like Ibsen's. Practically his whole life and energies were devoted to the theater; and his offerings, medicinal and bitter, have changed the history of the stage. The story of his life,—his birth March 20, 1828, in the little Norwegian village of Skien, the change in family circumstances from prosperity to poverty when the boy was eight years old, his studious and non-athletic boyhood, his apprenticeship to an apothecary in Grimstad, and his early attempts at dramatic composition,—all these items are well known. His spare hours were spent in preparation for entrance to Christiania University, where, at about the age of twenty, he formed a friendship with Björnson. About 1851 the violinist Ole Bull gave Ibsen the position of "theater poet" at the newly built National Theater in Bergen—a post which he held for six years. In 1857 he became director of the Norwegian Theater in Christiania; and in 1862, with *Love's Comedy,* became known in his own country as a playwright of promise. Seven years later, discouraged with the reception given to his work and out of sympathy with the social and intellectual ideals of his country, he left Norway, not to return for a period of nearly thirty years. He established himself first at Rome, later in Munich. Late in life he returned to Christiania, where he died May 23, 1906.

*Ibsen's plays.* The productive life of Ibsen is conveniently divided into three periods: the first ending in 1877 with the successful appearance of *The Pillars of Society;* the second covering the years in which he wrote most of the dramas of protest against social conditions, such as *Ghosts;* and the third, marked by the symbolic plays, *The Master Builder* and *When We Dead Awaken.* The first of the prose plays, *Love's Comedy* (1862) made an impression in Norway, and drew the eyes of thoughtful people to the new dramatist, though its satirical, mocking tone brought upon its author the charge of being a cynic and an atheist. The three historical plays, or dramatic poems, *Brand, Emperor and Galilean,* and *Peer Gynt,* written between 1866 and 1873, form a monumental epic. These compositions cannot be considered wholly or primarily for the stage; they are the poetic record of a long intellectual and spiritual struggle. In *Brand* there is the picture of the man who has not found the means of adjustment between the mechanical routine of daily living and the deeper claims of the soul; in *Emperor and Galilean* is a portrayal of the noblest type of pagan philosophy and manhood, illustrated in the Emperor

Julian, set off against the ideals of the Jewish Christ; and in *Peer Gynt* is a picture of the war within the soul of a man in whom are no roots of loyalty, faith, or steadfastness.

When *The Young Men's League* was produced, the occasion, like the first appearance of *Hernani,* became locally historic. The play deals with political theories, ideas of liberty and social justice; and in its presentation likenesses to living people were discovered, and fierce resentments were aroused. The tumult of hissing and applauding during the performance was so great that the authorities interfered. *The Pillars of Society,* Ibsen's fifteenth play, was the first to have a hearing throughout Europe. It was written in Munich, where it was performed in the summer of 1877. In the autumn it was enacted in all the theaters of Scandinavia, whence within a few months it spread over the continent, appearing in London before the end of the year. The late James Huneker, one of the most acute critics of the Norwegian seer, said: "The Northern Aristophanes, who never smiles as he lays on the lash, exposes in *The Pillars of Society* a varied row of whited sepulchres. . . . There is no mercy in Ibsen, and his breast has never harbored the milk of human kindness. This remote, objective art does not throw out tentacles of sympathy. It is too disdainful to make the slightest concession, hence the difficulty in convincing an audience that the poet is genuinely human."

*The Pillars of Society* proved, once for all, Ibsen's emancipation, first, from the thrall of romanticism, which he had pushed aside as of no more worth than a toy; and, secondly, from the domination of French technique, which he had mastered and surpassed. In the plays of the second period there are evident Ibsen's most mature gifts as a craftsman as well as that peculiar philosophy which made him the Jeremiah of the modern social world. In *An Enemy of the People* the struggle is between hypocrisy and greed on one side, and the ideal of personal honor on the other; in *Ghosts* there is an exposition of a fate-tragedy darker and more searching even than in Œdipus; and in each of the social dramas there is exposed, as under the pitiless lens of the microscope, some moral cancer. Ibsen forced his characters to scrutinize their past, the conditions of the society to which they belonged, and the methods by which they had gained their own petty ambitions, in order that they might pronounce judgment upon themselves. The action is still for the most part concerned with men's deeds and outward lives, in connection with society and the world; and his themes have largely to do with the moral and ethical relations of man with man.

In the third period the arena of the conflict has changed to the realm of the spirit; and the action illustrates some effort at self-realization, self-conquest, or self-annihilation. *The Master Builder* and *When We Dead Awaken* must explain themselves, if they are to be explained at all; for they are meaningless if they do not light, in the mind of the reader or spectator, a spark of the same clairvoyant insight with which they were written. In them are characters which, like certain living men and women, challenge and mystify even their closest friends and admirers. Throughout all the plays there are symbols—the wild duck, the mill race, the tower, or the open sea—which are but the external tokens of something less familiar and more important; and the dialogue often has a secondary meaning, not with the witty double *entendre* of the French school, but with suggestions of a world in which the spirit, ill at ease in material surroundings, will find its home.

It is significant that Ibsen should arrive, by his own route, at the very principles adopted by Sophocles and commended by Aristotle,—namely, the unities of time, place and action, with only the culminating events of the tragedy placed before the spectator. After the first period he wrote in prose, abolishing all such ancient and serviceable contrivances as servants discussing their masters' affairs, comic relief, asides and soliloquies. The characters in his later dramas are few, and there are no "veils of poetic imagery."

*Ibsen's moral ideals.* The principles of Ibsen's teaching, his moral ethic, was that honesty in facing facts is the first requisite of a decent life. Human nature has dark recesses which must be explored and illuminated; life has pitfalls which must be recognized to be avoided; and society has humbugs, hypocrisies, and obscure diseases which must be revealed before they can be cured. To recognize these facts is not pessimism; it is the moral obligation laid upon intelligent people. To face the problems thus exposed, however, requires courage, honesty, and faith in the ultimate worth of the human soul. Man must be educated until he is not only intelligent enough, but courageous enough to work out his salvation through patient endurance and nobler ideals. Democracy, as a cure-all, is just as much a failure as any other form of government; since the majority in politics, society, or religion is always torpid and content with easy measures. It is the intelligent and morally heroic minority which has always led, and always will lead, the human family on its upward march. Nevertheless, we alone can help ourselves; no help can come from without. Furthermore—and this is a vital point in understanding Ibsen—experience and life are a happiness in themselves, not merely a means to happiness; and in the end good must prevail. Such are some of the ideas that can be distilled from the substance of Ibsen's plays.

On the plane of practical methods Ibsen preached the emancipation of the individual, especially of woman. He laid great stress upon the principle of heredity, often perhaps to an extent that would be repudiated by the science of today. He made many studies of disordered minds, and analyzed relentlessly the common relationships—sister and brother, husband and wife, father and son. There is much in these relationships, he seems to say, that is based on sentimentalism, on a desire to dominate, on hypocrisy and lies. He pictured the unscrupulous financier, the artist who gives up love for the fancied demands of his art, the unmarried woman who has been the drudge and the unthanked burden-bearer—all with a cool detachment which cloaks, but does not conceal, the passionate moralist.

From the seventh decade of the last century to his last play in 1899, the storm of criticism, resentment, and denunciation scarcely ceased.[1] On the other hand, the prophet and artist

[1] The late William Archer, critic, author, and translator of several of the Ibsen plays, made an extraordinary collection of the epithets and curses showered upon the author of *Ghosts*.

which were united in Ibsen's nature found many champions and friends. In Germany he was hailed as the leader of the new era; in England his champion, William Archer, fought many a battle for him; but in the end no one could escape his example. Young playwrights learned from him, reformers adopted his ideas, and moralists quoted from him as from a sacred book. His plays scorched, but they fascinated the rising generation, and they stuck to the boards. Psychologists discovered a depth of meaning and of human understanding in his delineation of character. He did not found a school, for every school became his debtor. He did not have followers, for every succeeding playwright was forced in a measure to learn from him.

*August Strindberg.* 1849-1912. The greatest exponent of the so-called naturalistic school was Strindberg, born in Sweden in a home of extreme poverty. His childhood was stormy and unhappy, he was afflicted by periodic attacks of insanity, and for most of his life was under the spell of an erotic mania. Unable to complete his course at Upsala University, he nevertheless plunged into the study of chemistry and attained some recognition in that subject. Later we find him seeking the magic fluid which turns all base metals into gold. He was three times married and divorced; and in a published work he told the bitter story of his marital experiences with such frankness as to scandalize whatever public he had secured. In profession he was successively teacher, editor, actor. Passing through various stages of intellectual development, he was in turn a believer in the Christian religion, a free-thinker, a so-called atheist, a socialist, a dabbler in spiritualism,—and in each phase was undoubtedly sincere.

Strindberg was a poet and novelist as well as dramatist, his works in their collected edition filling forty volumes. His first play, *Master Olaf,* appeared in 1872, and with other early pieces belongs rather in the romantic class. In 1887 he produced *The Father,* probably the most powerful play of the naturalistic school; and, to one reader at least, one of the most terrible plays in existence. *The Countess Julia* is equally shocking in a different way: not primarily because it is pornographic, but because it reproduces with almost fiendish intensity the pain and disillusion which can come from thwarted desires and contaminated blood. Strindberg partially stated his own creed: "I find the joy of life in the powerful, terrible struggle of life; and the capability of experiencing something, of learning something, is a pleasure to me." He was bitterly opposed to what is called woman's emancipation, regarding woman's duty as, first, becoming wife and mother; and, second, administering to man's needs or clearing the path for his larger achievements. He believed that purity in man, and therefore in the state, could only be achieved at the cost of happiness and pleasure; that there was no possible reconcilement between man's desires and his personal morality.

The force and vigor of Strindberg's talent for dramatic writing was sufficient to overcome, to some extent, the abnormal and grisly nature of his plays. Furthermore, he could at will portray lovely and poetic scenes, as in *Swanwhite* and *Lucky Pehr,* which have much the same fanciful beauty as Maeterlinck's *Blue Bird.* He was specially skilful in one-act pieces, and could project characters that are clear-cut and powerful, winning from his countrymen the title of the "Shakespeare of Sweden."

*The dramatic awakening.* Ibsen proved to be merely the outstanding figure of a constantly increasing group of protestants against the emptiness and monotony of the earlier nineteenth century stage. The last quarter of the century witnessed an awakening from the long period of comparative insignificance. Playhouses began to multiply, audiences became more intelligent and critical, and men of talent began to turn in increasing number to the stage for the expression of their ideas. For the dramatist, there began a period of activity, experimentation and enlargement which has not yet reached its culmination. For the producers, there were several departures from the old methods, one of which was the organization of theater groups, both professional and amateur, for the patronage of plays which did not readily find a welcome on the commercial stage. In 1887 M. Antoine, a theater manager of independent personality and courage, established in Paris the *Théâtre Libre,* which became for a time the rallying point for all the protests against false classicism, sweet romanticism, and mechanical technique. His policy was to eliminate everything that seemed untrue to life, to present faithful studies of present-day social conditions, and to give no play, even the most successful, more than three consecutive nights. Above all things, the stage, theoretically at least, was to be free: every phase of life could be pictured, provided there were only life and sincerity in the portrayal; everything was to be tolerated except what was machine-made and rubber-stamped.

In the reaction against the old style of play the new playwrights often went to extremes, presenting scenes reeking with sex, characters drawn from the gutter, and dialogue that was coarse and brutal. Any play performed on the boards of the *Théâtre Libre* in the early days of its existence was fairly certain to be denounced as shocking by some one; but it was also fairly certain of finding intelligent, perhaps enthusiastic approval. Naturally such an opportunity as that offered by M. Antoine was sometimes abused; but the influence of his organization was markedly liberalizing and profitable.

Within a few years after the establishment of the *Théâtre Libre,* there was opened in Berlin *Die Freie Bühne* (1889), with the same purpose of providing an open forum for playwrights who could not get a hearing through the established managers. In London, Mr. J. E. Grein inaugurated the Independent Theater, and Miss Horniman a similar one in Manchester. Early in the present century, in Dublin, Mr. W. B. Yeats, Lady Gregory and others founded the Abbey Theater, whose purpose was not commercial but æsthetic and national. On these various stages were welcomed presentations of the struggles of real life or of imaginary worlds, interpreted in terms which had an interest for thoughtful and intelligent people. Dramatists everywhere now acknowledged important,— Strindberg, Ibsen, Björnson, Hauptmann, Shaw, Yeats, and Synge,—were first given a hearing in these free theaters. The first performance of Ibsen's *Ghosts* was given in Germany at *Die Freie Bühne* in 1889, in France at the *Théâtre Libre* in 1890, and in England at the Independent Theater in 1891.

Other plays, now known throughout Europe and America, show a similar history. Had it not been for the opportunity thus given for the performance of unusual plays, the drama of the nineteenth century would have been infinitely poorer. It is scarcely too much to say that since 1890 every young playwright with an individual point of view, and every new play unusual enough to provoke discussion, were first heard of through the independent and free theaters.

In addition to these organizations there sprang up everywhere, about the close of the nineteenth and the beginning of the present century, "little theater" groups, consisting sometimes of a few playwrights and actors who financed their own productions, sometimes of talented amateurs who were willing to risk something for the sake of the art. The "little" theaters were often small auditoriums with stage settings and lighting apparatus of the simplest description, needing only a meagre financial outlay for any single performance. These little theaters have virtually been workshops for experiment and practice, and have many times proved their value.

## CHAPTER XXXIV

# THE LAST FIFTY YEARS ON THE CONTINENT

> . . . when we have put before us one of those poignant scenes, or situations, or figures of human life, where good and evil, strength and weakness are so inextricably mixed, where all that might, that should turn out well does turn out so ill, then we cannot comprehend intellectually, do not try to, we can simply receive the impression emotionally or spiritually, we cannot but be seized by a mixture of pity and awe, as Aristotle says. And that feeling is our feeling for the Tragic.—EDWARD EVERETT HALE, JR., *Dramatists of Today.*

If the date 1900 be regarded for a moment as a turning point, then, for the dramatists, the twenty-five years preceding might justly be considered a period of siege or battle, and the years following a period of occupation. Before 1900, the radical writer for the stage often had to fight; since then he has simply had to answer the question, "Now that you have arrived, what have you to offer us?"

In general terms the answer has been, of course, the same old answer made by all the historic reformers of the stage, namely, the elimination of worn-out traditions and the substitution of new subjects and new forms. More particularly, the answer took a few well-defined shapes. The old guard of the earlier nineteenth century had stood for the carefully constructed plot *à la Scribe:* the newcomers therefore refused the domination of the well-made play, returning in some cases to a sprawling, spineless series of incidents; the old guard stood for a plentiful admixture of sentiment concerning deserving but consumptive harlots, kind burglars and noble bandits: the new school turned these figures into victims of social injustice, bad laws, or capitalistic greed; the old school preferred on the whole optimistic views of life, especially at the curtain; the new style was content to let the audience digest what was often a highly unpalatable dose, or, on occasion, ended the play with a sermon on the sins of society; the old-timers were strong for scenes in which mother-love, home, and the flag called forth eloquent speeches before the footlights; the new school regarded such devices with contempt. Satirists appeared, scoffing at the tameness or hypocrisies of the old régime; and side by side with them appeared also the romanticists, introducing the same old swashbuckling heroes and lovely heroines clothed in new cloaks and mantles.

## GERMANY AND AUSTRIA

As Germany had been among the first to recognize the force and virility of the work of Ibsen, so it was also one of the first to produce plays illustrative of the "new" ideas. In 1889, the year of the establishment of *Die Freie Bühne,* Gerhardt Hauptmann (born 1862) suddenly became nationally known through the production of a play called *Before Sunrise* (*Vor Sonnenaufgang*), depicting with painful realism the sufferings of a neurotic and sensitive youth during the difficulties attending adolescence. The performance, like that of Hugo's *Hernani* and Ibsen's *Pillars of Society,* aroused much excitement and almost brought on a battle between the old and the new schools. In the dramas immediately following, Hauptmann experimented with various themes; but in *The Weavers* (1892) he seems to have strained dramatic possibilities to their utmost. It is a series of brutal and grimy pictures of a company of toilers in a remote district, far from civilization, religion, or decency. There is no hero, scarcely a chief character. The place of hero is filled by the community, whose miseries and impotency in the face of capitalistic greed are portrayed with bitterness.

In *The Sunken Bell* (1896), a poetic drama, Hauptmann used the figures of German folk-lore in depicting an artist's struggles between his creative impulses and the calls of duty. Heinrich the bell-caster is drawn away from his home and family by the allurements of the mountains, where the beauty of the forest, the animals, the old magician, and the nymph Rauten-delein make him forget his former life. The priest calls him back, but the conflict has cost the life of his wife, the loss of his marvelous bell, which goes rolling down into the lake, and finally the life of Heinrich himself. It is full of romantic charm, with beautiful poetry and a few very effective scenes. There is perhaps no more poignant moment in the whole repertory of the stage than that in which is heard the tolling of the bell, at first muffled and distant then louder and more insistent, from its bed at the bottom of the lake.

Out of the score of dramas from the hand of Hauptmann, one other deserves special attention for its originality and beauty, namely, *Hannele's Journey to Heaven* (*Hanneles Him-melfahrt*), called by the author a dream-poem. It presents an almshouse child abused and neglected, at the moment when, after the delirium of fever, she first finds the delights and satis-factions of Heaven. There is the good Tailor with the white dress and the shoes for which she had longed, there is the kind Mother, and the Physician who takes her hand and leads her home. It is a tender picture, written in sincerity, which re-mains in the mind long after the details of many plots have been forgotten. Many other Hauptmann plays have had pro-duction in various parts of Europe and America; and, taken all in all, this writer must be considered the outstanding figure in German drama.

Hermann Sudermann (born 1857) has achieved European celebrity both as novelist and dramatist. From 1889, when *Honor* (*Die Ehre*) was produced, to about 1909, he shared laurels with Hauptmann, writing at least a score of plays, seven of which are in one act. Less poetic than Hauptmann, Suder-mann accepted the discipline of dramatic craftsmanship and built his plots with conscientious care. His people are not mere types, but recognizable figures of the world; and his plays deal with familiar questions: the antagonism between the ideals of the military aristocrat and the vulgar commoner, as in *Honor;* between the right to "live one's own life" and duty to family and society, as in *Sodoms Ende;* or, more happily, the peace that comes by voluntarily carrying one's share of a burden and accepting responsibilities, as in *Das Glück im Winkel*. Sudermann is perhaps a little heavy in treating the embroilments of sex, and too often opens to the spectator the drawing-rooms of fashionable, erotic females, or unfolds the liaisons of coldly sensual men of affairs; but he has power to chain the interest. Probably his most important play is *Magda* (*Heimat*, 1893), in which Mme Bernhardt, Signora Duse, Mrs. Patrick Campbell, Mrs. Fiske, Mme Modjeska, and various important German actresses have found a stellar rôle.

Other German or German-speaking writers have made interesting contributions not only to their native stage but to European and American theaters everywhere. Franz Wedekind (born 1864), in *The Awakening of Spring* (*Frühlingserwachen*), offered a serious but morbid study of youth, somewhat after the manner of Hauptmann's *Before Sunrise*. Now that the fever of the naturalistic school has somewhat abated, this play seems remarkable for its sincerity rather than for its dramatic interest. Of all the followers of the naturalistic method, Wedekind perhaps most strikingly illustrated its weakness,—the identification of life with depravity and vice.

Hugo von Hoffmannsthal (born 1874) turned away from realism and the modern schools to the classics and once again brought Electra, Clytemnestra, and Œdipus on the stage. Arthur Schnitzler, a physician of Vienna and a dramatist of European fame, is in his plays largely concerned with the portrayal of light, amusing love affairs. His *Anatol* has become widely known.

## FRANCE AND BELGIUM

In his zeal for a closer connection between life and literature, particularly literature in the form of drama and the novel, Zola introduced into his stories members of such outcast sections of society as had heretofore been largely ignored. He also advocated a "naturalistic" theater in which fellow creatures of all types should find sympathetic portrayal. Zola's plays were mediocre; but Henri Becque (1837-1899) was more successful in following Zola's program than the preceptor himself. In 1882 he demonstrated in *The Ravens* that an absorbingly interesting play could be written in a style absolutely contrary to the Scribe-Sardou pattern. It is drab and pessimistic, depicting vulgar and selfish people; it has no catchscenes for the gallery; and the whole plot is practically revealed in the first act. Like Becque's early plays, it was refused and almost scoffed at by theatrical managers; but when at last it reached the boards its success was sensational, and its author was hailed as a sort of leader of the new school.

Another sort of novelty was introduced to the Parisian stage by Eugène Brieux, born in Paris in 1858. The plays by which he is best known are *The Three Daughters of M. Dupont, The Red Robe,* and *Damaged Goods (Les Avariés).* M. Brieux's thesis seems to be: "Look now at all our hidden social evils: forced motherhood, motherhood avoided by illegal medical practices, venereal diseases transmitted to children, and sexual practices unfavorable to the race. Let us talk over these matters in a grave and scientific spirit in order to enlighten the world." The result was a series of revolting and dreary dramas beside which Ibsen seems almost invigorating. The evident sincerity of the author and the truth of his pictures of society are perhaps their best justification.

Reaction against the drabness of this out-clinic type of work for the theater was inevitable, and came from a wide variety of playwrights, among whom Rostand and Maeterlinck are preeminent. The early plays of Maurice Maeterlinck (born in Brussels in 1864), written in the one-act form, were for marionettes and had the atmosphere of a fairy tale. As his æsthetic philosophy crystallized, however, he evolved a theory of the stage somewhat as follows: drama has been slow in adapting itself to the changes in life and in thought; the time has come to cast aside the mechanical formula, most of the external action, and all theatrical "business" and trickery. The playwright should try rather to create atmosphere, to follow the ebb and flow of the spiritual currents of the soul, in the moments when it is under the control of the sub-conscious, "moments of ecstasy, of silent joys and luminous pauses." In a famous passage Maeterlinck asserts that an old man, sitting silent before the fire nursing his memories, may be quite as dramatic a figure as the romantic lover who strangles his rival. These silences, these pauses, must be interpreted, however; and it is this interpretation that Maeterlinck offers in his most characteristic dramas, such as *The Blind, The Intruder,* and *The Death of Tintagel.* In all these pieces the action has retreated into the soul; the atmosphere is all.

Maeterlinck, however, has made concessions to more popular ideas of stage-craft. There are eight or nine long dramas from his hand, the most notable among them being *Pelleas and Melisande, Sister Beatrice, Monna Vanna,* and *The Blue Bird. Pelleas and Melisande* (1892) is a story of the Rimini type, in which shadowy woods, dark castles, primitive punishments, and cruel passions fill the scene. It is doubtless more familiar through its use as a libretto for Debussy's opera than as spoken drama. *Sister Beatrice* (1901) is a modern miracle play illustrating the forgiveness and mercy of the Virgin quite according to medieval standards. In *Monna Vanna* (1902) the scene is placed in Italy at a time when the chieftains of rival cities were at war. The incident which marks the climax is a variation of the famous oriental situation in which the conquering general demands, as a tribute of war, the favorite wife of the vanquished king. In *Monna Vanna* the lady willingly offers to sacrifice herself in order to save the city; but the dénouement is, after all, a surprise. The play had an immediate success throughout Europe, but its performance was forbidden in London. By the year 1903 the unusual, somewhat abstruse ideas of the author had become sufficiently interesting to the Parisian public to warrant a *"Théâtre de Maeterlinck"*—formerly the *Gymnase. The Blue Bird,* performed in 1908 in Moscow and two years later in New York, preaches the simple lesson of contentment by means of a fairy story, staged with a delightful accompaniment of talking animals and excursions into fanciful worlds. In this, as in most of the Maeterlinck plays, there is a poetic, remote beauty, with pictures of a world which, though unfamiliar, still seems to be home.

The most distinguished theatrical event of the late nineteenth century was doubtless the production of *Cyrano de*

*Bergerac* (1897) whose author, Edmond Rostand (1864-1918), left at his death half a dozen dramas, all of them in verse and romantic in theme. His first work, called *The Fantastics* (*Les Romanesques*) is, oddly enough, a delicate satire on the perversions of the romantic school. *The Faraway Princess* and *The Samaritan Woman* provided Mme Bernhardt with interesting, if not distinguished, rôles. It is, however, by his last three dramas, *Cyrano de Bergerac, L'Aiglon,* and *Chanticler* that Rostand's name will be remembered. They stand alone in the roster of romantic plays; and each one, while stamped with its author's genius, yet has its own peculiar excellence. *Cyrano,* for example, is first of all a play with gorgeous poetry, full of wit and life; secondly, its plot, though somewhat improbable, is yet of such a nature as to tickle the fancy; and, thirdly, the author has been able to render fascinating a hero with peculiar misfortunes. The rôle has tempted some of the most gifted actors of contemporary and recent times. In *L'Aiglon* the author has taken one of the many eminent but insignificant creatures of history, and out of his futile dreamings made a tragedy which echoes the tragedies of all the dreamers of the world. In *Chanticler* quite a different feat was accomplished: under the guise of the feathered animals of the forest and barnyard, Rostand portrayed the optimistic captain who, believing that he and his work are essential to the proper running of the universe, suddenly finds that the sun rises and all the world's work goes on without his help. In each of these three plays the author attacked not only an interesting and subtle problem in psychology, but, especially in *Cyrano* and *Chanticler,* great difficulties in the way of stage representation. These difficulties were surmounted with precision and apparent ease. In the hands of Rostand the romantic play again offered an occasion for intense enjoyment,—an enjoyment in which the sense of truth still prevailed, and "reality" for a time was made synonymous with beauty.

## ITALY

The transition period between the old and the new drama of Italy was marked by two or three writers whose ability con-

Photograph by Arthur Kales

Interior, by Maurice Maeterlinck. Community Theater, Hollywood.

sisted chiefly of being able to sense the taste of the times. Most important of these transition writers was Giuseppe Giacosa (1847-1906) whose dramas, if not masterpieces, were generally interesting and workmanlike. His ideas and methods covered a wide range. One of his earliest plays, *A Game of Chess* (1871), founded on an old French legend and written in verse, is delicately idyllic in character. There followed several historical plays, which in turn were followed by several examples of social drama, represented by *Luise* (1883), in which the usual sexual difficulties were portrayed and the case solved by suicide. Coming under the influence of Becque, Augier, and other European "reformers," Giacosa more and more employed material drawn from contemporary life. Though he avoided violent action, yet he could set forth biting situations; and he came to be recognized as the chief exponent of the naturalistic school in Italy. *As the Leaves* is perhaps the best known of all his plays, it having been successful not only in Italy but elsewhere in Europe. He was the author also of the librettos for the operas of *La Bohème, Tosca,* and *Madame Butterfly.*

As in other parts of Europe, the revived interest in drama divided its followers into two camps: the romantics, on the one hand, and on the other the naturalists, who came in time to be called the Verists. Giacosa was never an extremist, but somewhat at home in both camps. Marco Praga (born 1862) considered Giacosa too "wholesome" and idealistic to be true to life. Praga disbelieved, or affected to disbelieve, in all goodness, purity, or faithfulness; and he was obsessed by sex and the allurements of illicit or extravagant passions. *The Virgins* and *The Ideal Wife* had considerable popularity. *The Enamoured Woman* was written especially for Eleanora Duse. Giovanni Verga (born 1840), author of *Cavallería Rusticana, In the Porter's Lodge, The Fox Hunt,* and other plays, was also much engaged with questions of sex, lust, and violence. He stated as his chief purposes, first, to simplify the action of drama and rid it of unnecessary conventions; secondly, to avoid literary ornaments and conceits in the dialogue. Verga's plays reflect a powerful and an honest mind, sincerely sympathetic with those who suffer; but his characters are too much pre-occupied with extravagant and lustful passions.

At the end of the nineteenth century doubtless the most notable name among Italian dramatists was that of Gabriele d'Annunzio (born 1863), whose contribution to the stage, like his life, has been interesting but contradictory. His early work included biblical plays in which the commonly accepted moral was reversed; and "dream plays" with splendid imagery but little action. His first long drama, *The Dead City* (*La Citta Morte*), is perhaps an attempt at a reconstruction of classic tragedy. It has a morbid theme of love between brother and sister, and for many readers only an equivocal value. *La Gioconda* (1898), based on an old legend, is, like *The Sunken Bell* of Hauptmann, a discussion of the needs of the artistic temperament in the male. The rôle of the wife in this play also had the advantage of being interpreted by Eleanora Duse. A drama called *Glory* (1899) was refused the stage even by the tolerant Italians. The ancient subject of *Phædra* has also attracted D'Annunzio. *The Daughter of Jorio* (1904) is prob-ably not only the most actable but also the most acceptable of all his works. D'Annunzio has virtuosity and color as a poet, and the ability to contrive effective situations and striking characters. This is well illustrated in his *Francesca da Rimini*. But he relies too much on words, and he is lacking in the social conscience which often renders even a mediocre work signifi-cant. Professor MacClintock describes him as "melancholy, lacking in humor, contemptuous of the people, one to whom faith, hope, charity are meaningless terms"; and one who "em-bodies the dead or dying past of his nation."[1]

Among the realists of Italy must be numbered Antonio Fogazzarro (1842-1911), novelist as well as dramatist, whose *Red Carnation* was counted a success; also the brothers Camillo and Gianino Traversi. The former achieved considerable fame as the author of *The Rozeno Family* (1891) in which a tragedy of low life is portrayed with sincerity. Following the example of the French, the brothers produced various one-act skits of the more or less risqué vaudeville type. Gianino later produced

[1] Landor MacClintock, *The Contemporary Drama of Italy.*

a long list of comedies in which situations of the Sheridan-Molière sort prevailed. Roberto Bracco (1862) has been a prolific writer for the stage, producing comedies, social dramas, psychological plays, and pure tragedies, some of which have traveled over Europe and into America. *The Hidden Spring* is concerned with social problems. *Don Pietro Carneso* and *Lost in Darkness* are considered among the best of his works. The former piece was produced in New York in 1914. Spectators have reported that the works of Bracco leave a profound impression of pessimism; also that with him there are still found many of the old-time stage devices, such as overheard conversations and lost letters.

Among the most provocative and stimulating of the present-day writers is Luigi Pirandello (born 1867), a Sicilian who studied in Germany and has won international honors as a dramatist. His plays, some of which are in one act, are called comedies, but they carry satire, psychological analysis, and often more than a touch of the tragic. Pirandello is a thoroughly trained craftsman. Among his titles are *Sicilian Limes, If Not Thus, Six Characters in Search of an Author,* and *Right You Are, If You Think You Are.* Under his humor lies the essentially melancholy temperament of the Sicilian; but beneath that is always the hint of something further, as if he would say, "Let us be kind and considerate, since life is not long, and the way is hard at best."

Sem Benelli (born 1877) is the author of at least seven dramas in verse. *The Bookworm* (1904) is, so far as the writer knows, his only play in prose, and also the only one dealing with contemporary modern life. All his other dramas are based on medieval or ancient legends, or semi-historical incidents, depicting the passions of hate, revenge, or some form of subtle cruelty. *The Supper of Jokes* (known on the English and American stage as *The Jest*) made a great sensation in Italy and in Europe generally. It is a play of intrigue, with sensuous and glittering scenes in which the naked passions of southern temperaments clash, take vengeance, and destroy themselves. *The Love of the Three Kings* (1910) is best known, at least outside of Italy, in its operatic form. Benelli has a sure eye for effective and thrilling situations, and at his best is poetic and imaginative. Moreover, he has been of service in substituting for the eleven-syllable line of verse a more vivid and flexible type, nearly resembling the English blank verse, in which the style is free from artificial ornaments.

## SPAIN

The old story of revolt against mechanical plots followed by a sudden fever of "realism" or "naturalism" was repeated in Spain, though in a somewhat milder form. As Giacosa in Italy represented the connecting link between the old drama and the new, so in Spain Jose Echegaray (1833-1916) formed a similar link. The play most familiar to theater-goers outside of Spain is his *El Gran Galeoto* (1908), known in English as *The World and His Wife*. It is a satire on the pettiness and cruelty of small-town respectability. The school of modern realism is further represented by Linares Rivas, whose work as dramatist has been carried on simultaneously with his activities as politician. Many of his plots hinge on domestic unhappiness. He is a satirist and a reformer; and he (with Benevente), has been accused of imitating the French. *Stifling* (*Aire de Fuera*), *The Claw* (*La Garra*), and *The Cage of the Lioness* (*La Jaula de la Leona*) are some of his titles.

Jose Benevente (born 1866), author of *The Passion Flower* (*La Malquerida*) and *The Bonds of Interest* (*Los Intereses Creados,* 1907), writes in prose, excludes physical action to a great extent, and probes deeply into the evils of society. The brothers Quintero are also exponents of realism and share with Benevente the credit of ridding the stage of much that was artificial and mechanical. *Concha the Clean* (*Concha la Limpia*) and *The House of Life* (*La Flor de la Vida*) are by the Quintero brothers; also several three-act pieces, each of which has but two characters.

Since the beginning of the present century symbolic and poetic drama has found special favor in Spain. Ramón Goy de Silva, Jacinto Grau Delgado, and Martínez Sierra have contributed to the species, the latter being known at the present moment (1927) in New York by *The Cradle Song* (*Canción de Cuna*),—a delicate and unusual play. The most widely known of the writers of poetic drama is perhaps Eduardo Marquina, who has been courageous enough to discard nearly everything in the way of theatrical tricks and trust to a well constructed plot. *The Poor Carpenter* (*El Pobrecito Carpintero*) well illustrates his poetic ability and his feeling for dramatic situation. Conditions in Spain, as elsewhere in Europe and in America, are in many respects more favorable for dramatic enterprise than at any time during the past century; and in Europe especially, with municipal theaters in almost every capital, a system of short runs and stock companies, the outlook for the theater is highly promising.

CHAPTER XXXV

# THE LAST FIFTY YEARS IN ENGLAND
## AND IRELAND

The drama, like the symphony, does not teach nor prove anything.—JOHN MILLINGTON SYNGE.

It has been noted in a previous chapter how the work of Sir
Arthur Pinero and of Mr. Henry Arthur Jones forms, in a
manner, a bridge between the pre-Ibsen and the post-Ibsen
drama of England. In the later years of the century there
was a marked rejuvenation of the theater; but there was no
such violent descent into the abysses of society as had appeared
in *The Weavers* of Hauptmann, nor any such pre-occupation
with morbid phases of life as had been seen in Wedekind's
*Awakening of Spring*. Nor was there, on the other hand, anything to parallel the jeweled brilliance of Rostand. One of the
most gifted writers, Oscar Wilde (1856-1900), was like Rostand in one respect, however: he seemed to be wholly unaffected by the revolutionary "schools" of the time. Wilde
wrote half a dozen comedies of social life, two of which, *The
Importance of Being Earnest* and *Lady Windermere's Fan,* are
masterpieces of their type. The Wilde plays, like those of
Congreve, are vehicles for epigram, witty repartee, and comments upon life and society which were thought bitterly caustic
in their day, and are still amusing. Underneath the verbal
fireworks is generally the solid structure of a well-built plot.
The one play not concerned with English life is *Salome,* originally written in French for Mme Bernhardt. It is ornate and
sumptuous in style, and possesses the theatrical effectiveness
peculiar to Wilde. After an initial performance in Paris in
1892 it was forbidden the French stage; but in 1901 it was
presented in Berlin, whence it has traveled to other parts of

Europe and to America. It has had the longest run in Germany of any English work. Wilde said of himself that he had broadened the field and enriched the characters of English drama.

*George Bernard Shaw.* Born 1856. The most conspicuous example of the social reformer of the English-speaking stage is, of course, Mr. Shaw, who though born in Dublin has spent most of his life in London. Mr. Shaw is novelist and journalist, as well as dramatist; and his connection with the stage began as dramatic critic. The necessity of attending the theater several evenings a week and witnessing the plays current on the London stage in the eighteen-nineties induced in him a sort of fever—resentment, disgust, and weariness combined. The remedy was for Mr. Shaw to write the plays himself. By the year 1898 he had scrutinized the social institutions of his day and discovered that the incomes of many pious people were derived from wicked sources, that the military hero is often a silly ass and a baby to boot, that the industrial world harbors injustices, and that men are often entrapped into marriage by clever women. These discoveries were not new: Mr. Shaw would be the first to point that out. For that very reason he saw that they could be used as themes for the theater. With his inexhaustible fluency and his renowned Irish wit, he was able to turn them into readable and, in some cases, actable plays. He began with "unpleasant" subjects, such as were exhibited in *Widowers' Houses* and *Mrs. Warren's Profession.* As *The Second Mrs. Tanqueray* had been the result of Sir Arthur Pinero's reaction to the Ibsen virus, so *Mrs. Warren* was the result of Shaw's inoculation. It was a courageous achievement for its time, though now it seems somewhat obvious and a little "dated." It was produced on the English stage through the enterprise of Messrs. Vedrenne and Barker, who belonged to the independent group. It was by means of other and more amusing plays, however, that Mr. Shaw found his larger public. In *Arms and the Man* he satirized delightfully the uniform-adoring female, making fun of the picture-book soldier and the pomposities of military heroes; in *Candida* he ridiculed the husband-wife-lover intrigue, turning the situation into half-earnest, half-extravagant comedy; in *The Man of Destiny* he showed Napoleon tricked by a clever woman; in *Cæsar and Cleopatra* he mocked at the long-accepted sanctities of history; in *St. Joan* he likewise gave his own interpretation of a half-legendary figure; in *Man and Superman* he created an amazing picture of the throw-back of even the most civilized persons under the stress of youth and love. In *Back to Methuselah* he put on the stage a five-hour study of the progress and failures of the human race. He could even use the conventionalized servants, the tea-parties and the stock situations of the early Victorians to advantage, turning them into laughable parodies of themselves. In one of his prefaces he says: ". . . far from taking an unsympathetic view of the popular demand for fun, for fashionable dresses, for a pretty scene or two, a little music, and even for a great ordering of drinks by people with an expensive air from an if-possible-comic-waiter, I was more than willing to show that the drama can humanize these things as easily as they, in undramatic hands, can dehumanize the drama."

Entertaining as Mr. Shaw, the dramatist, has been, he is primarily a salesman of ideas. He has written long plays with nothing in them but argument; and even in the best of his work he himself is the most conspicuous character. His courage and skill in attacking smug conventions and traditional prejudices amount to genius of the first order; and they were, to the stage of the late nineteenth century, of far more worth than a merely facile technique could possibly have been. He has afforded better entertainment than any other living preacher. If he has not created immortal characters he has been the gadfly of his generation, routing the slothful and stinging the sentimental. Like Ibsen, he is a passionate moralist; and, like Aristophanes, he has felt himself at liberty to attack anything. He has even cajoled and teased people into the habit of reading plays. Before Shaw almost nobody, except candidates for a Ph. D. in literature, ever read plays, new or old; now, roughly speaking, since the publication of *Plays Pleasant and Unpleasant* the reading of plays has become as much a matter of course as the reading of the weekly journals.

Shaw no longer shocks, however; he has become the venerable dean of the profession.

*Galsworthy and others.* The author of *Strife, Justice, The Pigeon,* and other plays, Mr. John Galsworthy (born 1867), was educated at Oxford, read law, and later won distinction both as novelist and critic. His first plays, *The Silver Box* (1906) and *Justice* (1910), placed him definitely in the ranks of reformers of social conditions; but he is less militant—possibly more bitter—than Mr. Shaw. With the courage of a crusader, he has the temperament of an æsthete and a recluse. Where Mr. Shaw is abusive, personal and partisan, Mr. Galsworthy is detached and objective; where Mr. Shaw used the bandwagon and trumpet, Mr. Galsworthy used the searchlight and scalpel. His plays are skilfully constructed, with true insight into character and good dialogue, showing, above all, the unsparing realist disdainful of the gewgaws of romanticism.

John Masefield, an Englishman who has served many years on the sea, has won his finest distinction in the field of narrative poetry. He is an uncompromising disciple of realism in drama. Among several more or less "literary" plays and dramatic poems, *The Tragedy of Nan* (1908) seems to be best adapted to the stage. It is, however, depressing and somewhat lacking in the vigor and driving power which alone can carry heavy tragic action. John Drinkwater, a well-known poet, is one of the few writers who have been successful in utilizing as heroes of their drama the figures of American history. His *Abraham Lincoln* was widely accepted, both in England and in the United States, as a sincere and moving picture of the great emancipator.

Another disciple of realism is Mr. Granville Barker, born in London in 1877, who has been both actor and manager, as well as dramatist. In 1904 he became associated with Mr. J. E. Vedrenne in the management of a London theater devoted largely to the production of plays not of the conventional sort. Mr. Barker has been instrumental in giving fine performances of Greek plays both in England and in the United States, and has himself written serious social dramas dealing with middle-class provincial people. He seems to avoid all appearance of a constructed plot, and to present life much as it appears to an onlooker, in its disjointed and sometimes fruitless scenes. The best of his offerings, up to the present time, are *The Madras House* and *Waste*. In *Prunella* (1904, in collaboration with Mr. Laurence Housman), he departed from his earlier practices and made concessions to the average spectator's love of romance and glamour.

A whimsical and humorous gift belongs to Sir James Barrie, born in Scotland in 1860, whose first plays appeared near the end of the nineteenth century. In common with the realists, Barrie has the power to produce local types of character, details of speech and conduct, and shades of temper, with uncanny exactitude. His tendency towards realism, however, goes no further. He has a careful regard for form, and he never allows his desire for truthfulness of characterization to lead him into depressing side-alleys. With subjects and people taken from small-town Scotch life, as in *Quality Street, The Little Minister* (dramatized from his novel), and *What Every Woman Knows,* he has been a valiant defender of a sort of sane idealism and happy fantasy. His romanticism does not belie or misrepresent the essentials of human nature. He has taken the old themes of the woman in revolt against too much domesticity, the brilliant public man who needs a lesson in humility, and the perfect servant who, by an unexpected turn of affairs, exchanges places with his master (*The Admirable Crichton*), and given them to the public with humor, sympathy, and quiet understanding. His *Peter Pan,* a fairy play, with the title rôle enacted by Miss Maude Adams, was one of the few dramas which could compete in popularity with Rostand's *Cyrano.*

Remembering the innumerable attempts and constant failures of nineteenth century writers to produce actable poetic drama, we should specially note the career of Mr. Stephen Phillips (born in England in 1867), and his success in that field. Mr. Phillips was for some years an actor, later a teacher. His *Herod,* played by Mr. Beerbohm Tree in London, has also been given successfully in Germany and in the United States. *The*

*Sin of David, Ulysses,* and *Paolo and Francesca* have found many admirers, in spite of the fact that poetic drama is still, as in the nineteenth century, a hazardous venture for the producer. Mr. Phillips has escaped, for the most part, the pitfalls which lay in the path of the nineteenth century poets, revealing the ability to create effective situations and to write verse suited to the stage.

## IRELAND

One of the results of the revival of interest in the Gaelic language and folk lore was the opening, in Dublin in 1899, of the Irish Literary Theater with a performance of *The Countess Cathleen* by Mr. W. B. Yeats. The policy of this organization was to give plays written by Irish dramatists upon national themes, but with English actors. Besides Mr. Yeats, Messrs. Edward Martyn, George Moore, and George Russell (A.E.) were associated in the undertaking. After producing one piece in Gaelic and six in English, the organization was discontinued. In 1901 there was established the Irish National Theater, whose policy differed from that of the earlier enterprise in one important point: namely, Irish actors were to be assembled and trained as a repertory company. The type of play, also, was to be restricted to works dealing with Irish peasant life, or with an imaginary world, with fairy stories, or with the great heroes of the past.

From these beginnings developed the Abbey Theater and the Irish Players, who, in a comparatively short time, gained considerable fame both in Britain and in America. The success of the movement was to a large extent due to the encouragement, managerial ability and devotion of Mr. W. B. Yeats; but working with him in close sympathy were also Lady Gregory, John Synge, Padraic Colum and a few others. Mr. Yeats' idea was to inaugurate a simple style of acting, in which words should be of more importance than gesture, movement, or scenery. Rhythmic and beautiful speech was to be cultivated, the importance of minor parts emphasized, and simple but suggestive settings used. Such ideas as these, almost unheard-of in the ordinary commercial theaters of 1901, have in recent years become the general property both of the "little" and the commercial theaters all over the world.

William Butler Yeats, born in Dublin in 1865, has written at least a dozen plays, nearly all of which are national in tone and content, mystical, and deeply poetic. He has avoided the stereotyped methods of obtaining stage effects, relying more upon the essential value of the situation. His work has sincerity and genuine beauty. *The Countess Cathleen* (1899), *The Land of Heart's Desire,* and *Cathleen ni Houlihan,* the best known of his plays, are all concerned with Celtic legends and national glories. Like several other modern writers, including Synge, Mr. Yeats has made a dramatic version of the story of Deirdre, the Irish Helen.

Lady Augusta Gregory, born in Ireland in 1859, has been until recently manager of the Abbey Theater and has had a large share in the creation of a national drama. Her first literary work was the re-writing of many of the Celtic legends; and it is upon the solid foundations of local character and folk lore that her plays are built. She is at her best in the short comedy, such as *Spreading the News* (1904), *The Workhouse Ward* (1908), and *Hyacinth Halvey* (1906), which have won a wide popularity. *The Rising of the Moon* (1907) has also been much admired for its fine simple style, its kindliness of temper, and its dramatic effectiveness. Besides writing more than a score of original plays, Lady Gregory has translated for the Irish stage pieces by Molière, Goldoni, and Sudermann.

The greatest playwright of the Irish movement, and one of the most distinguished dramatists of the past fifty years, was John Millington Synge (1871-1909). He was born in Ireland, led a sort of bohemian life in Paris, where he was discovered by Mr. Yeats and urged to turn his attention to Irish subjects, went to the Aran Islands for a considerable sojourn, and finally achieved notable success in his delineations of Celtic life and character. His plays were all written after 1903, and each one is based on a native legend or a characteristic incident. The language used is a kind of enhanced local dialect, picturesque and full of feeling. Mr. Ernest Boyd has re-

marked upon the skill with which Synge depicted the vaga-
bond life of the roads, the amusing and colorful "blackguard-
ism and rowdyism" of the country tramp. His scenes combine
realism with sardonic humor and imaginative strength. The
humor or tragedy lies always in the situation and not merely
in the words. *In the Shadow of the Glen* shows the suspicious
husband of a young and comely wife testing her faithfulness
by pretending to be dead and watching how she carries on at
the wake. *The Well of the Saints* portrays an old blind man
and woman, each thinking the other fine and handsome as in
youth, and shows what happens when they had their sight restored. *The Playboy of the Western World* (1907), an ex-
travaganza in which a bragging peasant boy is brought to book,
is perhaps Synge's most famous example of half-cynical humor
and romantic fantasy; while *Riders to the Sea* illustrates his
ability to portray relentless tragedy in a manner that has often
been compared to the power of the Greeks. "The creator of
*The Playboy* was something more than an exponent of peasant
drama. . . . Synge transformed reality until the real and the
ideal were one. It is this imaginative re-creation which en-
titles him to a place amongst the great dramatists of the world's
literature." [1]

Other writers, most of whom are still living, have added to
the repertory of the Irish Theater: Lennox Robinson, the present manager of the Abbey Theater, with *The Cross Roads* and
other plays; Seumas O'Kelly, with half a dozen pieces worthy
of attention; George Fitzmaurice, T. C. Murray, St. John
Ervine and others, some of whom have had productions in
London and New York. The most distinguished of the later
writers is probably Lord Dunsany, whose plays are enacted in
some unknown, half-oriental country, and whose characters
are neither Irish nor European but universal and typical. *A
Night at an Inn, The Golden Doom, King Argimenes,* and *The
Queen's Enemies* are all singularly original in theme and treatment, poetic in tone with realistic touches of character. *The
Gods of the Mountain* shows how seven beggars are induced
by their leader, a crafty rowdy, to impersonate the stone deities

[1] Ernest A. Boyd, *The Contemporary Drama of Ireland.*

who live on a distant hill, and who, according to the local belief, should one day come to life and visit the city. The beggars are successful in deceiving the people. They live on costly food and rare wines; but their day of reckoning comes when the real gods appear. It is a strikingly dramatic moment when the impostors, hearing the tread of the coming gods, begin to cower in their corners, and when at last each one in his own niche is slowly turned to stone.

Of all the local movements of recent years in the drama, none is more significant than that of the Irish stage, because of its national spirit and the sincerity of its aims. Mr. Yeats expressed as a prophecy what came to be recognized as a fact: "This theater cannot but be more interesting to people of other races because it is Irish, and, therefore, to some extent, stirred by emotions and thoughts not hitherto expressed in dramatic form."

## CHAPTER XXXVI

# RUSSIA

We should not go to the theater as we go to a chemist's or a dram-shop, but as we go to a dinner, where the food we need is taken with pleasure and excitement.—JOHN MILLINGTON SYNGE.

Long previous to the nineteenth century there was undoubtedly in Russia a native dramatic art—puppet shows, farces, and probably plays similar to the medieval mysteries; but so far the European world knows little about it. In the eighteenth century Alexander Sumarokov (1718-1777) produced both comedies and tragedies, the latter after the style of Racine and Voltaire, though he used plots based on native material. Sumarokov had numerous followers and disciples, among whom was no less a personage than Catherine II (called the Great), who wrote comedies in which she ridiculed the pomposities and hypocrisies of her courtiers. She even essayed a drama in the romantic style; but in her time and for a generation after, the influence of the French was paramount.

Pseudo-classicism, however, could not forever hold the Russian spirit; and the first important native tragedy, *Boris Godunov,* written in the third decade of the nineteenth century, was boldly composed in imitation of Shakespeare. Its author was Alexander Pushkin (1799-1837), who came from a wealthy, land-owning family, was several times embroiled in political difficulties, wrote an *Ode to Liberty* that was considered seditious, and was killed in a duel at the age of thirty-eight. Although Pushkin's work for the stage was but a minor part of his output, yet it was sufficient to turn the attention of contemporary and succeeding writers to the history of their own country. With his romantic treatment of national figures he combined truthfulness of detail. "Naturalness of scene," he wrote, "and naturalness of dialogue are the first principles of all true tragedy."

The dramatists of the middle years of the nineteenth century seem quite consistently to have striven to understand and portray the Russian character and the essential features of Russian life, with its crumbling feudal system, its vast army of peasants, its mysticism, its cruelty, and its enormous strength. Their genius showed itself for the most part in comedy rather than in tragedy. N. V. Gogol (1809-1852) has long been recognized as a humorist of the first rank. His comedy *The Inspector General* (*Revisor,* 1836) is one of the few world-famous pieces for the stage. The title of founder and creator of modern Russian drama is sometimes given to A. N. Ostrovsky (1823-1886), whose specialty was the portrayal of the merchant class in provincial districts. Ostrovsky, like Gogol, owes his fame to his power of shrewd observation and good-natured satire. Some of his titles are *Poverty is no Crime, Bad Days, The Snow Maiden,* and *The Storm,* the latter being considered his best work.

An important contribution to the national stage was made by the poet and dramatist Count Alexei Tolstoi (1817-1875), whose best known work is a trilogy based on historical material. The titles of the three plays are *The Death of Ivan the Terrible, Tsar Theodor,* and *Tsar Boris.* These plays appeared during the third decade of the nineteenth century and immediately became an important feature of the national repertory. They portray not only national figures, but also the conditions attendant upon despotic power, with its abuse and its glory, reminding the spectator somewhat of the heroic spectacles of Marlowe. Ivan Turgenev (1818-1883) produced a few dramas, but his best known works were in the field of fiction rather than for the stage.

After the tide of romanticism came to its height and passed, that of realism had its hour. Count Lyoff Tolstoi (1828-1910), better known as the writer of *Anna Karenina* and other novels, was the author of several dramas full of grim detail and pictures of suffering. *The Powers of Darkness* is a play of unmitigated horror; nevertheless, when it was performed

Striking climax of Act II in the "Habima" troupe's production of *The Dybbuk*, Ansky's play of Ghetto life. A synthesis of Hebrew and Russian stage art

in 1886, its effect was so great on the audience that after its close students waited outside the theater to catch sight of the author and to kiss his hand. Maxim Gorky (born 1868) has made himself, in a sense, the voice of an immense class hitherto submerged, but with each succeeding decade growing more and more articulate. Gorky's stage world—composed of thieves, prostitutes, and social outcasts of all kinds—is a half-savage, brutal place in which gross, titanic figures strive to make known their feelings and their dimly understood aspirations. *The Philistines* (1902) and *The Night Asylum* (also known as *In the Depths,* 1903) have been produced in many places outside of Russia. Even darker still is the world pictured by Leonid Andreyev (1871-1919), because for him there seems to be no light, no solace, no escape from sin. Normal desires were to him the clutch of the "abysmal brute," dragging men down to death and perdition. Andreyev's weakness as a dramatist consists in the vagueness of his characters, which are like the abstractions of a morality play. *The Black Masks* (1908) symbolizes the darkness which surrounds every human soul; the old question as to the meaning of life and its attendant sorrows is the underlying theme of *The Life of Man;* while *King Hunger* (1908) symbolizes the warfare between classes—the age-long conflict between the workers and the spenders. *He Who Gets Slapped,* a tragi-comedy based on the life of a circus clown, has had marked success outside of Russia. There is one quality of great worth in Andreyev: namely, his willingness to fight for intellectual and social liberty.

The most important dramatist which Russia has so far produced is Anton Chekhov (1860-1904), a physician of Moscow who left, besides many fine short stories, a few dramas which are strikingly original. Chekhov combined a naturalistic method with a philosophic mind and a humanitarian gentleness of temper. At least four of his plays—*The Sea Gull, The Cherry Orchard, Uncle Vanya,* and *The Three Sisters*—have become widely known throughout Europe and America, particularly through the interpretation of the Moscow Art Theater players. *The Cherry Orchard* is perhaps most typical both of the author's method and of his success in creating "atmosphere." The surviving members of an ancient land-holding family come back from Paris to find that their country place is about to be sold at auction for debts. A former peasant, now a prosperous factory owner, offers to buy their famous cherry orchard for a generous sum, and so save their fortunes; but family pride and a general spirit of procrastination will not permit them to trade with the social upstart. In their natures, sorrow over trouble and levity over responsibilities are inextricably mixed. They can take nothing seriously. They argue and talk it all over in their own charming fashion until finally the house is sold over their heads and the sound of the axe is heard in the beloved orchard. When they leave, with characteristic absent-mindedness they accidentally lock the faithful old servant into the empty and abandoned house. That is all: there is no struggle, nothing that could technically be called a plot; yet on the stage the representation is full of suspense and pathos. The author's conception is intense, though detached. There is no hint of social "problems" or blame for anybody or any party,—only a tender, acute delineation of weak, delightful people. Among the naturalists of the theater Chekhov and Synge alone have been able to achieve the classic tragic note. Their scenes rise out of human experiences, wherein love and tenderness and family relationships have had their due meed. Especially with Chekhov does one feel the presence of an understanding heart; nothing escapes his observation, yet all is rendered with sympathy and pity.

The fluctuations of Russian life in the nineteenth century were in many respects quite different from anything else in Europe. It is now scarcely more than sixty-five years since the abolition of the serf system, the result of which, long delayed, was the final dethronement of the landed aristocracy and the inauguration of a new social organization. Within the present century important revolutions have taken place; and the writers of today are, little by little, interpreting the spirit of the time. In the confusion and vagueness of much of the teaching, two main themes are constantly seen to be uppermost: individualism and religion. They preach the right of individuals to gratify personal desires, to take property or life, to rule others as they have been ruled, as long as power lasts. With this rampant individualism came also a revision of the code in sexual affairs and in family life,—a revision that has threatened to sweep away all tradition. Furthermore, Russian drama, like most of the modern Russian literature, reveals an intense preoccupation with religion. Some of the writers, like Andreyev, cried out that there is "no God, no consolation for this dark horror which is life"; but such a cry is of itself evidence of the search. There is a persistent mystical note,— the note of a belief that this material world is only the vestibule to another realm, and that poetry, art, and music can guide the soul thither. Above all, it must not be thought that the Russian drama is dying or decadent; on the contrary, it is developing before our eyes, and so, in a special sense, should be regarded as holding the seeds of the future.

## CHAPTER XXXVII

# DRAMA IN AMERICA

. . . real development is not leaving things behind, as on a road, but drawing life from them, as from a root.—GILBERT CHESTERTON, *All Things Considered.*

The history of drama in America is naturally bound up with that of England, owing partly to the use of a common language and the existence of a noble tradition in the mother country. The first play acted in America by a professional company is said to have been *The Recruiting Officer,* by George Farquhar, brought over from London in 1732. The visit of a company of English actors in 1752 was of great importance in stimulating interest in dramatic productions; but it was not until 1766 that a permanent playhouse, the Old Southwark of Philadelphia, appeared in America. In 1767 the John Street Theater was built in New York. According to Professor Arthur H. Quinn, of the University of Pennsylvania, the first play written by an American and performed by a professional company of actors on an American stage was *The Prince of Parthia,* a tragedy in blank verse by Thomas Godfrey (1736-1763), produced in 1767. In 1787 there was given a comedy called *The Contrast* [1] by Royall Tyler (1757-1826), who later became chief justice of the state of Vermont. *The Contrast* is in prose, with a prologue and catchy songs, and introduces the humorous figure of Jonathan, the clever Yankee.

Two years after the appearance of *The Contrast,* William Dunlap (1766-1839), an American, came forward with a comedy called *The Father;* and later he wrote or adapted half-a-hundred plays, among them a number from Kotzebue, Schiller, and other German playwrights. Two of his own dramas are

[1] Revived in 1912 in Brattleboro, Vermont, under the direction of Mrs. Otis Skinner.

352

on themes from American history. In the prologue to *André*
there is a hint of the tone taken by a long procession of dramatists from Plautus down:

> "She (the Muse) sings of wrongs long past. Men as they were
> To instruct, without reproach, the Men that are;
> Then judge the story by the genius shown,
> And praise, or damn it, for its worth alone."

Dunlap's most important claim to gratitude, however, is not
primarily based on his dramas, but rather upon the fact that
he wrote a *History of the Early American Theater,* which was
published in 1832.

During the latter part of the nineteenth century various companies of actors were organized, one of them for the express
purpose of giving plays "by Shakespeare and other well-estab-
lished authors." The Park Theater in New York was opened
in 1798 with a performance of *As You Like It;* and it was at
this playhouse that John Howard Payne (1791-1852) made
his début as an actor in 1809 as Norval in John Home's
*Douglas.* Although, in the grandiloquent fashion of the times,
Payne was later called "the American Roscius," yet it is not
for his acting that he is remembered, but as the author of
*Home, Sweet Home,*—a lyric included in the opera *Clari, or
The Maid of Milan,* which appeared in 1824. The song is
supposed to have been written in Tunis, North Africa. Among
his contributions to the stage are more than fifty plays, one
of which was done in collaboration with Washington Irving.
*Charles the Second* is a comedy of manners; while his *Brutus,*
a tragedy in blank verse, is generally considered the first drama
of importance written by an American.

*The early nineteenth century.* In the meantime several playhouses were built, stock companies were formed, and distinguished actors from England made profitable visits to
America. Edmund Kean came in 1820, his son Charles in
1830, MacCready in 1826, Junius Brutus Booth in 1821 and
in 1833, Charles and Fanny Kemble in 1832-33, and the elder
John Drew in 1845. The American actor Edwin Forrest made
his first appearance in 1826 as Othello, beginning a celebrated

career which continued for nearly fifty years. Two plays by American authors, *The Gladiator* by R. N. Bird (1806-1854) and *Metamora* by John A. Stone, were written for and success-fully produced by Forrest. *The Broker of Bogota,* also by Bird, first performed in 1834, was for more than thirty years included in Forrest's repertory. Bird's specialty was romantic tragedy in blank verse; but plays of other sorts, melodrama, historical pieces, and studies of Indian life, were not wholly lacking. Richard Penn Smith (1799-1854) had at least fifteen plays performed, two of which were taken to London. A prose drama called *Pocahontas and the Settlers of Virginia,* by George Washington Parke Custis (1781-1857), was produced in 1836 and had a "good" run of twelve nights. The poet Nathaniel P. Willis (1806-1867) had the distinction of having his comedy in verse, *Tortesa the Usurer* (1839), transferred to London. Few of these plays seem much worth while; but the same thing might be said of most other nineteenth-century dramatic productions. On the whole, it would appear that the American stage at this time was as creditable as that of any country in Europe with the exception of France.

*The mid-century.* One of the landmarks in American drama was the appearance of *Fashion* (1845) by Anna Cora Mowatt Ritchie (1819-1870). It is a satire on the pretensions of a newly-rich New York woman, who drags into her conversa-tion badly pronounced French phrases, boasts of her elegant European acquaintances, and is properly taken in by a slick hair-dresser who passes himself off as a French count.[2] It was highly successful, having the very unusual run of twenty-two nights. Edgar Allan Poe, writing for *The Broadway Journal,* called it a "very bad play," objecting especially to the use of asides. "Compared with the generality of modern drama," he wrote, "it is a good play; compared with most American drama it is a very good play; estimated by the natural principles of dramatic art, it is altogether unworthy of notice." Poe was somewhat jaundiced; for *Fashion* certainly is far from being contemptible. It is, moreover, the first successful instance of

[2] *Fashion* was revived in 1924 by the Provincetown Players in New York, when it ran for 235 performances.

a theatrical *genre* which belongs peculiarly to the American stage—shrewd, good-natured ridicule, the latest examples of which can be recognized in such plays as *The Show-Off* and *The First Year*.

It was the mode in England, as we know, for distinguished writers to try their hand at poetic drama; and we find in America George H. Boker (1833-1890) making his version of the oft-dramatized story of *Francesca da Rimini*. It was in blank verse, was first performed in 1855, and has twice been revived, once in 1882 by Lawrence Barrett, again in 1901 by Mr. Otis Skinner. Another and better known poet, Julia Ward Howe, (1819-1910) wrote a tragedy entitled *Leonora or The World's Own*, which was first performed in 1857 and considered a fine achievement.

*The second half of the century.* One of the visiting actors in the middle years of the century was Dion Boucicault (1822-1890), an Irishman who, at the age of nineteen, had written a successful comedy of society life called *London Assurance*. After two visits to the United States Boucicault again returned, founded a theater in Washington, and later the New Park Theater in New York, in which city he lived until his death in 1890. Authorities differ concerning the number of his plays; but they must have amounted to more than a hundred. Among them were such favorites as *The Octoroon, Streets o' London,* and the popular version of *Rip van Winkle,* which had its first performance in London in 1865. The actor Joseph Jefferson (1829-1905), who made the character of Rip familiar to at least two generations of play-goers, was in a way a link between the American stage and that of the eighteenth century; since, as a child of three years, he took his first rôle in a production of Sheridan's *Pizarro*.

The conditions of the American theater did not offer much encouragement to native playwrights, yet a few talented and persistent writers devoted some of their time to it. James A. Herne (1839-1901), an actor-manager, was successful with American characters and scenes, and won an honorable place in the dramatic history of his country. His first play, *Hearts of Oak,* appeared in 1879; his last, *Sag Harbor,* in 1900. His most popular piece, *Shore Acres,* had to wait almost ten years for a production; though in time it was recognized as a sincere and highly effective representation of American rural life. Denman Thompson in *The Old Homestead,* William C. De-Mille, and Steele Mackaye (1842-1894) are a few of the writers who helped to establish a native tradition. *Hazel Kirke* (1879), by Steele Mackaye, ran two years in New York, sent ten companies on the road, and lasted thirty years on the boards.

Bronson Howard (1842-1908) continued the use of native subjects. Howard was born in Detroit and came to the craft of the playwright *via* the columns of the New York *Tribune* and the *Evening Post.* He produced many successful plays during the last thirty years of the nineteenth century, including *Shenandoah,* a Civil War drama, *Saratoga, Young Mrs. Winthrop,* and *The Henrietta.* Though his plays now seem to belong to rather a remote age, and, like *Fashion,* are full of asides and soliloquies, yet in them there is a sound sense of stage values and an honest attempt to avoid artificiality of motive and emotion. Another successful playwright who came to the theater by way of the newspaper office is Mr. Augustus Thomas, born in St. Louis in 1859. His first play, *Alabama* (1890) was, as its title indicates, a study in local character. *In Mizzoura* and *Arizona* followed, then others, amounting to more than sixty. In *As a Man Thinks,* Mr. Thomas drama-tized a moral lesson; in *The Witching Hour* he performed the difficult feat of using telepathy as an integral factor in his plot. His pictures of local scenes, his characteristic humor, and his sincerity in the treatment of national subjects have sufficed to place Mr. Thomas at the head of the older school of American dramatists.

At about the turn of the century, probably the most widely known of American playwrights was Clyde Fitch (1865-1909), whose work includes *The Climbers, The Girl with the Green Eyes, The Truth, The City,* and many other titles. His very first play, *Beau Brummel* (1890), with the title rôle enacted by Richard Mansfield, was one of his greatest successes. He wrote more than fifty original pieces, adapted at least a dozen

French comedies for use in English, and found a hearing not only in America but also in England and France. With an excellent theater sense, good discipline in stage-craft, and constant industry in his chosen field, he made good use of the principles of technique according to nineteenth-century-French methods, and added measurably to the wealth of the American stage. Still another writer who made use of European technique while dealing with American themes was Mr. William Gillette, born in Hartford in 1855. Mr. Gillette has attained fame both as an actor and playwright. His most popular pieces were *Held by the Enemy* (1886) and *Secret Service* (1896), both Civil War plays, and the dramatization of Dr. Conan Doyle's masterpiece, *Sherlock Holmes* (1899).

*The Early Twentieth Century.* Several writers who earlier had attained distinction as poets also gained success on the stage. One of these was William Vaughn Moody (1869-1910), author of *The Great Divide* and *The Faith Healer*. The first of these plays, performed in Chicago in 1906, with Miss Margaret Anglin playing the principal woman rôle, created something like a sensation because of its dramatic first act, which portrays three men, in a Rocky Mountain mining camp, throwing dice to decide which of them shall take possession of a girl who has been stranded there. The need for a happy ending, or at least for the conventional wedding ring and "arty" bungalow, was too insistent then to allow the author to finish the piece with full sincerity; nevertheless the drama has a certain fine swing and bravado, especially in the early scenes.

When in 1910 the Shakespeare Memorial Theater in Stratford was dedicated, the opening production was a prize play, *The Piper,* by the American poet, Josephine Preston Peabody Marks. The drama shows how, after the Piper has been cheated by the burghers, he entices the children through a cave into an enchanted land; and how in the end he restores them to their homes. Other plays by Mrs. Marks are *Marlowe* and *The Wolf of Gubbio;* but interesting as these dramas are, they were not strong enough to break the spell which seems to ban poetic drama from the modern stage. Poets such as Olive Tilford Dargan, William Ellery Leonard, Ridgeley Torrence, and Edna St. Vincent Millay have gained, if not great popular successes, at least appreciative audiences in many little theaters.

The poet Mr. Percy Mackaye (born 1875), a son of the actor-manager Steele Mackaye, has experimented in many forms. His *Sappho and Phaon* has an intricate plot with a play within the play, and a Greek fable for its main subject. In *The Canterbury Pilgrims* he has woven a pleasant story around Chaucer's famous characters. *A Thousand Years Ago* is a romance of the Orient; while *Mater* and *Anti-Matrimony* are social comedies of the present day. *Jeanne d'Arc* has had many successful performances with Miss Julia Marlowe as the Maid. One of the best of Mr. Mackaye's works is *The Scarecrow,* founded on a fantastic New England legend. It has a fresh, vigorous theme, with opportunity for pathos, humor, irony; and as interpreted by Mr. Frank Reicher in the chief part it was a remarkable exhibition of virtuosity as well as a welcome change from the stereotyped creations of the stage. Mr. Mackaye has also made important contributions to the art of pageantry and to the production of outdoor masques.

Almost alone among writers for the stage stands Mr. Charles Rann Kennedy, an Englishman who has for some years made his home in New York, in that he has chosen in several cases to treat religious subjects. Mr. Kennedy's best known work, *The Servant in the House* (1908) shows by a sort of allegory the influence of the Man of Nazareth. *The Terrible Meek* (1911) might be called a modern mystery portraying in a very reverent manner the human side of the tragedy of the Cross. In *The Winter Feast* and *The Flower of the Palace of Han* the author has used respectively Scandinavian and Chinese legends. In the latter play the climax turns upon the sacrifice of the beloved wife in order to save the lives of the people of the kingdom. In *The Chastening* (1927) Mr. Kennedy has gone back to the life of Jesus for his theme. Another religious drama, *The Fool,* by Mr. Channing Pollock, is concerned with the difficulties the sincere clergyman encounters in carrying out the principles of love and forgiveness which he is supposed to preach.

Plays satirizing smart society have not been very numerous;

though *The New York Idea* (1909), by Mr. Langdon Mitchell, was a success in that field, as were also many of the pieces by Clyde Fitch. There have been serious pictures of social life, such as *The Easiest Way, Paid in Full,* and *Fine Feathers,* all by Eugene Walter; *The Boss* and *Salvation Nell,* by Edward Sheldon; *The Lion and the Mouse,* by Charles Klein; and *Kindling,* by Charles Kenyon. There are portrayals of the conflict between the younger and the older generations, such as *The Goose Hangs High,* by Louis Beach; plays founded on the biography of celebrated people, like *Georg Sand* and *A Road House in Arden,* by Philip Moeller; also studies of racial difficulties, as in *The Nigger* by Edward Sheldon. There have been odd but interesting and successful imitations, or adaptations of ideas from oriental sources, as in *Kismet,* by Edward Knoblaugh, and in *The Yellow Jacket,* by Hazelton and Benrimo, played with skill by Mr. and Mrs. Charles Coburn. Comedies by Jesse Lynch Williams, including *Why Marry?* and *Why Not?,* while in no sense imitations of Mr. Shaw, yet are in his vein, giving lively argumentative scenes concerning a much-discussed subject. Plays dealing with geographical sections have been numerous: *Desire Under the Elms,* by Mr. O'Neill; *Hell Bent for Heaven,* by Mr. Hatcher Hughes; *Sun Up,* by Miss Lulu Vollmer; *Icebound,* by Mr. Owen Davis; and *This Fine Pretty World,* by Mr. Mackaye. Mrs. Mary Austin, in *The Arrow Maker,* has given a fine study of one of the characteristic traditions of Indian life,—a subject which so far has been too seldom used. *Outward Bound,* by Mr. Sutton Vane, and *On Trial,* by Mr. Elmer Reizenstein, have both introduced novel themes and an arresting situation.

Among successful women writers for the stage are Miss Rachel Crothers, who has produced a long list of dramas dealing with contemporary life and character. Some of her titles are *A Man's World, Three of Us, Nice People, A Little Journey,* and, perhaps best of all, *Expressing Willie.* Zoë Akins, in *Declassée* and *The Moonflower,* has gone abroad for her atmosphere and has taken up again the theme of the discredited woman in society. Susan Glaspell, with *Inheritors,*

*Suppressed Desires,* and *The Verge,* has portrayed local types and situations in America with a sort of passionate concentration. Edith Ellis, Mary Austin, and Catherine Chisholm Cushing are well known in the dramatic field.

*Two types of comedy.* Without undue splitting of hairs it is perhaps possible, when looking back over a period of twenty-five years, to distinguish roughly two types of comedy which might be called, respectively, the comedy of the age of innocence and cartoon comedy. Plays of the first class are concerned, generally speaking, with pleasant people in more or less luxurious homes, with butlers, limousines, and expensive daughters largely in evidence. The quality of humor in this kind of play is flattering. If weaknesses are ridiculed, it is done with a touch of indulgent admiration. In this class belong Clare Kummer's play of wealthy American life called *A Successful Calamity,* Booth Tarkington's *Man from Home* and *Clarence,* and *Not So Long Ago,* by Arthur Richman.

Cartoon comedy, on the other hand, is apt to be concerned with humbler classes of people, and it does not handle them so indulgently. The satire, while still good-natured, has more acidity and bite. Characterization is often exaggerated as in a cartoon, but it is essentially truthful. The humor may be boisterous and vulgar, yet it belongs fundamentally to the tradition of Aristophanes, through Plautus and the medieval farce-comedy. The American stage has been rather rich in this type, with such old successes as *The College Widow* and *The County Chairman,* by George Ade; *The Chorus Lady, The Commuters,* and others, by James Forbes; the *Potash and Perlmutter* series, *Seven Days,* up to such recent contributions as *The Show-Off, Love 'em and Leave 'em,* and *God Loves Us.*

*Eugene O'Neill.* Born 1888. Among all these writers, many of them with undisputed gifts, the outstanding figure at the present time is Mr. Eugene O'Neill, the son of a popular actor, who first appeared in New York as a member of the Provincetown Players. In the ten years from 1915 to 1925, if report be true, Mr. O'Neill wrote something like fifty dramas, at least thirty-five of which have had some sort of production. Several of them have traveled to England and the continent. His first play was *Bound East for Cardiff;* but it was through the performance of *Beyond the Horizon* (1920) that the attention of the public was first specially attracted to him. Since that time the presentation of a new O'Neill play has been considered by many theater-goers as the most important event of the dramatic season. His subjects have been widely diverse. In *Desire Under the Elms* he has given a picture of the morbid cravings of a lonely and aspiring soul, too weak to attain his wish; in *The Hairy Ape* it is the confused and fierce struggles of strength which is mal-adjusted to its environment; in *Anna Christie* it is the story of a girl who lives by the sale of her body; but the sentimental vapor with which a Dumas would have enveloped his heroine has been changed to a more bracing and cutting atmosphere. Probably the most widely known of the O'Neill plays is *The Emperor Jones,* a drama which is strikingly original both in theme and treatment. Two comments on the work of Mr. O'Neill touch the secret of his thought. Mr. Percy Boynton, in *Some Contemporary Americans,* writes: "In selecting material for these plays, O'Neill has made no slightest concession to the popular liking for glad and sunny stuff . . . he presents grim life in a grim way. A play by O'Neill is the last possible resort for the matinée girl or the tired business man. But O'Neill has achieved his audience without regard to them. He deals with fundamental human emotions and experiences, he presents conditions faithfully, dodging none of the essential but unpleasant facts, and beneath all he shows an admiration for and a faith in the virtues of endurance and integrity." And Mr. Thomas H. Dickinson, in *The Playwrights of the New American Theater,* has given this word: "If I regard O'Neill correctly, he means that we all dream beyond our power, and that often the bad men, the failures, are those who have dreamed most bravely and most passionately."

*Conditions peculiar to America.* Up to this point, scarcely more than a century and a half of American drama has been considered, and that but briefly; and it may be well to pause for a moment to look at certain features which are or have been peculiar to the art on this side of the ocean. In the early days, of course, preoccupation with the practical difficulties of colonial and pioneer life made any theater impossible; also, social and recreational affairs were controlled for the most part by religious bodies, such as the Puritans in New England and the Society of Friends in Pennsylvania, which were officially opposed to theatrical entertainments. Later, when playhouses were fairly numerous, even up to 1891, the absence of copyright laws made it cheaper for producers to import European plays than to pay American writers for their work. During the nineteenth century the most powerful managers in New York, many of whom were of foreign birth, felt safer in gambling on a European play that had had some success than in taking a chance with an American product. The result was that native plays, such as have been mentioned in this chapter, were far outnumbered by adaptations, translations, and importations of all kinds.

This wholesale influx of foreign works would perhaps have been a good thing, had the conditions been such as to allow native playwrights to compete on equal terms, and if the imported plays had been presented honestly and artistically. As to the first point, it was manifestly impossible for American writers to compete with a highly finished European product which cost its purveyors little or nothing to import; and, regarding the second point, the plays, after they reached America, were often so manhandled and maltreated as to be unrecognizable as works of art at all. Managers, going to England for their wares, returned and gave to the public New York adaptations of London adaptations of Parisian or Viennese productions.[3] In addition to these drawbacks, actors of distinction were often content to repeat for many seasons their old successes. New York, now the center of theatrical production, has for half a century had a majority of foreigners in its population; and it has naturally been a bit cold to plays which did not bear the European stamp. Again, the art of acting has been largely left, until very recent days, to a hit-or-miss system, with few schools for training. Furthermore, nowhere in

[3] Of course this process of adaptation of European plays was extensively carried on in many countries other than America.

the country were there any municipal or state-endowed theaters such as have for many years existed in most European countries.

The miracle is that, in these circumstances, there was any native drama at all, and all the more honor to such writers as Herne, Mackaye, Howard and Mr. Thomas. That there was life in the American stage has of recent years been abundantly proved: first, because it has refused to assimilate any of the various schools, such as naturalism, verism, expressionism, and the like, which were obviously alien and would always have remained so; and, secondly, because with the early years of the present century it appears to have entered upon a genuinely creative period.

One of the first signs of renewed life was the growth of more or less independent "little theater" groups, which seemed to spring up almost simultaneously in different parts of the country. Before 1910 there were the Washington Square Players, the Provincetown Players, the Neighborhood Playhouse, and several studio groups in New York; there were "Peoples' Theaters" in North Carolina, North Dakota, Indianapolis, Los Angeles, Northampton, and elsewhere. The New Theater in New York (1909-1911) was not permanently successful; but later organizations have profited by the experience of its sponsors. Today the Theater Guild, depending for its resources mainly upon the annually renewed subscriptions of its clientele, has made interesting and daring experiments. The little theater groups have already produced distinguished playwrights; and foreign plays, while still eagerly sought and often enthusiastically received, are given as nearly as possible in their original setting and form.

Another proof of life in the American stage is the wide variety of subjects which find a welcome. The innumerable plays disporting sex and the English tea-table, which for some decades seemed to overwhelm it, are now giving place to pictures of the West and South, of different classes of society, of rural and small-town life, of Indians and their customs. Much of this product is ephemeral and superficial, to be sure; but those are qualities which apply to the great majority of plays everywhere. Many of the American pieces are written with keen observation and personal knowledge; and many of the playwrights who have already helped to produce what may fairly be called a national drama are still young and have not yet come to the height of their achievement. The wide diversity of subject and method, the use of local characters, and the discovery of dramatic material in American conditions and history,—these things are symptoms of health.

## CHAPTER XXXVIII

# LATEST PHASES OF DRAMA

The changes that can be traced in literary history are changes, not of poetry and its kinds, but of spiritual ideals.—JOHN ERSKINE, *The Kinds of Poetry.*

An impulse towards greater sincerity and strength on the stage, like a searching wind, followed everywhere in the wake of the Ibsen dramaturgy; and in the hurricane many flimsy or decaying accretions were swept away. The theater in every country was liberalized as to technique and conventions, and elevated in content and purpose. At this later date it seems that the work of many interesting modern playwrights—Shaw, Barker, Sudermann, O'Neill, and others—would have been impossible without this preliminary liberalizing force. The culminating excellence in drama of the realistic style was perhaps best illustrated in Russia in the combined work of Chekhov, as dramatist, and Stanislavsky, director of the Moscow Art Theater. This organization was preëminent for its conscientious attention to detail, for its smoothly articulated ensemble, and for its emphasis on the content of the play rather than upon any single actor or sensational scene. Everything done on the stage seemed "natural" and spontaneous; and, analogous to this carefully realistic setting were the dramas of Chekhov, which called for just such interpretation.

The impulse toward realism and truth, however, like every vigorous movement, brought on certain excesses: too much photographic detail in accessories, and a tendency toward the undue celebration of dull and insignificant affairs. It is no great feat for many play-goers of today to remember the time when the most successful "show" of the season seemed always to be the one which had the greatest number of genuine articles on display, such as sterling silver trophy cups, real books in the bookcase, or real tea for the afternoon ritual. Along with this realism in stage properties there was also an overwhelming tendency towards small-town and small-life subjects. Whether it were *The Truth, Bunty Pulls the Strings,* or *Business is Business,* the skill of the author was shown in the choice of everyday incidents, in depicting petty details, and in the glorification of the commonplace.

*Revolt against realism in stage settings.* Protests against this sort of thing came from two groups: artists who turned their attention to stage designs of more intrinsic value, and Little Theater managers who were forced to utilize small quarters and to avoid large financial outlay. These groups were united in the desire for more artistic stage effects; and the theater-loving world suddenly woke up to the fact that beauty of design, suggestiveness, and simplicity of impression on the boards are of more value than many silver trappings. Artists and producers, such as Max Reinhardt, Gordon Craig, R. E. Jones, Lee Simonson and others devised simple sets in which massed color and architectural lines offered picturesque and suggestive backgrounds. They prepared "unit" sets consisting perhaps of two pillars, an arch, and a shallow flight of steps, fashioned with movable parts so they could be made to represent several different scenes according to need. In the meantime the Little Theater managers had come to a similar result by a different route. The theory of the Little Theater was: better a bare stage than a clutter; and the frequent meagerness of financial backing was not always a hardship, for with simple means they often achieved beauty.

Naturally, the changes in stage accoutrements and in the style of acting did not stop with the achievement of simplicity. The needs of the new schools—expressionism, the grotesque, modernism, and the like—brought with them new and sometimes fantastic conceptions. Back scenes became cubistic designs, the gestures of the actors became rhythmical, angular, and statuesque, while the speech, formerly required to be natural and unaffected, was changed into staccato, artificial tones. One idea was to make the actor as nearly anonymous as possible; and Mr. Gordon Craig has gone so far as to advocate the abolition of living actors, thus making the presentation independent of the personal equation.

*Revolt against realism in subject.* The reaction against commonplace ideas and scenes in the drama itself, like the revolt against photographic accuracy in the stage picture, was not a national but a European affair, common to Germany, Italy, Russia, France, Spain and England; and of course the reaction also to some extent affected the American stage. The "movements," however, had certain national peculiarities and went by different names,—"expressionism" in Germany, the "grotesque" in Italy, "modernism" in Spain; and everywhere the reaction was closely allied with futurism and cubism in other arts. While differing in detail, these movements were all concerned with the one business of getting rid of reality, of escaping from the obvious and the natural, into the conventional, the stylistic and the unreal. The disciple of expressionism asks: why should not the spectators be included in the play? why should there always be three acts, or four? why not give Shakespeare in one act? why should one consider the death of a more-or-less important man tragic? why, in short, follow all the old conventions which have been worn out?

These ideas, and similar ones, were illustrated by various playwrights, such as the Capeks, in *R.U.R.* and *The Insect Play;* by Georg Kaiser in *Gas I* and *Gas II;* by Ernst Toller in *Massenmensch;* and by the American Elmer Rice in *The Adding Machine.* In the latter play, when Mr. Zero, put out of his accountant's job by the machine, murders his employer, the fact of the murder is conveyed to the audience by splashes of red suddenly appearing on the back-drop. In *Massenmensch* the purpose seems to be to dramatize the whole community, personalizing the force which makes men what they are. In *Gas I* the characters are more or less abstract figures: the Billionaire's son, who seems to symbolize the Idealist; the Gentleman in White, who personifies Terror; and the Gentleman in Black, who is Capital. The scene is a factory for making gas; and the action turns upon the impotence and insignificance of the Idealist in the face of the power which he generates in his factory. To the adherents of expressionism character is not the chief interest, but the expression of a mood; the ideal of beauty, instead of being a glorious sunset, a picture, a statue, a cathedral, or a symphony, is a racing automobile—symbol of energy and power.

In Italy the decadent romanticism illustrated by the D'Annunzio tradition was replaced by a movement similar to expressionism, with the additional touch of the grotesque—something analogous to the gargoyle in architecture. Furthermore, in Italy as elsewhere, radical ideas concerning the stage were accompanied by "futurism." The futurist believes in repudiating the past, with its ideals, morals, religion, history and faith. Make a jest of the sorrows of life. Turn topsy-turvy our customs and our "sacred" institutions, especially our rules of art, and invent something new.

In Russia one of the innovators was M. Tairov, manager of the Kamerny Theater, which opened in 1914. The purpose of the Kamerny players was that "the absolute essence of the play should be expressed; that all on the stage should conform to the new principle of construction; and that the acting should be freed from the natural and all signs of improvisation." On the stage of the Kamerny Theater, as on certain other European stages of radical tendency, the speech was highly conventionalized, and the scenery as far as possible from the appearance of actual life. The Russian stage, however, has not been left wholly to the experimentalists. Since the revolution the theaters have largely been nationalized,—that is, taken over by the workmen, the soldiers, and the peasant class; and in these theaters the modern schools have had very little foothold. A strict censorship has been established, and extreme or risqué pieces of every sort have been forbidden. Instead, there are regular performances of the plays of Schiller, Goldoni, Lope de Vega, and Shakespeare.

Benevente, one of the leading playwrights of modern Spain, does not indulge in radical experiments. Though he brings to the stage a fresh outlook and a modern philosophy of life, yet for the most part his plays are built upon solid nineteenth-century technique. The Quintero brothers represent the newer school, in that they have dispensed with some of the time-honored theatrical conventions; but both modernism and futurism on the Spanish stage seem at the present moment to be of far less interest than poetic drama.

*Change of conditions in America.* Though expressionistic plays have been written by American authors, and though futuristic settings have frequently been seen, yet it is impossible to identify any one of the movements described above with the American stage. Radical experiments have been made, revised, and abandoned,—and all, no doubt, to the future advantage of the art. Not one of the European growths has taken root; and this is as it should be. The American drama is drawing life from conditions peculiar to itself; and its plot material, its pictures of life, its implied philosophy, to be healthy and sincere, must evolve from the national melting-pot. The economic condition of the stage, however, has conspicuously improved. Although there is still no direct support from the government, yet in the past twenty years there has been a practical subsidizing of many groups of players. Private individuals have supplied well-equipped playhouses rent-free, and have in some cases supplemented this gift with substantial financial support. In various cities and towns certain theaters have been exempted from taxation; and a surprising number of schools of play-writing, acting, and practice production have come into existence. Chicago, St. Louis, and other cities have Civic theaters; Northampton, Ripon, Columbia and other towns have their own theaters, often with schools for playwriting and acting, and their own companies which go on tour at least within the boundaries of their own state; and North Carolina has made a state appropriation in support of its theater.

*Drama in colleges and universities.* It has long been a tradition for the college and the university to foster the theater; nevertheless, at the beginning of the present century it was rather a novelty when Harvard, Columbia, or the University of Pennsylvania staged a performance of a Greek play during Commencement Week. Today university productions are a matter of course. More time is given to the study of existing drama; and classes in the history of the play and in the technique of play-writing are included in literary courses in colleges large and small. Among the first college teachers to recognize the value of dramatic courses were Professor George Pierce Baker of Yale (formerly of Harvard), and Professor Emeritus Brander Matthews of Columbia, both of whom have already exerted great influence on American drama. Most of the larger colleges and state universities are sponsors for theater groups, supplying a practical workshop for study and production. It needs only a glance backward to the history of the Elizabethan stage to show how quickly and how generously such efforts contribute to the professional field.

*Most plays necessarily ephemeral.* In considering the great number of plays evolved during the long course of the drama, one must inevitably come to the conclusion that it is the very nature of the play to be ephemeral; and that it is only by the rarest combination of qualities that any play takes an important place in permanent literature. Motives of action, the things people laugh or cry over, range all the way from the extremely superficial and local to the deep and universal passions. Drama deals with them all, but mostly with the less profound. It is somewhat unreasonable to ask that a dramatist shall write with his eye on the next generation; and the lover of the theater has rightly been content if the dramatist has revealed with humor, intensity, or irony the human situation as he has seen it. The stage is naturally conservative, persisting in showing stock figures and stock situations long after they have ceased to be found in real life; and playwrights are constantly tempted to depend on them, instead of thinking and observing for themselves. Such playwrights have fallen into a quick oblivion; and when, with increasing years, any particular type has become too dull to be endured, there rise inevitably the so-called reformers to refresh and rejuvenate the stage. Keen observation and sympathetic revelation of genuine character, even without much technical skill, will often lift the degraded art back again into popularity.

Whenever the germinating forces are vigorous, there may be some things that are undesirable; and so it happens that what are called new movements are often associated with lapses

This Historic Building, used originally to house the University of North Carolina Library and later the School of Law, has been reconstructed and equipped as a permanent Home for The Carolina Playmakers. This is the first state-owned Theatre to be devoted to its own native Drama

from delicacy. Looking back for a few centuries, however, it is evident that the stage has become increasingly decent. Considering English plays alone, one can note that many pieces which were applauded in London during the Restoration, and long afterward, could not now be given even in the most tolerant cities of the civilized world.

Monsieur Stanislavsky in his memoirs relates how once every year his theater in Moscow was visited by a young peasant who came to the city for that express purpose and remained long enough to see all the offerings of the season. "Having seen our entire repertory, he folded his silk shirt, his velvet trousers and his boots, tied them in a bundle and returned to his home for the ensuing year. From there he would write numerous philosophical letters which helped him to digest and continue to live over the store of impressions which he had brought home with him from Moscow."

Aside from the applause in the theater itself, what more subtle and delightful mark of appreciation could be imagined?

# A BRIEF READING LIST FOR STUDENTS OF THE DRAMA

Since it is obviously more convenient for most American readers to obtain books in English, the following reading list has, with one exception, been limited to books in English, either original or in translation.

Archer, William .......... English Dramatists of Today
Archer, William .......... Playmaking
Aristotle .................. The Art of Poetry

Baker, George Pierce ...... Dramatic Technique
Baring, Maurice ........... Landmarks in Russian Literature
Björkman, Edwin ......... Voices of Tomorrow
Björkman, Edwin ......... Introduction to the English transla-
                           tion of Strindberg's plays
Boas, F. S. ............... Shakespeare and His Predecessors in
                           the English Drama
Boyd, Ernest .............. The Irish Literary Movement
Boyd, Ernest .............. The Contemporary Drama of Ireland
Brandes, George .......... Main Currents in Nineteenth Century
                           Literature
Brinkley, F. ............. Japan, Its History, Art, and Litera-
                           ture
Brooke, C. F. Tucker ...... The Tudor Drama
Brooke, Rupert ............ John Webster and the English Drama
Burton, Richard ........... The New American Drama
Butcher .................. Aspects of Greek Drama

Campbell, L. .............. Tragic Drama in Æschylus, Soph-
                           ocles and Shakespeare
Chamberlain .............. Classical Poetry of the Japanese
Chambers, E. K. .......... The Medieval Stage, 2 vols.
Chesterton, G. K. .......... George Bernard Shaw
Clark, Barrett ............ Continental Dramatists of Today
Clark, Barrett ............ A Story of the Modern Drama

Clark, Barrett ............European Theories of the Drama: an anthology from Aristotle to the present day

Collier, J. P. ..............History of English Dramatic Poetry, 3 vols.

Courtney, W. L. ..........The Idea of Tragedy in Ancient and Modern Drama

Creizenach, W. ...........History of Modern Drama

Cruttwell, C. T. ..........History of Roman Literature

Cunliffe, J. W. ...........The Influence of Seneca on Elizabethan Tragedy

Dill, S. ...................Roman Society in the Last Days of the Western Empire

Donaldson, J. W. .........The Theater of the Greeks

Doran, J. ................Their Majesties' Servants: annals of the English Stage, 3 vols.

Dryden, John .............Essay of Dramatic Poesy

Duff, J. Wright ...........A Literary History of Rome

Dukes, Ashley ............Modern Dramatists

Erskine, John ............The Kinds of Poetry

Filon, A. .................The Modern French Drama

Fleay, F. G. ..............A Chronicle History of the London Stage, 1559-1642

Flickinger, Roy H. ........The Greek Theater and Its Drama

Fraser ...................The Golden Bough

Freytag, Gustav ..........The Technique of the Drama

Gaspary, A. ..............History of Early Italian Literature

Genest ...................Some Account of the English Stage from 1660-1830

Giles, H. A. ..............History of Chinese Literature

Gobineau, Count ..........*Les Religions et les philosophies dans l'Asie central*

Gregory, Lady Augusta ....Our Irish Theater

Grosse ..................The Beginnings of Art

Haigh, A. E. .............The Attic Theater

Haigh, A. E. .............The Tragic Drama of the Greeks

Hale, E. E., Jr. ...........Dramatists of Today

Havemeyer, Loomis .......The Drama of Savage Peoples
Hawkins, F. ..............Annals of the Stage

Jebb .....................Greek Literature

Kincaid, Zoe .............Kabuki

Lee, Sir Sidney ...........Great Englishmen of the Sixteenth Century
Lessing, Gotthold E. ......Hamburg Dramaturgy
Lessing, O. E. ............Masters of Modern German Literature
Lewes, G. H. .............The Spanish Drama
Lowe, R. W. ..............Bibliographical Account of English Dramatic Literature (1888)

MacCurdy, Grace ..........Euripides
Macdonell, A. A. ..........A History of Sanskrit Literature
Macgowan, Kenneth ......The Theater of Tomorrow
Mackail, J. W. ............History of Latin Literature
Mackenzie, A. S. ..........The Evolution of Literature
Mantzius, Karl ............A History of Theatrical Art in Ancient and Modern Times, 5 vols.
Matthews, J. Brander ......The Development of the Drama
Matthews, J. Brander ......French Dramatists of the Nineteenth Century
Matthews, J. Brander ......The Life of Molière
Mayor, J. E. B. ...........Biographical Clue to Latin Literature
Moderwell, Hiram ........The Theater of Today
Moore, George ............Hail and Farewell
Moses, Montrose ..........The American Drama
Moulton, R. G. ............The Ancient Classical Drama
Murray, Gilbert ...........History of Ancient Greek Literature
Murray, Gilbert ...........Euripides and His Age

Neilson and Thorndike ....Facts About Shakespeare

Phelps, William L. ........Essays on Modern Dramatists
Pollard, A. W. ............English Miracle Plays, Moralities and Interludes
Price, W. T. ..............Analysis of Play Construction and Dramatic Principles

Robertson ................Elizabethan Literature
Ruhl, Arthur .............Second Nights

Schelling, F. E. ...........English Drama
Schelling, F. E. ...........Elizabethan Drama
Schlegel, A. W. von .......Dramatic Art and Literature
Seccombe .................The Age of Shakespeare
Sellar, W. Y. .............Roman Poets of the Republic and
                              Poets of the Augustan Age
Shaw, George Bernard ....The Quintessence of Ibsen
Shaw, George Bernard ....Dramatic Opinions and Essays
Shaw, George Bernard ....Preface to Three Plays by Brieux
Stoeskius, A. .............Naturalism in Recent German Litera-
                              ture
Stopes, M. C. .............The Plays of Old Japan
Symonds, J. Addington ....Predecessors of Shakspere in the
                              English Drama
Symonds, J. Addington ....The Renaissance in Italy
Symons, Arthur ..........Plays, Acting, and Music
Symons, Arthur ..........The Symbolist Movement in Litera-
                              ture

Thaler, Alwin ............Shakespeare to Sheridan
Thomas, E. ...............Maurice Maeterlinck
Thorndike, Ashley ........Tragedy
Thorndike, Ashley ........Literature in a Changing Age
Ticknor, G. ...............History of Spanish Literature, 2 vols.
Toulmin-Smith ............York Plays
Tyrrell, R. Y. ............Lectures on Latin Poetry

Vaughn, C. E. ............Types of Tragic Drama

Waley, Arthur ............The No Plays of Japan
Walkley, A. B. ............Drama and Life
Ward, A. W. ..............A History of English Dramatic Lit-
                              erature to the Death of Queen
                              Anne, 3 vols.
Witkowski, G. ............The German Drama of the Nineteenth
                              Century
Wilson, H. H. ............Select Specimens of the Theater of
                              the Hindus

Withington, Robert ........English Pageantry: an Historical
                                    Outline, 2 vols.
Woodbridge, Elizabeth .....The Drama, Its Laws and Technique
Wright, T. ...............Early Mysteries and Other Latin
                                    Poems of the 12th and 13th cen-
                                    turies

Yeats, William B. ..........Synge and the Ireland of His Time
                                    The Cutting of an Agate

## Eighth Century B.C. to End of Fourth Century A.D.

| DATE B.C. | CHINA | INDIA | GREECE | ROME | SYRIA |
|---|---|---|---|---|---|
| 700 | | | | | Job Cir. 722 |
| 500 | | | Æschylus | | |
| 499 | | | Sophocles | | |
| | | | Euripides | | |
| 400 | | | Aristophanes | | |
| 399 | | Dramatic | | | |
| 300 | Religious | Dialogues | Menander | | |
| 200 | | and | | Terence Plautus | |
| 100 | Pantomimic | | | | |
| Birth of Christ A.D. | Dances | Imitative Dances | | Seneca | |
| 100 | | The Toy Cart | | | |
| 200 | | | | | |
| 300 | | | | St. Gregory Nazianzen | |
| 400 | | | | | |

# DRAMA    CHART II

## Beginning Fifth Century A. D. to End of Fifteenth Century A.D.

| DATE A.D. | EUROPE | CHINA | JAPAN | INDIA |
|---|---|---|---|---|
| 401 | | | | Kalidasa (3 plays extant) (Sakuntala) |
| 500 | | | | |
| | | | | Important Period |
| 600 | | Plays about gods and national heroes | | |
| | | | | King Harsha (3 plays) |
| 700 | | | | |
| | | | | Bhavabuti (3 plays extant) |
| 800 | | The Pear Garden | | |
| 900 | Hroswitha Beginning of sacred drama (unwritten) | Singing actor appears | Chinese influence | The Great Nataka (14 acts) from Rama cycle |
| 1000 | | A few extant plays | Native *Kagura* dances | |
| 1100 | Oldest French Mystery | Kin and Yuen dynasties 600 plays extant | | Rise of the Moon of Knowledge (an Indian morality) |
| 1200 | Jean Bodel Rutebœuf | Orphan of House of Tchao Tr. 1735 | *No* Plays | |
| 1300 | Greatest period of Miracles of the Virgin | | Kiyotsugu 1355-1406 | The Martyr of Faith (slight similarity to Book of Job) |
| 1400 | Most spectacular period of mysteries | The Magic Lute | Motokiyo | |
| 1500 | 1st opera, 1499 | | | |

*Dramatic literature exceeds, in bulk, that of any other nation*

# CHART III

## DRAMA

### From the End of Fifteenth Century to 1900

| DATE A.D. | ENGLAND | FRANCE | GERMANY | SCANDINAVIA | SPAIN | ITALY | AMERICA |
|---|---|---|---|---|---|---|---|
| 1500 | | | Hans Sachs | | | Machiavelli Aretino Ariosto | |
| | The Scholar Poets Marlowe | Jodelle Garnier Hardy | | | Lope de Rueda | Trissino | |
| | Shakespeare | | | | | | |
| 1599 | | | | | | Tasso | |
| 1600 | Ben Jonson Beaumont and Fletcher | Corneille | | | Lope de Vega | Guarini | |
| | { Theaters Closed | Racine | | | Calderón | | |
| | | Molière | | | | | |
| 1699 | Dryden Congreve Addison's *Cato* | | | | | | |
| 1700 | | | Gottsched | | | | |
| | Goldsmith Sheridan | Voltaire | Lessing Schiller Goethe | Holberg | | Goldoni Alfieri | Thos. Godfrey Royall Tyler Wm. Dunlap |
| 1799 | | | | | | | |
| 1800 | Sheridan Knowles Bulwer-Lytton Tom Robertson H. A. Jones A. W. Pinero | Hugo Scribe Sardou Augier Dumas Rostand Brieux | Hebbel | | | | |
| | | | | Strindberg Ibsen | | Giacosa | Boucicault Bronson Howard Herne De Mille |
| | | | Hauptmann | | | | |

# A SUPPLEMENT

containing the names of important playwrights in Europe, America, and the Orient, with dates and representative plays; also notes as to the Cycles, manuscripts, etc., of the Middle Ages, and the building of the early English theaters.

Although the lists are far from being complete, yet an effort has been made to include those plays which have excited special interest on account of their novelty, timeliness, or genuine value.

## GREEK WRITERS BEFORE ÆSCHYLUS

THESPIS (legendary):
Born about the beginning of the 6th century at Icaria;
began to exhibit tragedies as early as 560 B.C.;
took part in the public contests at Athens in 534 B.C.

CHŒRILUS:
Began to produce plays about 523 B.C.;
wrote at least 160 plays;
won 13 victories in the contests;
no plays extant.

PRATINAS:
Died sometime before 467 B.C.;
competed against Æschylus in 499 B.C.;
said to have invented the satyric drama;
won the prize only once;
no plays extant.

PHRYNICUS:
Dates unknown;
won the first prize in tragedy 511 B.C.;
a few fragments extant.

## GREECE

ÆSCHYLUS:

Born 525 B.C.; died 456 B.C.;
wrote at least ninety plays;
won 13 victories, the first being in 484 B.C.;
defeated by Sophocles in 468 B.C.;
sixty certain titles known, twelve doubtful;
seven plays extant.

The seven surviving plays, in the probable order of their
composition, are:
The Suppliants
The Persians, exhibited in 472 B.C.
The Seven Against Thebes, exhibited in 467 B.C.
Prometheus Bound
Agamemnon
The Libation Pourers (*Choephori*)
The Benign Ones (*Eumenides*)

(The last three comprise The Orestean Trilogy.)

SOPHOCLES:

Born 495, died 406-5 B.C.;
won his first victory 468 B.C. against Æschylus;
wrote at least 110 plays;
won 18 victories at the City Dionysia, and probably as many at
lesser contests;
seven plays extant, in their probable chronology as follows:
Antigone
Ajax
The Maidens of Trachis (*Trachiniæ*)
Electra
Œdipus the King
Philoctetes (produced 409 B.C.)
Œdipus at Colonos

Euripides:

Born 485 or 480, died 406 B.C.;

began to write tragedies at the age of eighteen;

won third prize in the competitions in 455 B.C.;

won the first prize in 441 B.C.;

composed more than ninety plays;

won the prize four times during life, once after death;

died at the court of Archelaus in Macedonia;

composed one of the two satyr plays which have survived (*Cyclops*);

there are 18 accepted plays extant (*Rhesus,* not accepted by modern scholars, was also formerly attributed to him);

of the surviving plays, eight were selected for reading in the schools, and are enriched with the commentaries of ancient grammarians, called *scholia.* These eight are:

> Hecuba
> Orestes
> The Phœnician Women
> Andromache
> Medea
> Hippolytus
> Alcestis
> The Trojan Women

The ten other surviving plays, without *scholia,* are:

> Iphigenia in Tauris
> Iphigenia at Aulis
> The Suppliants
> Ion
> The Bacchantes
> Cyclops
> The Children of Hercules
> Helena
> The Mad Hercules
> Electra

## OLD COMEDY

CRATINAS:

Flourished about 450-422 B.C.;
called the inventor of Old Comedy;
entered the competitions 21 times;
won the prize nine times, once over Aristophanes;
no complete plays extant, only some titles and fragments.

CRATES:

About 499-425 B.C.;
was both actor and playwright;
no extant play.

EUPOLIS:

Said to have collaborated with Aristophanes in The Knights;
no extant play.

ARISTOPHANES:

Born about 446 or 450, died about 380 B.C.;
40 certain titles known;
11 plays extant, all except the Plutus generally classed with Old
   Comedy.

The plays are:

      The Acharnians
      The Knights
      The Clouds
      The Wasps
      Peace
      The Birds
      Lysistrata
      Women at the Thesmophoria (*Thesmophoriazusæ*)
      Plutus
      The Frogs
      Women in Council (*Ecclesiazusæ*)

## MIDDLE COMEDY

In addition to the Plutus of Aristophanes, there are the names
of 37 playwrights, among them

      Eubulus
      Antiphanes
      Alexis
      Hegemon (whose play, "The Battle of the Giants," was
      being given on the day the news was brought of the de-
      struction of the Sicilian fleet, in 413).

## NEW COMEDY

PHILEMON:
Flourished from 330 B.C.

MENANDER:
About 342-291 B.C.

DIPHILUS:
Contemporary of Menander.

POSIDIPPUS:
About 280 B.C.

RHINTHON OF TARENTUM:
About 300 B.C.

ARISTOTLE, 384-322 B.C.:
A native of Stagyra; critic and first teacher of dramatic principles.

## ROME

Five early Latin playwrights:

LIVIUS ANDRONICUS. First Latin play presented 240 B.C.
NÆVIUS, about 235 B.C.
ENNIUS, 239-169 B.C. Wrote 20 tragedies, large fragments preserved.
PACUVIUS, 220-130 B.C. Wrote 12 tragedies, one *prætexta*.
ATTIUS, or ACCIUS, died 94 B.C. Wrote 37 tragedies, fragments extant.

TITUS MACCIUS PLAUTUS, 254-184 B.C.
Most scholars recognize 20 extant plays, of which the most celebrated are:
Amphitryon (*Amphitruo*), a tragi-comedy
The Pot of Gold (*Aulularia*)
The Two Bacchuses (*Bacchidæ*)
The Captives (*Captivi*)
The Twins (*Menoechmi*)
The Haunted House (*Mostellaria*)
The Bragging Soldier (*Miles Gloriosus*)
The Cable (*Rudens*)
The Threepenny Bit (*Trinummus*)
The Comedy of Asses (*Asinaria*)
The Travelling Trunk (*Cistellaria.*)

Publius Terentius Afer, 193-158 b.c.
  Six plays extant, as follows:
      The Girl of Andros (*Andria*)
      The Mother-in-law (*Hecyra*)
      The Self-Tormentor (*Heauton Timorumenos*)
      The Eunuch (*Eunuchus*)
      Phormio
      The Brothers (*Adelphi*)

Lucius Annæus Seneca, 3 b.c.-65 a.d.
  Eight complete tragedies extant, and two fragments of tragedies;
    also one *prætexta* (authenticity questioned)
  The eight complete plays are:
      The Mad Hercules (*Hercules Furens*)
      Thyestes
      Phædra (same story as the Hippolytus)
      Œdipus
      The Trojan Women (*Troades*)
      Medea
      Agamemnon
      Hercules upon Mount Œta

# THE ORIENT

Drama of India:
  First period: development previous to 400 b.c.
    Bhasa, or Bhrata, playwright and critic, formulated rules for
      the art; left thirteen plays, which are known and published.
    Sudraka, a ruler to whom is attributed the play called, *The
      Toy Cart* (also called *The Little Clay Cart*).

  Second period: from 400 to 900 a.d.
    Kalidasa, probably about 400 a.d.; best known Indian play,
      *Sakuntala,* translated into English in the eighteenth century.
      Two other plays survive.
    Bhavabuti, early eighth century, from whom three plays sur-
      vive:
          Two treat of heroic adventures connected with the sev-
            enth incarnation of Vishnu;
          One is a love drama, sometimes called the *Romeo and
            Juliet* of the Hindus.

*The Signet of the Minister,* about 800, based on events which occurred soon after the invasion of India by Alexander; author unknown.

*The Binding of a Braid of Hair,* in six acts; author unknown; plot taken from the *Mahabarata.*

Rejacekhara, about 900; left four plays which are still in existence.

Third period: from 900 to the present.

Prabodha, end of eleventh century, left an allegorical play somewhat in the manner of the European morality, called *The Rise of the Moon of Knowledge;* six acts.

Other plays, farces, and dramatic poems exist, but only a few have so far been translated by western scholars.

## DRAMA OF CHINA:

School for singing and pantomimic dancing established in eighth century.

From 1200 to 1368, the most brilliant dramatic period, during the Kin and Yuen dynasties (Mongol).

A collection exists known as the *Hundred Plays of the Yuen Dynasty.* The titles of about six hundred other plays are known, also the names of eighty-five playwrights.

*The Little Orphan of the House of Tchao,* fourteenth century, author unknown, translated by a French Jesuit priest in 1735.

*The Story of the Magic Flute,* fourteenth century, author unknown.

*The Sorrows of Han,* based on a historical incident of 42 B.C. (played in America about 1910 by Miss Edith Wynne Matthison).

## DRAMA OF JAPAN:

The *No* theater:

Period of greatest brilliance, 14th and early 15th centuries.
Kwanami Kiotsugu, 1355-1406.
Seami Motokiyo, 1373-1455, son of Kiotsugu, manager and writer of *No* plays.

The popular theater of two kinds, legitimate and marionette; both developed to a great extent in the seventeenth century.

Chikamatsu Monzayamon, born about 1653, died about 1724; became a Ronin (rebel against a tyrannical lord); left fifty-one compositions for Marionettes, one of the best-known being *The Battles of Kokusenya.*

18th century: period of greatest achievement in popular drama.

Idzumo: died 1756.

Author of one of the many versions of *The Magazine of Faithful Retainers,* or *The Loyal Legion,* or *The Forty-seven Ronins,* founded on a historical event occurring in 1703.

Chikamatsu Hanni, son of the first Chikamatsu; playwright and manager.

## THE MIDDLE AGES

Drama in Europe quiescent for almost the entire first thousand years of our era.

Continuance of play-acting of a low sort, and occasional dramatic enterprises in the Church and monasteries.

Imitation and dialogue employed in the ritual of the Church in the fourth century.

"Living pictures" in the Church on festival days, fifth century.

Festivals which burlesqued the rites of the Church, such as,

The Feast of Fools

The Feast of the Ass

The Boy Bishop.

Occasional imitations of classic plays:

Roswitha (also Hroswitha, and Hrotsuit), tenth century, six plays extant.

Biblical plays established in some sections by the ninth century:

lasted until the sixteenth century;

most flourishing period: the fourteenth and fifteenth centuries.

## BIBLICAL PLAYS

BIBLICAL PLAYS

### FRANCE

Representatio Adæ (Representation of Adam) twelfth century, consisting of three plays called

> The Fall of Adam and Eve ⎫
> The Murder of Abel      ⎬ written in Norman French,
> The Prophecies of Christ ⎭   with rubrics in Latin.

Collection of Miracles of Our Lady, from the thirteenth or fourteenth century, containing the legends of

> Sister Beatrice
> The Juggler of Notre Dame
> Robert the Devil

Play of St. Nicholas, by Jean Bodel.

Miracle of St. Theophilus, by Rutebœuf, thirteenth century, probably the first of the French Mary plays.

Acts of the Apostles, more than ten times as long as a Shakespeare play.

Octavian and Sybilline prophecies counted as sacred subjects.

Manuscript preserved at Orleans, from thirteenth century, includes ten plays:

> Four on the miracles of St. Nicholas
> Adoration of the Magi
> Appearance of Christ on the Road to Emmaus
> Conversion of St. Paul
> Raising of Lazarus
> An Easter Play
> A Christmas Play

According to Stoddart's Bibliography, there are in France, still unedited, 15 manuscripts of cycles of plays, each containing from 4,000 to 37,000 lines.

### GERMANY

Earliest miracles belong to the thirteenth century. Performance of *The Ten Virgins* at Eisenach, 1322. (Play lost.)

### ITALY

Earliest record of an Italian mystery, 1243.

Earliest sacred play known to be written, *Abraham and Isaac*, by Feo Belcari, 1449.

ENGLAND

Sacred plays and fragments of plays surviving:

*Harrowing of Hell,* earliest extant play, with three manuscripts, all belonging to the fourteenth century.

*Abraham and Isaac,* an East Midland play, discovered recently, belonging to the fourteenth century.

*Ludus Filiorum Israel,* 1350, performed at Cambridge.

Two manuscripts from Norwich, sixteenth century:

> Creation of Eve
> Fall of Adam and Eve

The Cycles:

Chester:

> Earliest manuscript belongs to the year 1591, but was compiled or composed probably as early as 1340.
>
> Authorship attributed to Don Randall, monk of Chester Abbey, who is supposed to be identical with Randulf Higden, author of the *Polychronicon.* Died 1364. Manuscript shows marks of having been combined with other similar works.
>
> Known to have been produced as early as 1328.
>
> Acted at Whitsuntide.
>
> Complete edition made for the Shakespeare Society in 1843.

York:

> Manuscript dates from about 1430, but was composed probably a century earlier.
>
> Originally consisted of forty-eight plays, some of which are now missing.
>
> Follows Bible narrative closely.
>
> Has five pieces almost identical with the Towneley plays on the same subject. These plays are:
>
> > The Departure of the Israelites
> > Christ in the Temple
> > The Descent into Hell
> > The Resurrection
> > The Last Judgment
>
> Played on Corpus Christi Day. Very popular.
>
> Edited and printed in 1885 by Lucy Toulmin-Smith.
>
> Manuscript in the possession of Lord Ashburnham.

Coventry:
  Greater part of manuscript written in 1468.
  Manuscript in the British Museum; has been edited by
    Halliwell-Phillips.
  As divided by the editor it consists of forty-two plays.
    Not all were performed in any one year.
  Most dramatic plays are *Woman Taken in Adultery,* and
    the *Death of Herod.*
  This Cycle exceeded all others in fame in the fifteenth
    century.

Towneley (sometimes called Wakefield):
  About the middle of the fourteenth century.
  Called Towneley from name of family who once pos-
    sessed the MS.
  MS. now owned by Bernard Quaritch.
  Contains five plays identical with five of York (see above).
  Consists of thirty-two plays in present form; has two
    Shepherd plays, one with the farce *Mak the Sheep
    Stealer.*

Beverley:
  Early fifteenth century. Only few remnants preserved.

Newcastle:
  One play extant, *Building of the Ark,* with five charac-
    ters, fifteenth century.

### MORALITIES AND MEDIEVAL SECULAR PLAYS

THE MORALITY:
  Earliest extant example in England, *Castle of Perseverance,*
    fifteenth century.
  *Everyman,* probably of Dutch origin, belongs to time of Ed-
    ward IV, fourteenth century.
  *Condemnation of Banquets,* by Nicolas de la Chesnaye, French.

LIGHT COMEDY:
  Adam de la Halle, French, 13th century.
    Le Jeu d'Adam.
    Le Jeu Robin et Marion, called the first light opera.

The Farce:
  *Mak the Sheep Stealer,* in Towneley Cycle, English.
  *The Wash Tub,* French.
  *The Farce of Pierre Pathelin,* 15th century, French.
  85 Shrovetide plays extant, by Hans Sachs, 1494-1576, German.

The Interludes:
  Examples by
    Nicholas Udall,
    John Bale,
    John Heywood (1497-1580).

The Puppet Show:
  Flourished especially in 15th century.

Travesties of Rituals, Like The Feast of the Ass
  Known as early as 10th century.
  Flourished for nearly five centuries.

## NATIONAL DRAMA
### ITALY BEFORE 1700

Tragedy:
  Sofonisba, 1515, by Gian Giorgio Trissino, 1478-1550.
  Rosamunda, by Rucellai.
  Canace, by Speron Sperone.

Comedy:
  Calandra (based upon the Menœchmi of Plautus), by Bibbiena, 1470-1520.
  Cortigiana and other plays, by Aretino, 1492-1556.
  Mandragola, and Clizia, by Machiavelli, 1469-1527.
  Suppositi, Negromante, and other plays, by Ariosto, 1474-1533.

Pastorals:
  Aminta, by Torquato Tasso, 1544-1595.
  Pastor Fido, by Giovanni Guarini, 1537-1612.

#### SPAIN BEFORE 1700

Early tragedy, Celestina, or the Tragedy of Calisto and Melibœa, late 15th century.
Lope de Rueda, "Father of Spanish Drama," between 1544 and 1567.

Lope de Vega, 1562-1635:
    1800 dramas.
    400 sacred plays (*autos sacramentales*).
Guillen de Castro, from whom Corneille borrowed material for the
    *Cid*.
Calderón de la Barca, 1600-1681:
    108 dramas.
    73 sacred plays (*autos sacramentales*).
        Some of the important plays are:
            Devotion to the Cross
            Origin, Loss, and Restoration of the Virgin
            Purgatory of St. Patrick
            The Wonderful Magician
            Life Is a Dream
            Love Triumphant over Death

### TRAGEDY IN FRANCE BEFORE 1700

Early writers of tragedies:
    Jodelle, 1532-1573.
    Robert Garnier, 1534-1590.
    Alexander Hardy, 1560-1631—Court poet to Henry IV—1200
    plays.

Pierre Corneille, 1606-1684:
    Thirty plays, among which are:
        Mélite
        The Cid
        The Liar (*Le Menteur*)
        Les Horaces
        Cinna
        Polyeucte

Jean Racine, 1639-1699:
    Thébaide
    Alexandre
    Andromaque
    Bérénice
    Athalie
    Phèdre
    Esther
    Mithridate
    Iphigénie

COMEDY IN FRANCE BEFORE 1700

Jean Baptiste de Poquelin de Molière, 1621-1673
  Best known plays:
      L'Étourdi
      Docteur Amoureux
      Les Précieuses Ridicules
      Sganarelle
      L'École des Maris
      L'École des Femmes
      Tartuffe
      Don Juan
      Médicin malgré lui
      Le Misanthrope
      Tartuffe (2nd)
      L'Avare
      Georges Dandin
      Monsieur de Pourceaugnac
      Les Bourgeois Gentilhomme
      Les Fourbéries de Scapin
      Les Femmes savantes
      La Contesse d'Escarbognas
      Le Malade Imaginaire


THE KINDS OF ENGLISH DRAMA BEFORE 1700

INTERLUDE: Represented by
  John Heywood, cir. 1497-1580
      The Play of the Weather
      Plays Witty and Witless
      The Play of Love
      Merry Play between Johan the Husband, Tyb his Wife, and
          Sir John the Priest
      The Four P's


EARLIEST COMEDIES: Represented by
  Ralph Roister Doister, by Nicholas Udall, written between 1534
      and 1541, printed in 1566
  Gammer Gurton's Needle, attributed to
      John Still, to John Bridges, and to William Stevenson
          (about 1566)

EARLIEST TRAGEDIES:
  Gorboduc (Ferrex and Porrex) by
        Thomas Norton and          } 1561
        Thomas Sackville, Earl of Dorset
  Misfortunes of Arthur, Thomas Hughes.
  Tamburlaine, Christopher Marlowe, 1587.

TRAGEDY OF BLOOD:
  The Spanish Tragedy, 1587, Thomas Kyd.

DOMESTIC TRAGEDY: based on local and nearly contemporary events
  Arden of Faversham, 1592, anonymous.
  A Woman Killed with Kindness, Thomas Heywood, 1603.
  A Warning for Fair Women, anonymous.

CHRONICLE AND HISTORY PLAYS: partially represented by
  Tamburlaine, 1587, Christopher Marlowe.
  Edward Second, Marlowe, 1594.
  Battle of Alcazar, 1594, George Peele.
  True Tragedies of Marius and Sylla, 1594, Thomas Lodge.

ROMANTIC COMEDIES:
  Promos and Cassandra, 1578, George Whetstone.
  James IV, Robert Greene.
  Friar Bacon and Friar Bungay, Robert Greene.
  As You Like It, Shakespeare.
  Twelfth Night, Shakespeare.
  A Pleasant Comedie of Fair Em, Robert Greene.
  A Merry Devil of Edmonton, anonymous (1604 approximately).
  The Shoemaker's Holiday, Thomas Dekker.
  Old Fortunatus, Thomas Dekker.

PASTORAL COMEDY:
  The Queen's Arcadia, 1605, Samuel Daniel.
  Hymen's Triumph, 1614, Samuel Daniel.
  The Faithful Shepherdess, John Fletcher.
  The Sad Shepherd (unfinished), Ben Jonson.

COURT COMEDIES: Represented by
John Lyly in his six comedies:
Campaspe (based on an incident in the life of Alexander the Great)
Sapho and Phao ⎫
Endimion ⎬ from Latin mythology
Midas ⎭
Gallathea
Love's Metamorphosis
The Woman in the Moon

COURT MASQUES: written by
Ben Jonson
John Fletcher
Thomas Heywood
George Chapman
Thomas Marston
Samuel Daniel
John Ford
Thomas Campion

## PATENTS AND THEATERS IN ENGLAND

First royal patent issued to the "Servants of Lord Leicester," 1574.
Six companies licensed, 1578.
Lord Leicester went with his players to Germany, 1585.

Playhouses:
The Theater (first house in England regularly designed for plays), built 1576, pulled down 1598, in Shoreditch, public.
The Curtain, built 1576, in Shoreditch, public.
Newington Butts, owned by Henslowe, public.
The Rose, built 1592, destroyed probably in 1647, used by the Chapel Children, private.
The Globe, built 1598, burned 1613, rebuilt 1614, pulled down by Puritans 1644, public.
Fortune, built 1599, burned 1621, rebuilt probably in 1622, destroyed about 1661, public.
Red Bull, built about 1599, rebuilt about 1630, destroyed about 1663, private.
Hope, or Bear Garden, built as theater 1613, destroyed about 1644.

Cockpit, or Phœnix, built about 1615 in Drury Lane, destroyed sometime after 1663.

Salisbury Court, or Whitefriars, built 1629.

## THE SCHOLAR POETS

JOHN LYLY, 1552-1601—Court Comedies
  Endimion ⎫
  Midas ⎪
  Sapho and Phao ⎪
  Alexander and Campaspe ⎬ in prose—euphuistic
  Gallathea ⎪
  Mother Bombie ⎭
  The Woman in the Moon—in blank verse

ROBERT GREENE, 1561-1592
  Orlando Furioso
  Honorable History of Friar Bacon and Friar Bungay
  Looking Glass for London (with Lodge)

THOMAS NASH, 1567-1601
  Isle of Dogs
  Tragedy of Dido (with Marlowe)
  Summer's Last Will and Testament

GEORGE PEELE, 1558-1598
  Edward I (Chronicle Play)
  Battle of Alcazar
  David and Bathsabe
  Old Wives' Tale

THOMAS LODGE, 1556-1625
  Looking Glass for London (with Greene)
  Wounds of Civil War

THOMAS KYD, c.1557-c.1595
  The Spanish Tragedy
  Soliman and Perseda
  The First Hamlet (authorship uncertain but attributed to Kyd, 1589)

CHRISTOPHER MARLOWE, 1564-1593
  Tamburlaine (two parts)
  Doctor Faustus
  Massacre at Paris

The Jew of Malta
Edward II
Tragedy of Dido (with Nash)

WILLIAM SHAKESPEARE, 1564-1616
Earliest dramatic production probably Henry VI, in collaboration.

Chronology of plays, according to Neilson and Thorndike:

### First Period

Henry VI (Part I) ..........................1590-1
Love's Labour's Lost ........................1591
Comedy of Errors ...........................1591
Two Gentlemen of Verona ...................1591-2
Henry VI (Part II) ..........................1590-2
Henry VI (Part III) .........................1590-2
Richard III ................................1593
King John ..................................1593
Titus Andronicus ...........................1593-4

### Second Period

Midsummer Night's Dream ...................1594-5
Richard II .................................1595
Romeo and Juliet ..........................1594-5
Merchant of Venice .........................1595-6
Taming of the Shrew ........................1596-7
Henry IV (Part I) ..........................1597
Merry Wives of Windsor ....................1598
Henry IV (Part II) .........................1598
Much Ado About Nothing ...................1599
Henry V ....................................1599
Julius Cæsar ...............................1599
As You Like It .............................1599-1600
Twelfth Night ..............................1601

### Third Period

Troilus and Cressida .........................1601-2
All's Well That Ends Well ...................1602
Hamlet .....................................1602-3
Measure for Measure ........................1603
Othello ....................................1604
King Lear ..................................1605-6

### Fourth Period

Macbeth ....................................1606
Timon of Athens ..........................1607
Pericles ...................................1607–8
Antony and Cleopatra ....................1607–8
Coriolanus ...............................1609
Cymbeline ...............................1610
Winter's Tale ............................1611
Tempest ..................................1611
Henry VIII .............................1612
Two Noble Kinsmen .....................1612–13

First Folio, published by Heminge and Condell, 1623 contained 37 plays. Pericles was not included.

## DRAMATISTS OF THE REIGNS OF JAMES AND CHARLES I, WITH REPRESENTATIVE PLAYS

Ben Jonson, 1574-1637. Poet laureate
  Every Man in His Humour
  Sejanus, His Fall
  Volpone, or The Fox
  The Alchemist (satirizing the prevailing passion for the occult)
  Bartholomew Fair
  Eastward Hoe (with Marston and Chapman)

Francis Beaumont, 1584-1616 ⎱
John Fletcher, 1579-1625     ⎰ Joint plays:
  Philaster, or Love Lies a-Bleeding
  The Maid's Tragedy
  King and No King
  The Knight of the Burning Pestle
By Fletcher alone, or with collaborators other than Beaumont:
  I. Pure comedies:
        Rule a Wife and Have a Wife (underplot from
          Cervantes)
        Wit Without Money
        The Wild Goose Chase
        The Chances (partly from Cervantes)
        The Noble Gentleman (with some other author)
  II. Heroic or romantic dramas:
        The Knight of Malta (with Massinger)
        The Pilgrim
        The Loyal Subject
        A Wife for a Month
        Love's Pilgrimage (with Shirley and Jonson, from
          Cervantes)
        The Lover's Progress (revised by Massinger)
  III. Mixed comedy and romance:
        The Spanish Curate (with Massinger)
        Monsieur Thomas
        The Custom of the Country (with Massinger, from
          Cervantes)

The Elder Brother (with Massinger)
The Little French Lawyer (with Massinger)
The Humorous Lieutenant (from Plutarch)
Women Pleased
Beggar's Bush (with Massinger)
The Fair Maid of the Inn (with Massinger)
The Two Noble Kinsmen (with Shakespeare)
Henry VIII (with Shakespeare)

THOMAS DEKKER, 1570-cir. 1637:
The Shoemaker's Holiday
Old Fortunatus
Satiromastix
Westward Hoe (with Webster)
Northward Hoe (with Sir Thomas Wyatt)
The Roaring Girl (with Middleton)
The Virgin Martyr (with Massinger)
The Sun's Darling (with Ford)
The Witch of Edmonton (with Ford)

THOMAS HEYWOOD, 1570-1650:
The Captives, or The Lost Recovered
If You Know Not Me, You Know Nobody
Four Prentices of London
A Woman Killed with Kindness
A Pleasant Conceited Comedie, Wherein is shewed how a Man
May Choose a Good Wife from a Bad

THOMAS MIDDLETON, 1570-1627:
A Trick to Catch the Old One
Michaelmas Term
The Family of Love
Your Fine Gallants
A Mad World, My Masters
The Changeling (with Rowley)

JOHN FORD, 1586-1640:
The Broken Heart
The Lover's Melancholy

JOHN WEBSTER, 1580-c.1625:
The Duchess of Malfy
The White Devil
Northward Hoe (with Dekker)
Westward Hoe (with Dekker)

GEORGE CHAPMAN, 1559-1634:
All Fools (from two plays by Terence)
The Blind Beggar of Alexandria
The Revenge of Bussy D'Ambois
The Widow's Tears
The Gentleman Usher
Eastward Hoe (with Jonson and Marston)
The Ball (with Shirley)

PHILIP MASSINGER, 1583-1640:
A New Way to Pay Old Debts
The Fatal Dowry (plagiarized and produced by Rowe under the name of *The Fair Penitent*)
(See Fletcher and Dekker for collaborations)

JOHN MARSTON, 1575-1634:
History of Antonio and Mellida (in two parts)
Histriomastix
Jack Drum's Entertainment (doubtful)
What You Will
Eastward Hoe (with Jonson and Chapman)

JAMES SHIRLEY, 1596-1666:
At least 43 plays
The Ball (with Chapman)
Hyde Park
The Cardinal

CYRIL TOURNEUR, cir. 1575-1626:
The Atheist's Tragedy
The Revenger's Tragedy
Theaters closed 1642-1660.

RESTORATION PLAYWRIGHTS, WITH REPRESENTATIVE PLAYS:

Lord Orrery, 1621-1679
The Black Prince
Tryphon
Herod the Great
Altemira

John Dryden, 1631-1700
Left at least twenty-seven plays, partially represented by Comedies:

The Wild Gallant
Marriage à la Mode
Limberham, the Kind Keeper
Tragi-comedies:
The Rival Ladies
The Spanish Fryar, or the Double Discovery
Love Triumphant, or Love Will Prevail
Heroic Plays:
The Indian Queen (with Howard)
The Indian Emperor, or The Conquest of Mexico
Tyrannick Love, or The Royal Martyr
Aureng-zebe
The Conquest of Granada (two parts)
Tragedies:
The Tempest, or The Enchanted Island (revision of Shakespeare)
All for Love, or The World Well Lost (revision of Antony and Cleopatra by Shakespeare)
Troilus and Cressida, or Truth Found Too Late (revision of Shakespeare)
Œdipus
The Duke of Guise
Don Sebastian
Cleomenes

William Wycherley, 1640-1716:
The Country Wife
The Plain Dealer

Sir George Etherege, c. 1635-1691:
The Comicall Revenge, or Love in a Tub
The Man of the Mode, or Sir Fopling Flutter
She Would If She Could

William Congreve, 1670-1729:
The Old Bachelor
The Mourning Bride
Love for Love
The Way of the World
The Double Dealer

Sir John Vanbrugh, 1666-1726:
The Relapse
The Provoked Wife

George Farquhar, 1677-1707:
  The Beaux' Stratagem
  The Recruiting Officer

Thomas Otway, 1652-1685:
  Venice Preserved
  The Orphan

WOMEN PLAYWRIGHTS:
  Mrs. Aphra Behn, 1640-1689:
    Left eighteen plays, among them
      The Forced Marriage
      The Amorous Prince
      The Dutch Lover
      The Town Fop

  Mrs. Mary Manley, 1672-1724:
    Left several plays

  Mrs. Susannah Centlivre, 1667-1723:
    The Platonic Lady
    The Busybody
    A Bold Stroke for a Wife

OTHER PLAYWRIGHTS:
  Sir Charles Sedley, 1639(?)-1701
  Edward Ravenscroft, fl. 1671-1697
  Thomas Shadwell, 1642(?)-1692
  Thomas D'Urfey, 1653-1723
  Thomas Southerne, 1660-1746
  Nicholas Rowe, 1674-1718
  Elkanah Settle, 1648-1724
  Nathaniel Lee, 1653(?)-1692
  John Crowne, died 1703(?)
  John Dennis, 1657-1734

FAMOUS ACTORS AND ACTRESSES OF THE RESTORATION STAGE:
  Thomas Betterton, 1635(?)-1710
  Michael Mohun, about 1625-1684
  Edward Kynaston, about 1640-1706
  Robert Nokes, died 1673
  James Nokes (comedian) died about 1692
  Mrs. Elizabeth Barry, 1658-1713
  Mrs. Anne Bracegirdle, 1663-1748
  Mrs. Eleanor Gwynne, 1650-1687

## ENGLAND

Prominent Playwrights of the 18th Century, with Representative Plays:

Joseph Addison, 1672-1719:
   Cato, 1713

Sir Richard Steele, 1672-1729:
   The Funeral, or Grief à la Mode.  1701
   The Lying Lover, 1703 (from Corneille's *Menteur*)
   The Tender Husband, 1705
   The Conscious Lovers, 1722 (from Terence's *Andria*)

John Gay, 1685-1732:
   The Beggar's Opera, 1728

George Lillo, 1693-1739:
   The London Merchant, or The History of George Barnwell, 1731
   Fatal Curiosity, 1736

Edward Moore, 1712-1757:
   The Gamester, 1753

Henry Fielding, 1707-1754:
   The Rehearsal
   The Pasquin
   The Critic
   The Coffee House Politician
   The Letter Writers
   The Modern Husband
   The Universal Gallant

Samuel Foote, 1720-1777:
   The Minor
   The Liar

James Townley, 1714-1778:
   High Life Below Stairs

Arthur Murphy, 1727-1805:
The Apprentice
The Spouter
The Upholsterer
Three Weeks After Marriage

Charles Macklin, 1697-1797:
The Man of the World
Benjamin Hoadly, 1706-1757
The Suspicious Husband, 1747

James Thompson, 1700-1749:
Sophonisba
Agamemnon
Tancred and Sigismunda
Alfred (a masque)

Colley Cibber (poet laureate) 1671-1757:
The Careless Husband
The Non-juror (a political adaptation of Molière's Tartuffe)
Last part of Vanbrugh's Provoked Wife

George Colman, the Elder, 1732-1794:
The Clandestine Marriage
The Deuce Is in Him
The English Merchant
The Jealous Wife
The Musical Lady
Philaster
Polly Honeycombe

George Colman, the Younger, 1762-1836:
The Poor Gentleman
John Bull
The Heir-at-Law

Richard Cumberland, 1732-1811:
Produced 37 plays, among them
The Wheel of Fortune
The Brothers
The West Indian
The Choleric Man
The Fashionable Lover

Thomas Holcroft, 1745-1809:
  The Follies of a Day (translation of *The Marriage of Figaro* by Beaumarchais)
  The Road to Ruin
  The Deserted Daughter (founded on an earlier play, *The Fashionable Lover,* by Cumberland)

Hugh Kelly, 1739-1777:
  Clementina
  False Delicacy
  The Man of Reason
  The School for Wives
  A Word to the Wise

Matthew (Monk) Lewis, 1775-1818:
  The Castle Spectre, 1797
  Alphonso, King of Castile
  Adelgitha

Mrs. Elizabeth Inchbald, 1753-1821 (actress as well as playwright)
    Such Things Are

Oliver Goldsmith, 1728-1774:
  The Good Natured Man
  She Stoops to Conquer

Richard Brinsley Sheridan, 1751-1816:
  The Rivals
  St. Patrick's Day, or The Scheming Lieutenant
  The Duenna
  The School for Scandal
  The Critic, or a Tragedy Rehearsed
  A Trip to Scarborough
  Pizarro (based on *Die Spanier in Peru,* by Kotzebue)

#### WRITERS OF CLASSICAL POETIC TRAGEDY, FOLLOWING IN THE STEPS OF ADDISON

| Name | Play |
|---|---|
| Young | Busiris, 1719<br>The Revenge, 1721 |
| Thompson | Sophonisba, 1730<br>Agamemnon, 1738 |

Mallet ................... Eurydice, 1731
Brooke ................... Gustavus Vasa, 1739
Gray .................... Agrippina (a fragment) 1742
Johnson ................. Irene, 1749
Smollett ................. The Regicide, 1749
Motley ................... Antiochus, 1721
Fenton ................... Mariamne, 1723
West .................... Hecuba, 1726
C. Johnson .............. Medea, 1731
Tracey .................. Periander, 1731
Jeffrey ................. Mérope, 1731
Mason ................... Elfrida, 1752
Crisp ................... Virginia, 1754
Whitehead .............. Creusa, 1754

Home ................ { Agis
                       { The Fatal Discovery
                       { Alonzo
                       { Douglas, 1756

Hoole ................... Cleonice, 1775

## REPRESENTATIVE PLAYWRIGHTS AND PLAYS IN THE EIGHTEENTH CENTURY

FRANCE:

Bernard de Boivier de Fontenelle, 1657-1757:
Eight comedies

Jean François Regnard, 1655-1709:
Folies amoureuses
Légataire universel and several other comedies

Charles Rivière Dufresny, 1648-1724:
Joyeuse
Coquette du village
Malade sans maladie

Florent Cartien Dancourt, 1661-1725:
Les fonds perdues
Chevalier à la mode

Prosper Jolyot Crébillon (Crébillon the Elder), 1674-1763
Idoménée
Atrée
Rhadamiste et Zénobie

François Marie Arouet (Voltaire), 1694-1778:
  Wrote more than fifty plays, among them
    Œdipé
    Oreste
    Zaïre
    The Death of Cæsar
    Alzire
    The Phantasm (based on the life of Mahomet)
    Mérope
    Tancrède
    The Orphan of China (based on a Chinese play)
Alain-Réné Lesage, 1668-1747:
  Wrote many farce-operettas wholly or in part, among them
    Crispin rival de son maître
    Turcaret

Alexis Piron, 1698-1773:
  Le métromanie
  Vaudevilles

Philippe Destouches, 1680-1754:
  Le philosophe marié
  Le glorieux

Pierre Carlet de Chamberlain de Marivaux, 1688-1763:
  Wrote more than thirty plays, among them
    Le jeu de l'amour et du hasard
    Le legs
    Les fausses confidences

Pierre Claude Nivelle de la Chaussée, 1691 or 92-1754:
  La fausse antipathie
  Le préjugé à la mode
  Mélanide
  L'École des mères
  La gouvernante

Denis Diderot, 1713-1784:
  Le fils naturel
  Le père de famille

Jean Jacques Rousseau, 1712-1778:
  Le devin du village

Michael Jean Sedaine, 1719-1797:
  Le philosophe sans le savoir
  La gageure imprévue and other comedies

Pierre Augustin Caron de Beaumarchais, 1732-1799:
Le barbier de Seville
Le marriage de Figaro
Eugénie
Les deux amis
La mère coupable

Pompignan, author of Didon
Saurin, author of Spartacus
Pierre de Belloy, author of Siege de Calais, Titus, Zelmire
Jean François Ducis, adapted six Shakespeare plays for the French stage
Jean François de la Harpe, also made adaptations of Shakespeare

ITALY:

Pietro Bonaventura Trepassi, known as Metastasio, 1698-1782:
Left fifteen lyric dramas, among them
Dido Abandoned (*Dido abandonata*)
In the Reign of Attilus

Carlo Goldoni, 1707-1803:
Left about one hundred and sixty comedies, among them
The Coffee House
The True Friend
The Mistress of the Inn (*La Locandiera*)
Carlo Gozzi, 1722-1806:
The Loves of the Three Melarancie
The Little Angel of Belverde

Vittorio Alfieri, 1749-1803:
Left at least nineteen plays, among them
Virginia
The Conspiracy of the Pozzi
Timoleon
The First Brutus
The Second Brutus

SPAIN:
Huerta, 1734-1787:
Raquel (a tragedy)

Gaspar Melchior de Jovellanos, 1744-1811:
The Honest Criminal (a comedy)

Nicolas Fernandez de Moratin (Moratin the Elder), 1737-1780:
  The Female Coxcomb (*Petimetra*) 1762
  Hormesinda

Leandro Fernandez de Moratin, 1760-1828:
  The Old Man and the Maiden
  The New Comedy
  The Baron
  The Female Hypocrite
  The Girl's Yes

Ramon de la Cruz, 1731-1791:
  Left at least three hundred dramatic pieces
  Farces most successful

GERMANY:
  Gotthold Ephraim Lessing, 1729-1781:
    Most important plays are
      Miss Sara Sampson
      Minna von Barnhelm
      Nathan the Wise
      Emilia Galotti

  August Friedrich von Kotzebue, 1761-1819:
    Left about two hundred plays, among them
      The Crusader
      The Stranger (English title of *Menschenhass und Reue*)
      The Spaniards in Peru

  Johann Wolfgang von Goethe, 1749-1832:
    Tragedies:
      Clavigo
      Egmont
      Faust
      Götz von Berlichingen
      Iphigenia
      The Natural Daughter
      Prometheus
      Stella
      Tasso
    Also six comedies, five satirical dramas, three operettas, five
    festival plays, several masques, two serious plays (not com-
    monly classed with the tragedies) *Künstler's Erdenwallen*
    and *Künstler's Vergötterung,* and at least two translations
    from Voltaire.

Johann Friedrich von Schiller, 1759-1805:
The Robbers
Love and Intrigue (*Kabale und Liebe*)
Don Carlos
Wallenstein's Camp ⎫
The Piccolomini ⎬ belong together
The Death of Wallenstein ⎭
Marie Stuart
The Bride of Messina
The Maid of Orleans
Wilhelm Tell

SCANDINAVIA:
Ludwig Holberg, 1684-1754:
Left thirty-four plays, among them
The Arabian Powder
Without Head or Tail
Witchcraft
The Busy Man
The Fickle-minded Woman
Jean de France
The Political Pewterer
The Fortunate Shipwreck
Erasmus Montanus

Johannes Evald, 1743-1781:
Adam and Eve
Rolfe Krage
The Brutal Applauders

Johan Herman Wessel, 1742-1785:
Love Without Stockings

## THE NINETEENTH AND TWENTIETH CENTURIES

FRANCE:
Guilbert de Pixérecourt, 1773-1844:
Wrote at least one hundred and twenty plays, half of which
were melodramas

Frederic Soulié, 1800-1847:
  Writer of melodramas of violent type
    La closerie des Genets

Alexandre Dumas, the Elder, 1803-1870:
  Henry III and his court
  Antony
  Christine
  La tour de Nesle
  Richard Darlington
  Angèle
  Kean

Victor Hugo, 1802-1885:
  Cromwell
  Marion Delorme
  Hernani, 1830
  Le roi s'amuse (basis of Verdi's opera Rigoletto)
  Lucrèce Borgia
  Marie Tudor
  Angélo
  Ruy Blas (often counted Hugo's finest play), 1838
  Les Burgraves
  Les jumeaux
  Torquemada

Eugène Scribe, 1791-1861:
  Either alone or in collaboration, he wrote about four hundred
    dramatic pieces, among them
      Mon oncle César
      La petite sœur
      Le mariage d'argent
      Zoë, ou l'amant prété (*Loan of a Lover* in English)
      Valérie
      La Czarine
      Adrienne Lecouvreur

Émile Augier, 1820-1889:
  Ciguë, 1844
  L'Aventurière
  Gabrielle

Le gendre de Monsieur Poirier (with Jules Sandeau), 1854
Les effrontés
Le fils de Giboyer
Maître Guérin
Paul Forestier
Les Fourchambault

Alexandre Dumas, the younger, 1824-1895:
Wrote at least twelve important plays between 1852 and 1876
La dame aux camélias, 1852 (Camille in English, La Traviata in Verdi's opera)
Diane de Lys
Le demi-monde
La question d'argent
Le fils naturel
Un père prodigue
L'Ami des femmes
Les idées de Mme Aubray
Une visite de noces
La princesse Georges
La femme de Claude
Monsieur Alphonse
L'Etrangère
Denise
Françillon

Victorien Sardou, 1831-1908:
Wrote more than forty plays, among them
Les pattes de mouche, 1861 (adapted into English under the titles of A Scrap of Paper, and Adventures of a Love Letter)
Nos intimes (adapted into English under the titles of Friends or Foes, Bosom Friends, Peril)
Dora (in English called Diplomacy)
Maison neuve
Cléopatra
Divorçons
Odette
L'Oncle Sam
Fédora
Madame Sans-Gène
La Tosca

Patrie
La haine
Famille Benoiton
Nos bons villageois

Octave Feuillet, 1821-1890:
Either alone or in collaboration wrote about twenty plays
Tentation, 1860 (adapted by Boucicault as Led Astray)
Sphinx
Palma, ou la nuit du Vendrédi-Saint
Dalila
Julie

Eugène Labiche, 1815-1888:
Wrote many farces and light comedies (Box and Cox borrowed by Morton, Little Toddlekins borrowed by Charles Matthews)
Voyage de Monsieur Perrichon

Ludovic Halévy, 1834-1908:
Wrote librettos for opera, including *Carmen* for Bizet, and many other plays, collaborating with
Henri Meilhac, 1832-1897:
Plays by the two authors include
Froufrou
La cigale
La boule
La petite mère

Alfred de Vigny, 1799-1863 (translator of Shakespeare):
Chatterton

Alfred de Musset, 1810-1857:
Fantasio
Un Caprice
On ne badine pas avec l'amour

Henri Becque, 1837-1899:
The Parisian Woman
The Ravens (*Les corbeaux*)
Michael Pauper
Honest Women
Widowed
The Start

François de Curel, 1854-
  The New Idol
  The Beat of the Wing
  The Dance Before the Mirror
  The Wise Man's Folly

Eugène Brieux, 1858-
  Blanchette
  The School for Mothers-in-law
  The Three Daughters of Monsieur Dupont
  The Red Robe
  Les avariés (known in English as Damaged Goods)

Paul Hervieu, 1857-1915
  The Nippers
  The Passing of the Torch
  The Labyrinth
  The Awakening
  Destiny Is Master

Henri Lavedan, 1859-
  The Family
  The Medici
  The Duel
  Sire
  The King's Dog
  Petard

Maurice Donnay, 1854-
  Lysistrata
  The Lovers
  The Other Danger
  The Return from Jerusalem
  Molière's Household

Edmond Rostand, 1864-1918
  The Sacred Wood
  The Romantics
  The Faraway Princess
  The Samaritan Woman
  Cyrano de Bergerac
  L'Aiglon
  Chantecler
  Don Juan's Last Night

Germany and Austria:
  Christian Grabbe, 1801-1836:
    Frederick Barbarossa
    Henry Sixth
    Don Juan and Faust


  August Platen (Count von Platen-Hallermund) 1796-1835:
    Writer of comedies and parodies
      The Fatal Fork
      Romantic Œdipus


  Heinrich von Kleist, 1777-1811:
    The Schroffenstein Family (same theme as Romeo and Juliet)
    Amphitryon
    Penthesilea
    Katie of Heilbronn
    The Broken Jug
    The Battle of Arminius
    The Prince of Homburg ⎫
    Robert Guiscard (a fragment) ⎬ posthumous


  Franz Grillparzer, 1791-1872:
    The Ancestress (*Die Ahnfrau*)
    Sappho
    The Golden Fleece ⎫
    Jason          ⎬ a trilogy
    Medea        ⎭
    King Ottokar's Fortune and End
    A True Servant of His Master
    The Waves of Love and the Sea (theme of Hero and Leander)
    Dream Is a Life (*Der Traum ein Leben*)
    Woe to Him Who Lies
      Three tragedies appeared after the author's death


  Karl Gutzkow, 1811-1878:
    Queue and Sword, 1843
    The Prototype of Tartuffe
    Uriel Acosta
    The King's Lieutenant

Friedrich Hebbel, 1813-1863:
Genoveva
Maria Magdalena
Herod and Mariamne
Gyges and His Ring
Agnes Bernauer

Otto Ludwig, 1813-1865:
The Maccabees
The Hereditary Forrester
The Niebelungs (a trilogy which won the Schiller prize in 1862)

Ernst von Wildenbruch, 1845-1909:
The Karlovingians
Christopher Marlowe
The Mennonite
The Songs of Euripides

Gerhardt Hauptmann, 1862-
Before Sunrise, 1889
Lonely Lives
The Weavers, 1892
Hannele
The Sunken Bell
Florian Geyer
Drayman Henschell
Poor Henry
Rose Bernd

Hermann Sudermann, 1857-
Honor
John the Baptist
St. John's Fire
Storm-Brother Socrates
The Flower Boat
The Woman Friend
Raschoffs, The
Heimat (in English Magda)
The Joy of Living (*Es lebe das Leben*)

Arthur Schnitzler, 1862-
   Anatol
   The Green Cockatoo
   The Legacy
   Light o' Love
   The Mate
   Beatrice's Veil
   Living Hours
   Literature
   The Lonely Way
   Intermezzo
   The Countess Mizzi
   Young Medardus
   Professor Bernhardi
   The Big Scene
   The Sisters

Hermann Bahr, 1863-
   The Poor Fool
   The Fawn
   The Concert
   The Little Dance
   The Phantom
   The Gay Soap Boiler
   The Voice
   The Monster
   Light o' Marriage

Franz Wedekind, 1864-
   The Earth Spirit
   The Awakening of Spring

Hugo von Hofmannsthal, 1874-
   Death and the Fool
   Yesterday
   The Rose Cavalier
   The Woman Without a Shadow
   Helen
   Elektra
   Œdipus

Belgium:

Maurice Maeterlinck, 1864-
  The Princess Maleine
  The Blind
  The Intruder
  Joyzelle
  Sister Beatrice
  Monna Vanna
  The Miracle of St. Anthony
  Pelléas and Mélisande
  The Blue Bird
  Mary Magdalene

Holland:

Herman Heijermans, 1864-
  The Good Hope
  Shackles
  All Souls
  The Sleeping Beauty
  Jubilee
  The Ghetto
  Saltimbank

Hungary:

Ferenc Molnar, 1878-
  The Devil
  Liliom
  The Guardsman (also known as Where Ignorance is Bliss)
  The Swan
  Fashions for Men
  The Wolf (known as The Phantom Rival)
  The Play's the Thing

Spain:

José Echegaray, 1833-1916:
  The Great Galeoto (in English The World and His Wife)
  Mariana
  Madman or Saint (also known as Folly or Saintliness)
  The Son of Don Juan
  The Madman Divine
  The Street Singer
  Always Ridiculous

Benito Peréz-Galdos, 1845-1920:
  Doña Perfecta
  The Grandfather
  The Duchess of San Quentin
  Electra

Jacinto Benevente, 1866-
  The Bonds of Interest
  The Passion Flower
  The Prince That Learned Everything Out of Books
  Saturday Night
  In the Clouds
  The Truth
  The Soul of the Princess
  The Magic of an Hour
  The Field of Ermine

Martinez Sierra, director of Theatro Esclava in Madrid:
  The Cradle Song

The Quintero brothers:
  Conchá the Clean
  The House of Life

Eduardo Marquina:
  The Poor Carpenter

Jacinto Grau:
  Count Alareos

Ramon Goy de la Silva:
  The Kingdom of Silence
  The Court of the White Crow

ITALY:
  Giuseppe Giacosa, 1847-1906:
    A Game of Chess
    Sad Loves
    The Husband in Love with His Wife
    The Cat's Claw
    The Rights of the Soul (also known as Sacred Ground)
    As the Leaves
    The Stronger

Gabriele d'Annunzio, 1864-
The Dead City
La Gioconda
Glory
Francesca da Rimini
The Daughter of Jorio
More Than Love
The Ship
Phædra

Luigi Pirandello, 1867-
Sicilian Limes
"If Not Thus—!"
Cap and Bells
Right You Are, If You Think You Are
The Pleasure of Honesty
Each in His Own Way
Naked
Signora Morli
All for the Good
Henry IV
Six Characters in Search of an Author

NORWAY:

Björnsterne Björnson, 1832-1910:
Between the Battles
Lame Hunda
Sigurd Slembe (a trilogy)
Maria Stuart of Scotland
The Newly Wedded Pair
The Editor
The King
Bankruptcy
A Gauntlet

Henrik Ibsen, 1828-1906:
Love's Comedy, 1862
The Pretenders
Brand, 1866
Emperor and Galilean (in two parts)

The Young Men's League
The Pillars of Society (1877)
A Doll's House
Ghosts
An Enemy of the People
The Wild Duck
Rosmersholm
The Lady from the Sea
John Gabriel Borkman
Hedda Gabler
Little Eyolf
The Master Builder
When We Dead Awaken

SWEDEN:
  August Strindberg, 1849-1912:
    Master Olaf, 1872
    The Father
    Countess Julia
    The Stronger
    Easter
    Gustavus Vasa
    Charles XII

DENMARK:
  Adam Öhlenschläger, 1779-1850:
    The Legend of Aladdin
    The Play of St. John's Eve
    Earl Haakon
    Corregio

  Johann Heiberg, 1791-1860:
    King Solomon and Jorgen the Hatter
    The April Fools
    The Critic and the Beast
    The Flying Post
    The Elf Hill, 1828 (an important national play)

  Hans Christian Andersen, 1805-1875:
    Love on the Nikolai Tower

  Edvard Brandes
    A Visit

Peter Nansen
  Judith's Marriage

Hjalmarl Bergstrom, 1868-1914:
  Karen Borneman
  Ida's Wedding
  In the Swim
  The Way to God
  The Day of Trial
  What People Talk Of

ENGLAND:
  Joanna Baillie, 1762-1851:
    Plays on the Passions (3 vols.)

  James Sheridan Knowles, 1784-1862:
    Wrote more than one hundred plays, among them
      Virginius
      The Hunchback
      William Tell
      John of Procida
      The Daughter
      The Love Chase

  Edward Bulwer, first Lord Lytton, 1803-1873:
    The Lady of Lyons
    Richelieu
    Cromwell
    Money
    Not so Bad as We Seem
    The Rightful Heir

  John Madison Morton, 1811-1891:
    Wrote nearly one hundred farces, among them
      Box and Cox (taken from Labiche)
      Speed the Plough (in which originated "Mrs. Grundy")

  Thomas Robertson, 1829-1871:
    David Garrick
    Caste
    School
    Society
    Ours
    M. P.

Tom Taylor, 1817-1880:
 Wrote more than one hundred plays, among them
  Still Waters Run Deep
  The Ticket-of-Leave Man
  The Overland Route
  Joan of Arc
  Masks and Faces
  The King's Rival

G. R. Sims
 Lights o' London

### LITERARY OR "CLOSET" DRAMAS, ENGLISH

William Wordsworth, 1770-1850:
 The Borderers

Samuel Taylor Coleridge, 1772-1834:
 Translations from Schiller
 Osorio, produced under the title Remorse
 Zapolya

Walter Savage Landor, 1775-1864:
 Count Julian

Percy Bysshe Shelley, 1792-1822:
 Prometheus Unbound
 The Cenci

George Gordon, Lord Byron, 1788-1824:
 Manfred
 Cain
 Sardanapalus
 Werner

Richard H. Horne, 1803-1884:
 Cosmo de' Medici
 The Death of Marlowe
 Gregory the Seventh

Matthew Arnold
 Mérope, 1858

William Morris, 1834-1896:
Love Is Enough (a morality) 1873

Alfred Lord Tennyson, 1809-1892:
Queen Mary
Harold
The Falcon
The Cup
Becket (acted 1881, published 1884)

Robert Browning, 1812-1889:
Strafford, 1837
The Blot on the 'Scutcheon
In a Balcony
Colombe's Birthday

Algernon Swinburne, 1837-1909:
Bothwell, 1874
Chastelard
Mary Stuart
Erechtheus
Locrine
Marino Faliero
Sisters: A Tragedy

Thomas Hardy, 1840-
The Dynasts (3 parts)

Arthur Wing Pinero, 1855-
Wrote many plays, among them
The Money Spinner
Lords and Commons
The Magistrate
The Schoolmistress
Sweet Lavender
The Profligate
The Cabinet Minister
Iris
Letty
The Gay Lord Quex
The Second Mrs. Tanqueray
His House in Order
The Thunderbolt
Mid-channel

Henry Arthur Jones, 1851-
  The Silver King
  Wealth
  The Middle Man
  Michael and His Lost Angel
  The Liars
  Mrs. Dane's Defense
  The Case of Rebellious Susan
  The Evangelist

Sidney Grundy, 1848-
  A Fool's Paradise
  A White Lie
  The Greatest of These
  The Seat of Honor

R. C. Carton, 1856-
  Liberty Hall
  Lord and Lady Algy
  Wheels within Wheels
  Mr. Preedy and the Countess

Oscar Wilde, 1856-1900:
  Salome (written in French for Sarah Bernhardt) 1893
  Lady Windemere's Fan
  A Woman of No Importance
  An Ideal Husband
  The Importance of Being Earnest

George Bernard Shaw, 1856-
  Mrs. Warren's Profession
  Widowers' Houses
  You Never Can Tell
  Cæsar and Cleopatra
  Man and Superman
  Candida
  The Man of Destiny
  Back to Methuselah
  Androcles and the Lion
  Saint Joan

Sir James M. Barrie, 1860-
  Quality Street
  The Admirable Crichton
  Little Mary
  Peter Pan
  Alice-sit-by-the-Fire
  What Every Woman Knows
  The Legend of Leonora
  The Will
  The Twelve-pound Look
  A Kiss for Cinderella
  Dear Brutus

John Galsworthy, 1867-
  The Silver Box
  Justice
  The Pigeon
  The Little Man
  Strife

Granville Barker, 1877-
  The Marrying of Ann Leete
  The Voysey Inheritance
  Waste
  The Madras House
  Prunella (with Laurence Housman)
  Anatol (adapted from Schnitzler)

C. Haddon Chambers, 1860-1921:
  The Tyranny of Tears
  The Golden Silence
  Passers-by
  The Saving Grace
  Sir Anthony

Hubert Henry Davies, 1869-1917:
  Cousin Kate
  The Mollusc
  Lady Epping's Lawsuit
  A Single Man
  Doormats
  Outcast
  Captain Drew on Leave

Stephen Phillips, 1867-
  Paolo and Francesca
  Herod
  Ulysses
  The Son of David
  Nero
  The King
  Pietro of Siena
  Armageddon

St. John Hankin, 1860-1909:
  The Return of the Prodigal
  The Charity That Began at Home
  The Last of the De Mullins
  The Constant Lover
  The Cassilis Engagement

John Masefield, 1875-
  The Tragedy of Nan
  The Tragedy of Pompey the Great
  Mrs. Harrison
  Good Friday
  Melloney Hotspur

Stanley Houghton, 1881-1913:
  The Younger Generation
  Hindle Wakes
  The Hillarys
  The Dear Departed
  Independent Means

Elizabeth Baker
  Chains
  Cupid in Clapham
  Over a Garden Wall

Somerset Maugham, 1874-
  Our Betters
  The Circle
  Loaves and Fishes
  Lady Frederick
  East of Suez
  Home and Beauty
  The Camel's Back

IRELAND:

William Butler Yeats, 1865-
Cathleen ni Houlihan
The Hour Glass
The Pot of Broth
The Land of Heart's Desire

Lady Augusta Gregory:
Has written many plays on Irish folk-themes, also made translations of Goldoni, Molière, Sudermann and Hyde
Spreading the News
Hyacinth Halvey
The Workhouse Ward
The Rising of the Moon
The Gaol Gate

John M. Synge, 1871-1909:
In the Shadow of the Glen
Riders to the Sea
The Well of the Saints
The Tinker's Wedding
The Playboy of the Western World
Deirdre of the Sorrows

Lord Dunsany, 1878-
The Gods of the Mountain
If
The Golden Doom
The Queen's Enemies
The Glittering Gate
A Night at an Inn

St. John Ervine, 1883-
Mixed Marriage
Jane Clegg
John Ferguson

RUSSIA:

Alexander Sumarakov, 1718-1777:
Wrote comedies and tragedies in the French style

Alexander Pushkin, 1799-1837:
Boris Godunov

N. V. Gogol, 1809-1852:
  The Inspector-General (Revisor, 1836)

A. N. Ostrovsky, 1823-1886:
  (Called the "father of modern Russian drama")
    Poverty Is No Crime
    Bad Days
    The Snow Maiden
    The Storm

Count Alexei Tolstoi, 1817-1875:
  Best known work a trilogy, consisting of
    The Death of Ivan the Terrible
    Tsar Theodor
    Tsar Boris

Count Leo Tolstoi, 1828-1910:
  The Powers of Darkness
  The Live Corpse
  The Light That Shines in Darkness
  The Fruits of Culture

Maxim Gorky, 1868-
  The Night Asylum (also called In the Depths)
  A Country House
  Children of the Sun
  Barbarians
  The Judge

Feodor Sologub:
  The Triumph of Death

Leonid Andreyev, 1871-1919:
  The Black Masks
  The Life of Man
  King Hunger
  Anathema
  Gaudeamus
  The Parrot
  Youth
  He Who Gets Slapped
  Requiem
  The Waltz of the Dogs

AMERICA:
First American theater opened in New York, 1761.
First permanent theater built, the Old Southwark in Philadelphia, 1766.
The John Street Theater in New York, built 1767.

First play written by an American to have a professional performance on an American stage:
The Prince of Parthia, by Thomas Godfrey, 1767.
First comedy by an American:
The Contrast, by Royall Tyler, 1787.

William Dunlap, 1766-1839:
The Father, 1789
Leicester, 1794
Andre
A History of the Early American Theater, published 1832

John Howard Payne, 1791-1852:
Charles the Second
Brutus
Clari, the Maid of Milan

Richard Penn Smith, 1799-1854

R. N. Bird, 1806-1854:
The Gladiator
The Broker of Bogota

George Washington Parke Custis, 1781-1857:
Pocohontas and the Settlers of Virginia

John A. Stone:
Metamora

N. P. Willis, 1806-1867:
Tortesa the Usurer

Julia Ward Howe, 1819-1910:
Leonora or The World's Own

George H. Boker, 1833-1890:
Francesca da Rimini

Dion Boucicault, 1822-1890 (Irish-American):
Opened Park Theater, New York, 1876.
Wrote many plays, among them
  London Assurance (before coming to New York, probably
    with Brougham)
  The Octoroon
  Streets o' London
  Foul Play
  Rip Van Winkle
  The Colleen Bawn
  The Shaughraun

Anna Cora Mowatt Ritchie, 1819-1870:
Fashion
Armand

James A. Herne, 1839-1901:
Hearts of Oak
The Minute Men
Marjorie Fleming
Shore Acres, written 1844, produced first as The Hawthornes
Sag Harbor

Bartley Campbell, 1845-1888:
My Partner
Fairfax
The Galley Slave
Matrimony

Bronson Howard, 1842-1908:
Saratoga, 1870
Moorcraft
The Banker's Daughter
Hurricanes
Young Mrs. Winthrop
The Henrietta
Shenandoah
Aristocracy, 1892

Augustus Thomas, 1859-
Alabama
In Mizzoura
Arizona
The Earl of Pawtucket
Mrs. Leffingwell's Boots
The Witching Hour
As a Man Thinks

William Gillette, 1855-
Held by the Enemy
Secret Service
Too Much Johnson
Sherlock Holmes

Denman Thompson:
The Old Homestead

Steele Mackaye, 1842-1894:
Hazel Kirke

David Belasco:
Heart of Maryland
The Girl of the Golden West
The Return of Peter Grimm

Clyde Fitch, 1865-1909:
Captain Jinks of the Horse Marines
Beau Brummel
The Climbers
The Girl with the Green Eyes
The City
The Truth

William Vaughn Moody, 1869-1910:
The Great Divide
The Faith Healer

Langdon Mitchell:
The New York Idea

Percy Mackaye, 1875-
The Canterbury Pilgrims
Jeanne d'Arc
Sappho and Phaon
Mater

Anti-Matrimony
The Scarecrow
A Thousand Years Ago
This Fine Pretty World

Josephine Preston Peabody Marks:
The Piper
Marlowe
The Wolf of Gubbio

Mary Austin:
The Arrow Maker

Rachel Crothers:
Three of Us
A Man's World
Nice People
Old Lady 31
Expressing Willie

Booth Tarkington, 1869-
The Man from Home (with Leon Wilson)
Clarence
Mister Antonio
The Intimate Strangers

Eugene Walter:
Paid in Full
The Easiest Way
Fine Feathers
The Challenge

Edward Sheldon:
Salvation Nell
The Boss
The Nigger
Romance
The Garden of Paradise

Charles Rann Kennedy:
The Servant in the House
The Terrible Meek
The Winter Feast
The Flower of the Palace of Han
The Chastening

Charles Kenyon:
  Kindling

Jesse Lynch Williams:
  Why Marry?
  Why Not?

George M. Cohan, 1878-
  Broadway Jones
  Get-Rich-Quick Wallingford
  Seven Keys to Baldpate
  The Tavern
  Hit-the-Trail Halliday

Susan Glaspell:
  Inheritors
  Suppressed Desires
  The Verge

Charles Klein:
  The Lion and the Mouse

Sutton Vane:
  Outward Bound

Elmer Reizenstein:
  On Trial

Elmer Rice:
  The Adding Machine

Zoë Akins:
  Declassée
  The Moonflower

Hatcher Hughes:
  Hell Bent for Heaven

Lulu Vollmer:
  Sun Up

Owen Davis:
  Icebound

Louis Beach:
  The Goose Hangs High

Philip Moeller:
  Georg Sand
  A Road House in Arden
  Helena's Husband

Clare Kummer:
  Good Gracious, Annabelle
  A Successful Calamity

Eugene O'Neill, 1888-
  Bound East for Cardiff
  Beyond the Horizon
  Desire Under the Elms
  The Emperor Jones
  The Hairy Ape
  The Great God Brown
  All God's Chillun Got Wings
  Anna Christie
  Diff'rent

Paul Green:
  In Abraham's Bosom
  The Field God

# INDEX

*Italicized references indicate titles of plays or of books.*

Abbey Theater, founding of, 343
  one of the independent group, 324
*Abraham Lincoln,* Drinkwater, 341
Absence of naturalism on the Kamerny stage, 368
Abstract figures in recent drama, 367
Academy of Arcadians (Italy), 277
Academy Theater at Strassburg, 281
Acte, 91
Acting companies organized in America, 353
Action in Greek plays, 68
Actors and actresses of note (eighteenth century), 260
Actors' position, in China, 105
  in Greece, 75
  in Rome, 91
Actors, first appearance of professional, 158
*Acts of the Apostles,* 131
Adams, Maude, 342
*Adding Machine, The,* Rice, 367
Addison, Joseph, 261
*Adelchi,* Manzoni, 314
Adultery, theme of French plays, 294
  in Dumas' plays, 300
Æschylus, life of, 27
  changes made by, 31
  chorus of, 32
  patriotic and religious ideas of, 33
  eclipse of, 33
  how regarded by ancients, 33
  honored by Athenians, 34

Æsopus, 81
*Agamemnon,* Æschylus, 30
*Ahnfrau, Die,* Grillparzer, 311
*Ajax,* Sophocles, 37
Akins, Zöe, 359
*Alabama,* Thomas, 356
Alemanni, 149
Alfieri, Vittorio, 277
Alleyn, Edward (note), 236
*All for Love or The World Well Lost,* Dryden, 253
*Alphonsus of Germany,* 196
Amadis of Gaul, legends of, 13
Ambidexter, 186
"American Roscius," The, 353
American stage in the nineteenth century, 354
*Aminta,* Tasso, 157
  model for English pastorals, 201
*Amphitruo,* Plautus, imitated, 187
*Anatol,* Schnitzler, 329
*Ancestress, The,* Grillparzer, 311
*André,* Dunlap, quoted, 353
Andersen, Hans Christian, 315
Andreyev, Leonid, 349
*Andromaque,* Racine, 175
*Angelo,* Hugo, 296
Anglin, Margaret, 357
*Anna Christie,* O'Neill, 361
*Annales, or a General Chronicle of England from Brute until the present Yeare of Christ 1580,* by Walsingham, 15
d'Annunzio, Gabriele, 334
Anonymous writers of sacred plays, 120
Anticipation of theories of Ibsen, 312

*Antigone,* Sophocles, 36
  imitated in Italian, 149
  use of legend, 12
*Anti-Matrimony,* Mackaye, 358
Antoine, Monsieur, 323
*Antonio Foscarini,* Niccolini, 314
*Antony and Cleopatra* rewritten, 253
*Antony,* Dumas, 294
  Garnier, 192
Appearance of lay actors in sacred plays, 125
Appearance of women on London stage, 250
*Appius and Virginia* (interlude), 186
Appurtenances of the romantic play, 294
Arabian story-tellers, 14
Aran Islands, 344
Arcadia, 157
Archer, William (note), 321
Arden, Mary, 224
*Arden of Faversham,* authorship of, 196
Aretino, Peter, 152
Arion, 19
Ariosto, 151
Aristophanes, his life and works, 52
  conservatism of, 53
  as critic, 55
Aristotle, opinion of tragic poets, 61
  dramatic principles, 62
  principles perverted, 64
*Arizona,* Thomas, 356
*Arms and the Man,* Shaw, 339
*Arnoldo di Brescia,* Niccolini, 314
Arouet, François Marie, 269
*Arrow Maker, The,* Austin, 359
*Arraignment of Paris, The,* Peele, 217
*Ars Poetica,* Horace, 89
Arthur, King, legends of, 13
*Art of Poetry, The,* Gottsched, 282
*As a Man Thinks,* Thomas, 356

Asides and soliloquies, 356
*As the Leaves,* Giacosa, 333
*As You Like It,* type of romantic comedy, 201
  in America, 353
Atellanæ, 79
*Athalie,* Racine, 173
*Atheist's Tragedy, The,* Tourneur, 244
*Attila,* Corneille, 171
Attius, or Accius, 81
Audiences, in Athens, 76
  in Rome, 93
  in Elizabethan London, 212
Augier, Emile, 297
Authorship of *Arden of Faversham,* 197
Austin, Mary, 359
Auto sacramentale, 130
  performance forbidden, 279
*Avariés, Les,* Brieux, 330
*Aventurière,* Augier, 298
Awakening, The Dramatic, 323
*Awakening of Spring, The,* Wedekind, 329

*Back to Methuselah,* Shaw, 340
Bacon, Francis, collaboration of, 192
  quoted, 302
*Bad Days,* Ostrovsky, 348
Baillie, Joanna, 303
Baker, George P., leader of study of drama in America, 370
  quoted, 310
Bale, John, life and work, 184
  importance of, 143
Ballads in Spain, 159
Ballad-opera in England, 262
Bandello, version of *Romeo and Juliet* by, 231
Barbarossa, legend used by Hugo, 296
*Barber of Seville, The,* Beaumarchais, 275
Barker, Granville, 341
Barrett, Lawrence, 355

Barrie, Sir James, 342
*Battle of Alcazar, The,* Peele, 200
  quoted, 217
*Battle of the Corn, The,* 4
*Battles of Kokusenya, The,* Chika-
  matsu, 110
*Bauble Shop, The,* Jones, 308
Bayes (Dryden), 254
Bazoche du Palais, La, 141
*Beau Brummel,* Fitch, 356
Beaumarchais, 274
  plays used as opera librettos, 276
Beaumont, Francis, 237
Beccari, 157
*Becket,* Tennyson, 307
Becque, Henri, 329
Bedlam Beggars, Poor Toms, or
  Abraham Men, 189
*Before Sunrise,* Hauptmann, 327
*Beggar's Opera, The,* Gay, 262
Beginning of a national drama in
  Denmark, 291
Behn, Mrs. Aphra, 258
Belcari, Feo, 128
Belloy, criticism of sacred plays,
  269
Benelli, Sem, 335
Benevente, José, 336
  not in radical group, 368
*Benign Ones, The,* Æschylus, 30
Bergen, Theater of, 318
Bernhardt, Sara, 332
*Bertram, or the Castle of St. Aldo-
  brand,* 303
Bethlehem plays, 119
*Beyond the Horizon,* O'Neill, 361
Bhasa, or Bhrata, 99
Bhavabuti, 101
Bibbiena, Cardinal, 150
*Binding of a Braid of Hair, The,*
  102
Bird, R. N., 354
*Birth of Tragedy, The,* Nietzsche,
  20
Biographical plays, American, 359
Bizet, 301
Björnson, Björnstjerne, 316

Blackfriars Theater, 210
*Black Masks, The,* Andreyev, 349
Blank verse, first use in England,
  191
  as used by Greene, 216
  improved by Marlowe, 221
*Blind, The,* Maeterlinck, 331
*Blue Beard,* Gozzi, 277
*Blue Bird, The,* Maeterlinck, 331
Blue-stockings of the Renaissance,
  169
Bobadil, Captain, 156, 236
Boccaccio, 14
*Bohême, La,* Giacosa, 333
Boileau, an admirer of Racine, 175
  theory of drama, 175
  translated into Spanish, 278
Boker, George H., 355
*Bonds of Interest, The,* Benevente,
  336
*Book of Heroes (Heldenbuch),* 13
*Bookworm, The,* Benelli, 335
Booth, Junius Brutus, 353
*Boris Godunov,* Pushkin, 347
*Boss, The,* Sheldon, 359
Botta, on Spanish romances, 14
Boucicault, Dion, 355
*Bound East for Cardiff,* O'Neill,
  361
Bourgogne, Hotel de, form of
  stage, 181
Bovio, Giovanni, 314
Bowdlerization of Shakespeare,
  261
Boyd, Ernest A., quoted on Synge,
  344
Boyle, Richard, Earl of Orrery,
  251
Boynton, Percy, quoted on O'Neill,
  361
Bracco, Roberto, 335
Bragging Captain, The, 156
*Brand,* Ibsen, 318
*Breaking a Butterfly,* Jones, 308
*Bride of Messina, The,* Schiller,
  289
Brieux, Eugene, 330

Brisbarre, Edouard, 305
Bridges, Dr. John, 188
*Broker of Bogota, The*, Bird, 254
Brotherhood of the Passion, 127
Brooke, C. Tucker, opinion of Greene's play, 201
on seventeenth-century drama, 235
Brooke, Arthur, 231
Brooke, Stopford, on Marlowe, 219
Browning, Robert, closet drama, 306
Brunetière, on the influence of the *précieuses*, 170
*Brutal Applauders, The*, Ewald, 291
*Brutus*, Voltaire, 270
Büchner, Georg, 311
*Building of the Ark, The*, 133
Bulwer, Edward, Lord Lytton, 304
Burbage, Richard, builder of Globe Theater, 210
Burbage, James, one of the "Servants" of the Earl of Leicester, 208
*Burgraves, Les*, Hugo, 296
*Bushido* (note), 106
*Bussy d'Ambois*, Chapman, 241
Byron's defence of *Bertram*, 303
eulogy of Sheridan, 266
closet plays, 306

Cabell, James Branch, on Marlowe, 222
on Restoration drama, 249
*Cabinet Minister, The*, Pinero, 307
*Cadmus and Hermione*, 250
*Cæsar and Cleopatra*, Shaw, 340
*Cage of the Lioness, The*, Rivas, 336
*Caius Gracchus*, Knowles, 304
*Calandra*, Bibbiena, 150
Calderón de la Barca, Life of, 164
as court poet, 165
sacred plays of, 165
Calverley, Walter, 198

*Cambises King of Percia* (interlude), 186
*Candida*, Shaw, 339
*Canterbury Pilgrims, The*, Mackaye, 358
Capell, Edward, on the authorship of *Edward III*, 199
Capeks, The, 367
Captain Bobadil, 156, 236
Capitano Metamoros, 156
Capitaine Fracasse, Le, 156
Captain Horribilicribilifax, 156
*Captives, The*, Plautus, 83
imitated, 187
*Cardinall, The*, Shirley, 245
Cardinal Wolsey, 184
Carlyle, Thomas, on books, 9
*Carmen*, 301
Caron, Pierre Augustin (Beaumarchais), 274
"Cartoon" comedy, 360
*Case Is Altered, The*, Jonson, 236
Casket scene, source of, 232
*Caste*, Robertson, 305
*Castle of Perseverance, The*, 139
*Castle Spectre, The*, Lewis, 302
Catalogues and records of Greek plays, 64
Catchwords from Shakespeare, 223
Catherine the Great, as playwright, 347
*Cathleen ni Houlihan*, Yeats, 344
*Cato*, Addison, 261
Cause of the War of the Theaters, 241
*Cavalleria Rusticana*, Verga, 333
Caxton, William, 183
*Celestine, or The Tragedy of Callisto and Melibœa*, 159
Cellini, Benvenuto, 182
Celtic legends rewritten, 344
Centilivre, Mrs. Susannah, 258
Cervantes, 160
Change of verse-form in Benelli, 336
*Chanticler*, Rostand, 332

Chapman, J. J., on Shakespeare, 233

Chapman, George, 241

Characteristics of d'Annunzio's plays, 334
  of Barrie's plays, 342
  of Cyrano de Bergerac, 332
  of plays by the elder Dumas, 294
  of Elizabethan drama, 245
  of English melodrama, 303
  of Marlowe's plays, 221
  of Pinero's plays, 308
  of Wilde's plays, 338
  of Yeats' plays, 344

Character of the morality, 138

Charlemagne, legends of, 13

*Charles the Second,* Payne and Irving, 353

Charles Second restored, 249

*Chastening, The,* Kennedy, 358

Chekhov, Anton, 349

*Cherry Orchard, The,* Chekhov, 349

Chesterton, Gilbert, quoted, 352

Chettle, collaborator with Munday, 200

Chikamatsu, 109

Children of the Chapel Royal, licensed, 209
  producers of court comedies, 202

Children of Shakespeare, 224

Children of St. Paul's, licensed, 209

Chinese drama, subjects of, 103
  theory of, 103

Choerilus, 23

*Chorus Lady, The,* Forbes, 360

Chorus in Æschylean tragedy, 32

Christiania University, 318

*Christ at the Feast of Purim,* Bovio, 314

Christmas plays, 119
  performed at Constance, 132

"Christopher North" on Miss Baillie, 304

Chronicle and history play, 198 ff.

*Chronicles of England, Scotland and Ireland,* Walsingham, 15

*Chronicle of Matthew Paris,* 15

Cibber, Colley, manager of Drury Lane Theater, 260

Cid, The Legend of, 16

*Cid, The,* Corneille, 170
  Guillem de Castro, 171

*Ciguë,* Augier, 297

Cinthio, source of *Othello* plot, 232

*Circe,* Calderon, 165

City Dionysia, Athens, 73

*City, The,* Fitch, 356

*Civil Death,* Giacometti, 313

Civic theaters in America, 369

Civil War dramas, 356, 357

Claque, in Athens, 76

*Clarence,* Tarkington, 360    [353

*Clari, the Maid of Milan,* Payne,

Classic tragedy in England, 261

Classic themes on modern German stage, 329

Classicism in Spain, 159

Classic drama imitated in monasteries, 116
  in Germany, 287

"Classic," two meanings, 67

*Cleopatra,* Cossa, 314
  Daniel, 192
  Jodelle, 168

*Clerical Error, A,* Jones, 308

*Climbers, The,* Fitch, 356

*Clizia,* Machiavelli, 151

*Clavigo,* Goethe, 286

*Claw, The,* Rivas, 336

Cloak-and-Sword dramas, 161

"Clockmaker to the King," 275

Closet drama in England, 306

Closing of London playhouses, 248

Coat-of-arms granted to Shakespeare, 225

Coburn, Mr. and Mrs., 359

Coleman, Mrs., 250

Collaboration among French playwrights, 298
  of Beaumont and Fletcher, 237

*College Widow, The,* Ade, 360
Collier's attack on the stage, 258
Collier's list of plays (Elizabethan), 204
Colman the elder, George, 264
Colman the younger, George, 304
Colum, Padraic, 343
Comedietta, 268
Commedia dell' Arte, 153
  subjects of, 154
  actors in, 155
  decline of, 276
Comédie larmoyante, 268
  of La Chaussée, 273
Comedies of the Restoration, 255 ff.
Comedy in France (1640-1658), 178
  eighteenth century, 273
*Comedy of Errors, The,* 227
"Comedy of humours," 236
Comédie-vaudeville in France, 297
*Comicall Historie of Alphonsus, King of Arragon,* Greene, 215
*Commodye of pacient and meeke Grissill,* 186
*Commuters, The,* Forbes, 360
Comparison between the Victorian and modern schools, 326
Companies of actors (Elizabethan), 209
Comparison of *Doctor Faustus* and *Faust,* 287
Compensation received by Otway, 255
Competitions in Greece, 73
Competition in tragedy, first public, 22
Composition of Elizabethan plays, 211
Comus, character of, 51
*Concha the Clean,* Quintero, 336
Condell, Henry, 228
*Condemnation of Banquets, The,* 139
Condemnation of the theater (Elizabethan), 246
  (Roman), 95

Condition of Danish stage in eighteenth century, 316
Conditions peculiar to American drama, 361
Conflict, the material of epic and drama, 9
Congreve, William, 256
  visited by Voltaire, 270
Conservatism of the stage, 370
Construction of the morality, 139
*Contrast, The,* Tyler, 352
"Contamination," meaning of, 65
*Contention of Two Famous Houses of York and Lancaster,* 199
*Conquest of Granada, The,* Dryden, 252
Copenhagen, playhouse in, 290
*Corbeaux, Les,* Becque, 330
*Coriolanus,* source of plot, 232
*Cornelia,* Garnier, 192
"Corneille of the Boulevards," 293
Corneille, Pierre, 170, 171
Corneille, Thomas, 177
Correction of errors in First Folio, 230
Corregio, Niccola da, 157
*Countess Cathleen, The,* Yeats, 343, 344
*Countess of Carmagnola, The,* Manzoni, 314
*Countess Julia, The,* Strindberg, 322
*Country Wife, The,* Wycherley, 255
*County Chairman, The,* Ade, 360
Cossa, Pietro, 314
Court comedies (Elizabethan), 202 ff.
Court masques (Elizabethan), 203
Court Revels, minutes of, 205
Covent Garden, 260
Corydon and Thyrsis, 157
*Cradle Song, The,* Sierra, 337
Craig, Gordon, 366
Cratinas, 52
*Creation and Flood,* 144

Crébillon the elder, 269
Creed of Strindberg, 323
Criharsha, plays attributed to, 102
Critic, The, Sheridan, 267 (note), 254
Critical and Historical Essays, Macdowell, 6
Criticisms of Ibsen, 321
Cromwell, Thomas, play on subject of, 200
Cromwell, preface to, 295
Cross Roads, The, Robinson, 345
Crothers, Rachel, 359
Cruttwell, on Roman drama, 59
Cubistic designs on stage, 366
Cumberland, Richard, 264
Curtain Theater built, 210
Cushing, Catherine C., 360
Custis, George Washington Parke, 354
Cycles of plays in England, 133
Cyclops, The, Euripides, 46
"Cynthia," 202
Cymbeline, 227
  source of plot, 232
Cyrano de Bergerac, Rostand, 331

Damaged Goods, Brieux, 330
Dance of Life, The, Ellis, quoted, 3
Dancing an ancient art, 4
Dancourt, 269
Daniel, Samuel, 192
  author of pastorals, 201
Danish pension given to Hebbel, 312
Daughter of Iorio, The, D'Annunzio, 334
Davenant, William, 250          [305
David Garrick, play by Robertson,
David and Bathsabe, Peele, 218
Davis, Owen, 359
Dead City, The, D'Annunzio, 334
Death of Danton, The, Büchner, 311
Death of Tintagiles, The, Maeterlinck, 331

Death of Ivan the Terrible, The, Tolstoi, 348
Death of Robert Earl of Huntington, The, Munday and Chettle, 200
Debt of modern writers to Ibsen, 322
Dearth of arts in Germany in seventeenth century, 280
Decameron, as source of plots, 232
  legends preserved in, 14
Declassée, Akins, 359
Decline of classic drama, reasons for, 95
  of romanticism in France, 296
Defence of Poesy, A, Sidney, 205
Deirdre, Yeats, 344
Dekker, Thomas, 240
Delgado, Jacinto Grau, 336
DeMille, William C., 356
Demi-mondaines, on French stage, 299
Demi-monde, Le, Dumas, 300
De Montfort, Baillie, 304
Depravity portrayed in Italian comedies, 151
Desire Under the Elms, O'Neill, 359, 361
Destouches, 273
Devotion to the Cross, The, Calderón, 165
Dewey, John, on standards of art, 68
Diane de Lys, Dumas, 300
Diary, Henslowe's (note), 236
Diccon the Bedlam, 189
Dickinson, Thomas H., on O'Neill, 361
Diderot, Denis, 274
  opinion of The London Merchant, 263
Dido abandonata, Metastasio, 277
Die Spanier in Peru, Kotzebue, 285
Difficult questions of play-authorship, 230
Dill, on Roman Society, 91

Dionysiac festivals, 19, 74
 procession, 7, 74
 time of, 75
Dionysus, impersonated, 7
Disappearance of biblical plays, 136
Discovery of ancient literatures, 147
Distinction between miracle and mystery, 127
Dithyrambic Hymn, 7
 subjects of, 21
 chorus, 19
Divorçons, Sardou, 300
Doctor, The, in Italian comedy, 155
Doctor Faustus, Marlowe, 219 ff.
 in Germany, 221, 281, 287
Dodsley, 133
Doll's House, A, Ibsen, adapted, 308
Domestic tragedy, 196
Domestic "triangle" as subject for plots, 306
Don Carlos, Schiller, 289
Don Juan and Faust, Grabbe, 311
Don Pietro Carneso, Bracco, 335
Don Roderigo, tales of, 14
Double Dealer, The, Congreve, 256
Douglas, Home, 261
 author inspired by Maffei, 277
 performed in America, 253
Dovizio, Cardinal Bibbiena, 150
Dowden, on Shakespeare, 227
Downfall of Robert, Earl of Huntington, 200
Drama defined, 3
Dramatic Awakening, The, 323
Dramatis personæ of melodrama, 293
Drame, 268
Drame bourgeois, 274
Dream device in plays, 216, 311
Dream Is a Life, Grillparzer, 311
Drew, John, 353

Drinkwater, John, 341
 on eighteenth century drama in England, 267
Drum with primitive dancing, 7
Drury Lane Theater, 260
 under Sheridan, 266
Dryden, John, 252
Duchess of Malfy, The, Webster, 242
Duchess of Portsmouth, friend of Otway, 255
Ducis, translator of Shakespeare, 273
Duenna, The, Sheridan, 267
Dufresny, 269
Duke of Gothland, The, Grabbe, 311
Duke of Hesse, employment of English players, 281
Dumas the younger, Alexandre, 299
Dumas the elder, Alexandre, 294
Dumb show in medieval plays, 144
 in Battle of Alcazar, 218
 in Gorboduc, 191
Dunlap, William, 352
Dunsany, Lord, 345
Duse, Eleanora, in Praga's plays, 333
Dynasts, The, Hardy, 306
Dying Cato, The, Gottsched, 282

Earl of Dorset (Thomas Sackville), 190
Earl of Orrery, 251
Earl Haakon, Öhlenschläger, 315
Earl of Southampton, 227
Earliest Faust story, 220
Early death of Scholar Poets, 215
Early English tragedy, 189 ff.
Easiest Way, The, Walter, 359
Easter plays, 119
 dialogue from, 115
Eastward Hoe, Marston, 242
Eccyclema, 72
Echegaray, José, 336

Eclipse of drama in England in nineteenth century, 302
in Spain, 278

*Eddas, The,* as source of plot material, 13

Editors of Shakespeare, 230, 231

Editions of the Faust story, 220

Education of Victor Hugo, 294

*Edward First,* Peele, 199, 217

*Edward Second,* Marlowe, 199, 219

*Edward Third,* 199

*Edward Fourth,* Heywood, 199

Effect of Ibsen's dramaturgy, 365

*Egmont,* Goethe, 287

Egyptian Passion play, 6

*Ehre, Die,* Sudermann, 328

Eighteenth century represented by Voltaire, 272

*Electra,* Sophocles, 39

*El Gran Galeoto,* Echegaray, 336

Elizabethan drama, forces that shaped, 183
public, taste of, 204
performances compared with Athenian, 213

Ellis, Edith, 360

Ellis, Havelock, on primitive dancing, 3

*El Pobrecito Carpintero,* Marquina, 337

*Emilia Galotti,* Lessing, 284

*Emperor and Galilean,* Ibsen, 318

*Emperor Jones, The,* O'Neill, 361

*Enamoured Woman, The,* Praga, 333

*Endimion,* Lyly, 202                    [319

*Enemy of the People, An,* Ibsen,

*Enfants sans souci,* 141

England, lack of culture in sixteenth century, 182

English actors in America, 353

English comedians in Germany, 281

"English Euripides," The, 254

English influence on Voltaire, 271
in Germany, 282

English plays in Germany, 281
company in America, 352

Ennius, 80

Ephemeral character of most drama, 370

*Epic Cycle,* 11

Erasmus in England, 182

Erskine, John, quoted, 268, 365
on Racine, 175

Ervine, St. John, 345

*Esther,* Racine, 173

Etherege, Sir George, 255

*Eugénie,* Beaumarchais, 275

Eulenspiegel as clown, 281

*Euphues, the Anatomy of Wit,* 202
*His England,* 202

Euripides, 45-50

European influence in Restoration plays, 257

European plays brought to America, 362

*Everyman,* 139

*Every Man in His Humour,* Jonson, 236

Ewald, Johannes, 291

Experimentation on the American stage, 369

"Expressionism," 367

*Expressing Willie,* Crothers, 359

Extant manuscripts of sacred drama in England, 132

Extent of work of Scribe, 297

*Faith Healer, The,* Moody, 357

*Faithful Shepherdess, The,* Fletcher, 202

*Falconer of Pietro Ardena, The,* Marenco, 314

*False Delicacy,* Kelly, 264

False sentimentalism concerning the life of the harlot, 299

*Famous Victories of Henry V,* 199

*The Fantastics,* Rostand, 332

*Faraway Princess, The,* Rostand, 332

Farquhar, George, 256

*Fashion,* Ritchie, 354
*Fatall Dowry, The,* Massinger and Field, 243
*Fatal Fork, The,* Platen, 311
Fate motive in *Romeo and Juliet,* 231
in Ghosts, 319
"Father of Danish literature," 291
*Father, The,* Dunlap, 352
Strindberg, 322
Faust legend, 16
development of legend, 219, 220
Goethe's poem, 287 ff.
as opera, 288
early versions of, 287
"Feasts" in England, 182
Feast of the Ass, origin of, 116
Feast of Fools, origin of, 116
*Female Coxcomb, The,* Moratin, 279
*Ferrex and Porrex,* 190
Fescennine songs, 78
Feuillet, Octave, 301
Field, Nathaniel, 343
Fielding, Henry, 263
Figaro, servant in *The Barber of Seville,* 275
*Figaro, The Marriage of,* Beaumarchais, 275
*Fils de Giboyer, Le,* Augier, 298
*Fils naturel, Le,* Diderot, 274
Financing a medieval play, 127
*Fine Feathers,* Walter, 359
First appearance of nationalism in German theater, 286
*First Folio, The,* 228
First *Hamlet,* The, 196, 210
American play acted by a professional company, 352
English morality, 138
formal play in Rome, 80
good historical play in English, 199
important American drama, 353
royal patents granted, 208
*First Part of Jeronimo,* etc., 194
Fitch, Clyde, 356

Fitzmaurice, George, 345
Fletcher, John, 237 ff.
as collaborator with Shakespeare, 227
Flickinger, Roy, on Greek drama, 13, 61
*Flower of the Palace of Han, The,* 358
Flutter, Sir Fopling, 255
Fogazzaro, Antonio, 334
Folk-lore in Hauptmann's plays, 327
Fontenelle, 268
quoted on Corneille, 172
*Fool, The,* Pollock, 358
Foote, Samuel, 263
Forbes, James, 360
Forces in Elizabethan drama, 183
Ford, John, 244
Foreign movements not assimilated in America, 363
Foreign plays in London, 261
Forerunners, The, 23
Forrest, Edwin, 353
Fortune Theater built (note), 210, 236
*Forty-seven Ronins, The Story of,* 110
"Founder of Russian drama," 348
Founders of the Irish Literary Theater, 343
*Four Elements, The,* 184
*Four P's, The,* Heywood, 185
*Fox Hunt, The,* Verga, 333
*Francesca da Rimini,* Boker, 355
D'Annunzio, 334
Fraternity of the Bazoche, 127
Freie Bühne, Die, 324
French Academy, founded, 171
classic influence in England, 191
comedy influenced by Spain and Italy, 178
drama in Italy, 313
drama in Spain, 278
imitations driven from Danish stage, 291
influence in Russia, 347

French plays adapted by Fitch, 357
plays performed in London, 250
plays in Copenhagen, 290
plays in Leipzig, 282
technique adopted by Pinero and Jones, 308
vaudevilles in Denmark, 315
Freytag, Gustav, 312
*Friar Bacon and Friar Bungay,* 201, 216
Friendship between Goethe and Schiller, 286, 289
Frischlin, Nicodemus, 281
*Frogs, The,* Aristophanes, 54, 55
*Froufrou,* Halévy and Meilhac, 301
*Frühlingserwachen,* Wedekind, 329
"Futurism" in drama, 368

*Gabrielle,* Augier, 298
Galsworthy, John, 341
*Game of Chess, A,* Giacosa, 333
*Gamester, The,* Moore, 263
influence in France, 274
*Gammer Gurton's Needle,* 188
Garnier, Robert, 168
admired in England, 191
Garrick, David, manager of Drury Lane, 260
*Gas I* and *Gas II,* Kaiser, 367
Gascoigne, George, 187
Gay, John, 262
Gellert, Christian, 282
Gelosi, The, in Paris, 177
*Gendre de Monsieur Poirier, Le,* Augier, 298
*Genoveva,* Hebbel, 312
Geoffrey of Monmouth, as source of plots, 15, 232
*George Barnwell, The History of,* Lillo, 262
*George Sand,* Moeller, 359
*George a Greene, Pinner of Wakefield,* 200
German clowns, 281
German editors of Shakespeare, 231

German plays in America, 352
*Gesta Romanorum,* source of plots, 232
*Ghosts,* Ibsen, 318
first performance of, 324
Giacometti, Pietro, 313
Giacosa, Giuseppe, 333
*Gigantomachia,* 57
Gillette, William, 357
*Gioconda, La,* D'Annunzio, 334
*Giovanni da Procida,* Niccolini, 314
*Girl of Andros, The,* translated, 187
*Girl with the Green Eyes, The,* Fitch, 356
*Gladiator, The,* Bird, 354
*Glance Towards Shakespeare, A,* quoted, 233
Glaspell, Susan, 359
Globe Theater, 210
*Glorieux, Le,* Destouches, 273
"Glorification of the harlot," 298
*Glory,* D'Annunzio, 334
*Gluck im Winkel, Das,* Sudermann, 329
Godard, Jean, 177
*God Loves Us,* 360
*God's Merciful Promises,* 184
*Gods of the Mountain, The,* Dunsany, 345
Godfrey, Thomas, 352
Goethe, Johann Wolfgang von, 285
connection with the Weimar Theater, 288
quoted on Shakespeare, 223
Gogol, N. V., 348
*Golden Doom, The,* Dunsany, 345
*Golden Fleece, The,* Grillparzer, 311
Goldoni, Carlo, 276
Goldsmith, Oliver, 264
*Good Natured Man, The,* Goldsmith, 265
*Goose Hangs High, The,* Beach, 359
*Gorboduc,* 190

Gorky, Maxim, 349

Gosson, Stephen, criticism on sixteenth century plays, 205

Gottsched, Johann Christoph, 281

*Götz von Berlichingen,* Goethe, 286

Gozzi, Carlo, 276

Grabbe, Christian, 311

Grahame, Kenneth, on Carnival mummers, 138

*Great Divide, The,* Moody, 357

Greene, Robert, 215
 author of romantic comedy, 201

Greek comedy, general nature of, 59

Greek drama, subjects of, 70
 Helen, in Faust, 288
 myths collected, 11
 plays in England and America, 341
 theater, description of, 71
 treatment of love, 70

Gregory, Lady, work of, 344
 founder of Abbey Theater, 324

Grein, J. E., 324

Grillparzer, Franz, 310

Grimstad, home of Ibsen, 318

*Groatsworth o' Wit, A,* Greene, 225

"Grotesquerie," 367

Grundy, Mrs., origin of, 305

*Guardians, The,* Menander, 58

Guarini, 157

Gubernatis, Angelo de, 314

Guilds in medieval drama, 135

*Gull's Horn Book, The,* Dekker, 240

Gummere, F. C., quoted, 244

Gutzkow, Karl, 312

*Guzman,* Orrery, 252

*Gyges and His Ring,* Hebbel, 312

Gymnase Théâtre, scene of Scribe's successes, 297

Haigh, quoted on Æschylus, 32

*Hairy Ape, The,* O'Neill, 361

Hale, E. E., Jr., on tragedy, 326

Halévy, Ludovic, 301

Hall, John, married Judith Shakespeare, 226

*Hamburg Dramaturgy,* Lessing, 283

*Hamlet,* Shakespeare, 227
 source of plot, 232

*Hannele's Journey to Heaven,* Hauptmann, 328

Hans Wurst, coarseness of, 281

Haphazard, 186                [329

*Happiness in a Corner,* Sudermann,

Hardy, Alexander, influence of, 168

Harlequin, 156

Hardy, Thomas, 306

*Harrowing of Hell, The,* 133

Hauptmann, Gerhardt, 327

Havemeyer, Loomis, on drama of savage peoples, 4

Haymarket Theater, 260

*Hazel Kirke,* Mackaye, 356

Hazelton and Benrimo, 359

*Hearts of Oak,* Herne, 355

Hebbel, Friedrich, 312

Hebbel's protest against artificial drama, 317

Heiberg, Johan Ludwig, 315

*Heimat,* Sudermann, 329

Heinrich the Bell-caster, 327

*Heir at Law, The,* Colman, 304

*Held by the Enemy,* Gillette, 357

*Heldenbuch,* 13

*Helena,* Euripides, 46            [359

*Hell Bent for Heaven,* Hughes,

Heminge, John, editor of the *First Folio,* 228

*Hemlock, The,* Augier, 297

*Henrietta, The,* Howard, 356

*Henry V,* Shakespeare, 199

*Henri III et sa cour,* Dumas, 294

*Henry VI,* Shakespeare, 199, 225

Henslowe's employment of playwrights, 211

Henslowe as producer, 196
 as manager (note), 236
 concerning Dekker, 240

*Hereditary Forester, The,* Ludwig, 312

*Hernani,* Hugo, 295

Herne, James A., 355

*Hero and Leander,* Marlowe, 219

*Herod,* Phillips, 244

Heroes of the Restoration drama, 257

Heroic, drama, 251
drama parodied, 253
couplet, 251

*He Who Gets Slapped,* Andreyev, 349

Heywood, John, 185
as writer of interludes, 144
author of tragedy of blood, 197

*Hidden Spring, The,* Bracco, 335

*High Life Below Stairs,* Townley, 264

Hindu play, quotation from, 99

*Hippolytus,* Euripides, 46
Seneca, 148

*Historia Brevis,* Walsingham, 15

*Historia Britonum,* source of *Gorboduc,* 190

*Historia Regum Brittanniæ,* 15

Historical drama in Italy, 314

Historical themes, importance of, 17

*History of the Early American Theater,* Dunlap, 353

History as plot material, 15

*Histriomastix,* Marston, 242

*Histrio,* origin of word, 78

Hoffman, 196

Hoffmannsthal, Hugo von, 329

Hofteufel, J. C., 280

Holberg, Ludwig, 290
influenced by Italian comedy, 157

Holinshed's *Chronicle,* source of *Arden of Faversham,* 197
source of *Macbeth,* 232
general popularity of, 15

Homeric poems, as source of plots, 11

*Home Sweet Home,* Payne, 353

Home, John, 261

Howe, Julia Ward, 355

*Honest Criminal, The,* Jovellanos, 278

*Honor,* Sudermann, 328

Honors bestowed on Voltaire, 270

Hope Theater, 210

Hopi Indians, Rain Dance, 6

Horace, maxims of, 90

Horniman, Miss, theater in Manchester, 324

Hotel de Bourgogne, patronized by Richelieu, 168

House of Atreus, legend, 11

*House of Life, The,* Quintero, 336

Housman, Laurence, collaborator with Barker, 342

Howard, Bronson, 356

Howard, Sir Robert, 252

Hughes, Hatcher, 359

Hughes, Thomas, 192

Hugo, Victor, 294

*Humanity,* an interlude, 139

*Hunchback, The,* Knowles, 304

*Hundred Plays of the Kin and Yuen Dynasties,* 103

Huneker, James, on Ibsen, 317

*Hyacinth Halvey,* Gregory, 344

Ibsen, Henrik, 317
"adapted" in England, 308
in Germany, 322
friendship with Björnson, 318
influence on English writers, 308
liberation from French technique, 319

*Icebound,* Davis, 359

*Ideal Wife, The,* Praga, 333

*Idomenée,* Crebillon, 269

*If Not Thus,* Pirandello, 335

*Iliad,* translation dedicated to Congreve, 256                [280

Imitation, of Plautus in Germany, of Shakespeare in Russia, 347
of oriental plays, 359

Importance, of Beaumont and Fletcher, 239
of Voltaire, 272

*Importance of Being Earnest, The,* Wilde, 338

*In a Balcony,* Browning, 307

Increasing, decency of the stage, 371

refinement of French stage, 172

Indebtedness of playwrights to Lope de Vega, 163

Independent theaters, 323

*Indian Queen, The,* Dryden, 252

*Indian Emperor, The, or the Conquest of Mexico by the Spaniards,* Dryden, 252

Indian legends in American plays, 359

*Inez de Castro,* Hugo, 294

Influence, of Lope de Vega, 162

of Dryden, 253

of Lillo and Moore in Europe, 262

of Lessing in Germany, 285

of romanticism in Italy, 314

of Shaw, 340

of Pushkin in Russia, 347

of the Théâtre Libre, 324

*Inheritors, The,* Glaspell, 359

*In Mizzoura,* Thomas, 356

Inscription on monument at Stratford, 226

*Insect Play, The,* the Capeks, 367

*Inspector General, The,* Gogol, 348

*Interlude of Vice Concerning Horestes,* Pikering, 186

Interlude, subjects of, 184

*Interlude de Clerico et Puella,* 143

Interpretation, of Aristotle, Lessing, 284

of Chekhov's plays, 365

*In the Depths,* Gorky, 349

*In the Porter's Lodge,* Verga, 333

*In the Shadow of the Glen,* Synge, 345

Introduction to the *First Folio,* 229

*Intruder, The,* Maeterlinck, 331

"Invention" of the actor, 21

Inventory of a Perugian monastery, 128

Iphigenia, theme used, 12

*Iphigenia in Tauris,* Goethe, 287

imitated in Italian, 149

Irving, Washington, as collaborator, 128

*Isle of Dogs, The,* Nash, 218

Italian, comedy, 149, 150

tragedy, early, 148

opera in England, 262

players in Germany, 281

Italians histrionic rather than dramatic, 313

Italy, as the home of learning, 177

*Iris,* Pinero, 308

"Irish Helen," The, 344

Irish, Literary Theater, 343

National Theater, 343

Players, 343

Irony in Greek drama, 70

Irving, Sir Henry, 307

*Jack Juggler,* 187

Jacob, Edward, on authorship of *Arden of Faversham,* 197

James II, denunciation of actors, 259

*James IV, King of Scotland,* Greene, 216

Jameson, Storm, quoted, 292

Japanese drama, brilliant period of, 106

*Jeanne d'Arc,* Mackaye, 358

Jefferson, Joseph, 355

*Jest, The,* Benelli, 335

*Jew of Malta, The,* Marlowe, 219

as type of tragedy of blood, 196

first performed, 210

*Job* as drama, 10

*Jocasta,* Dolce, translated, 187

Jodelle, 168

*John a Kent and John a Cumber,* Munday, 201

John Street Theater built, 352

Joint plays of Beaumont and Fletcher, 238

Jones, Henry Arthur, 308

Jones, Inigo, 204

Jones, R. E., 366

Jones, Sir William, 99

Jonson, Ben, 235
eulogy on Shakespeare, 229
influence of later writers, 237
involved in the War of the Theaters, 169
as writer of masques, 204

Jovellanos, Gaspar Melchor de, 278

*Judith* (Apocrypha), regarded as drama, 280

*Judith,* Hebbel, 312

Juggler of Notre Dame, legend of, 123

*Jumeaux, Les,* Hugo, 296

*Justice,* Galsworthy, 341

Julian the Apostate, attitude towards theater, 91

*Kabale und Liebe,* Schiller, 289

Kalidasa, 101

Kamerny Theater, 368

Kean, Charles, visit to America, 353

Kean, Edmund, visit to America, 353

Kelly, Hugh, 264

Kemble, Charles and Fanny, in America, 353

Kemble, John, in *De Montfort,* 304
in *The Stranger,* 285

Kennedy, Charles Rann, 358

"Kidnapping," school of comedy, 152

Killigrew, Thomas, 250

*Kindling,* Kenyon, 359

*King Argimenes,* Dunsany, 345

*King Hunger,* Andreyev, 349

*King John,* Shakespeare, 198

*King John,* Bale, 198

*King John,* interlude, 186

*King Lear,* "improved," 264

*King Lear,* Shakespeare, 227

"King Leir," source of, 15

Kiotsugu, Kwanami, 108

*Kismet,* Knoblauch, 359

Kleist, Heinrich von, 310

Klinger, Friedrich von (note), 282

Klopstock in Denmark, 291

Knighthood and chivalry in drama, 286

Knights of the Round Table, legends of, 13

Knoblauch, Edward, 359

Knowles, James Sheridan, 304

*Komos,* 7

Kotzebue, August Friedrich, 285

Kummer, Clare, 360

Kyd, Thomas, life and work, 214

Kyd's *Spanish Tragedy,* 194

Labdacidæ myth, 12

La Chaussée, Pierre Claude de, 273

La Cruz, Ramon de, 279

*L'Aiglon,* Rostand, 332

*Lady of Lyons, The,* Bulwer, 304

*Lady Windermere's Fan,* Wilde, 338

*Land of Heart's Desire, The,* Yeats, 344

Landgrave of Cassel, built first court theater, 281

Lang, Andrew, on Molière, 177

Language, in Synge's plays, 344
in Hindu plays, 100

Larrivey, Pierre de, 177

Lasca, Il, criticism of Italian comedy, 153

Latin, plays given before Queen Elizabeth, 190
in Germany, 281
playwrights after Seneca, 91
tragedies given in England, 190

*Lazzi,* in Commedia del' Arte, 154

Leaders in dramatic study in America, 370

*Lear,* source of plot, 232

Legge, Doctor, 199

*Legend of Aladdin,* 315

Legend of the House of Atreus, 11

Legends included in the *Epic Cycle*, 11
Leipzig School, The, 282
*L'Enfant Prodigue*, Voltaire, 270
Length of French miracles, 123
*Leonard*, Brisbarre and Nus, 305
*Leonora or the World's Own*, Howe, 355
Leo X, patron of the theater, 150
built theater in Rome, 152
Le Sage, 273
Lessing, Gotthold Ephraim, 283
encouraged by *Barnwell*, 263
*Letters to Piso*, Horace, 89
Lewis, "Monk," 302
"Lewter" impersonated, 184
*Liar, The*, Corneille, 171
*Liar, The*, Foote, 263
*Libation Pourers, The*, Æschylus, 30
Liberty extolled in *Cato*, 261
Librettos of Metastasio, 277
Licensing, Elizabethan plays, 208, 247
Act, The, 263
*Life and Death of Thomas Lord Cromwell*, 200
Life of Ibsen, 317
*Life of Man, The*, Andreyev, 349
*Life Is a Dream*, Calderón, 165
Lillo, George, 262
Lines on Shakespeare's tomb, 226
Linley, Elizabeth, 265
*Lion and the Mouse, The*, Klein, 359
*Little Journey, A*, Crothers, 359
Literary or "closet" drama in England, 306
*Little Clay Cart, The*, probable date, 100
*Little Orphan of the House of Tchao, The*, 105
*Little Minister, The*, Barrie, 342
"Little Theater" movement, 325
used by Fielding, 263
Livius Andronicus, producer of the first formal play in Rome, 80

Livy, source of plots, 15
*Locrine*, 194
Lodge, Thomas, 214
*London Assurance*, Boucicault, 355
London in Shakespeare's time, 225
*London Merchant, The*, Lillo, 262
in France, 274
*Looking Glass for London, A*, Lodge and Greene, 215
Lope de Rueda, 160
Lope de Vega, 160-163
*Lord Governance and Lady Public Weal*, 184
Lord Lytton (Edward Bulwer), 304
*Lost in Darkness*, Bracco, 335
Louis XIV and Molière, 178
*Love and Intrigue*, Schiller, 289
*Love for Love*, Congreve, 256
*Love Is Enough*, Morris, 306
Love of liberty, in Alfieri, 278
in Voltaire, 272
*Love of the Three Kings*, Benelli, 335
*Love without Stockings*, Wessel, 291
*Love's Comedy*, Ibsen, 318
*Love's Labour's Lost*, Shakespeare, 227
original in plot, 231
*Love's Martir*, Marston and Jonson, 241
*Lucrece*, Shakespeare, 227
*Lucrèce Borgia*, Hugo, 296
*Lucky Pehr*, Strindberg, 323
Ludwig, Otto, 312
*Luise*, Giacosa, 333
Lully, operas produced in London, 250
*Lust's Dominion*, 196      [280
Luther's opinion of the theater,
Lyly, John, author of court comedies, 202, 214
Lynd, Robert, quoted, 177

*Macbeth*, Shakespeare, 227
source of plot, 232

MacCready, William, 353
MacDowell, Edward A., quoted, 6
MacGowan, Kenneth, on the nature of drama, 280
Machiavelli, 151
"Machine," The, 72
MacKail, J. W., on Latin poetry, 78
MacKaye, Percy, 357
Mackaye, Steele, 356
Macklin, Charles, 264
Mad World, My Masters, A, Middleton, 242
Mad Hercules, The, Seneca, 87
Madame Butterfly, Giacosa, 333
Madras House, The, Barker, 342
Maeterlinck, Maurice, 330
Maffei, Scipione, 277
Magazine of Faithful Retainers, The, 110
Magda, Sudermann, 329
Magistrate, The, Pinero, 307
Mahabharata, The, source of plots, 13
Maid of Orleans, The, Schiller, 289
Maidens of Trachis, The, Sophocles, 38
Mak the Sheep Stealer, 142
Malade imaginaire, Le, Molière, 179
Malay play, 3
Malquerida, La, Benevente, 336
Man and Superman, Shaw, 340
Man from Home, The, Tarkington and Wilson, 360
Man of Destiny, The, Shaw, 340
Man of the World, The, Macklin, 264
Manchester Theater, The, 324
Mandragola, Machiavelli, 151
Manly, Mrs., 258
Mannheim Theater, The, 289
Man's World, A, Crothers, 359
Mansfield, Richard, 356
"Mansions" on medieval stage, 126

Mantzius, Karl, on English sacred plays, 134
Manzoni, Alessandro, 313
Masqueraders, The, Pinero, 308
Matthew Merigreek, 188
Matthews, Brander, leader of dramatic study in America, 370
    quoted on Molière, 181
    quoted on Lope de Vega, 162
    on Greek drama, 77
    on Aristophanes, 51
Matthison, Edith Wynne, in Everyman (note), 139
    in Chinese play (note), 106
Marais, Theater in the, 169
Marenco, Leopoldo, 314
Margery Mumblecrust, 188
Marguerite, in Faust, 288
Mariage d'Olympe, Augier, 299
Maria Stuart in Scotland, Björnson, 316
Marie Antoinette, actor in Figaro, 275
Marie Antoinette, Giacometti, 313
Marionette plays in Germany, 281
    in Japan, 109
Marie Tudor, Hugo, 296
"Marivaudage," 273
Marviaux, Pierre Carlet de, 273
Marks, Josephine Preston Peabody, 357
Marlowe, Christopher, life and work, 218 ff.
    improvement of blank verse, 221
    improvement of chronicle play, 199
Marlowe, Julia, in Jeanne d'Arc, 358
Marlowe, Mrs. Marks, 357
Marquina, Edouardo, 337
Marriage of Figaro, The, Beaumarchais, 275
Marston, John, 241
Martyrdoms of the Apostles, 125
Mary Magdalen plays, 127
Mary Magdalene, Hebbel, 317
Masefield, John, 341

Masks, used by Thespis, 22
  in Italian comedy, 155
Masque, Elizabethan, 203
Masques in America, 358
*Massacre of Paris, The,* Marlowe, 219
*Massenmensch,* Toller, 367
Massinger, Philip, 243
*Master Builder, The,* Ibsen, 318
*Master Olaf,* Strindberg, 322
Masuccio, 231
*Mater,* Mackaye, 358
Maturin, Charles Robert, 302
"Maturin's Bedlam," 303
*Measure for Measure,* source of plot, 232
*Medea,* Seneca, 87
  Grillparzer, 311
Medieval, sacred drama, 133 ff.
  cycles, 133
  farces, subjects of, 142
  stage, arrangement of, 126
  romances, source of, 13
  secular plays, 140
  puppet plays, 144
Mediocrity of sacred plays, 136
Meilhac, Henri, 301
*Melampe,* Holberg, 290
Melodrama, in France, 293
  in Italy, 313
Menander, 58
*Menœchmi,* given at Ferrara, 148
*Menschenhass und Reue,* Kotzebue, 285
Mermaid Tavern group, 235
*Merope,* Maffei, 277
  Voltaire, 270
*Merry Devil of Edmonton,* 201
*Merry Play between Johan the Husband,* etc., 185
*Merry Wives of Windsor,* Shakespeare, 231
*Messaline,* Cossa, 314
Messenger, in pseudo-classic plays, 272
  praised by Sidney, 193
*Metamora,* Stone, 354

Metastasio, 277
*Michael and His Lost Angel,* Jones, 308
*Midchannel,* Pinero, 308
Middle Comedy, names of writers preserved, 57
Middleton, Thomas, 242
Miles Gloriosus, 156
  imitated by Udall, 187
Millar, J. H., quoted, 260
Mimes in Rome, 94
*Minna von Barnhelm,* Lessing, 283
*Minor, The,* Foote, 263
*Miracle of Theophilus,* 219
  an earlier Faust, 122
Miracles, of St. Nicholas, 124
  of Our Lady, 122
Miracle plays, in France, 122
  leave the altar, 124
*Miseries of Enforced Marriage, The,* 198
*Misfortunes of Arthur, The,* 192
*Miss Sara Sampson,* Lessing, 283
Mode of giving seventeenth century plays, 181
Modern miracle play, 331
"Modernism," 367
Moeller, Philip, 359
Molière, Jean Baptiste de Poquelin de, life and work, 178 ff.
  and the critics, 180
  influenced by Italian comedy, 157
  influence on later playwrights, 181
Monasteries broken up, 189
*Money,* Bulwer, 304
*Monna Vanna,* Maeterlinck, 331
  theme (note), 110
Moody, William Vaughn, 357
*Moonflower, The,* Akins, 359
Moore, Edward, 263
Moral ideals of Ibsen, 320
Morality, The, 138
  construction of, 139
Moratin the younger, 279
Moratin the elder, 278

More, Sir Thomas, subject of play, 200

Morton, James Madison, 305

Moscow Art Theater, 349, 365

Motokiyo, Seami, 108

Mountjoy, Christopher, 226

*Mourning Bride, The,* Congreve, 256

Movable machinery on London stage, 250

*Mrs. Warren's Profession,* Shaw, 339

Munday, Anthony, 200

Murray, Gilbert, on Greek tragedy, 48

Murray, T. C., 345

Murphy, Arthur, in sentimental comedy, 264

Murry, J. Middleton, literary aspects of drama, 61

Music in early sacred plays, 121

Mussato of Padua, 148

Musset, Alfred de, 301

Mystical note in Russian drama, 351

Mythology, as source of plots, 10

Nævius, 80

Naogeorg, Thomas, 280

Nash, Thomas, 218

*Nathan the Wise,* Lessing, 284

"Nationalist" school in Germany, 283

Nationalization of Russian theaters, 368

Native subjects used in America, 356

"Naturalistic" theater advocated by Zola, 329

"Naturalist" school represented by Strindberg, 322

Nature of early sacred plays, 121

Neilson and Thorndike, on Elizabethan drama, 207

Neo-classic school, strength of, 176

*Nero,* Cossa, 314

Neuber, Frederika C., 282

New Comedy, Greek, 57

New England legend in play, 358

New Place, purchased by Shakespeare, 225

New Park Theater founded, 355

New Century Theater in New York, 363

*New York Idea, The,* Mitchell, 359

"New Shakespeare," The, 304

*New Way to Pay Old Debts, A,* Massinger, 243

Newington Butts, Theater, 210
  scene of first productions, 200

*Nibelungs, Song of the,* 13

Niccolini, Giovanni, 314

*Nice People,* Crothers, 359

Nietzsche, quoted, 20

*Nigger, The,* Sheldon, 359

*Night Asylum, The,* Gorky, 349

*Night at an Inn, A,* Dunsany, 345

*Nobleman, The,* Tourneur, 244

Nomenclature in biblical plays, general, 118
  in England, 132
  in France, 122
  in Germany, 129
  in Italy, 128
  in Spain, 130

Nomenclature in secular plays in Germany, 141

*No* plays of Japan, 106, 107
  founded on sacred legends, 13

*No* play quoted, 99

Non-commercial theaters, 324

North, Sir Thomas, translator of Plutarch, 15, 232

Norse mythology first used in drama, 315

"Northern Aristophanes," 319

Norton, Thomas, 190

Norwegian theater in Christiania, 318

*Nos Intimes,* Sardou, 300

*Not So Long Ago,* Richman, 360

*Novelle,* Italian, as source of plots, 14

*Numancia,* Cervantes, 160
Nus, Eugene, 305

Oberammergau (note), 136
Objections to playhouses (Elizabethan), 208
*Octoroon, The,* Boucicault, 355
*Œdipe,* Voltaire, 269
*Œdipus the King,* Sophocles, 39
*Œdipus,* Dryden, 253
  Corneille, 171
  use of plot, 40
*Œdipus at Colonos,* Sophocles, 42
Öhlenschläger, Adam, 315
O'Kelly, Seumas, 345
*Old Bachelor, The,* Congreve, 256
Old Comedy, chorus granted, 52
  Greek, 52 ff.
*Old Fortunatus,* Dekker, 240
*Old Homestead, The,* Thompson, 356
Old Southwark Theater built, 352
Old Testament Prophets, in sacred plays, 120
*Old Wives' Tale, The,* Peele, 218
Ole Bull, patron of Ibsen, 318
Oliphant, Mrs., concerning *Bertram,* 303
O'Neill, Eugene, 360
*On Trial,* Reizenstein, 359
Opportunity given by independent theaters, 325
*Oresteia, The,* Æschylus, 11, 30
*Orestes,* Rucellai, 149
Orestes, theme used, 12
*Oreste,* Voltaire, 271
Origin of Faust legend, 219
*Orlando Furioso* versified, 215
*Oroonoko,* Behn, 258
*Orphan, The,* Otway, 254
*Orphan of the House of Tchao, The Little,* 106, 270
Ostrovsky, A. N., 348
*Othello,* Shakespeare, 227
  source of plot, 232
  played by Forrest, 353
Otway, Thomas, 254

*Outward Bound,* Vane, 359
Ownership of plays (Elizabethan), 211

Pacuvius, 81
Pageants in England, 134
*Paid in Full,* Walter, 359
*Palace of Pleasure, The,* 14
*Palliatæ,* 80
Pamphlets against theaters, 248
*Pandosto,* Greene, 215
Pantalone, 155
Pantomimes in Rome, 94
*Paolo and Francesca,* Phillips, 343
Paracelsus, 220                    [252
*Paradise Lost* arranged for opera,
Parallelism in Chinese poetry, 104
Park Theater opened, 353
Parody, of Euripides, 53
  of heroic drama, 253
*Passion of Christ,* 136
*Passion Flower, The,* Benevente, 336
*Pastor Fido,* Guarini, 157
  as model for English pastorals, 201
Pastoral drama in Italy, 157
Pastorals (Elizabethan), 201
*Pattes de mouche, Les,* Sardou, 300
Payne, John Howard, 353
Paynter, William, 14, 231
Peele, George, 217
*Peer Gynt,* Ibsen, 318
*Pelleas and Melisande,* Maeterlinck, 331
Peoples' theaters in America, 363
Performances (Elizabethan), time and manner, 212
Pepys, Samuel, plays witnessed by, 251
*Père de famille, Le,* Diderot, 274
*Pericles,* in Shakespeare canon, 229
Periods of Shakespeare's activity, 227
*Persians, The,* Æschylus, 28
*Peter Pan,* Barrie, 342

*Petimetra,* Moratin, 279

*Petronius,* on a Roman banquet, 89
as source of plots, 241

*Phèdre,* Racine, 176

*Philaster,* Beaumont and Fletcher, 238

Philemon, Greek playwright, 58

Philip II, forbade secular plays, 161

*Philistines, The,* Gorky, 349

Phillips, Stephen, 342

*Philosophe marié, Le,* Destouches, 273

Philosophy of Ibsen, 321

*Philotas,* Daniel, 192

*Philoctetes,* Sophocles, 41

Phrynicus, 23

Pickle-herring as clown, 281

*Pierre Pathelin, Farce of,* 142

Pierrot, 156

*Pigeon, The,* Galsworthy, 341

Pigments, used by Thespis, 22

Pikering, writer of interludes, 186

*Pillars of Society,* Ibsen, 318

Pinero, Sir Arthur Wing, 307

Pindemonte brothers, 314

*Piper, The,* Mrs. Marks, 357

Piracy, of plays, 211
of Lessing's Essays, 283
of Elizabethan successes, 305

Pirandello, Luigi, 335

Piron, 273

Pisistratidæ, caused myths to be collected, 11

Pixérécourt, Guilbert de, 293

*Pizarro,* Sheridan, 285
Jefferson as actor in, 355

Plagiarism, charged against Shakespeare, 225

Plague, visitations of, 246
performances forbidden during, 208

*Plain Dealer, The,* Wycherley, 255

Platen, Count von, writer of parodies, 311

*Plautus and His Century,* Cossa, 314

Plautus, rediscovered, 148

Plautus, plots, themes, and life, 82, 83, 84

*Playboy of the Western World, The,* Synge, 345

*Play of the Pardoner and the Friar,* 185

*Play of the Ten Virgins* (German), 123, 129

Play-acting, in Christian ritual, 115

Playbills (Elizabethan), 212

Playhouses (Elizabethan), 210

Plays of special localities in America, 359

*Plays on the Passions,* Baillie, 303

*Plays Pleasant and Unpleasant,* Shaw, 340

Playwrights, of the Elizabethan stage, 225
introduced by the independent theaters, 324

Playwriting, a family tradition, 66

*Pleasant Commodie of Fair Em, The,* Greene, 201

Plutarch, as source of plots, 15
used by Shakespeare, 232
translated into English, 15

*Plutus,* Aristophanes, performed in England, 186
at Zurich, 280
Holberg, 290

*Pocohontas and the Settlers of Virginia,* Custis, 354

Poe, Edgar Allan, criticism on *Fashion,* 354

*Poetaster, The,* Jonson, 241

Poetic drama, revived in Spain, 336, 369
unsuited to the stage, 306
in America, 357
in England, 306

Poggio, Bracciolini, 148

Policy, of the Irish theater, 343
of the Leipzig School, 282

Political, struggles unfavorable to drama, 313
unity in the Middle Ages, 117

Political situation in Norway and Denmark, 290

*Political Pewterers, The,* Holberg, 290

Pollock, Channing, 358

*Polly,* Gay, 262

Pompignan, 269

*Poor Carpenter, The,* Marquina, 337

Pope, as editor of Shakespeare, 230

Popular heroes, plays concerning, 200

Popularity, of theater in Elizabethan London, 207
of the study of the classics in France, 167
of Sheridan's *Pizarro,* 302
of melodrama in France, 293
of *Mrs. Tanqueray,* 308
of French plays in England, 305
of *Salome* by Wilde, 338
of sacred plays, 120

Porpora, teacher of Metastasio, 277

Position of Sophocles among the ancients, 42

*Poverty Is No Crime,* Ostrovsky, 348

*Potash and Perlmutter* plays, Glass, 360

*Powers of Darkness, The,* Tolstoi, 348

Practice of "improving," Shakespeare, 251

*Prætextæ,* 80

Praga, Marco, 333

Praise of Elizabeth in plays, 218

Pratinas, 23

*Précieuses ridicules, Les,* Molière, 179

*Précieuses, Les,* influence of, 169

*Prefaces* of Dryden, 253

Prémaire, Joseph, discoverer of Chinese play, 105

Presenter, The, 218

Preservation of Greek plays, 64

Prestige of French plays, 268

Price of admission to Elizabethan theater, 212

Primitive, plays, a school for youth, 6
nature of medieval drama, 118

*Primo amoroso,* in Italian comedy, 156

*Prince of Parthia,* Godfrey, 352

Principles of the drama, Freytag, 312
Hugo, 295
Lessing, 284

*Prinz von Homburg,* Kleist, 310

Prizes in Greek competitions, 73

*Proagon,* 74

*Prodigal Son, The,* Waldis, 130

Productions on the Weimar stage, 288

Professional actors more esteemed, 210

Progress of dramatic art in cycles, 17

*Prometheus Bound,* Æschylus, 29

Prometheus, legend used, 12

*Promos and Cassandra,* lost version of, 205

Protest against classicism in France, 168

*Proteus,* Æschylus, 30

Provincetown Players, 363, 354 (note)

*Prunella,* Barker and Housmann, 342

Pseudo-classicism, in Voltaire, 271
parodied, 311

*Punch and Sir John Spendall,* 144

Punchinello, 155

Puppet shows, in England, 144
in Japan, 109
in Germany, 281

Purity of the Elizabethan stage, 209

Pursuit of learning in Elizabethan England, 183

Pushkin, Alexander, 347

*Quality Street,* Barrie, 342

Quartos, The, 227

Queen Elizabeth's, learning, 183
policy regarding playhouses, 209

*Queen Dido,* Marlowe and Nash, 219

Queen Mary's attitude towards the theater, 208

*Queen's Enemies, The,* Dunsany, 345

Quinault, 178
produced in London, 250

Quiney, Thomas, 226

Quinn, Arthur H., authority on American drama, 352

Quintero brothers, 336, 368

Racial conflicts represented in American plays, 359

Racine, Jean, life and work, 172-175

Rain Dance of the Hopi Indians, 6

Raleigh, Sir Walter, on Shakespeare, 223

Ralph Roister Doister, 188
reincarnation of the bragging soldier, 156

Rambouillet, Marquise de, 169

*Ravens, The,* Becque, 330

Realism on the American stage, 365

Rebhun, Paul, 130, 280

Recitations from Terence, Book of, 187

*Recruiting Officer, The,* performed in America, 352

Red Bull Theater, 210

*Red Robe, The,* Brieux, 330

*Red Carnation, The,* Fogazzaro, 334

Rediscovery of ancient plays, 148

Regnard, 269

Regulation of troupes of actors (Elizabethan), 208

*Rehearsal, The,* parody on heroic drama, 254

Reicher, Frank, 358

Reinhardt, Max, 366

Rejuvenation of English theater, 338

Religious, plays in America, 358
unity in the Middle Ages, 117

Renewed life in American drama, 363

Replies to *A Short View,* 259

Repudiation of the "well-made play," 326

Restoration, The, 249
comedy, 257
wits, 255

Restrictions on Spanish theater removed, 278

*Revisor,* Gogol, 348

Revival, of classic rules and subjects, 148
of poetic drama in England, 303

*Revenge of Bussy d'Ambois, The,* Chapman, 241

*Revenger's Tragedy, The,* Tourneur, 244

Revolt, against artificial drama in Spain, 336
against realism in stage settings, 366
against traditional stage business, 367

*Rhadamiste et Zénobie,* Crébillon the elder, 269

*Rhesus* (sometimes attributed to Euripides), 46

Rhymed couplet, The, 251

*Ricardus Tertius,* Dr. Legge, 199

*Richard Savage,* Gutzkow, 312

*Richelieu,* Bulwer, 304

Richman, Arthur, 360

*Riders to the Sea,* Synge, 345

*Right You Are, if You Think You Are,* Pirandello, 335

*Rigoletto,* Verdi, 295

*Rip Van Winkle,* Boucicault, 355

*Rise of the Moon of Knowledge, The* (Hindu play), 102

*Rising of the Moon, The,* Gregory, 344

Ritchie, Anna Cora Mowatt, 354

*Rivals, The,* Sheridan, 266

Rivas, Linares, 336

*Road House in Arden, A,* Moeller, 359

*Robbers, The,* Schiller, 288

Robertson, Thomas, 305

Robin Hood, plays, 200
  medieval play, 142

Robinson, Lennox, 345

*Roi s'amuse, Le,* Hugo, 295

Romantic, School in Germany, 286
  comedies (Elizabethan), 201

Romanticism, defined, 292
  in France, 293
  in Italy, 313
  in work of Barrie, 342
  in work of Rostand, 332

*Romantic Œdipus,* Platen, 311

Roman, spectacles, 93
  plays, time, costumes, stage-settings, 92
  plays, how financed, 94

*Romeo and Juliet,* first stage version, 205
  rewritten, 177
  source of plot, 14, 231

Roo, John, imprisoned, 184

*Rosamunda d'Ingliterra,* Niccolini, 314

Rose Theater, built, 210

Round Table, Knights of the, 13

Roscius, 81

Rostand, Edmond, 332

Roswitha, imitator of Terence, 85 (note), 116

Rotebœuf, 122

Rousseau, opinion of *Barnwell,* 263

Rowe, Nicholas, editor of Shakespeare, 230

Royal protection of stage, 247

*Rozeno Family, The,* Traversi, 334

Rucellai, 149

*R.U.R.,* The Capeks, 367

Russian drama reflects national life, 350

*Ruy Blas,* Hugo, 296


Sachs, Hans, 143

Sackville, Thomas, 190

Sacred books as sources of plot, 13

Sacred plays brought to England, 132

*Sacre rappresentazione,* 128

*Sag Harbor,* Herne, 355

*Saint Paul,* Bovio, 314

St. Hilary, writer of Latin plays, 116

*Sad Shepherd, The,* Jonson, 202

Saint-Beuve, comment on Racine, 175

St. Francis of Assisi, presenter of Christmas play, 119

*Sakuntala,* Kalidasa, 102
  translated into English, 99
  source of plot, 13

Saladin, in *Nathan the Wise,* 284

*Salome,* Wilde, 338

*Salvation Nell,* Sheldon, 359

Salvini, in *Civil Death,* 313

*Samaritan Woman, The,* Rostand, 332

Sandeau, Jules, 298

Sanskrit drama, brilliant period of, 101

Santayana, George, on the function of poetry, 27

*Sappho and Phaon,* Mackaye, 358

*Saratoga,* Howard, 356

Sardou, Victorien, 300

*Satiromastix,* Dekker, 241

*Saturae,* 79

Satyr-play, 23

Saurin, 269

*Scarecrow, The,* Mackaye, 358

Scarron, 178

Scenes of violence, in Japanese plays, 109
  in Chinese plays, 104
  in tragedy of blood, 193
  absence of in Greek plays, 69

Scenery, on the Elizabethan stage, 212
costumes and finance in sacred drama, 135
Schiller, Johann Friedrich von, 288
opinion of Lessing, 285
Schlegel's criticism of Holberg, 291
Schnitzler, Arthur, 329
Scholar Poets, The, 214
*School for Scandal, The,* Sheridan, 266
School of Salamanca, 278
*Schroffenstein Family, The,* Kleist, 310
Schlegel, on national themes, 17
Screen scene, origin of, 266
Scribe, Eugène, 296
*Sea Gull, The,* Chekhov, 349
Second Folio, plays included in, 229
*Second Mrs. Tanqueray, The,* Pinero, 308
*Secret Service,* Gillette, 357
Sedition, as clown, 186
Seeds of drama in "closet plays," 307
Seneca, life and work, 86, 87
translated into English, 88
rediscovered in Middle Ages, 148
as model in France, 167
influence of, 88
Sentimental Comedy (English), 264
*Servant in the House, The,* Kennedy, 358
"Servants" licensed to give plays, 208, 210
*Seven Days,* 360
*Seven Against Thebes, The,* Æschylus, 29
Sex, in English drama, 306
in plays of Dumas the younger, 300
Shakespeare, John, 224
Judith, marriage of, 226

Shakespeare, Susannah, marriage of, 226
Shakespeare, William, life and work, 224 ff.
as actor, 225
"improved," 251, 272
produced in France, 272
representative of his time, 232
translated into German, 283
Shakespeare Memorial Theater, 357
Shakespeare's, adaptability to the stage, 233
ideal of women, 234
influence on Goethe, 286
use of historical material, 16
versatility, 232
Shakespearean editors, 230, 231
"Shakespeare of Sweden," 323
Shaw, G. Bernard, 339
as moralist, 340
quoted, 122
Sheldon, Edward, 359
*Shenandoah,* Howard, 356
Sheridan, Richard Brinsley, 265
as manager of Drury Lane Theater, 260
(note), 254
*Sherlock Holmes,* Gillette, 357
*She Stoops to Conquer,* Goldsmith, 265
Shirley, James, 244
*Shoemaker's Holiday, The,* Dekker, 240
*Shore Acres,* Herne, 356
Shoreditch, site of Elizabethan theaters, 210
*Shorn Lamb, The,* Menander, 58
Short-hand copies, 229
*Short View, A,* Collier, 258
Shrovetide plays, subjects of, 141
*Show-Off, The,* 360
*Sicilian Limes,* Pirandello, 335
*Sidney Buddulph,* Mrs. Sheridan, 265
Sidney, Sir Philip, on tragedy, 205
Siddons, Mrs., in *DeMontfort,* 304

*Siege of Rhodes, The,* panorama, 250

Sierra, Martínez, 336

*Signet of the Minister, The* (Hindu play), 102

Silva, Ramon Goy de la, 336

*Silver Box, The,* Galsworthy, 341

Simmias of Thebes, on Sophocles, 35

Simonson, Lee, 366

*Sin of David, The,* Phillips, 343

Singing actor, The (Chinese), 103

Sir Fretful Plagiary, 264

*Sister Beatrice,* Maeterlinck, 331

Sister Beatrice, legend used, 123

*Six Characters in Search of an Author,* Pirandello, 335

Skênê, origin of, 22

Skien, birthplace of Ibsen, 317

Skinner, Otis, 355

Skinner, Mrs. Otis (note), 352

*Sleeping Beauty, The,* Gozzi, 277

"Slice of life" in *drame bourgeois,* 293

Slow progress of reforms, 285

Small-town life portrayed in plays, 366

Smith, Richard Penn, 354

*Snow Maiden, The,* Ostrovsky, 348

Social drama in France, 296

*Societa del Gonfalone,* 128

*Société des Sottes,* 141

Society satirized in American plays, 358

*Society,* Robertson, 305

*Sodom's End,* Sudermann, 328

*Sofonisba,* Trissino, 15, 149
imitated, 189
as model in France, 167

*Sofonisba,* Corneille, 171

*Soliman and Perseda,* possibly by Kyd, 196

Solon's opinion of the Thespian play, 22

Sonnets of Shakespeare, 227

Sophocles, life and work, 35, 36
changes made by, 43

Sophocles, extracts from, 43

*Sophonisba,* Marston, 242

*Sorrows of Han, The,* 106

*Soul After Death, A,* Heiberg, 315

Soulié, Frederick, 293

Sources, of story material used in drama, 9
of plots used in Fletcher's plays, 239
of Shakespeare's plays, 231

Southwark, playhouses in, 210

Spanish drama, weaknesses of, 165

*Spanish Fryar, The,* Dryden, 252

*Spanish Tragedy, The,* Kyd, 194

"Spanish Molière," The, 279

Specimens of tragedy of blood, 196

*Speed the Plough,* Morton, 305

*Spirit, Will, and Understanding,* 139

*Spreading the News,* Gregory, 344

Spurious plays in Shakespeare canon, 229

Stage, appliances in Greek theater, 72
machinery in Elizabethan theater, 212
seats in Elizabethan theater, 212
in "Little Theaters," 325
machinery in medieval plays, 130
setting in early Greek plays, 31
setting in Hindu plays, 101

Stanislavsky, director, 365

State as manager in Greece, 73

*Stella,* Goethe, 286

Stevenson, R. L., on *Hernani,* 295

*Stifling,* Rivas, 336

Still, Dr. John, 188

*Still Waters Run Deep,* Taylor, 305

Stone, John A., 354

*Story of the Magic Lute, The,* 106

Stock characters, in Italian comedy, 150
in Greek comedy, 58
in miracle plays, 124

Storm and Stress School, 282

*Storm, The,* Ostrovsky, 348

*Story of the Three Rings,* 284

Stow, as source-book for plots, 15

*Strafford,* Browning, 307

*Stranger, The,* Kotzebue, 285

Stratford-on-Avon, 224

*Streets o' London,* Boucicault, 355

Strength of the neo-classic school, 176

*Strife,* Galsworthy, 341

Strindberg, August, 322

Structure of the miracle play, 123

Study, of drama in colleges, 369

of classics in France before 1700, 167

Stukeley, Sir Thomas, as subject of plays, 200

death portrayed, 218

*Sturm und Drang* period (note), 282

Subjects, used by Holberg, 290

used by O'Neill, 361

of medieval puppet plays, 144

Subsidization of American stage, 369

*Successful Calamity, A,* Kummer, 360

Sudermann, Hermann, 328

Sudraka, plays attributed to, 100

Sumarokov, Alexander, 347

Sumatra war play, 5

*Summary of English Chronicles, A,* Stow, 15

*Summer's Last Will and Testament,* Nash, 218

*Sun Up,* Vollmer, 359

*Sun's Darling, The,* Ford and Dekker, 244

*Sunken Bell, The,* Hauptmann, 327

Superiority of Italian literature during the early Renaissance, 187

Superstitions treated in Holberg's plays, 290

*Supper of Jokes, A (The Jest),* Benelli, 335

*Suppliants, The,* Æschylus, 28

*Suppositi,* Ariosto, 152

translated, 187

*Suppressed Desires,* Glaspell, 360

Suppression of playhouses (Elizabethan), 248

*Survey of London,* Walsingham, 15

*Susanna,* Rebhun, 130

Susarion, 52

*Swanwhite,* Strindberg, 323

*Sweet Lavender,* Pinero, 307

Swinburne, on *Arden of Faversham,* 197

on Marlowe, 219

as writer of closet drama, 307

Symbolism in Ibsen, 320

Symonds, J. A., on the influence of the classics, 193

on the nature of art, 19

on sacred plays in Italy, 128

on sacred plays in England, 132

on the Renaissance in Italy, 147

on the Renaissance in England, 182

Symons, Arthur, on Racine, 176

Sympathetic magic, 4

Synge, John M., 344

on the nature of drama, 338

on the nature of art, 347

Tairov, manager of Russian theater, 368

*Tale of a Tub, The,* Jonson, 236

*Tamburlaine,* Marlowe, at Newington Butts playhouse, 219

first performance of, 210

fixed the type, 200

*Taming of the Shrew, The,* first performance of, 210

early version of, 216

*Tancred and Gismunda,* lost version of, 205

*Tancrède,* Voltaire, 270

Tarkington, Booth, 360

Tasso, Torquato, 157

Taylor, Henry Osborne, on Roman society, 89

Taylor, Tom, 305

Teaching in Ibsen's plays, 319

"Tea-table" drama, 307

"Tearful comedy," 264

*Technique of the Drama,* Freytag, 312

Temperament of Pirandello, 335

*Tempest, The,* Shakespeare, 227
rewritten, 253

"Tendenz-drama," in Germany, 311

Tennyson, Alfred, 307

Telepathy, used in play, 356

Terence, life and work, 84, 85
imitated by Roswitha, 85
rediscovered, 148

*Terrible Meek, The,* Kennedy, 358

*Terza rima,* rhyme scheme (note), 149

Thayer, William Roscoe, on Elizabethan plays, 239

*Théâtre historique,* 294

Theater The, built, 210

Theater Guild, The, 363

*Théâtre Libre,* 323

Theaters and playhouses, in Rome, 93
in ancient Greece, 66

*Théâtre de Maeterlinck,* 331

Theatrical exhibitions given by Alexander the Great, 65

Themes, used by Shaw, 339
used by Synge, 345
used by Björnson, 316
used by Rostand, 332
used by Maeterlinck, 331
used by Dunsany, 345
of unconscious drama, 8
of story-tellers, 16
of Elizabethan plays, 245

Theobald's edition of Shakespeare, 231

*Théodora,* Sardou, 300

Theory of the stage, Alfieri, 277
Joanna Baillie, 303
Diderot, 274
Dumas the younger, 300

Theory of the stage, Hugo, 295
Hebbel, 312
Ibsen, 320
Lessing, 284
Maeterlinck, 330
Praga, 333
Shaw, 340
Verga, 333
Yeats, 343

Thespis, life and work, 20

Thespian changes, importance of, 22

Thespian play, character of, 21

*This Fine Pretty World,* Mackaye, 359

Thomas, Augustus, 356

Thompson, Denman, 356

Thorpe the bookseller, on Marlowe, 219

*Thousand Years Ago, A,* Mackaye, 358

*Three Daughters of M. Dupont, The,* Brieux, 330

*Three of Us,* Crothers, 359

Three periods of Ibsen's work, 318

*Three Sisters, The,* Chekhov, 349

*Ticket-of-Leave Man, The,* Taylor, 305

Tieck, on authorship of *Arden of Faversham,* 197

"Tiger's heart wrapped in a woman's hide," 225

*Timon of Athens,* source of plot, 232

Tintoretto, attack on Aretino, 152

*Titus Andronicus,* type of tragedy of blood, 196

*Titus Andronicus,* Shakespeare, 227

*Tobit,* regarded as drama, 280

*Togatæ,* 80

Tolstoi, Count Alexei, 348

Tolstoi, Count Lyoff, 348

*Torments of the Damned, The,* 129

*Tortesa the Usurer,* Willis, 354

*Torquato Tasso,* Goethe, 287

*Torquemada,* Hugo, 296

*Tosca, La,* Sardou, 300
*Tosca, La,* Giacosa, 333
*Tour de Nesle, Le,* Dumas, 294
Tourneur, Cyril, 244
Townley, James, 264
*Tragédie bourgeois,* 268
*Tragedy of Nan, The,* Masefield, 341
Tragedy of blood, 193-195
Transition period in Italy, 332
Translations, by Lady Gregory, 344
    of Seneca and Plautus, 187
Traversi brothers, 334
*Traytor, The,* Shirley, 245
*Trick to Catch the Old One, A,* Middleton, 242
Trilogy, The, 30
*Trimalchio's Dinner,* quoted, 89
*Trip to Scarborough, A,* Sheridan, 266
Trissino, Gian Giorgio, 149
*Triumph of Peace, The,* Shirley, 245
    Jonson, 204
Triumphs (*trionfo*) in Italy, 129
*Trojan Women, The,* Seneca, 87
*Troublesome Reign of King John, The,* 198
*True Tragedie of Richard Third,* 198
True spirit of classicism in Marlowe and Shakespeare, 222
*Truth, The,* Fitch, 356
*Tsar Boris,* Tolstoi, 348
*Tsar Theodor,* Tolstoi, 348
*Turcaret,* LeSage, 273
Turgenev, Ivan, 348
Turnèbe, Odet de, 177
*Twelfth Night,* type of romantic comedy, 201
Twelve lost plays of Plautus, 186
*Two Gentlemen of Verona,* Shakespeare, 227
*Two Tragedies in One,* 197
Tyler, Royall, 352
*Tyrannick Love,* Dryden, 252
Types of American comedy, 360

Udall, Nicholas, and the first English comedy, 187
    as writer of interludes, 144
    editor of Latin reader, 187
*Ulysses,* Phillips, 343
*Uncle Vanya,* Chekhov, 349
Unconscious drama, significance of, 7
*Une nuit de garde nationale,* Scribe, 296
Unfamiliar themes used by Voltaire, 270
Unities, The Three, 63
    in Hindu plays, 101
University production of plays, 370
University Wits, The, 214
Upsala University, 322
*Uriel Acosta,* Gutzkow, 312

*Valérie,* Scribe, 297
Vanbrugh, Sir John, 256
Vane, Sutton, 359
Variation is text of the *Folios,* 229
Variety, of subjects in American drama, 363
    of plots in Voltaire, 270
Vaudeville in France, 296
*Vaudeville-comédie* in Italy, 334
Vaughn, C. E., on Spanish drama, 159
    on Racine, 175
Vedrenne, J. E., 341
    and Barker, 339
*Venice Preserved,* Otway, 254
    quoted, 254
*Venus and Adonis,* Shakespeare, 227
Verdi, composer of *Rigoletto,* 295
Verga, Giovanni, 333
Verse used in early English tragedy, 149
"Virgin Queen" praised, 202
*Virgins, The,* Praga, 333
"Verists," The, 333
Verse-forms in *Romeo and Juliet,* 232

Vice, as comic figure, 186
  as clown in Germany, 281
Vigny, Alfred de, 301
*Virgin Martir, The,* Dekker and
    Massinger, 243
*Virginius,* Knowles, 304
Vittoria Corombona, Webster, 242
Vogue, of classicism in England,
    261
  of Kotzebue in England, 302
Vollmer, Lulu, 359
Voltaire, life and work, 269-271
  employment of Lessing, 283
  in praise of *Cato,* 261
Voltaire's, "classic" formula, 271
  opinion of Shakespeare, 271
*Vor Sonnenaufgang,* Hauptmann,
    327
Vulgarities of clown abolished,
    282

*Wagnerbuch* added to Faust leg-
    end, 220
Waldis, anti-papal playwright, 130
Wallace, G. M., concerning Shake-
    speare, 226
*Wallenstein* plays, Schiller, 289
War dances of primitive people, 5
*Warning for Fair Women, A,* 196
  quoted, 246
*War of the Giants, The,* Hegemon,
    57
War of the Theaters, The, 240
  Marston involved in, 242
Washington, play dedicated to, 278
Washington Square Players, 363
  (note), 106
*Wash Tub, The,* 142
*Waste,* Barker, 342
*Way of the World, The,* Con-
    greve, 256
Webster, John, 242
*Weavers, The,* Hauptmann, 327
Wedekind, Franz, 329
Weimar Court Theater, 286
*Well of the Saints, The,* Synge,
    345

Wells, H. G., on ancient drama,
    45
Wessel, Johan Herman, 291
*What Every Woman Knows,* Bar-
    rie, 342
*What You Will,* Marston, 242
*Wheel of Fortune, The,* Cumber-
    land, 264
*When We Dead Awaken,* Ibsen,
    318
*White Devil, The,* Webster, 242
*Why Marry,* Williams, 359
*Why Not,* Williams, 359
*Widow's Tears, The,* Chapman, 241
*Widowers' Houses,* Shaw, 339
Wilde, Oscar, 338
Wieland, Martin, 283
*Wilhelm Tell,* Schiller, 289
Williams, Jesse Lynch, 359
Willis, Nathaniel P., 354
Wilson, "Christopher North," on
    Miss Baillie, 304
*Winter Feast, The,* Kennedy, 358
*Winter's Tale, A,* founded on *Pan-
    dosto,* 215
*Wise and Foolish Virgins, The,*
    122
*Witch of Edmonton, The,* 244
*Witching Hour, The,* Thomas,
    356
*Wolf of Gubbio, The,* Marks,
    357
Wolfenbüttel, associated with Les-
    sing, 283
*Woman Killed with Kindness, A,*
    Heywood, 197
Women, playwrights, seventeenth
    century, 258
  playwrights in America, 359
  actors in Hindu plays, 101
  actors in England, 213
"Wonders" of the medieval stage,
    131
Wordsworth, William, on popular
    taste, 292
*Workhouse Ward, The,* Gregory,
    344

Workshops provided by Little Theaters, 325

World and His Wife, The, Echegaray, 336

World Runs on Wheels, The, Chapman, 241

Workmanship of Corneille, 171

Wounds of Civil War, The, Lodge and Greene, 215

Wright, quoted on Hernani, 295

Writers of court comedies, 203

Writers of poetic drama, English, 306

American, 357

Wycherley, William, 255

Xenophon of Ephesus, 231

Yarington, Robert, 197

Yeats, W. B., 344
    founder of Irish National Theater, 324, 343
    quoted on Irish theater, 346

Yellow Jacket, The, Hazelton and Benrimo, 359

Yorkshire Tragedy, A, 196, 198

Young, Mrs. Winthrop, Howard, 356

Young Men's League, first performance of, 319

Young, Stark, on the Greek theater, 72

Zaïre, Voltaire, 270

Zanni, in Italian comedy, 156

Zola, as preacher of "naturalism," 317

Zwingli, 280